A Handbook on Chinese Language Structure

SCANDINAVIAN UNIVERSITY BOOKS

Universitetsforlaget, Oslo, Bergen, Tromsö

Munksgaard, København

Esselte Studium, Stockholm, Göteborg, Lund

A HANDBOOK ON CHINESE LANGUAGE STRUCTURE

by

Henry Henne

Ole Bjørn Rongen

Lars Jul Hansen

Universitetsforlaget

Oslo – Bergen – Tromsö

© Universitetsforlaget 1977
ISBN 82-00-02406-7

Cover design by Per Syversen

Distribution offices:

NORWAY
Universitetsforlaget
Postbox 6589-Rodeløkka
Oslo 5

UNITED KINGDOM
Global Book Resources Ltd.
37, Queen Street
Henley on Thames
Oxon RG9 1AJ

UNITED STATES and **CANADA**
Columbia University Press
136 South Broadway
Irvington-on-Hudson
New York 10533

Printed in the United Kingdom

PREFACE

In this *Handbook* an attempt is made to present an outline of Modern Chinese language structure. Its purpose is twofold: to be a reference grammar for students of Chinese, and to serve as an introduction to the main features of Chinese for the benefit of people interested in acquiring some knowledge of the structure of the language from a descriptive point of view.

Our approach owes a great deal to *A Grammar of Spoken Chinese* by Yuan Ren Chao (1968), a pioneering and comprehensive work to which we hope our volume will serve as an introduction.

This book is the result of teamwork undertaken by members of the East Asian Institute of the University of Oslo. Although each co-author has contributed to some extent to all the chapters, Chapters I to V were in the main written by Henry Henne, Chapters VI to IX by Ole Bjørn Rongen, and Chapters X to XII by Lars Jul Hansen. Liu Baisha has rendered invaluable assistance in checking the Chinese examples. We are indebted to Eli Hofvind for the typing of the manuscript and the arrangement of the index.

Valuable suggestions and criticism, for which we are extremely grateful, have been received from cand. mag. Birthe Arendrup and from Professor Søren Egerod, both at the East Asian Institute, University of Copenhagen. In addition we are much indebted to Professor Hugh M. Stimson, of Yale University, who saw the text in proof, and gave advice on a number of specific points.

March, 1977

Henry Henne
Lars Jul Hansen
Ole Bjørn Rongen

TABLE OF CONTENTS

CHAPTER I

SOME BASIC TERMS AND DEFINITIONS

D. THE WORD

CHAPTER II
THE SENTENCE

A. GENERAL

B. INTONATION

CHAPTER III

THE CLAUSE   93–99

CHAPTER IV

THE PHRASE   100–102

CHAPTER VIII
VERBAL SYNTACTICAL CONSTRUCTIONS

CHAPTER IX
ADVERBS AND THEIR FUNCTIONS

CHAPTER X

NOMINAL STRUCTURE

CHAPTER XI

CLASSES OF NOMINALS

CHAPTER XII

NOMINAL SYNTACTICAL CONSTRUCTIONS

CHAPTER I

SOME BASIC TERMS
AND DEFINITIONS

This chapter presents, in concentrated form, an outline of the description of Chinese grammar which will be further elaborated in the rest of the book. It may be read as a preliminary orientation to the material, or, alternatively, as a resumé to be studied at the very end. Without entering into too many details, it aims at pinpointing the descriptive terms of major importance, and includes, in a fairly succinct form, explanations of the meanings of those terms as used in this book. A limited number of examples are provided.

A. Levels of Grammatical Analysis

1. Analysis is carried out on five **levels** of descending order: the sentence, the clause, the phrase, the word, and the morpheme. In addition, the term "expression" is used as an operational term covering words and phrases.

2.1. A **sentence** is a grammatically independent sequence bounded by major pauses and characterized by one of three intonational patterns. A sentence contains at least one predicate and consists of one or more clauses. For further details see B (p. 3).

2.2. A **clause** is any sequence which has the form of a simple sentence (B 1.2) and which is either a sentence or an immediate constituent (Ch. II. F 2, pp. 64–77) of a sentence. A clause which in a given context is a sentence is said to *function* as a sentence (sentence-clause). A clause which is not functioning as a sentence in a given context forms part of a compound sentence (B 1.3), i.e. is a sentence component. Such a clause does not carry the intonation characteristic of a sentence unless it is the *final* clause in a sentence. For further details see B (p. 3).

2.3. A **phrase** is a stress and pause group which contains a nuclear stress; it may be any sequence which has the segmental form of a simple sentence or a clause, and which is either a clause or an immediate constituent of a clause. A phrase which in a given context is a clause/sentence is said to *function* as a clause/sentence. A phrase which is not functioning as a clause/sentence in a given context forms part of a clause. A phrase consists of two or more words. For further details see C (p. 8).

Examples: *Hén$_1$ hǎo$_2$*. "Very$_1$ good$_2$." is a sentence containing one clause, which consists of one phrase. The same can be said of *Zhèiguán$_1$ bǐ$_2$*. "This (item)$_1$ pen$_2$." But in *Zhèiguán$_1$ bǐ$_2$, hén$_3$ hǎo$_4$*. "This$_1$ pen$_2$ is$_4$ very$_3$ good$_4$." we have a sentence which is also a clause, that is, the clause functions as a sentence, but the clause includes two phrases. In the first two examples the phrases function as sentences; in the last example they do not function as such. *Zìláishuǐ$_1$ bǐ$_2$ hěn$_3$ guì$_4$; qiānbǐ$_5$ gāngbǐ$_6$ bú$_7$ dà$_8$ guì$_9$*. "Fountain$_1$ pens$_2$ are$_4$ (very$_3$) expensive$_4$; pencils$_5$ [and] (ordinary) pens$_6$ are$_9$ not$_7$ very$_8$ expensive$_9$." is a sentence containing two clauses; each clause consists of two phrases: $1 + 2, 3 + 4; 5 + 6, 7 + 8 + 9$.

2.4. A **word** is a unit which is primarily a constituent of a phrase. A (free) word which in a given context is a clause/sentence is said to *function* as such: *Hǎo*. "OK". A *free word* is a unit which can occur as a sentence (i.e. as an independent utterance, bounded by major pauses): *Wénhuà* "culture" and *děngzhe* "is waiting" are free words. A *bound word* can never occur independently as a sentence/clause, only as a constituent of a sentence, a clause, or another word. *Le* in the clause/sentence *Tā$_1$ chī fàn$_2$ le$_3$*. "He$_1$ has$_3$ eaten$_2$." is a bound word.

2.5. An **expression** is a word or a phrase, or several phrases joined in a grammatical construct. It may function as a clause/sentence or as a constituent of such a unit. A free word is said to be a *minimal expression*. A phrase is an *expansion* of a minimal expression. *Hěn duō$_1$ de$_2$ shū$_3$*. "Many$_1$ (marker$_2$) books$_3$." is an expression expanded from *shū*.

2.6. A **morpheme** is a minimal linguistic unit which has form as well as meaning; it may be a (free or bound) word or the constituent of a word. Most morphemes are coterminous with a syllable ("monosyllabic"). Some morphemes are dissyllabic; others are subsyllabic (less than a syllable). *Nán* "male person" and *nǚ* "female" are both morphemes, but neither are free words; they can only occur as constituents of words and are thus said to be *bound morphemes* (but note that *nánnǚ* "men and women" is a free word). *Shān* "mountain" is a morpheme which is also a free word, but *gŭ* "valley" is a bound morpheme. *Mădá* (or: *mótuō*) "motor" and *kāfēi* "coffee" are examples of bisyllabic morphemes; *Sūwéiāi* "Soviet" and *qiăogélì* "chocolate" are trisyllabic morphemes. In *bàr* "handle" and *(yí)xiàr* "one stroke", -*r* (a suffix) is a morpheme which is less than a syllable. Some morphemes are *tonic* (they occur with an inherent tone if stressed), others are *atonic* (they never occur with an inherent tone, and they have zero stress). Some morphemes have more than one shape (the morpheme *-men* in *wŏmen* has a reduced form *m*: *wŏm* "we"). Some morphemes have a lexical meaning (*rén* "human being"), others (such as *-zhe* in *dĕngzhe* "is waiting") have only a grammatical meaning, i.e. function.

B. The Sentence and the Clause

1.1. Structure, form, and type. A sentence is *simple* or *compound*, depending on whether it has one or more clauses. Depending on whether or not it contains a topic (major subject), it is a *major sentence* (with topic), or a *minor* sentence (with a predicate only). The sentence is said to have a vocative, an exclamatory, an interrogative, an imperative, or a declarative *form*, depending on the form of the predicate. Depending on whether or not the predicate contains a verb as its nucleus, it is a *verbal* sentence (in the former case) or a *non-verbal* sentence (in the latter case). Depending on whether the non-omissible verbal nucleus of the predicate (the central) is negatable, negated, negative, or ambivalent, a verbal sentence is said to represent a *negatable*, a *negated*, *negative*, or *ambivalent type* respectively (cp. 5.1). All non-verbal sentences are of the *non-negatable type*.

1.2. A simple sentence consists of one clause: *Tā$_1$ míngtian$_2$ lái$_3$.* "He$_1$ is coming$_3$ tomorrow$_2$."; *Wŏ$_1$ yào$_2$ bāng$_3$ nǐmen de$_4$ máng$_5$.* "I$_1$ want to$_2$ help$_3$ (your$_4$ hurry$_5$ =) you".

1.3. A compound sentence consists of more than one clause; a sentence-final intonation does not occur between the clauses. A marker (B 4.3) may or may not occur between clauses. Examples: *Wŏ$_1$ bù$_2$ dŏng$_3$ Zhōngwén$_4$; zhí$_5$ hăo$_6$ qíng$_7$ ni$_8$ fānyi$_9$ fanyi$_{10}$.* "I$_1$ don't$_2$ understand$_3$ Chinese$_4$, [so it] is best$_{5,6}$ to ask$_7$ you$_8$ to interpret$_9$ (a little$_{10}$)." (unmarked); *Wŏmen$_1$ gēn$_2$ ni$_3$ qù$_4$, kéyi$_5$; dànshi$_6$ wŏmen$_7$ déi$_8$ zăo$_9$ diar$_{10}$ huílai$_{11}$.* "We$_1$ can$_5$ go$_4$ with$_2$ you$_3$, but$_6$ we$_7$ must$_8$ be back$_{11}$ somewhat$_{10}$ early$_9$." (marked by *dànshi*).

1.4. A major sentence/clause contains a topic subject (major subject) as well as a predicate. A *minor* sentence contains a predicate only. Note that a sentence, whether major or minor, must contain a predicate. *Xuésheng₁ méi₂ lái₃.* "The students₁ didn't₂ come₃." is a major sentence; *Méi₁ lái₂.*" ["Someone] didn't₁ come₂.", and *Shì zhēn₁ de₂.* "It is₁ (something which is₂) true₁." are minor sentences.

2.1. The occurrence of a *predicate* in a sentence/clause is called **predication**.

2.2. A sentence contains at least one **predicate**. *Méi lái* in *Xuésheng méi lái.* "The students didn't come." is a predicate; so is *Běijīng rén* in *Tā₁ fùqin₂ Běijīng₃ rén₄.* "Her₁ father₂ [is] ([a] Peking₃ man₄ =) from Peking." In a compound sentence each clause contains a separate *clause predicate*.

3.1. The endocentric sentence: *the predicate as center.* A predicate functions either as a sentence/clause alone, or as an immediate constituent of a sentence/clause. It may have the *form* of a sentence/clause, of a phrase (and is then a *complex predicate*), or it may consist of a single word (and is, in that case, a *simple predicate*), but it may not have the form of zero. In other words, if a sentence/clause does not contain a topic (major subject) and a predieate, it contains at least a predicate. The predicate may be *verbal* (if its nucleus is a verb) or *non-verbal* (i.e. mostly *nominal*) if its nucleus is non-verbal. As an immediate constituent of a sentence/clause it forms the second *partner* of a constitute, with a *topic subject* (B 8) as the first partner. A constitute consisting of a topic subject and a predicate is an *endocentric* construction in which the predicate is the *center*. The predicate is thus a non-omissible part of the sentence, i.e. it is presupposed by the subject. In other words the predicate is an essential part of the sentence/clause in which it occurs; it functions as a *comment* on the topic subject and tends to carry the main load of information given in the clause/sentence. *Kéyi.* "[It] is all right." is a simple, minor, verbal sentence which consists of a simple predicate. *Bú₁ dà₂ hǎo₃ ba₄!* "[That] is₃ not₁ very₂ good₃!₄" is the same kind of sentence, but with a complex predicate. *Zhèi₁ liǎngge₂ dōngxi₃, shémme₄ fēnbie₅ yě₆ méi₇ yǒu₈.* "[As to] these₁ two₂ things₃, there is₈ (not₇ even₆ any₄ =) no difference₅." is a simple, major, verbal sentence with the predicate in major clause form. *Xuésheng₁ lái₂.* "The students₁ are coming₂." is a simple, major, verbal sentence with a simple predicate.

3.2. A predicate may or may not contain a *central*. A central can occur only in the predicate, never in the topic subject. For predicates containing no central, see B 6, p. 6.

3.3. In a verbal sentence the non-omissible center of the predicate is the **central**. A simple sentence contains one central; a compound sentence contains one central in each clause. In an ambivalent sentence (5.5, p. 6) there is a composite central. A central is said to be negatable, negated, negative, or ambivalent. Words and phrases placed before the central are said to occur *precentrally*; if they occur after the central, they are said to occur *postcentrally*.

3.4. A central is always a *verb*. No verb is always a central in all of its occurrences. A verb which is a modifier or a constituent of a modifier is not a central. In $Tā_1$ $xǐhuan_2$ $zhòng_3$ $huār_4$. "He_1 $likes_2$ to $raise_3$ $flowers_4$." *xǐhuan* is the central (negatable). $Tā_1$ $zuò_2$ de_3 $nèige_4$ $fēijī_5$, $diàode_6$ $háili_7$ le_8. "The_4 $plane_5$ $which_3$ he_1 was on_2, has_8 $fallen_6$ [into] the $ocean_7$." has *diàode* as its central; the potential central *zuò* is part of the modifier. *Chī* is the central in $Yòng_1$ $kuàizi_2$ $chī_3$ $fàn_4$. "[Someone] $eats_3$ ($food_4$) $with_1$ $chopsticks_2$."

4.1. A **modifier** is an immediate constituent which enters into a type of endocentric construction called modification. The modifier is a descriptive element in the widest sense. A construct consisting of two immediate constituents, of which one partner is the center (and therefore non-omissible) and the other partner is a satellite (i.e. it presupposes the other, and is therefore omissible) is called a *modifier + modified construct.* A modifier can have the segmental form of a sentence/clause, a phrase, or a word (and within a word, the form of a morpheme). *Hǎishang* in *hǎishang de chuán* "the ships on the sea" modifies *chuán* (*de* is a marker); $Zài_1$ $Huánghé_2$ $fùjìn_3$ $zhù_4$. "[Someone] $lives_4$ $near_{1,3}$ the Yellow $River_2$." contains *zhù* as an element modified by the preceding words (here there is no marker).

A verb with its modifiers is a *verbal phrase* or *expression* (p. 9). A nominal with its modifiers is a *nominal phrase* (p. 9).

4.2. A modifier + modified construct is said to be **marked** or **unmarked**. A typical marker is *de: hǎishang de chuán* "ships on the sea". $Wǔjiàn_1$ $xíngli_2$ "five $pieces_1$ [of] $luggage_2$" is an example of unmarked modification.

4.3. A **marker** is a bound word whose function is to signal some specific syntactical relation between sentences/clauses, phrases, or words. Markers form a closed class. They are *pure* or *impure*. A pure marker has only grammatical function. An impure marker has a lexical meaning in addition to its grammatical function. *De* is a pure marker; *suírán* "although" is an impure marker.

4.4. Whereas modification involves **subordination** of one constituent to another (satellite and center), **coordination** is a construction in which both constituents are centers. Whereas the order of constituents in a subordinative construction is irreversible (= fixed order), the order of the constituents in a coordinative construction is, in principle, reversible (= no fixed order). Clauses, phrases, words, and morphemes can enter into coordinative constructions. As in the case of subordination (modification), coordination may be marked or unmarked. *Nǐ*₁ *wǒ*₂ *tā*₃ "you₁, I₂ [and] he₃" is an example of unmarked coordination; *nǐ gen wǒ gen tā* is a parallel utterance with a marker *gen* included.

5.1. The verbal sentence: Sentence types. Depending on whether the predicate central is *negatable, negated, negative,* or *ambivalent,* a sentence is said to be of the negatable, the negated, the negative, or the ambivalent **type.**

5.2. A central is said to be *negatable* if it occurs in non-negated form (i.e. not modified by any of the negators *bù* "not" or *méi* "not (yet)"). In such a case the sentence is said to be a negatable sentence. Examples of negatable centrals are: *Lái.* "[He] is coming."; *Hǎo.* "It's OK."

5.3. A central is said to be *negated* if it occurs with a modifying negator. *Méi lái.* "[He] hasn't come."; *Bú qù.* "[I] am not going." are examples of negated centrals. Such sentences are said to be negated sentences.

5.4. A central is said to be *negative* if it is non-negatable, but otherwise has all (or most) of the (verbal) functions of other centrals. This class has only one member: the word *méi* "there is/are not". Note that the negator *méi* modifies a central, whereas the verb *méi* is itself a central. *Méi* in *Méi*₁ *qián*₂. "(There is no₁ =) [someone] does not have₁ money₂." is a negative central, whereas *méi* is a negator in *Méi lái.* "Hasn't come."

5.5. A central is said to be *ambivalent* if it consists of two coordinated immediate constituents, i.e. if it is a constellation of two lexically identical verbs, the first of which is in the negatable (i.e. non-negated) form, and the other is in the negated form, so as to form two juxtaposed alternatives. This construction is one of the syntactical patterns of questions (ambivalent sentences): *Lái*₁ *bu*₂ *lai*₃. "(comes not comes =) Is₁ [someone] coming₁,₃ ([or] not₂)?" Similarly: *Yǒu*₁ *mei*₂ *you*₃. "([There] is₁/is₃ not₂ =) is/are there (any)?"

6. The non-verbal sentence. A sentence which contains no predicate central is a non-negatable, non-negated sentence. Its predicate usually consists of a nominal phrase. *Jiār jiǎr.* "Today is what date?" is an example.

7.1. Sentence forms. Depending on the *form* of the predicate, a sentence is said to represent a *vocative,* an *exclamatory,* an *interrogative,* an *imperative,* or a *declarative* form.

7.2. A sentence in the **vocative** form is a minor sentence which typically consists of a nominal or a nominal phrase. It is characterized by intonation and by a reduced pitch range. Sometimes a vocative particle *a* is added. The function of the vocative is to attract the listener's attention: *Wáng xiansheng!* "Mr. Wang!"

7.3. A sentence in the **exclamatory** form typically consists of an interjection, and is characterized by having intonation and stress, but no tone. Its function is to express emotion or some other psychological state on the part of the speaker: *E!* "hm!"; *Zaogao!* "What a mess!, Oh gosh!".

7.4. A sentence in the **interrogative** form conforms to one of five patterns:

a) It contains one of a limited number of question words: $Zhè_1$ $shì_2$ $shémme_3$? "What$_3$ is$_2$ this$_1$?"; $Shéi_1$ $huì_2$ $shuō_3$ $Zhōngguo$ $huà_4$. "Who$_1$ can$_2$ speak$_3$ Chinese$_4$?". *Shémme* and *shéi* are question words.

b) Its predicate contains an ambivalent central (B 5.5).

c) Its predicate contains two coordinated centrals so as to form a disjunctive question "or": $Tā_1$ $chī_2$ $fàn_3$ $chī_4$ $miàn_5$. "[Does] he$_1$ eat$_2$ rice$_3$ [or] [does] he eat$_4$ noodles$_5$?"

d) Its predicate contains one of a limited number of final interrogative particles: $Zhèige_1$ $hǎo_2$ ma_3. "Is$_2$ this one$_1$ all right$_2$?$_3$".

e) The intonation ends on a rather high level; none of the features mentioned under **a)** to **d)** are present. The sentence in this case has the segmental form of a declarative sentence, but is clearly and distinctly a question: $Nǐ_1$ $yòu_2$ $lái_3$ le_4. "[So] you$_1$ are already$_{2,4}$ back$_3$ again$_2$?"

7.5. A sentence in the **imperative** form typically consists of a verb with or without a modifier; it may also include a subject. It is characterized by a high-level intonation, sometimes in connection with the final particle *a*. Its function is to effect compliance: $Bié_1$ $dòng_2$! "Don't$_1$ move$_2$!".

7.6. A sentence in the **declarative** form lacks the special intonational features which are characteristic of vocative, exclamatory, and imperative sentence forms, but shares those found under interrogative sentences of types **a)**, **b)**, and **c)**. Declarative sentences have a falling intonation toward the end, with a marked drop on the last syllable. Their function is to state a fact, to inform, to describe, etc. Sentences of this form in a series are more common in formal speech than in ordinary conversation. Examples are: $Mǎ$ $xiansheng$. "Mr. Ma." (as an answer to the question: "Who is that gentleman?"); $Nèixie_1$ $shìqing_2$, $wǒ_3$ $yìdiǎr_4$ $yě_5$ $bú_6$ $jìde_7$ le_8. "[As far as] those$_1$ things$_2$ [are concerned], I$_3$ cannot$_6$ remember$_7$ (even$_5$) a single$_4$ [thing] (any more$_8$)."

8.1. A sentence that contains a **topic subject** (major sentence subject) is a major sentence (B. 1.4). A compound sentence may contain separate subjects in each of its clauses. Such subjects are *clause subjects*. In a simple sentence clause subject and sentence subject coincide.

8.2. A subject may have the *form* of a (major or minor) clause, a phrase, a word, or zero. It may be verbal (if its nucleus is a verb), or non-verbal (if its nucleus is a nominal). A final intonation does not occur within or after a subject. It forms, with a predicate as its second partner, an endocentric construction in which the predicate is the center. A subject is, in fact, a more or less common attribute to the predicate; if it occurs, it is regularly found in a precentral position. Since the subject is an omissible partner of the constitute, and never occurs without a predicate, its potential zero form is a natural consequence. The subject often has a rather loose formal and semantic connection with the predicate, and is separated or separable from it by a pause or by one of a few phrase particles, or by both. The function of the subject is to indicate, in a general way, the topic or the subject matter of the sentence/clause in the widest sense, and it may contain a specification as to actor, time, place, or may give other circumstantial reference to the general conceptual framework within which the action or the state of affairs expressed in the predicate takes place/does not take place, exists/does not exist, is valid/is not valid, etc. Examples: $T\bar{a}_1$, $dár_2$ $xi\check{a}o_3$. "(He$_1$, the courage$_2$ is small$_3$ =) he's quite a coward." (predicate in clause form, topic subject *tā*); $Z\grave{a}i_1$ $n\grave{a}r_2$ a, $t\bar{a}$ de_3 $shu\bar{o}_4$ $Zh\bar{o}ngguo_5$ $hu\grave{a}_6$ de_7 $j\bar{\imath}hui_8$ $h\acute{e}n_9$ $sh\check{a}o_{10}$. "(In$_1$ that place$_2$ =) there his$_3$ opportunities$_8$ of$_7$ speaking$_4$ [the] Chinese$_5$ (language$_6$) are few$_{9,10}$." (predicate in clause form; topic subject a verbal expression; *zài nàr*); $K\grave{a}n_1$ $xi\grave{a}nd\grave{a}i_2$ $xi\check{a}oshu\bar{o}r_3$ de_4 $sh\acute{\imath}hou_5$, $du\bar{o}_6$. "(The times$_5$ ... were many$_6$ =) [we] often$_{5,6}$ read$_1$ modern$_2$ novels$_3$." (predicate a word; subject a nominal phrase).

C. The Phrase

1.1. Phrases which are constituents of a sentence/clause are separated or separable from each other by minor pauses. In $Xi\grave{a}nz\grave{a}i_1$ de_2 $Zh\bar{o}ngguo_3$, $m\acute{\imath}x\grave{\imath}n_4$ de_5 $r\acute{e}n_6$, $sh\check{a}odu\bar{o}_7$ le_8. "[In] China$_3$ (of$_2$) nowadays$_1$ superstitious$_{4,5}$ people$_6$ have become$_8$ much fewer$_7$ [than before].", two minor pauses are possible between the three phrases; the second pause is not likely to occur unless the first occurs. Within phrases, pauses may, in slow speech, occur between free words.

1.2. A phrase may function as a topic subject or as a constituent of the same, as a predicate or as a constituent of the same, or as an adverbial.

1.3. A phrase consists of a *nucleus* with its modifiers. If the nucleus is a verbal expression, it is a **verbal phrase**; if the nucleus is a nominal expression, it is a **nominal phrase**. *Kànzhe*$_1$ *bào*$_2$. "[Someone] is reading$_1$ the newspaper$_2$." is a verbal phrase; *zhèibǎ*$_1$ *dāo*$_2$ "this$_1$ knife$_2$" is a nominal phrase. In *Tā*$_1$ *yòng*$_2$ *kuàizi*$_3$ *chī*$_4$ *fàn*$_5$. "She$_1$ eats$_4$ (rice$_5$) with$_2$ chopsticks$_3$.", the verbal expression *yòng kuàizi* functions·as an adverbial.

1.4. Phrases may stand in **coordination** with or in **subordination** tò each other (in the latter case one is said to modify another). In *Tīng*$_1$ *yīnyuè*$_2$, *niàn*$_3$ *shī*$_4$, *hén*$_5$ *yǒu*$_6$ *yìsi*$_7$. "To listen$_1$ [to] music$_2$ [and] read$_3$ poetry$_4$ is$_6$ very$_5$ interesting$_7$." two coordinated phrases make up the topic subject; both are, as a whole, subordinate to the predicate, which consists of one phrase.

1.5. A **nucleus** is the center of the phrase, i.e. a (simple, complex, or compound) word. The nucleus of a phrase may be identical with the central of a predicate (sentence); in that case the nucleus may serve as the center of a nest of modifications. An ambivalent central is for practical purposes counted as one composite nucleus. Phrase components other than that which is nuclear are said to occur in *prenuclear* or *postnuclear* position. *Bù*$_1$ *xūyào*$_2$ *hěn*$_3$ *duō*$_4$ *de*$_5$ *fángzi*$_6$. "[We] don't$_1$ need$_2$ (very$_3$) many$_4$ (of$_5$) rooms$_6$." contains the nucleus (and central) *xūyào* with a prenuclear (modifier) *bù* and the postnuclear nominal construct *hěn duō de fángzi* (object). The nucleus of the predicate phrase is the sentence central if the predicate is a verbal phrase: *Zhèijiān*$_1$, *wǒ*$_2$ *zuótian*$_3$ *kànguo*$_4$ *le*$_5$. "This one$_1$ (= this room) I$_2$ saw$_{4,5}$ yesterday$_3$." (*kànguo* is nucleus/central). If the predicate is a nominal phrase, the nucleus of the phrase as well as that of the sentence is a nominal nucleus: *Tā*$_1$ *érzi*$_2$, *chàbuduō*$_3$ *liǎngsuì*$_4$ *le*$_5$. "His$_1$ son$_2$ [is] already$_5$ about$_3$ two years$_4$ [old]." (*liǎngsuì* is the nucleus of the phrase/sentence). Note that such a sentence has no central, but it has a nucleus.

1.6. The function of a phrase in a larger context depends on its relative position in regard to the sentence central. Thus a *verbal phrase* in *precentral position* is either a topic subject or a modifier that is part of a verbal expression: *Zhòng*$_1$ *huār*$_2$, *hěn róngyi*$_3$. "To plant$_1$ flowers$_2$ is easy$_3$." (topic subject); *Ná*$_1$ *gāngbǐ*$_2$ *xiě*$_3$ *zì*$_4$. "To write$_3$ (characters$_4$) with$_1$ a pen$_2$."; *Dào*$_1$ *Rìběn*$_2$ *qù*$_3$. "To go$_3$ to$_1$ Japan$_2$." (*ná gāngbǐ* and *dào Rìběn* are constituents of a verbal expressions in series construction, see p. 11 for definition). A *verbal phrase* in *postcentral position* is often a constituent of an object or a predicative complement: *bù hǎo* is part of an object in clause form in: *Wǒ$_1$ shuō$_2$ zhè$_3$ bù$_4$ hǎo$_5$*. "I$_1$ say$_2$ this one$_3$ is$_5$ no$_4$ good$_5$."; *bù hǎo* is a complement in *Xiě de bù hǎo.* "[He] does not write well." A *nominal phrase* in *precentral position* is typically a sentence topic subject or a "small" subject (i.e. a subject forming part of the predicate): *Wǒ de$_1$ péngyou$_2$, shìlì$_3$ hěn dà$_4$.* "(As far as) my$_1$ friend$_2$ (is concerned, his) influence$_3$ is great$_4$." = "My friend is very influential." (*wǒ de péngyou* is the sentence topic subject; *shìlì* is the "small" subject within the predication). A *nominal phrase* in *postcentral position* is typically an object (direct or indirect): *Wǒ$_1$ zhǎobudào$_2$ nèige$_3$ rén$_4$.* "I$_1$ cannot find$_2$ that$_3$ man$_4$." (object: *nèige rén*); *Wǒ$_1$ gěile$_2$ ta$_3$ (yì)diǎr$_4$ qián$_5$.* "I$_1$ gave$_2$ him$_3$ some$_4$ money$_5$." (two objects); *Wǒ$_1$ nálai$_2$ tā$_3$ sònggei$_4$ wo$_5$ de$_6$ (nèiben$_7$) shū$_8$.* "I$_1$ will bring$_2$ the$_7$ book$_8$ which$_6$ he$_3$ sent$_4$ me$_5$." (the object is a nominal expression).

2.1. Types of verbal phrases. If the verb nucleus of a phrase is a transitive/intransitive action verb (also called a functive verb), the phrase is said to be a *transitive/intransitive action verb phrase*. If the verb nucleus of a phrase is a transitive/intransitive quality verb, the phrase is said to be a *transitive/intransitive quality verb phrase*. If the verb nucleus of a phrase is one of the two existential verbs *yǒu* and *méi*, the phrase is said to be an *existential verb phrase*. If the verb nucleus of a phrase is a classificatory verb, the phrase is said to be a *classificatory verb phrase*. If in a verbal expressions in series construction (C 2.8) the nucleus of a phrase serves as a coverb (D 3.4.3), the phrase is said to be a *coverbal phrase*. If the verb nucleus of a phrase is a modal verb, the phrase is said to be a *modal verb phrase.*

2.2. A transitive action verb phrase consists of a transitive action verb with or without its prenuclear modifiers, and with or without one or more postnuclear nominal expressions as object(s). The immediate phrase constituents are the verb and its modifier(s), if any, as the first partner, and the postnuclear elements as the second. If there are two objects (nominal phrases), the verb and the first object form the first immediate constituent, and the other object the second immediate constituent of the phrase. If the phrase serves as a predicate, it may also include one or more predicate particles (aspectual or modal). In the latter case the particle forms an immediate constituent with the rest of the phrase: *Chīle$_1$ fàn$_2$ le$_3$/ma$_4$.* "Has$_1$ [someone] (already$_3$) eaten$_1$ (food$_2$)?$_4$" (modal particle *ma*). *Hái$_1$ méi$_2$ dào$_3$ Běijīng$_4$.* "[He] has not$_2$ yet$_1$ arrived$_3$ [in] Peking$_4$." is a transitive action verb phrase with nucleus *dào*, with prenuclear modifiers *hái* and *méi* and with object *Běijīng. Hái$_1$*

méi$_2$ *dào*$_3$. "[Someone] has not$_2$ yet$_1$ arrived$_3$." represents the same type of phrase, but without an object. *Hái*$_1$ *méi*$_2$ *géi*$_3$ *wo*$_4$ *nèiben*$_5$ *shū*$_6$. "[He] has not$_2$ yet$_1$ given$_3$ me$_4$ that$_5$ book$_6$." contains two objects. In *Nǐ*$_1$ *shuō*$_2$ *Zhōngguo*$_3$ *huà*$_4$, *hén*$_5$ *hǎo*$_6$. "It is (very$_5$) good$_6$ [that] you$_1$ speak$_2$ (China$_3$ words$_4$) Chinese." the action verb phrase *shuō Zhōngguo huà* forms part of the subject. *Gěi*$_1$ *ta*$_2$ *liángběn*$_3$ *shū*$_4$, *yě*$_5$ *xíng*$_6$. "It will be all right$_6$ too$_5$ [if you] give$_1$ him$_2$ two$_3$ books$_4$." (the subject verbal phrase contains two objects).

2.3. An **intransitive action verb phrase** consists of an intransitive action verb with or without its prenuclear modifiers, and sometimes with a nominal expression as its object. Such objects are selectively limited to certain types: semantically cognate objects (*Zǒule*$_1$ *hěn*$_2$ *duō*$_3$ *de*$_4$ *lù*$_5$. "Has done$_1$ a lot$_{2,3}$ of$_4$ walking$_{1,5}$."), or objects mostly designating destination, origin, etc. (*Fēi*$_1$ *Běijīng*$_2$. "Fly$_1$ [to] Peking$_2$."). The verb in these cases is sometimes used in a causative sense: *Lái*$_1$ *chá*$_2$. "Bring$_1$ tea$_2$."

2.4. A **transitive quality verb phrase** consists of a transitive quality verb with or without prenuclear modifiers, and with or without a nominal expression as an object: *hén xǐhuan ta* in *Wó*$_1$ *hén*$_2$ *xǐhuan*$_3$ *ta*$_4$. "I$_1$ like$_3$ him$_4$ very much$_2$." is an example.

2.5. An **intransitive quality verb phrase** consists of an intransitive quality verb with or without prenuclear modifiers (indicating degree), and sometimes an object (usually indicating a quantity): *hén*$_1$ *hǎo*$_2$ "very$_1$ good$_2$"; *zuì*$_1$ *dà*$_2$ "(is most$_1$ big$_2$ =) is the biggest"; *Nǐ*$_1$ *zài*$_2$ *dàzhe*$_3$ *diǎr*$_4$ *shēngr*$_5$, *shuō*$_6$ *ba*$_7$. "Will you$_1$, please$_7$, (again$_2$) speak$_6$ (making$_3$ [your] voice$_5$ a little$_4$ bigger$_3$ =) a little louder."

2.6. An **existential verb phrase** consists of one of the two existential verbs *yǒu* "there is" and *méi* "there is not" with or without prenuclear modifiers, and usually a nominal expression as its object: *Yǒu qián.* "(There is =) I/you (etc.) have money."; *Tā méi gōngfu.* "(As for him, there is . . . =) he has no time."

2.7. A **classificatory verb phrase** consists of a classificatory verb (usually *shì* "it is") with or without prenuclear modifiers, and often followed by a nominal expression as its object: *Shì*$_1$ *wǒ*$_2$ *de*$_3$ *péngyou*$_4$. "[He] is$_1$ my$_{2,3}$ friend$_4$".

2.8. A **coverbal phrase** is a verbal phrase in a precentral position, functioning as a modifier of the following verbal phrase, so as to form a construction (named by Chao Yuan-ren *verbal expressions in series*). Being of an essentially adverbial nature, a coverbal phrase indicates some circumstantial specification such as time, place, purpose, benefit, means, manner, etc. In the following examples the verbs *zài, cóng, yòng*, and *gēn* are coverbs (i.e. nuclei in coverbal phrases): $zài_1$ $xuéxiào_2$ $niàn_3$ $sh\bar{u}_4$ "to study$_3$ (books$_4$) at$_1$ school$_2$"; $cóng_1$ $B\check{e}ij\bar{\imath}ng_2$ $lái_3$ "to come$_3$ from$_1$ Peking$_2$"; $yòng_1$ $kuàizi_2$ $ch\bar{\imath}_3$ $fàn_4$ "to eat$_3$ (food$_4$) with$_1$ chopsticks$_2$"; $g\bar{e}n_1$ wo_2 $qù_3$ "to go$_3$ with$_1$ me$_2$". A special type of such a precentral coverbal phrase, with a higher degree of grammatical formalization, is the use of the "pretransitive" coverb $b\check{a}$ "take" followed by a nominal expression: $B\check{a}_1$ $zhèige_2$ $bi\check{a}o_3$ $xi\bar{u}lih\check{a}o_4$. "(Take$_1$ this$_2$ watch$_3$ [and] repair$_4$ [it] =) repair this watch."

2.9. A **modal verb phrase** consists of a modal verb with or without its prenuclear modifiers and a following verbal expression: $Bù_1$ $y\bar{\imath}ngd\bar{a}ng_2$ $nèmmo_3$ $shu\bar{o}_4$. "[You] should$_2$ not$_1$ talk$_4$ like that$_3$."

3. An **object** is a nominal expression or a clause-like sequence which occurs in a post-verbal (i.e. postcentral or postnuclear) position. It occurs as a second immediate constituent in an endocentric construction with the verb as the center. Certain transitive verbs can take two objects (i.e. two nominal expressions); in this case the last object forms a second immediate constituent, with the verb and the first object as the first immediate constituent. A single object generally designates the goal toward which the action indicated by the verb is directed, and is, if not otherwise specified, of indefinite reference. In the case of a double object the first object indicates a person who receives something or for whose benefit or detriment the action indicated by the verb is carried out. Examples of objects: $Mài_1$ $sh\bar{u}_2$. "Sell$_1$ books$_2$." (single object: one word); $Xi\check{e}le_1$ $y\grave{\imath}f\bar{e}ng_2$ $xìn_3$. "Wrote$_1$ a$_2$ letter$_3$." (single object: a nominal expression); $T\bar{a}_1$ $shu\bar{o}_2$, $t\bar{a}_3$ $bú_4$ $yuànyi_5$ $qù_6$. "He$_1$ says$_2$ he$_3$ is$_5$ not$_4$ willing to$_5$ go$_6$." (single object: object in the segmental form of a major clause); $Wó_1$ $g\check{e}i_2$ ta_3 $li\check{a}ngkuài_4$ $qián_5$. "I$_1$ give$_2$ him$_3$ two$_4$ dollars$_5$." (double object); $Kànle_1$ $liángy\check{a}n_2$. "[He] gave$_1$ two glances$_2$." (cognate object indicating "number of times"); $Xiào_1$ $yíxiào_2$. "[He] smiled$_1$ a smile$_2$, smiled a little." (cognate object containing a repetition of the verb itself; tentative aspect).

4.1. A **nominal phrase** has a nominal (D 4.1) as its nucleus, or contains a phrase marker *de* specifying its function. Nominal phrases are: $li\check{a}ngkuài_1$ $qián_2$ "two$_1$ dollars$_2$" (nucleus: $qián$); $xi\check{a}o_1$ $háizi_2$ "little$_1$ child$_2$" (nucleus: $háizi$); $zh\check{a}obudào_1$ de_2 $sh\bar{u}_3$ "the book$_3$ which$_2$ [I] cannot find$_1$" (nucleus: $sh\bar{u}$); $dào_1$ $Nánj\bar{\imath}ng_2$ de_3 $lù_4$ "the road$_4$ which$_3$ goes to$_1$ Nanking$_2$" (nucleus: $lù$); $gèrén$ de_1 $wèntí_2$ "personal$_1$ problems$_2$" (nucleus: $wèntí$). Some nominal phrases have no clearcut nominal nucleus, but have instead a special nominal marker *de*: $mài_1$ $sh\bar{u}_2$ de_3 "(sell$_1$ book$_2$ -er$_3$ =) bookseller"; $t\bar{a}_1$ $shu\bar{o}_2$ de_3 "what$_3$ he$_1$ said$_2$".

4.2. **The prenuclear modifier** in a nominal phrase is a nominal or verbal expression, or a subject + predicate construction. An example of the latter is: $ní_1$ $xiě_2$ de_3 $zì_4$ "the characters$_4$ which$_3$ you$_1$ wrote$_2$".

4.3. When two or more nominals occur in a sequence so as to form one or more nominal phrases, the constituents may stand in a **subordinative** or a **coordinative** relation. a) If there is only one nucleus, that nucleus is the last constituent: $jīngjì_1$ $jiànshè_2$ "economic$_1$ construction$_2$"; $xīnwén_1$ $jìzhě_2$ "news$_1$ reporter$_2$". b) If there are several nuclei, they stand in coordination with one another. Coordination may be marked or unmarked. Examples: $fēngsú_1$ $xíguàn_2$ "customs$_1$ [and] habits$_2$"; $shūrù_1$ $shūchū_2$ "imports$_1$ [and] exports$_2$"; $nǐ_1$ gen_2 $wǒ_3$ "you$_1$ and$_2$ I$_3$" (*gen* is a marker of coordination). In the absence of markers both types of relationships are established by mere juxtaposition. Possible ambiguities are usually resolved by the context. A special case of coordination is *apposition*: $wǒmen_1$ $Zhōngguo$ $rén_2$ "we$_1$ Chinese$_2$"; $Běijīng$ $Zhōngguo$ (de) $shǒudū$ "Peking, the capital of China". In the case of subordination, if the modifier is a nominal, a marker may or may not be included (sometimes with a difference in meaning: $Zhōngguó$ $Yínháng$ "the Bank of China"; $Zhōngguó$ de $yínháng$ "banks in China"). If the modifier is a single quality verb, the marker is not required ($gāo$ $shān$ or $gāo$ de $shān$ "high mountains"). But if the verb is further modified, the marker is inserted: $hěn$ $gāo$ de $shān$. With an action verb as a modifier a marker is almost invariably required: $yòng_1$ de_2 $bǐ_3$ "the pen$_3$ which$_2$ was used$_1$". If a longer expression consisting of several phrases is a modifier, a marker is required.

5. An expression which functions as a predicate may include one or more **predicative particles**. They are of two types, aspectual or modal, and occur in sentence-final position. If in a sentence both types of particles are present, the modal particle occupies the absolute final position, whereas the aspectual particle occupies the prefinal position. Generally the aspect particle *le* indicates the speaker's realization of a situation as new; the modal particles usually modulate or color the preceding sequence (question, advice, assumption, etc.) $Jǐsuì_1$ le_2. "(How many years$_1$ =) how old [is he/she] now$_2$?" (aspect particle with a nominal expression); $Yǐjīng_1$ $liùsuì_2$ le_3 ma_4. "[Is he/she] already$_1$ six years$_2$ [old]?$_4$" (*le$_3$* indicating realization of new situation; *ma* modal particle of question; particles bound with a nominal phrase). In this sentence the particle *ma* is an immediate constituent with the whole of the preceding; on the next level of analysis *le* is an immediate constituent with $yǐjīng$ $liùsuì$. Further examples: $Chīle_1$ $fàn_2$ le_3. "[Someone] has eaten$_{1,3}$ (food$_2$)." (aspect particle with verbal phrase); $Nǐ_1$, $zài_2$ $Chóngqìng_3$ $zhùle_4$ $sānnián_5$ le_6 ma_7. "Have$_4$ you$_1$ been living$_4$ in$_2$

Chungking$_3$ [for] three years$_5$ now$_6$?$_7$" (particles *le* and *ma* with verbal and coverbal phrase); *Wǒmen$_1$, zǒu$_2$ ba$_3$.* "Let$_3$ us$_1$ go$_2$." (predicate verb with modal particle *ba*); *Wǒ$_1$, yě$_2$ yào$_3$ qù$_4$ ne$_5$.* "I$_1$, too$_2$, want to$_3$ go$_4$ [there], [don't you see!$_5$]."

D. The Word

1. **A word** is 1) free or bound, 2) simple, compound, or complex (derived), 3) primary or secondary. A word is a member of a word class; by class overlap, a word may be a member of more than one word class.

1.1. **A free word** is a minimal pause group bounded by potential pauses. It is the smallest unit which can occur as a sentence or as a syntactic constituent of a sentence. It is the smallest unit which has the capability of permutation, i.e. it can, as a unit, change position within a sentence. Most bisyllabic words are free.

1.2. **Bound words** (not to be confused with bound morphemes, cp. A 2.6) are particles and markers. They are bound to phrases, clauses, or sentences. The marker *de* and particles *le*, *ne* and *ba* are examples.

1.3. **A simple word** consists of one root morpheme (monosyllabic or polysyllabic): *rén* "person"; *dǎ* "to hit"; *zuì* "most"; *dōngxi* "thing"; *àsīpīlíng* "aspirin"; *kāfēi* "coffee".

1.4. **A compound word** is an endocentric or exocentric construct containing more than one (very often two) root morphemes, either of which may or may not occur in other contexts as free words: *mìfēng* "bee" and *fēngmì* "honey" are compound words consisting of the (otherwise) free words *mì* "honey" and *fēng* "bee"; *lìshǐ* "history" is a compound consisting of *lì* "calendar" and *shǐ* "history", both of which are bound morphemes — these examples are endocentric; *dǒngshi* "board member" is an exocentric compound consisting of the bound morpheme *dǒng* "arrange" and the (otherwise) free morpheme *shì* "matter, affair".

1.5. **A complex word** consists of at least one root morpheme and an affix (usually a derivational suffix). A *suffix* is a member of a listable class of purely grammatical morphemes which are attached to roots or combinations of roots. Suffixes are always bound and usually atonic, and their chief function is to indicate the class membership of the word as a whole. Examples of complex words are: *shítou* "stone" (*-tou* is a nominal suffix), *cuòr* "a mistake" (*cuò* "to be wrong" + nominal suffix *-r*), *pùzi* "a store" (nominal suffix *-zi*), *děngzhe* "is waiting" (verbal suffix *-zhe*).

1.6. A primary word is either a monosyllabic free word (*lái* "to come") or a bisyllabic word in which at least one constituent is a bound morpheme (*jīntian* "today"). If one morpheme is a bound root morpheme and the other a suffix, the word is a *primary derived word* (*jìngzi* "a mirror", from a bound root *jìng*).

1.7. A secondary word is either 1) a compound consisting of free morphemes, or 2) a free root morpheme plus an affix. In *huǒchē* "train" both morphemes (*huǒ* "fire" and *chē* "car") are free; *lóngzi* "a deaf person" consists of the root (free word) *lóng* "to be deaf" plus the suffix *-zi*. In the latter case the word is a *secondary derived word*.

1.8. Any word which contains an affix (usually a suffix) is said to be a **derived word**.

2.1. Depending partly on morphological structure and partly on selection, words are members of **word classes**. *Dīngzi* "a nail" is marked as a nominal by the suffix *-zi*; *dǎ* "to hit", and *rén* "person" are a verb and a nominal respectively simply because of the feature of arbitrary selection. *Bìng* "to be sick, a sickness" is a verb as well as a nominal by virtue of selection.

2.2. For our purposes six word classes are set up: *verbs, nominals, adverbs, interjections, particles*, and *markers*. The last two classes consist of grammatical words; the other classes are lexical. Among lexical words a basic distinction may be made between verbs on the one hand and non-verbs (nominals, adverbs, interjections) on the other. Some words (*pǎo* "to run", *dà* "to be big", *kànjian* "to see") are verbs in all their occurrences; others are non-verbs in all their occurrences (*shū* "book", *diǎnxin* "sweets", *yǐjing* "already"). There are numerous cases of class overlap, especially in the case of nominals and verbs, and verbs and adverbs (*xiāng* "to be fragrant; fragrance").

3.1. A verb is a word which is negatable or negative (cp. B 5.2). In most cases verbs also take one of the aspectual suffixes (*-le, -zhe, -guo, -qilai*). Verbs are simple or compound (D 3.5).

3.2. Verbs may be divided into two main categories: 1) *description* verbs (these are lexical and form an open class); 2) *relation verbs* (of limited membership; function is mainly grammatical). Some verbs are members of both categories.

3.3. Description verbs are of two kinds: 1) *action verbs* (also called *functive verbs*); 2) *quality verbs*. Relation verbs are of four kinds: 1) *existential* verbs *yǒu* and *méi*; 2) *classificatory verbs*; 3) *coverbs*; 4) *modal verbs*.

3.3.1. Action verbs and quality verbs are *transitive* or *intransitive*.

Classifactory verbs and coverbs are transitive. Modal verbs mostly take action verbs as their "objects". The difference between transitivity and intransitivity is not absolute, but is rather a matter of degree. *Transitive* verbs, whether they are action verbs, quality verbs, classificatory verbs, or coverbs, regularly and frequently take a wide variety of objects (lexical compatibility is the limiting factor). Some transitive verbs take two objects: *Sòngle$_1$ ta$_2$ sānběn$_3$ shū$_4$.* "[I] sent$_1$ him$_2$ three$_3$ books$_4$." Examples of transitive action verbs are *chī* "to eat", *mǎi* "to buy", *zuò* "to make", *sòng* "to send". Transitive quality verbs are *xǐhuan* "to like", *xiāngxìn* "to believe", *ài* "to love".

Intransitive verbs regularly and frequently occur without an object; if an object is actually attached, it is likely to be a cognate object (e.g. *kàn yikan* "(to take a look =) to glance (at)"), or some specification as to quantification (extent) or destination: *Shuō$_1$ liǎngcì$_2$* "to say$_1$ [it] twice$_2$"; *Bìngle$_1$ sāntiān$_2$.* "[He] was sick$_1$ [for] three days$_2$." Intransitive verbs used transitively often take on a causative sense: *Lái$_1$ chá$_2$!* "Bring$_1$ [some] tea$_2$!" By class overlap some verbs are transitive as well as intransitive (*duǎn*: 1) "to be short" (*Yìtiáo$_1$ hén$_2$ duǎn de$_3$ lù$_4$.* "A$_1$ quite$_2$ short$_3$ road$_4$."); 2) "to be short of = to owe (money)": *Wǒ$_1$ hái$_2$ duǎnzhe$_3$ ta$_4$ wǔkuài$_5$ qián$_6$.* "I$_1$ still$_2$ owe$_3$ him$_4$ five$_5$ dollars$_6$."

3.3.2. An **action verb** is modifiable by the word *bié* "don't!", and can, in general, take any of the aspect suffixes (*-le* for perfective aspect, *-zhe* for durative aspect, *-guo* for indefinite aspect of the past: *xiěle/xiězhe/xiěguo yìfēng xìn* "has written/is writing/has once (in the past) written a letter"). Further, verbs of this category form a tentative aspect by reduplication (monosyllabics: *kànkan* "just look", *xiǎngxiang* "just think"; note that the second syllable has neutral tone; bisyllabics: *tǎolun taolun* "discuss a little"). Semantically, action verbs denote an action in the widest sense: *gǔn* "to roll", *yǎn* "to perform", *dài* "to wear" (a hat, etc.).

3.3.3. A **quality verb** is a verb which is modifiable by the adverbs of degree *hěn* "very" and *zuì* "most". They do not normally take the aspect suffix *-zhe*, but can be reduplicated ("vivid reduplication"): *hǎohāorde* "extremely good"; *qīngqīngchǔchū* (of *qīngchu* "clear") "perfectly clear". Quality verbs, when not further modified, regularly serve as modifiers of nominals without an explicit marker: *hǎo shū* "good books". Quality verbs are mostly translatable as adjectives.

3.4. Relation verbs form a closed class; they have primarily grammatical functions.

3.4.1. The verbs *yǒu* "to exist, to be, to have", and its negative counterpart *méi* are here classified together as **existential verbs**. The verb *yǒu* is regularly negatable only by the negator *méi*: *Méi yǒu*. "There isn't/aren't any; he/she/they has/have none." The verb *méi*, being negative, is non-negatable.

3.4.2. A classificatory verb is not, in general, modifiable by *bié* or *hěn*. Although transitive, verbs of this class do not take the "pretransitive construction" with *bǎ*. Classificatory verbs are *shì* "to be (identical with, equal to)", *xìng* "to be named (so and so)", and some others.

3.4.3. A coverb is a member of a limited class of verbs which occur as first members of a verbal expressions in series construction. They are transitive, and form, with their objects, adverbial modifications of the verb central. *Yòng* in *yòng₁ kuàizi₂ chī₃ fàn₄* "to eat$_{3,4}$ with$_1$ chopsticks$_2$" functions as a coverb.

3.4.4. A modal verb is a member of a limited class of verbs which occur before action verbs or verbal expressions, adding a semantic value of modality ("can, will, must") to the expression as a whole. Modal verbs do not usually take aspect suffixes. *Huì* in *huì₁ shuō₂ Zhōngguo huà₃* "can$_1$ speak$_2$ Chinese$_3$" is a modal verb.

3.5.1. A verb which contains only one root morpheme is a **simple verb**: *děng* "wait", *zhuā* "to snatch". A verb which contains more than one root morpheme is a *compound verb*.

3.5.2. Compound verbs are extremely numerous and represent many types. The internal structure of a compound verb conforms to one of the following morphological types: **a)** the first immediate constituent modifies the second (*subordinate compound*, type I): *lìyòng* ("profit" + "use" =) "make use of, apply", *qīngshì* ("to be light" + "look, view" =) "look down upon, despise"; **b)** the second immediate constituent is subordinate to the first (historically an object, *subordinate compound*, type II): *dòngshēn* ("move" + "body" =) "to start" *tíyì* ("bring up" + "discussion" =) "to propose"; **c)** the two constituents stand in coordination, and are sometimes synonymous or near-synonymous (*coordinate compound*): *cúnzài* ("exist" + "be present, exist" =) "to exist"; **d)** the second constituent gives the result of the action indicated by the first (*resultative compound*) *shuōmíngbai* (*shuō* "speak" + *míngbai* "understand" =) "explain"; **e)** the second immediate constituent gives the result of the action indicated by the first, but a potential infix is inserted between the constituents (*potential resultative compound*): *kànbudǒng* ("read" + "not" + "understand" =) "be unable to understand when reading"; **f)** the second immediate constituent gives the direction of the action indicated by the first verb (*directional compound*): *pǎochuqu* ("run" + "go out" + "go away" =) "to run out (from here)"; **g)** the second immediate constituent gives the direction of the action indicated by the first verb, but a potential infix is inserted between the constituents (*potential directional compound*): *nádeshànglái* ("take" + "can" + "go up" + "come" =) "can take (or: bring) [it] up here". In type d) the element *míngbai* is called a *resultative complement*; in type e) (*bù*)*dǒng* is called a *potential resultative complement*; in type f) *chuqu* is called a *directional complement*; in type g) (*de*)*shànglái* is called a *potential directional complement*.

4.1. A **nominal** is a word which is non-negatable and which occurs in precentral position (very often as a major subject) as well as in post-central position (very often as the object of the central verb). It is generally modifiable by other nominals, nominal or verbal phrases, and by quality verbs. Like verbs, but unlike adverbs, interjections, particles, and markers, a nominal often serves as the nucleus of a phrase. Like interjections, but unlike particles and markers, and to some extent adverbs, it is usually a free word. *Xiǎo háizi* is a subject in *Xiǎo₁ háizi₂ zài₃ jiāli₄*. "The little₁ child₂ is₃ at₃ home₄.", but is an object in *Jiāli₁ yóu₂ xiǎo₃ háizi₄*. "[At] home₁ there are₂ small₃ children₄."; the quality verb *xiǎo* modifies *háizi* without specific marking. Nominals are simple, complex, or compound.

4.2. **Simple nominals** are either nouns or pronouns; they consist of one morpheme: *rén* "person", *shū* "book", *kāfēi* "coffee".

4.3. **Compound nominals** conform, as regards internal structure, to one of the following main types: **a)** the first immediate constituent modifies the second (*subordinate compound type I*): *huǒchē* ("fire" + "car" =) "train"; *wòchē* ("to sleep" + "car" =) "wagon-lit"; *dàren* ("to be big" + "man" =) "adult person"; *zhèige* ("this" + measure: "piece" =) "this one"; *sānjiàn* ("three" + "pieces" =) "three items (e.g. of baggage)" (the last two examples are determinative compounds); **b)** the second immediate constituent (historically an object) is dependent on the first constituent (*subordinate compound type II*): *lǐngshì* ("to guide, direct" + "affairs" =) "a consul"; **c)** the two immediate constituents stand in coordination (*coordinative compounds*): *shānshuǐ* ("mountains" + "water" =) "landscape"; *jiàoshòu* ("teach" + "transmit" =) "professor"; *chángduǎn* ("to be long" + "to be short" =) "length".

4.4. A **complex nominal** ends in one of a small number of suffixes: *mào-zi* "a hat"; *lí-ba* "a fence" (nouns); *zhuō-shang* "on the table" (place word); *nǐ-men* "you (plur.)" (pronoun).

4.5. A nominal is a) a *noun*, b) a *pronoun*, c) a *determinative compound*, d) a *place word*, or e) a *time word*.

4.5.1. A **noun** is a nominal which is modifiable by a determinative compound. Examples are *rén, qián*, and *wèntí* respectively in *zhèige rén* "this person", *liangkuài qián* "two dollars", *nèizhŏng wèntí* "that (kind of) problem". Depending on the determinative compound with which they can be combined, nouns can be divided into a number of subgroups (mass nouns, abstract nouns, etc.). Like other nominals, nouns are neutral in regard to number; a single, non-modified noun tends to have a collective meaning (*rén* "people", *xìn* "letters"). Singularization or individualization can be established by a determinative compound as modifier: *yíwèi₁ xiānsheng₂* "a₁ gentleman₂". An explicit "plural" (actually a collective) can be expressed by the suffix *-men* added to nouns denoting persons: *xuéshengmen* "students".

4.5.2. A **pronoun** is a substitute for a nominal: *wŏ* "I", *nĭ* "you", *tā* "he/she/it" (also with the "plural" suffix *-men*: *wŏmen* "we", etc.); *shéi* "who?"; *zhèi* "this (one)". Pronouns rarely take modifiers.

4.5.3. A **determinative compound** is either 1) a demonstrative + a measure (*zhèige* "this (one)"), or 2) a numeral + a measure (*sānge* "three (pieces or items)"). Very often a noun is modified by a demonstrative followed by a numeral + measure compound: *zhèi sānge rén* "these three people". A *demonstrative* is a pronoun: *zhè* "this", *nà* "that". It is a free word. *Numerals* and *measures* are not free words, but bound morphemes which are used in word-formation (numerals are used freely only when naming numbers and when counting). Determinative compounds have as one of their chief functions the modification of nouns: *wŭjiàn₁ shì₂* "five₁ things₂ (matters)", *zhèitiáo₁ lù₂* "this₁ road₂". Note that a further modifier, in the form of a word, a phrase, or a clause, can be inserted between the determinative compound and the noun: *zhèi₁ wŭjiàn₂ zhòngyào₃ de₄ shì₅* "these₁ five₂ important₃,₄ matters₅"; *nĭ₁ jiè₂ de₃ nèi₄ liángbĕn₅ shū₆* "those₄ two₅ books₆ which₃ you₁ borrowed₂".

4.5.4. A **place word** is a nominal (including place names, which are actually proper names) which can occur as an object after the verbs *zài* "to be at/on/in" and *dào* "to arrive in/at". Practically all place words are compound or complex. Marked place words are complex (i.e. they contain a localizer suffix): *zài₁ zhuōzishang₂* "on₁ [the] table₂", *zài₁ qiántou₂* "in₁ front₂". A noun denoting a place is not necessarily a place word unless a localizer suffix is added.

4.5.5. A **time word** is a nominal which can occur not only after *zài* and *dào* (similar to place words), but also after *dĕngdao* "until", and between *cóng* "from" and *qĭ* "begin(ning)": *dĕngdao₁ míngtian₂* "wait until₁ tomorrow₂", *cóng₁ Hàncháo₂ qĭ₃* "beginning₃ with₁ [the] Han Dynasty₂". Some time words are compound (*xiànzài* "now"), others are complex, i.e. they contain a suffix (*jiār* "today").

5. An **adverb** is a non-negatable (and generally non-modifiable) word which occurs in the preverbal position (unipositionally). Being a non-nuclear unit, an adverb is typically a modifier (or a constituent of a modifier) of a verb or a verbal expression.

Examples are: *hěn* in *hén$_1$ hǎo$_2$* "(very$_1$) good$_2$"; *bù* in *bù hén hǎo* (in which *bù* is an immediate constituent with *hén hǎo*, and *hěn* with *hǎo*); *hěn$_1$ bù$_2$-hǎo$_3$* "(very much$_1$ not$_2$ good$_3$" =) extremely bad" (in which *hěn* is an immediate constituent with *bù-hǎo*); *dàgài* in *dàgài$_1$ méi$_2$ yǒu$_3$ guānxi$_4$* "[it] probably$_1$ has$_3$ no$_2$ (connection =) importance$_4$"; *gāngcái* in *gāngcái$_1$ láile$_2$* "[someone] just$_1$ came$_2$". Adverbs are either complex (i.e. marked by a suffix, e.g. *dāngrán* "of course") or simple (i.e. not marked by a suffix, e.g. *zuì* in *zuì dà* "(the) biggest"). If phrases and words which are not primarily adverbs occur in an adverbial position, they are said to function adverbially: *Hòulái$_1$, tiān$_2$ jiù$_3$ qīng$_4$ le$_5$.* "Afterwards$_1$ [the] (sky =) weather$_2$ (then$_3$) cleared$_{4,5}$." A few quality verbs function adverbially so frequently that the dual function of these verbs may be considered as a case of class overlap: *Bú$_1$ dà$_2$ dǒng$_3$* "[someone] does not$_1$ understand$_3$ well$_2$." Adverbs commonly express degree, manner, scope, negation, etc.

6. An **interjection** is a free word with exclamatory value, which lacks tone, but has intonation and stress: *Wei!* "Hello!"

7. A **particle** is a bound word which is usually atonic, and whose function is grammatical. A particle never occurs at the beginning of a sentence, and is mostly bound to subject or predicate phrases or words. If bound to predicate phrases, particles are either aspectual or modal. In the following example, *a* is a subject particle: *Zhèige$_1$ rén$_2$ a, yídìng$_3$ bú$_4$ shì$_5$ yíge$_6$ Zhōngguo rén$_7$.* "He$_{1,2}$ is$_5$ definitely$_3$ not$_4$ a$_6$ Chinese$_7$." *Ma* is bound to the predicate in: *Nǐ$_1$ rènshi$_2$ ta$_3$ ma$_4$.* "Do$_2$ you$_1$ know$_2$ him$_3$?$_4$"

8. A **marker** is a bound word which has grammatical function. It indicates the relation between constituents such as words, phrases, clauses, and sometimes sentences, or it may mark off a phrase in such a way that it functions differently from the way it normally does. A subordinative marker before nominals is *de*: *wǒ de$_1$ shū$_2$* "my$_1$ book$_2$"; *wǒ$_1$ zhǎobudào$_2$ de$_3$ shū$_4$* "the book$_4$ which$_3$ I$_1$ cannot find$_2$"; *nǐ$_1$ gāngcái$_2$ gēn$_3$ ta$_4$ shuō$_5$ huà$_6$ de$_7$ (nèige$_8$) nüren$_9$* "(that =) the$_8$ woman$_9$ (with$_3$ her$_4$ =) with whom you$_1$ just$_2$ talked$_5$ (words$_6$)". A subordinative marker between verbs is *de*: *zǒu$_1$ de$_2$ kuài$_3$* "to walk$_1$ fast$_3$". A coordinative marker is *gen* (mostly between nominals): *nǐ$_1$ gen$_2$ wǒ$_3$* "You$_1$ and$_2$ I$_3$". A nominalizing marker, which is often used to turn verbal expressions into nominal expressions, is *de*: *zuò$_1$ mǎimai$_2$*

de_3 ("("do"$_1$ + "business"$_2$ + "one who"$_3$ =) a businessman". Other markers are sometimes called "impure" because, in addition to their grammatical class meaning, they have a more or less clearly defined lexical meaning. This category includes *yàoshi*, a subject marker (at or near the beginning of the sequence to which it is bound), which includes the conditional meaning "if", *suírán* (including the concessive meaning "although"), and *yīnwei* (including cause or reason "because"; this marker sometimes occurs in the predicate). A marker occurring at the beginning of a sentence or between two clauses, is *dànshi* "but"; it indicates a difference or other contrast of meaning with the preceding sequence: $Nǐ_1$ $qù_2$ $kéyi_3$, $dànshi_4$ $déi_5$ $záo_6$ $diǎr_7$ $huílai_8$. "You$_1$ may$_3$ go$_2$, but$_4$ [you] must$_5$ be back$_8$ (a little$_7$) early$_6$."

CHAPTER II

THE SENTENCE

A. General

1. In Chinese, as in other languages, speech, whether in the form of a talk or a conversation, is a *chain* of linguistic material occurring in a given context. Such a chain consists of components, which we may call *major segments*. Segments of this kind are of varying lengths, and may have varying degrees of complexity. In a sequence like

$Zhè_1$ $shì_2$ $nǐ$ de_3 $hùzhào_4$. $Nǐ_5$ $zài_6$ $zhèr_7$ $kéyi_8$ $tíngliú_9$ $sānge_{10}$ $yuè_{11}$. "$This_1$ is_2 $your_3$ $passport_4$. You_5 can_8 $stay_9$ (at_6 this $place_7$ =) $here_7$ [for] $three_{10}$ $months_{11}$."

two major segments can be discerned. They are set off against each other by a break, here indicated by a full stop. Each such major segment is a *sentence*.

Within each sentence a number of *minor segments* can be identified. Examples of such minor segments are *hùzhào*, *nǐ de hùzhào*, *zài zhèr*, *tíngliú*, *sānge yuè*, *tíngliú sānge yuè*, etc. Minor segments are words, or a group of words that belong together. All segments, major or minor, simple or complex, which occur and reoccur in various contexts with the same or approximately the same form and meaning, are *grammatical forms*.

Pauses between major segments are in principle obligatory. Pauses between minor segments may occur, but with less regularity.

2. The *sentence* is, within a chain of speech, the largest segment of language material about which specific descriptive statements of a linguistic type can be made. It is independent in the sense that it does not stand in grammatical construction with other segments (although it may logically or psychologically be more or less closely tied to preceding or succeeding sentences). It is complete in the sense that it forms a structured grammatical whole, it forms a semantically complete entity, and it is characterized by certain accentual patterns. Structural signals

22

like pauses and accentual features are manifested in close interplay, and this generally makes it possible, without much difficulty, to decide where the cuts between sentences are to be made.

3. The total accentual "profile" (the suprasegmental features) of the sentence consists of 1) intonations, 2) tones, 3) stresses. Of these, tones are phonemes which form part of morphemic shapes, and thus operate inside syllables. They contribute very significantly to the impressionistic "image" of the whole sentence. Intonation, on the other hand, is a sentence/clause feature, and is not tied to a morpheme or even a word as such. Tone and intonation should be kept strictly apart. They are easily mixed up, because both involve musical pitch. Stress belongs with words as well as with phrases and sentences. All three are of fundamental importance in Chinese. Intonation and stress are part of grammar and are therefore dealt with in some detail in the following. Tones fall within the sphere of phonology, and are therefore not dealt with in this book.

4. Sentences may be described according to their *type*, *form* and *structure*.

a) As far as *type* is concerned the most basic distinction is between *verbal* and *non-verbal* sentences. Most sentences are verbal sentences. Among verbal sentences four subtypes can be distinguished, viz. negatable, negated, negative, and ambivalent. Non-verbal sentences are for the most part nominal sentences.

b) Sentence *form* is vocative, exclamatory, interrogative, imperative, or declarative.

Note that type *and* form are both necessary to describe a given sentence. *Zhè shì nǐ de hùzhào.* (see p. 22), is a verbal/declarative sentence or, more precisely, a negatable/declarative sentence. *Nǐ yǒu mei you qián.* "Do you have some money?" is a verbal (ambivalent)/interrogative sentence. *Jīntian lǐbàiwǔ.* "Today is Friday." is a non-verbal/declarative sentence. *Wáng xiansheng!* "Mr. Wang!" is a non-verbal vocative sentence.

c) Sentence *structure* depends on the parts of which the sentence is made up. A sentence is said to be *simple* if it consists of only one clause. The sentences quoted under b) are all simple sentences. A sentence which is not simple is *compound*, i.e. it consists of several clauses. There is no definite limit to the number of clauses which may be included in one sentence; in some styles there may be five or six. Note that some simple sentences may be long, whereas some compound sentences may be quite short. *Zhèige$_1$ fázi$_2$ hǎo$_3$; nèige$_4$ fázi$_5$ bù$_6$ hǎo$_7$.* "This$_1$ way$_2$ (of doing it) is good$_3$; that$_4$ way$_5$ is$_7$ no$_6$ good$_7$." is a compound sentence. *Zài$_1$ hěn$_2$ duō$_3$ nián$_4$ yǐqián$_5$, Zhōngguo$_6$ yǒu$_7$ yīge$_8$ qīngnián$_9$, líkāile$_{10}$*

jiāxiāng$_{11}$ dào$_{12}$ Nányáng$_{13}$ qù$_{14}$ móushēng$_{15}$. "(Very$_2$) many$_3$ years$_4$ ago$_{1,5}$ there was$_7$ [in] China$_6$ a$_8$ young man$_9$ [who] left$_{10}$ [his] home village$_{11}$ [and] went to$_{12,14}$ (the Southern Seas$_{13}$ =) Southeast Asia to make a living$_{15}$." is a simple sentence.

From the point of view of structure a distinction should also be made between *major* and *minor* sentences. Any sentence must contain at least one predicate. *Minor sentences* contain a predicate and nothing else (*Hǎojíle*. "Extremely good."; *Kéyi$_1$ tíngliú$_2$ sānge$_3$ yuè$_4$*. "[You] may$_1$ stay$_2$ [for] three$_3$ months$_4$."). *Major* sentences contain a sentence topic subject as well as a predicate. Examples of major sentences: *Chē$_1$ lái$_2$ le$_3$*. "The car$_1$ (has$_3$ arrived$_2$ =) is here."; *Zhōngguo$_1$ sīchóu$_2$ shēng-chǎn$_3$, yǐjīng$_4$ yóu$_5$ háojǐ$_6$ qiānnián$_7$ de$_8$ lìshǐ$_9$ le$_{10}$*. "Chinese$_1$ silk and silk material$_2$ production$_3$ (already$_{4,10}$) has$_5$ several$_6$ thousand years$_7$ of$_8$ history$_9$."

In the following main sections of this chapter we shall deal with the Chinese sentence according to the following outline:

B. Intonation

1. TONE AND INTONATION

It is common knowledge that Chinese is a tonal language, i.e. that it contains a class of phonemes (sometimes called *tonemes*) characterized, not by vocalic or consonantal values, but by musical pitch. It is thus quite natural that attention has been focused on the tones. Unfortunately this has resulted in another, equally important part of the accentual system of Chinese, viz. intonation, being largely overlooked or at least given insufficient attention. In a tonal language like Chinese, intonation is a far more elusive phenomenon to observe and describe than in languages where pitch is manifested only in the form of intonational patterns, as in English. Thus the importance of intonation as a feature of Chinese speech was not generally recognized until fairly recently. For these reasons our present knowledge of Chinese intonation is rather limited and a great deal of research in this area remains to be done. We can deal with it here only on a very elementary level.

Tone is an immediate constituent of the morpheme; it operates within the framework of the syllable. Intonation, on the other hand, is an immediate constituent of larger segments of speech, such as clauses and sentences. In principle no utterance is possible without intonation as part of the total phonetic shape. In a short sentence consisting of only two or three words, intonation is somewhat hard to hear and identify; in longer sentences, particularly compound sentences, intonational features manifest themselves more clearly.

2. THE FUNCTION OF INTONATION

Intonation is a suprasegmental feature, i.e. it transcends the morpheme and word boundaries, and covers a whole sequence in an umbrella-like fashion. It thus incorporates a stretch of speech into a unit of a higher order. Without changing the lexical values of the words or morphemes, it influences the meaning and function of the sequence as a whole and colors it with additional content, such as the speaker's own attitude to what he or she is saying. Intonation is thus a linguistic signal which is an integrated part of speech, and which serves to clarify and facilitate perception. It is best thought of as being morphemic in nature, and is thus part of grammar.

There is a close interplay between intonation and pausal features. A given intonation is bounded by major pauses. Two sentences or two clauses are not combined under one intonation; but a topic subject plus a predicate may be combined, and usually is, into one syntactic whole by means of one intonation. Intonation and pause signal indicate where one sentence ends and another begins, and thus where to make a cut between clauses. It is probably true that a listener who is not familiar with the language, but pays attention to these signals on a purely impressionistic basis, will be able to determine, with a fairly high degree of probability, the number of clauses and sentences in a given sequence in Chinese.

Intonation also influences the shape of tones. It does not fundamentally change them so that the distinctions are lost, but modifies their pitches and contours in various ways, especially at the end of a clause or a sentence. Together with another suprasegmental feature, stress, intonation is the main factor which decides the actual manifestation of tones in a context. These manifestations in many cases differ considerably from those which occur with morphemes uttered in isolation.

Intonation may be said to have three basic functions: 1) to help tie together what belongs together; 2) to help keep separate what is to be kept separate; 3) to indicate the speaker's own attitude to what he or she is saying.

3. THE FORM OF INTONATION

Intonation is manifested and is describable in terms of three criteria: a) *pitch range*; b) *pitch level*; c) *pitch contour*.

Pitch range is wide or narrow. Range here means the extent of possible variation in pitch of voice. In ordinary, unemotional speech such variation takes place within a relatively narrow scope; in other types of speech the range is much wider.

Pitch level is high, low, or medium. Level in this context refers to the level of the pitch range as such. In ordinary speech the pitch level may be heard as medium, with a narrow range. In other types of speech the level may be high or low (various types of emotional speech); any pitch level with a wide range usually indicates emotional or emphatic speech.

Pitch contour is even, rising, or falling. An intonation contour, as used here, means the deflections of the voice within a given voice range; in Chinese such contours occur on the last syllables or on the very last syllable of a sequence, i.e. the pause group within which the intonation operates.

The various combinations of these possibilities give rise to a large number of possible intonations. There are, however, two basic types of intonation and any spoken sentence can be classified as belonging to one of them: an intonation is either emphatic or non-emphatic.

An *emphatic* intonation stands apart in respect of either pitch range or pitch level. In the former case it is characterized by a rather wide pitch range; thus, tone intervals are larger and tone contours are more distinct than in non-emphatic intonations. In the latter case the pitch level is raised or lowered (and the range naturally narrower). An emphatic intonation can be said to convey some degree of emotional intensity. A *non-emphatic* intonation lacks the special features mentioned above. It is characterized by a relatively narrow range and a medium pitch level; the tones are somewhat flattened. Impressionistically, non-emphatic intonation strikes the ear as far less colorful and lively than emphatic intonation. It is typical of ordinary, plain conversation, and may, for lack of a better term, be called "normal" intonation.

4. EMPHATIC INTONATION

Emphatic intonation usually involves emphatic stress on at least one word in the sequence.

$Qǐng_1$ $tíng_2$ $yíxiàr_3$! $Wǒ_4$ $yào_5$ $xià$ $qù_6$! "Please$_1$ stop$_2$ (one moment$_3$)! I$_4$ want to$_5$ get off$_6$!"

Nà₁ zhēn₂ zāogāo₃ le₄! Zěmmo₅ bàn₆ ne₇! "What a₂ mess₃ (is₃ that₁) now₄! How₅ can₆ [we] fix it₆?!₇"

In these sentences, which are spoken with emphatic intonation, the words *tíng, xià, zāogāo,* and *zěmmo* are likely to have emphatic stress.

Under the term emphatic intonation we subsume several varieties of intonation which reflect the speaker's own special attitude to what he or she is saying, or his or her immediate reaction to a statement or some phenomenon. It will not be possible for us to go into detail here. We shall only suggest a few of the possibilities:

Nèige₁ rén₂ a, shémme yě₃ bù₄ dǒng₅! "[Oh], that₁ man₂ doesn't₄ understand₅ anything at all₃!" (spoken with medium pitch, a rather wide voice range, expressing complaint or perplexity).

Zhāng xiānsheng₁ a, zhēn de₂ huì₃ shuō₄ Yīngguó huà₅! "Mr. Chang₁ can₃ really₂ speak₄ English₅!" (spoken with a relatively low pitch, a narrow pitch range, expressing admiration or praise).

Shì₁ xiàwǔ₂ sìdiǎn₃ zhōng₄ lái₆ de₇ a₈?! "[It] was₁ [at] four₃ o'clock₄ [in] the afternoon₂ [that he] came₆?₈ (he was one who...₇)" (spoken with a rather high pitch, expressing a repeated question).

It should be understood that a sentence with emphatic intonation is not necessarily segmentally different from a sentence with a non-emphatic intonation. Intonation is a suprasegmental feature which is imposed by the speaker "on top of" the segmental features. The replacement of an emphatic intonation by a non-emphatic intonation produces a different sentence. A sentence with non-emphatic intonation is usually a sentence in the declarative or interrogative form; a sentence with emphatic intonation is a sentence in the exclamatory or imperative form.

Zhèijiān₁ wūzili₂ zhēn₃ lěng₄. "It's cold₃,₄ in₂ this₁ room₂." (non-emphatic intonation: a declarative sentence, a neutral statement of fact).
Zhèijiān wūzili zhēn lěng! "How cold it is in this room!" (emphatic intonation, exclamatory sentence).

Similarly, with alternative intonations:

Wǒ₁ zuòle₂ yíjiàn₃ huài shì₄ le₅./Wǒ zuòle yíjiàn huài shì le! "I₁ have done₂,₅ something₃ bad₄./!"
Jīnnián₁ hái₂ méi xiàguo₃ zèmme₄ dà de₅ xuě₆ ne. "There hasn't been₃ such₄ a heavy₅ snow₆ yet₂ this year₁."
Jīnnián hái méi xiàguo zèmme dà de xuě ne! "Oh, surely there hasn't been such a heavy snow yet this year!"

5. NON-EMPHATIC INTONATION

Let us consider the following sentence:

$Tā_1$ $dàgài_2$ $míngtian_3$ $xiàwǔ_4$ $dào_5$ $Běijīng_6$ $lái_7$. "He$_1$ probably$_2$ comes$_7$ to$_5$ Peking$_6$ tomorrow$_3$ afternoon$_4$."

If we assume that the last syllable *lái* is not spoken as an atonic syllable in this context, i.e. that it has stress and tone, there are two rising tones in the sentence: *míng* in *míngtian* and *lái* at the end. The rising tone on *lái* is perceptably lower than that on *míng*, but it does have a rising contour. A similar phenomenon is heard in the following example, where high even tones are involved:

$Wǒ$ de_1 $diànhuà_2$ $hàomǎ_3$ $shì_4$ $sānbǎi$ $sānshísān_5$. "My$_1$ telephone$_2$ number$_3$ is$_4$ 333$_5$."

In this sentence, not only is the even tone on the last syllable *sān* lower than that on the preceding syllables *sān* (in *sānbǎi* and *sānshí-*), but it may even fall slightly towards the end.

This phenomenon is an effect of intonation. A sentence which has a medium pitch level, a narrow pitch range, and an even contour except at the very end, where a falling trend sets in, is said to have *Intonation I*. Since sentences frequently end on this downward trend, this feature may be called a regular sentence-terminal intonation curve. Followed by an obligatory pause it signals a major cut between sentences. Intonation I is a typical feature of declarative sentences, but is not limited to sentences of this form. Many interrogative sentences, especially those which contain a question word and those with ambivalent centrals, are also spoken with this intonation. In this book a period (.) is used to denote Intonation I. Examples:

Declarative sentences:

$Qǐng$ ni_1 $wèn_2$ $tā_3$ $jiū_4$ $zài_5$ $nǎr_6$. "Please$_1$ ask$_2$ where$_6$ his$_3$ house$_4$ is$_5$."
$Qián$ $xiānsheng_1$ $bú_2$ $dào_3$ $Měiguó_4$ $lái_5$. "Mr. Ch'ien$_1$ is$_5$ not$_2$ coming$_5$ to$_3$ America$_4$."
$Zhè_1$ shi_2 $wǒ_3$ $zài_4$ $túshūguǎn_5$ $jiè_6$ de_7 $shū_8$. "This$_1$ is$_2$ the book$_8$ (which$_7$) I$_3$ borrowed$_6$ at$_4$ the library$_5$."

Interrogative sentences:

$Gāo$ $xiānsheng_1$ $zhǎo_2$ $shéi_3$ qu_4 le_5. "Whom$_3$ has$_5$ Mr. Kao$_1$ gone$_4$ to visit$_2$?"

Nǐ₁ wèi shémme₂ bú₃ qù₄. "Why₂ are₄ you₁ not₃ going₄?"
Nǐ₁ rènshi bu renshi₂ Gāo xiānsheng₃. "Do₂ you₁ know₂ Mr. Kao₃?"
Túshūguǎn₁ lí₂ gōngyuán₃ yuǎn₄ ma₅. "Is₄ the library₁ far₄ from₂
the park₃?₅"

It should be noted, however, that very often interrogative sentences
ending in *ma* have a raised pitch level. It is the whole sentence, not only
the last word, which is affected.

Students whose native language makes extensive use of special
intonation in questions (for example, a rising trend at the end of the
sentence) should take care not to continue this habit when speaking
Chinese. If, for example, a speaker has in mind an English sentence: "Is
this radio expensive?" (with a rising intonation contour at the end) he
may easily transfer this intonation unconsciously into Chinese, saying:

*Zhèige wúxiàndiàn guí ma?

instead of

Zhèige wúxiàndiàn guì ma.

Another common mistake is to replace a rising or an even *tone* on the
last syllable of a Chinese declarative sentence with a falling *tone*. It
should be kept in mind that the tone of the last syllable in a declarative
Chinese sentence is only slightly modified, not fundamentally changed,
by the Chinese Intonation I. For example, the English sentence "He says
he has no money." has a typically falling intonation at the end
(intonation of statement). The corresponding sentence in Chinese runs as
follows:

Tā shuō tā méi yǒu qián.

where the rising *tone* on *qián* is kept, although the pitch level on *qián* is
lower than that on *méi*. The pronunciation to be avoided in Chinese is:

*Tā shuō tā méi yǒu qiàn.

Similarly, in the following examples:

Zhōngguohuà₁ fāyīn₂ hěn₃ nán₄. "The pronunciation₂ [of] Chinese₁
is₄ (very₃) difficult₄."
Wǒ₁ yào₂ niàn₃ liǎngge₄ xīngqī₅ shū₆. "I₁ am going to₂ study₃
(books₆) [for] two₄ weeks₅."

care should be taken not to pronounce the last syllables as **nàn* and **shù*
respectively.

Intonation is an important feature of Chinese sentences, but it is equally important to remember that in Chinese *intonation must not be allowed to replace tones.* Figuratively speaking, tones "swim" or "float" on an intonational "wave". A high tone is higher if it occurs on or near the top of a wave than when it occurs at a point where the "wave" recedes toward the end, but it does not lose its fundamental character except where it occurs with zero stress.

Intonation I is a regular feature of simple sentences. In compound sentences, however, only the last clause receives this terminal intonation. Clauses in a compound sentence are not separated by terminal intonation contour and final pause. In a compound sentence the general pitch level of the first clause(s) is slightly higher than that of the final clause, and the terminal contour at the end is replaced by a sustained contour. This intonation may be called *Intonation II.* In a sentence consisting of two clauses we thus get the following intonation pattern:

Clause I	*Clause II*
1. Slightly higher pitch level	1. Slightly lower pitch level
2. No final drop in pitch	2. A final drop in pitch
3. No final pause	3. Final pause

Intonation II is thus a signal of non-finality; it enables the listener to anticipate that something is to follow in the same sentence. Examples of sentences consisting of several clauses, illustrating the combination of Intonation II + Intonation I:

Nèizuò$_1$ shān$_2$ hěn$_3$ gāo$_4$; nǐ$_5$ pádeshàngqù$_6$ ma$_7$. "That$_1$ mountain$_2$ is$_4$ very$_3$ high$_4$, can$_6$ you$_5$ climb$_6$ [it]?$_7$"

Xīngqīrì$_1$ háizimen$_2$ dào$_3$ dòngwùyuán$_4$ qù$_5$ wár$_6$ le$_7$; tāmen$_8$ wár de$_9$ hěn gāoxìng$_{10}$. "[On] Sunday$_1$ the children$_2$ went$_{5,7}$ to$_3$ the zoo$_4$ to play$_6$, [and] they$_8$ had a wonderful time$_{10}$ playing$_9$."

Péngyou$_1$ lái$_2$ le$_3$; wǒmen$_4$ pǎoxia$_5$ lóuxià$_6$ qu$_7$ huānyíng$_8$ tamen$_9$. "[Our] friends$_1$ have come$_{2,3}$, we$_4$ run$_{5,7}$ downstairs$_6$ to welcome$_8$ them$_9$."

It should be clearly understood that sequences of this type can be spoken as one or as two sentences. Whether we are in fact dealing with one or with two sentences in each case depends on intonation and pause. In this book a semicolon (;) is used to indicate Intonation II. Alternative ways of pronouncing the sentences given as examples above would be:

Nèizuò shān hěn gāo. Nǐ pádeshàngqù ma.
Xīngqīrì háizimen dào dòngwùyuán qù wár le.
Tāmen wár de hěn gāoxìng. (etc.)

In each case the alternative chosen depends on the speaker's mood and inclination. The alternatives are synonymous as far as denotation is concerned; the difference (if any) lies in the connotation. It has more to do with style than with grammar in the conventional sense.

Very often clauses which are combined into one sentence (coordinated clauses) contain explicit markers of coordination. First clauses in such compound sentences show the same intonational features that have been described for non-final clauses above: their non-final, non-conclusive character is manifested by the presence of Intonation II:

Dàgài$_1$ shì$_2$ nèiyang$_3$ (ba); kěshi$_4$ bú$_5$ quèshí$_6$. "[It] is$_2$ probably$_1$ so$_3$, but$_4$ [it] is$_6$ not$_5$ certain$_6$." (marker *kěshi*).

Tīngshuō$_1$ Hángzhou$_2$ zhēn$_3$ shì$_4$ yīge$_5$ hén$_6$ měilì de$_7$ chéngshì$_8$; suóyi$_9$ yīnggāi$_{10}$ dào nàr$_{11}$ qù$_{12}$. "[I] have heard$_1$ [that] Hangchou$_2$ is$_4$ really$_3$ a$_5$ very$_6$ beautiful$_7$ city$_8$, so therefore$_9$ [I] ought to$_{10}$ go$_{12}$ there$_{11}$."

Although Intonation II is not primarily a sentence terminal intonation, it sometimes occurs with this function. Its effect is to give to the sentence an overtone of non-conclusiveness; it indicates doubt or at least a lack of complete certainty:

Yéxú$_1$ wǒ$_2$ míngtian$_3$ qù$_4$; "Maybe$_1$ I$_2$ will go$_4$ tomorrow$_3$, (but) . . ."

In contrast to this,

Yéxú wǒ míngtian qù. "I may well go tomorrow." (neutral statement, intonation I).

In addition to the two intonations which have been dealt with above we shall here briefly mention still another, which is limited to questions. In the subsection on sentence forms (Ch. II E 3, pp. 55–60) it is mentioned that most interrogative sentences are formed by means of a question word (*shéi*, etc.), a particle (*ma*), or an ambivalent central (type: *lái bu lái*). In subsection (e), p. 60, a special high intonation is described, which, when imposed on a sentence which is segmentally of declarative form, results in an interrogative sentence. In other words, it is possible to form an interrogative sentence by intonation alone. This intonation, which we may call *Intonation III*, has a high trend throughout, and a minor rising contour at the end. This intonation is mostly used to form rhetorical questions. Examples of *Intonation III*:

Nĭ$_1$ bù$_2$ xĭhuan$_3$ kàn$_4$ xì$_5$?? "You$_1$ don't$_2$ like$_3$ to go to$_4$ the theater$_5$?"

*Zhè*₁ *shì*₂ *nǐ*₃ *mǎi*₄ *de*₅?? "(Is₂ this₁ something which₅ you₃ bought₄ =) did you buy this?"

In connection with a following major pause each of the intonations I, II, and III are terminal intonations. In practice, however, Intonation I is by far the most common sentence-final signal. The primary function of Intonation II is to indicate non-finality; it is thus most commonly found in non-final clauses. Its occurrence as a terminal intonation is limited to cases where doubt or indefiniteness is indicated.

C. Stress

1. GENERAL

The categories of the accentual system of Standard Chinese are intonation, tone, and stress. They are closely interwoven into an organic whole; their coexistence results in a more complex accentual system than those of, for example, English or Russian. Differences of stress in Chinese should not be thought of primarily in terms of differences in *loudness*, although primary and secondary (and especially emphatic) stress are characterized by a stronger articulatory energy than is zero stress. Stress influences the length of a syllable, the tone intervals, the vowel quality (and sometimes the consonant quality). Stressed syllables are more *prominent*, but not necessarily louder, than unstressed syllables.

Stress other than zero stress can fall on any *tonic* morpheme, whereas zero stress can fall on tonic as well as atonic morphemes. But zero stress is invariably put on atonic morphemes. In other words, the fact that a given morpheme occurs in a given context with zero stress (and neutral tone) does not in itself indicate that it is an atonic morpheme. *Bai* in *míngbai* "understands" is a tonic morpheme which in this particular word receives zero stress and neutral tone. *Zhe* in *děngzhe* "is waiting" is an atonic morpheme and occurs here, as always, with zero stress and neutral tone. Atonicity and zero stress coincide, just as tonicity and potential non-zero stress coincide. Atonic morphemes form a closed class (particles, markers, some affixes); tonic morphemes form an open class and are thus listable only in a comprehensive lexicon. In other words, the occurrence of neutral tone means either 1) tonicity with incidental zero stress, or 2) atonicity with automatic zero stress.

The directional complement *shangqu* in *pǎoshangqu* "to run up there" has zero stress on both syllables. But in the potential compounds *pǎobushàngqù* "cannot run up there" and *pǎodeshàngqù* "can run up there" the directional complement has stress (and tone). This shows that *shangqu* consists of tonic morphemes. But the infixes *bu* and *de* do not attract stress, since as atonic morphemes they are automatically assigned zero stress.

2. EMPHATIC AND NON-EMPHATIC STRESS

Emphatic speech involves longer than average duration of a syllable, and extra wide pitch range. It focuses special attention on a given word by giving it an increased prominence. This kind of stress will be dealt with in more detail later in this section (p. 41). Non-emphatic stress is the most common type in ordinary conversation.

3. NON-EMPHATIC STRESS

For our purposes it is most practical to distinguish between three stress levels in non-emphatic speech. Listed on the basis of relative prominence, in decreasing order, they are: 1) *primary* stress; 2) *secondary* stress; 3) *zero* stress. Apart from the degree of prominence, syllables with primary and secondary stress do not differ from each other phonologically. Zero stress has a more radical effect on the syllable: lack of tonal contour, modification, especially of vowel quality, and a greatly reduced length. All syllables occurring in Standard Chinese (except for emphatic speech) contain one of these levels.

Whenever, in the rest of this section, examples are given, the symbol [ˈ] before a syllable with a tone sign indicates primary stress. In the case of secondary stress the presence of the tone sign alone, without any other symbol, means secondary stress; absence of any sign implies zero stress. Thus: *máo*ˈ*bǐ* = secondary + primary; ˈ*gōngren* = primary + zero. Later a special notation will be introduced for indicating a phonetic difference between a weaker and stronger secondary stress.

4. DISTRIBUTION OF STRESS IN
PHRASES, WORDS, AND SYLLABLES

The following possibilities exist:

a) A *monosyllabic word* which is tonic receives *primary* stress when spoken in isolation: ˈ*shì*. "yes"; ˈ*nàr*. "there".

b) A *bisyllabic* word which consists of one morpheme follows, when spoken in isolation, either model 1: *primary* + *zero* (ˈ*bōli*. "glass";

ˈpútao. "grapes") or model 2: *secondary + primary* (mǎˈdá. or móˈtuō. "motor"; léiˈdá. "radar").

c) A *complex* word ending in a suffix follows the pattern: *primary + zero* when spoken in isolation: ˈshuāzi. "a brush"; ˈshítou. "stone"; ˈláile. "has come"; ˈxiězhe. "is writing".

d) A *compound* word which is bisyllabic, follows, when spoken in isolation, one of two models: 1) *secondary + primary*, or 2) *primary + zero*. Neither phonological nor grammatical criteria yield a basis for predicting the pattern in each case; model 1 represents a lexical majority group. Some words vacillate between the two models: máoˈdùn. or ˈmáodun. "to be inconsistent"; tiáoˈjiàn. or ˈtiáojian. "condition". Examples of model 1: mínˈzú. "nation"; huǒˈchē. "train"; bìˈyè. "to graduate"; fāˈxiàn. "to discover"; gāngˈcái. "just now". Examples of model 2: ˈwàiguo. "foreign country"; ˈxiāngxia. "in the country(side)"; ˈkànjian. "to see"; ˈcōngming. "to be clever". Many reduplicated forms follow model 2: ˈmèimei. "younger sister"; ˈxièxie. "thank you".

e) A *phrase* consisting of two monosyllabics follows one of the models indicated under d). Model 1: *secondary + primary*: (subject + predicate constructions:) wǒ ˈlái. "I'm coming"; nǐ ˈkàn. "you see"; tāng ˈrè. "the soup is hot"; (verb + object:) shuō ˈhuà. "to speak"; xià ˈyǔ. "it's raining"; (other verbal phrases:) hén ˈhǎo. "very good"; bú ˈcuò. "not bad"; qù ˈmǎi. "go and buy"; hui ˈxiě. "can write"; (nominal phrases:) hǎo ˈshū. "a good book"; tiān ˈdì. "heaven and earth". Model 2: *primary + zero*: ˈguì le. "it has become expensive now"; ˈhǎo ma. "is it OK?"; ˈmà ta. "scold him".

f) Relatively close-knit *trisyllabic* word-like forms. Some of these are on the borderline between words and phrases; they will be dealt with here as compounds. From the point of view of stress, four types will be described. In some forms of this type two secondary stresses may occur in consecutive syllables without an intermediary pause. In such cases the first secondary stress is stronger than the second. For example, in dǎzìjī "type-writer" the first two syllables both have secondary stress; dǎ has a slightly stronger stress than zì. We use the sign [ˌ] before the syllable which has the stronger secondary stress as a reminder notation: ˌdǎziˈjī.

Type 1. *secondary + secondary + primary*: ˌhánshùˈbiǎo. "thermometer"; ˌhuǒchēˈzhàn. "railway station"; ˌjiāngxuéˈjīn. "scholarship"; ˌtúshūˈguǎn. "library".

Type 2. *secondary + primary + zero*: kànˈwánle. "has finished reading"; lèiˈjíle. "has become awfully tired"; hēiˈbǎnshang. "on the blackboard"; váˈshuāzi. "toothbrush".

Type 3. *secondary + zero + primary:* shuìbu|zháo. "cannot fall asleep"; gănde|shàng. "can catch up with"; dòufu|jiàng. "beancurd soup"; dòngwu|xué. "zoology".

Type 4. *primary + zero + zero:* |páshanglai. "can climb up here"; |liaobude. "is wonderful"; |péngyoumen. "friends"; |wūzili. "in the room".

g) *Phrases and clauses* consisting of three syllables and without internal pauses generally exhibit the same stress patterns as those given under **f)**.

Type 1. ₁wǒ méi |kōngr. "I don't have time"; ₁ zhēn bù |hǎo. "really no good"; ₁dǎ diàn|huà. "makes a telephone call". Here belong personal names like ₁Yè Jīng|guó and place names like ₁Héběi |shěng. "Hopei province" and ₁Běijīng |shì. "Peking City".

Type 2. bú |rènde. "doesn't know (him)"; zhēn |kuàihuo. "is really happy"; zài |nàr ba? "it is there, I suppose?"; yòng |kuàizi. "use chopsticks"; xìng |Bái de. "one whose surname is Pai"; wǒ |lèi le. "I have become tired"; méi |fázi. "there is no way (of doing it)".

Type 3. háizi |lái. "the children are coming"; sānge |rén "three people"; kuài de |duō "is much faster"; xiězhe |xìn. "is writing letters"; chéngli |zhù. "lives in the city"; tā de |shū. "his books"; yàoshi |shuō. "if you say (it)"; hǎodiar |xiě. "writes a little better".

Type 4. |shuìzhe ne. "he's sleeping; |duìle ba. "that's right, isn't it?"; |Wáng xiansheng. "Mr. Wang"; |xíng bu xing. "is it all right?"; |kànjian ta. "sees him"; |wǒmen de. "ours"; |hǎo zhene. "it's awfully good!".

h) *Words of more than three syllables* are for the most part special formations, such as reduplicated verbs and verbs with double complements. Examples of reduplicated forms: ₁gāngānjìng|jìng. (strong secondary + weak secondary + weak secondary + primary) "really clean", míngmíngbāibāir. "very clearly". Verbs with complements: ₁pábu₁shàng|lái. "cannot climb up here"; ₁dǎbu₁qǐ|lái. "cannot start fighting".

i) *Four-syllabic* sequences are usually phrases or clauses, not words. We shall here consider only a few types of frequently occurring phrases, such as, for example: guǎngbō diàntái. "broadcasting station".

Type 1. If each of the immediate constituents are of the secondary + primary stress type (model 1 as described under **d**)), the primary stress of the first constituent is reduced to a secondary stress. Thus: ˌguǎngˈbō + diànˈtái > ˌguǎngbō diànˈtái. (strong secondary + weak secondary + weak secondary + primary). Similarly: ˌgōnggòng qiˈchē. "a bus"; ˌlüxíng zhīˈpiào. "traveller's check"; ˌyāpiàn zhànˈzhēng. "the Opium War"; kāishǐ gōngˈzuò. "to start working"; ˌzēngjiā shēngˈchǎn. "to increase production".

Type 2. If one or both of the immediate constituents have zero stress (and neutral tone) on one of its (their) syllables, zero stress is usually retained also in the resulting phrase: ˌxiāngxia ˈhuódong. "life in the country"; ˌxiāomiè ˈQīngchao. "destroy the Ch'ing Dynasty"; ˌháizi ˈpíqi. "a child's temper; childishness"; ˌgēbei ˈzhǒuzi. "the elbow".

5. STRESS TYPES IN WORDS

The patterns described in paragraph 4 (subsections **a, b, c, d, f,** and **h**) illustrate what may be called *word stress.* Most words in Standard Chinese have a relatively fixed stress pattern, but variant forms occur. The vast majority of words fall into the categories which have just been described. By way of summary we can list the following *stress types*:

I. Monosyllabic words

1. Tonic: ˈhǎo. "OK"; ˈdà. "it is big"; ˈrén. "people"; ˈnàr. "there".
2. *Atonic*: de (marker); ma. (interrogative particle).

II. Bisyllabic words

3. ˈpútao. "grapes"; ˈshítou. "stone"; ˈshuāzi. "a brush"; ˈláile. "has come"; ˈyuèliang. "moon"; ˈshēngyin. "a sound"; ˈmèimei. "younger sister"; ˈkànjian. "sees"; ˈdànshi. "but".
4. ˌguóˈwài. "abroad"; ˌhuǒˈchē. "train"; ˌmínˈzú. "nation"; ˌyīngˈgāi. "ought to"; ˌshuōˈwán. "finish speaking"; ˌjiǎnˈzhí. "simple, simply"; ˌgāngˈcái. "just now".

III. Trisyllabic words

5. ˌhuǒchē ˈzhàn. "railway station"; ˌyòuzhèngˈjú. "post office".
6. ˌkànˈwánle. "has finished reading"; ˌcāˈgānjing. "to wipe clean"; ˌhēiˈbǎnshang. "on the blackboard".
7. ˌkàndeˈjiàn. "can see (it)"; ˌguǒziˈjiàng. "marmelade"; ˌyánjiuˈsuǒ. "research institute".

8. ˈ*páshanglai.* "to climb up there"; ˈ*péngyoumen.* "friends"; ˈ*wūzili.* "in the room".

IV. Words having more than three syllables

9. ˌ*gāngānjìng*ˈ*jìng.* "is perfectly clean".
10. ˌ*tīngbu*ˈ*qīngchu.* "cannot hear very well".
11. ˈ*pábushàng*ˈ*lái.* "cannot climb up here".
12. ˈ*páshanglaile.* "came climbing up here".

Reviewing these types, two generalizations can be made: 1) Every word (except atonic words) contains a primary stress; no word contains more than one. 2) The placing of primary stress on a given syllable in a word is unpredictable, except in bisyllabic words which end in a suffix. It may, for example, fall on the first syllable, as in ˈ*péngyoumen* or ˈ*pútao*, on the second, as in *kàn*ˈ*wánle*, or on the last, as in *huǒ*ˈ*chē* or *kànde*ˈ*jiàn*. Contrasts like ˈ*jìnlai* "to come in" versus ˌ*jìn*ˈ*lái* "recently", ˈ*dàyi* "to be careless" versus ˌ*dà*ˈ*yì* ("big idea" >) "tenor; general trend (of something)" show that the placing of primary accent is an important element in word formation. Note that non-emphatic stress in words is always predictable if it is known which syllables are tonic and which are not.

A word has a primary stress, and this stress is a *fixed* stress. Taking the position of fixed stress as a criterion, and choosing the symbols F for fixed stress, s_1 for strong secondary stress, s_2 for weak secondary stress, and o for zero stress, we can arrange the word stress formulae of polysyllabic words in the way shown in Table I.

TABLE I. Stress formulae of polysyllabic words

Formula	F placed on	Stress formula	Example	Stress type
1	first syllable	F o	*shítou, cōngming*	3
2		F o o	*páshanglai, péngyoumen*	8
3		F o o o	*páshanglaile*	12
4	second syllable	s_1 F	*huǒchē, kànwán, gāngcái*	4
5		s_1 F o	*kànwánle, hēibǎnshang*	6
6	third syllable	s_1 s_2 F	*huǒchēzhàn*	5
7		s_1 o F	*kàndejiàn, dòngwuxué*	7
8		s_1 o F o	*tīngbuqīngchu*	10
9	fourth syllable	s_1 s_2 s_2 F	*gāngānjìngjìng*	9
10		s_1 o s_2 F	*pábushànglái*	11

From this it can be seen that:

1) After F only o occurs.

2) Except for formulae 7, 8, and 10, which are mostly of specific morphological types, the occurrence of o is limited to after F.

3) s occurs only before F; the maximum number is three; s_1 occurs before s_2 if both are present.

4) F occurs on the last stressed syllable, whether or not it is final.

5) Five formulae have F on the last syllable; five formulae have zero on the last syllable(s).

6) There is no relation between stress pattern and grammatical function.

7) If in a given word the position of F is known, most other stress features are predictable. It follows that the student should take care to notice the placement of F whenever he learns a new word.

6. PHRASE STRESS

Some examples of phrase stress were given in 4 e, g, and i, although that paragraph deals chiefly with word stress. The stress pattern of a phrase as a whole does not differ basically from that of a word if it is spoken without pauses and if it is of no more than three or four syllables. But since many phrases are longer than the sequences dealt with in terms of our ten-word stress formulae, the stress patterns of phrases tend to be a little more complex. What is of importance is to be aware of the fact that stress plays a significant role, not only in words, but in syntactical constructions like phrases and sentences.

In the following we give an outline of the ways in which stress features are manifested in phrases:

a) A single tonic word spoken as a phrase retains its basic word stress: $^{\mid}$*láile.* "he came"; $_{\mid}$*kànbu$^{\mid}$jiàn.* "[I] cannot see [it] ".

b) If a word enters a phrase as a *part* of the phrase, certain adjustments of stress occur. A syllable with zero word stress naturally retains its zero stress if it — or the word of which it is a part — is incorporated into a phrase. Thus: *Náchulai$_1$ běnzi$_2$ le$_3$.* "[She] has taken out$_{1,3}$ her notebook$_2$." Syllables with word stress other than zero retain some degree of stress when entering a phrase. But as a general rule, in a phrase spoken as a phonological unit, i.e. without intervening pauses, all primary stresses except the last are reduced to secondary stresses. An example of this was given above in 4 e, p. 34: $_{\mid}$*Tāng $^{\mid}$rè.* "The soup is hot.", where *tāng* carries secondary stress. Similarly, if a sentence like

Kèren₁ lái₂ le₃. "The guests₁ have arrived₂,₃." is spoken as one phrase, with no pause after *kèren*, it will have the following stress pattern: ₗ*Kèren* ˈ*lái le*. The primary word stress on ˈ*kèren* when spoken in isolation is reduced to a secondary (phrase) stress, whereas the primary word stress on *lái*, which is the last primary stress in the phrase, is retained. Both zero stresses, on *rén* and *le*, are kept. But if the same sentence is spoken as two phrases, with a pause (or a pause particle) between each, each one-word phrase retains its primary stress: ˈ*Kèren a*, ˈ*lái le*. "The guests – they've come." In longer phrases the same basic pattern occurs:

> ₗ*Nèige₁* ₗ*zhàoxiang* ₗ*jī₂ de₃* ˈ*jiàqian₄*. "The price₄ of₃ that₁ camera₂."
> ₗ*Zhè₁ shì₂ (yī)ge₃ hén₄* ₗ*hǎo₅ de* ˈ*fázi₆*. "This₁ is₂ a₃ very₄ good₅ way (of doing it)₆."
> ₗ*Xiàwu₁* ₗ*liángdiǎn* ˈ*zhōng₂*. "[At] two o'clock₂ in the afternoon₁."
> ₗ*Qíng₁ ni₂* ₗ*zài₃* ˈ*shuō₄ yibian₅*. "[I] (ask₁ you₂ to =) please₁ say₄ [it] once₅ again₃."
> ₗ*Tā₁ hén₂* ₗ*xǐhuan₃* ₗ*shuō* ˈ*huà₄*. "He₁ likes₃ very much₂ to talk₄."

Note that in all examples primary stress is indicated by the symbol [ˈ], strong secondary by the symbol [ₗ], weak secondary by a tone symbol without any stress sign, and zero stress by no tone symbol and no stress sign.

The retention of the last primary word stress and the reduction of the other primary stresses is a significant feature. It may be interpreted as an effect of a pattern of a higher order than word stress, a pattern overlaying the whole grammatical construction and binding it into one unit with a special rhythm. This rhythmic stress pattern, which is typical of the phrase, may be termed *phrase stress*. It consists of an arrangement of various degrees of stress under one *dominant* stress on the last non-neutral tone in the sequence. This dominant stress is not in itself a part of the word stress as such, but is a separate phonological component of the phrase structure. It is a structural signal which establishes the sequence as a group of words belonging together. The phrase is thus a *stress group*; the group usually coincides with a grammatical construction (attribute + head; verb + object, etc.). Such stress groups are a constant feature of Chinese speech. They are bounded by pauses.

The dominant stress is also, in the same way as word stress, a *fixed* stress, since it is always the *last* primary word stress of the sequence which attracts it. Both fixed stresses have grammatical function: word stress is part of word-formation and thus belongs in the area of morphology; phrase stress establishes units of a higher order, i.e. it forms part of syntax.

The dominant stress in a stress group may be termed *nuclear stress*. Connected speech is punctuated by nuclear stresses. Such stresses form rhythmic peaks; these are spaced in such a manner as to form fairly clearcut units based on stress rhythm.

7. SENTENCE STRESS

A short sentence may consist of only one stress group: $_|$Wŏmen$_1$ cān$_|$guānle$_2$ $_|$jǐge$_3$ $_|$gōng$^|$chǎng$_4$. "We$_1$ visited$_2$ several$_3$ factories$_4$."; $_|$Tàiyang$_1$ $^|$chū$_2$ lai$_3$ le$_4$! "The sun$_1$ (has$_4$ come$_3$ =) is up$_2$!". Such sentences naturally have only one nuclear stress; in addition, an intonation contour signals the end of a sentence. There is, on the whole, a close interplay between stress and intonation.

Longer sentences usually consist of several stress groups, separated by pauses. In such sentences at least two stress groups materialize. The major sentence type is built according to the model:

Stress group I + pause + stress group II + pause + stress group III + pause + . . .

Examples of such sentences:

$_|$Wŏ$_1$ zuì$_2$ $_|$zhù$^|$zhòng$_3$ de$_4$, $_|$shì$_5$ $_|$xuéxi$_6$ Zhōng$^|$wén$_7$. "What$_4$ I$_1$ consider$_3$ most$_2$ important$_3$ is$_5$ to study$_6$ Chinese$_7$."
$_|$Nèige$_1$ $^|$wàiguoren$_2$, $_|$huì$_3$ $_|$shuō$_4$ jiǎn$_|$dān de$_5$ $^|$huà$_6$, $_|$hái$_7$ méi$_8$ $_|$shuō$^|$guàn$_9$. "That$_1$ foreigner$_2$ (can$_3$ speak$_4$ simple$_5$ words$_6$ =) has some elementary language knowledge, [but] (has not$_8$ yet$_7$ spoken into a habit$_9$ =) has not got sufficient speaking practice."
$_|$Jiāng$^|$lái$_1$, yí$_|$dìng$_2$ $_|$yǒu$_3$ qù$_4$ $_|$Zhōngguo$_5$ de$_6$ xī$^|$wàng$_7$. "In the future$_1$ [we] have$_3$ the hope$_7$ of$_6$ definitely$_2$ going$_4$ to$_4$ China$_5$."
$^|$Zuótian$_1$, $_|$zhège$_2$ $^|$huì$_3$, nǐ$_4^-$ $_|$cān$^|$jiā$_5$ le$_6$ ma$_7$. "This$_2$ meeting$_3$ yesterday$_1$, did$_6$ you$_4$ attend$_{5,6}$ [it] ?$_7$"
$_|$Zài$_1$ $^|$Zhōngguo$_2$, $_|$lǚxíng$_3$ $_|$zhī$^|$piào$_4$, $_|$kéyi bu $_|$kéyi$_5$ $^|$yòng$_6$. "Can$_5$ [one] use$_6$ travellers'$_3$ checks$_4$ in$_1$ China$_2$?$_5$"
$_|$Tā de$_1$ $_|$Zhōngguo$^|$huà$_2$, $_|$yìtiān$_3$ $_|$bǐ$_4$ yìtiān$_5$ $_|$jìn$^|$bù$_6$. "His$_1$ Chinese$_2$ is making progress$_6$ day$_3$ by$_4$ day$_5$."

A given sentence may be spoken in a number of different ways. A stress group is also a pause group, and the distribution of pauses in a sentence thus has a decisive effect on the number of phrases and nuclear stresses it contains. Beyond the general rule that short sentences tend to have few such groups and longer sentences tend to have a larger number, it is hard to give precise details. Nor is it possible to indicate how many syllables can be included in one phrase, but it is likely that in ordinary speech few phrases have more than ten syllables.

A very important factor for the distribution of stress is tempo. The examples given in this and preceding sections illustrate a type of speech which, for lack of a better term, may be called normal, i.e. a type of speech which contains neither the element of "fast speech" nor that of "slow speech". Phenomena connected with tempo are very complex, and they fall outside the scope of this survey. It should be mentioned, however, that rhythm in fast speech may differ greatly from the patterns outlined above. Secondary stresses are often flattened out or modified in other ways, whereas primary stresses usually remain on the last stressed syllables.

8. EMPHATIC STRESS

The stress patterns outlined above are characteristic of non-emphatic speech, i.e. speech in which no particular word or syllable is meant to be the focus of special attention. In Chinese as in other languages it is possible for a speaker to single out a specific word in a sequence in order to emphasize it. This can be achieved by giving it a special prominence by means of *emphatic stress*. A syllable with emphatic stress is recognized by its longer duration and its extra wide pitch range as compared to other syllables; emphatic stress also involves a certain amount of increased energy in articulation.

Emphatic stress may in principle fall on any tonic syllable, but only rarely on an atonic syllable. Since it is usually a word as a whole that is emphasized in this manner, emphatic stress tends to fall on that syllable in a given word which would normally get primary stress.

Some examples will be sufficient to indicate the possibilities (the syllable carrying emphatic stress is indicated by the symbol ["]):

> "*Wǒ de* ₗ*yīfu dōu* ₗ*chuān*ˡ*pò le.* "MY clothes are all worn out." (not those of the others).
> ₗ*Wǒ de* "*yīfu dōu* ₗ*chuān*ˡ*pò le.* "My CLOTHES are all worn out." (not my shoes).
> ₗ*Wǒ de* ₗ*yīfu* "*dōu* ₗ*chuān*ˡ*pò le.* "My clothes are ALL worn out."
> ₗ*Wǒ de* ₗ*yīfu dōu* "*chuān*ˡ*pò le.* "My clothes have all been WORN out." (they have not just been wilfully torn to pieces).
> ₗ*Wǒ de* ₗ*yīfu dōu* ₗ*chuān*"*pò le.* "My clothes have all been worn OUT." (they are just rags).

D. Sentence Types

1. VERBAL AND NON-VERBAL SENTENCES

A sentence whose predicate contains a verb as its center, is a *verbal* sentence. Such sentences are:

Zhōngguo$_1$ fàn$_2$ hǎochī$_3$. "Chinese$_1$ food$_2$ tastes good$_3$."
Zhāng xiansheng$_1$ shì$_2$ Húnanrén$_3$. "Mr. Chang$_1$ is$_2$ (a Hunan man$_3$ =) from Hunan."
Wǒ$_1$ péngyou$_2$ xǐhuan$_3$ huà$_4$ huàr$_5$. "My$_1$ friend$_2$ likes$_3$ to paint$_4$ (paintings$_5$)."
Wǒ$_1$ fùqin$_2$ mǔqin$_3$ dōu$_4$ qùguo$_5$ Zhōngguo$_6$. "My$_1$ father$_2$ [and my] mother$_3$ have$_5$ both$_4$ been to$_5$ China$_6$."

The verbs are: *hǎochī, shì, xǐhuan, qùguo.*

A sentence which has no verb as the center of its predicate, is a *non-verbal* sentence:

Zhèiben$_1$ shū$_2$, liǎngkuài$_3$ qián$_4$. "This$_1$ book$_2$ [costs] two$_3$ dollars$_4$".

2. NEGATION

The verbal sentences quoted above are all in the affirmative. They are said to be *negatable.* Negation in this context is to be understood as direct contradiction or denial of a statement or other utterance. Such a negation is effected by inserting a negative adverb in the predicate. The negative adverbs are *bù* and *méi* (in imperative sentences: *bié*). The negatable sentences in Section 1 are negated in the following way:

Zhōngguo fàn bù hǎochī. "Chinese food *does not* taste good."
Zhāng-xiansheng bú shì Húnanrén. "Mr. Chang is *not* from Hunan."
Wǒ péngyou bù xǐhuan huà huàr. "My friend does *not* like to paint."
Wǒ fùqin mǔqin dōu méi qùguo Zhōngguo. "My father and mother (both) have *not* been to China."

Regarding the use of the negative adverbs *bù* and *méi* the following rules are the most important:

a) The verb *yǒu* "to have, to exist" is negated by *méi:*

Wó$_1$ yǒu$_2$ qián$_3$. "I$_1$ have$_2$ [some] money$_3$.": *Wǒ méi yǒu qián.* "I don't have [any] money."

Zhōngguo$_1$ *nánbù*$_2$ *yǒu*$_3$ *láohu*$_4$. "[In] the southern part$_2$ of China$_1$ there are$_3$ tigers$_4$.": *Zhōngguo nánbù méi yǒu láohu.* "There are no tigers in the southern part of China."

Huì$_1$ *shuō*$_2$ *Rìben huà*$_3$ *de*$_4$ *rén*$_5$ *yé*$_6$ *yǒu*$_7$. "There are$_7$ also$_6$ some people$_5$ who$_4$ can$_1$ speak$_2$ Japanese$_3$.": *Huì shuō Rìben huà de rén yě méi yǒu.* "There are not (even) any people who can speak Japanese."

b) A verb form which contains the perfective aspect suffix *-le* has as its negated counterpart the verb form without the suffix, preceded by *méi*:

Tā$_1$ *nálaile*$_2$ *yìbēi*$_3$ *chá*$_4$. "He$_1$ brought$_2$ a cup of$_3$ tea$_4$.": *Tā* **méi** *nálai yìbēi chá.* "He has not brought a cup of tea."

Wǒmen$_1$ *zuótian*$_2$ *mǎile*$_3$ *sānběn*$_4$ *shū*$_5$. "We$_1$ bought$_3$ three$_4$ books$_5$ yesterday$_2$.": *Wǒmen zuótian* **méi** *mǎi sānběn shū.* "We did not buy three books yesterday."

Xiǎole$_1$ *yícùn*$_2$. "Has become$_1$ one inch$_2$ smaller$_1$.": **Méi** *xiǎo yícùn.* "Has not become one inch smaller."

Méi is also used to negate a sentence which contains a perfective verb form and the final particle *le*:

Tā$_1$ *yùbeile*$_2$ *gōngkè*$_3$ *le*$_4$. "He$_1$ has prepared$_{2,4}$ [his] lessons$_3$.": *Tā méi yùbei gōngkè.* "He has not prepared his lessons."

Tā$_1$ *chūqu*$_2$ *le*$_3$. "He$_1$ has gone out$_{2,3}$.": *Tā méi chūqu.* "He has not gone out."

It should be noted that in the examples quoted under **b)** the modal verb *méiyou* can replace the negative adverb *méi*:

Tā méiyou nálai yìbēi chá.
Wǒmen méiyou mǎi sānběn shū., etc.

c) A verb form which contains the aspect suffix *-guo* or *-zhe* is negated by *méi*; the suffix remains in the negated form:

Qùguo$_1$ *Zhōngguo*$_2$ "Has (some time in the past) been to$_1$ China$_2$.": *Méi qùguo Zhōngguo* "Has not (ever) been to China."

Tā$_1$ *kànguo*$_2$ *Hónglóumèng*$_3$. "He$_1$ has read$_2$ (the novel) 'The Dream of the Red Chamber$_3$'.": *Ta méi kànguo Hónglóumèng.* "He has not read 'The Dream . . .'."

d) With a corresponding difference of meaning, *bù* or *méi* may alternatively negate a verb, as exemplified in the following sentences (note that the forms with *méi* can also have *méiyou*):

Tā₁ bù₂ chūqu₃. "He₁ is₃ not₂ going out₃.": *Tā méi/méiyou chūqu.* "He has not gone out.", *or*: "He did not go out."

Tā₁ bù₂ lái₃. "He₁ is₃ not₂ coming₃.": *Tā méi/méiyou lái.* "He has not come.", *or*: "He did not come."

Tā₁ bú₂ yùbei₃ gōngkè₄. "He₁ does not₂ prepare₃ his lessons₄.": *Tā méi/méiyou yùbei gōngkè.* "He has not prepared (*or*: did not prepare) his lessons."

Wǒ₁ bú₂ gàosong₃ ta₄. "I₁ am not going to₂ tell₃ him₄.": *Wǒ méi/méiyou gàosong ta.* "I have not told (did not tell) him."

3. NEGATABLE AND NEGATED SENTENCES

A sentence whose predicate contains a non-negated verb as its center is a *negatable* sentence: *Zhōngguofàn hǎochī. Wó yǒu qián.* A verbal sentence whose predicate contains a negated verb as its center is a *negated* sentence. Negatable and negated sentences are two important *sentence types*.

It should be noted that even a negated sentence can be further negated. For example, in the sentence: *Zhōngguofàn bù hǎochī.* another negated element can be introduced:

Zhōngguofàn, bú shì bù hǎochī (dànshi wǒ bú è). "It is not that Chinese food is not tasty, (but I am not hungry)."

Note that the negation *bú-* in the phrase *Néng₁ búqù₂.* "[I] may₁ stay home₂." does not affect the whole sentence in the same way as *bù* in *Bù₁ néng₂ qù₃.* "[I] cannot₁,₂ go₃". *Búqù* is probably to be taken as a compound; it is not the negated, but the opposite action of *qù* (i.e. "not-go" = "stay (home)"). The negated counterpart of *Néng búqù.* is *Bù néng búqù.* "I cannot stay (home); I have to go." In the same way, while *Bù hén hǎo.* "Not very good." is the negated form of *Hén hǎo.* "Very good.", *Hěn bùhao.* ("Very not-good" =) "Very bad." (since "bad" is the opposite of "good") consists of the modifier *hěn* + the compound verb *bùhǎo.*

4. AMBIVALENT SENTENCES

A third sentence type, which is characteristically Chinese, contains a negatable verb form followed by the negated form of the same verb or by *méiyou* (the latter form usually in the neutral tone): *Lái bu lai*. "Is he coming?"; *Yŏu mei you*. "Is/are there any?; Do you/does he (etc.) have any?" The two forms, which occur in simple juxtaposition, yield a sentence which is neither simply negatable nor simply negated, but a combination of both. It may thus be termed *ambivalent*.[1]

Such a sentence states two mutually exclusive alternatives: 1) "he comes", 2) "he does not come" and thus suggests the idea of a *question*. All ambivalent sentences are interrogative sentences; the answer is formed by deleting one of the alternatives: *Ní dŏng bu dong*. "Do you understand?". Answers: 1) *Dŏng*. "Yes."; 2) *Bù dŏng*. "No." *Ní yŏu qián mei you*. "Do you have any money?" *Yŏu*. "Yes."; *Méi yŏu*. "No." Since all ambivalent sentences are questions, they will be further dealt with in Section E, Sentence forms. Here we give some examples of the use:

> *Dà bu da*. "Is it big?" Answers: 1) (*Hĕn*) *dà*. "Yes."; 2) *Bú dà*. "No."
> *Nĭ₁ xīn₂ măi de₃ màozi₄, héshì bu heshi₅*. "Is₅ your₁ newly₂ bought₃ hat₄ suitable₅?" Answers: 1) *Héshì*. "Yes."; 2) *Bù héshì*. "No."
> *Kàndejiàn kànbujiàn*. "Can you see (it)?" Answers: 1) *Kàndejiàn*. "Yes."; 2) *Kànbujiàn*. "No."
> *Nĭ shì bu shi Wáng Guódào*. "Are you Wang Kuo-tao?" Answers: 1) *Shì*. "Yes."; 2) *Bú shì*. "No."
> *Nĭ₁ kànle₂ nèige₃ diànyĭngr₄ meiyou*. "Have₂ you₁ seen₂ that₃ film₄?" Answers: 1) (*Yĭjīng*) *kànle*. "Yes (I have already).."; 2) (*Hái*) *méiyŏu*. "No (not yet)."
> *Nĭ yào chī fàn bu yao*. "Do you want to eat?" Answers: 1) *Yào*. "Yes."; 2) *Bú yào*. "No."
> *Nĭmen chīguo Zhōngguofàn meiyou*. "Have you ever eaten Chinese food?" Answers: 1) *Chīguo*. "Yes."; 2) *Méi chīguo*. "No."
> *Nĭ zhīdao bu zhidao tāmen mĕi yīge xīngqī shàng jĭ táng*. "Do you know how many classes they attend every week?" Answers: 1) *Zhīdao*. "Yes."; 2) *Bù zhīdao*. "No."

5. NEGATIVE SENTENCES

A sentence which has the negative verb *méi* as the center of its predicate is a negative sentence. *Méi* "there is not, there are not" is the contrary of *yŏu* "there is, there are". Care should be taken to keep the verb *méi*

---

[1] The term was suggested by Professor S. Egerod.

apart from the negative adverb *méi* as in *méi you*.[1] The verb *méi* has an intrinsically negative value and is thus non-negatable; in this respect it is an exception to the general rule that verbs are negatable. In most respects it has the syntactical functions of a verb; it is most commonly followed by an object, but never occurs finally in a sentence. Examples are:

Wǒmen$_1$ *zuò*$_2$ *fēijī*$_3$ *huòzhe*$_4$ *zuò*$_5$ *huǒchē*$_6$, *duì*$_7$ *wǒ*$_8$ *méi*$_9$ *guānxi*$_{10}$. "[Whether] we$_1$ go by$_2$ plane$_3$ or$_4$ by$_5$ train$_6$ (has no$_9$ connection$_{10}$ =) does not matter to$_7$ me$_8$."

Zhōngguo$_1$ *běibù*$_2$ *méi*$_3$ *láohu*$_4$. "[In] the northern part$_2$ [of] China$_1$ there are no$_3$ tigers$_4$."

Méi$_1$ *fázi*$_2$ *xiūlǐ*$_3$ *zhèliàng*$_4$ *qìchē*$_5$. "There is no$_1$ way$_2$ [of] repairing$_3$ this$_4$ car$_5$."

6. NON-VERBAL SENTENCES

Since negation, in the sense in which we use it in this book, is a way of modifying verbs, and thus presupposes the presence of a verb in the predicate, non-verbal sentences are non-negatable. Such sentences are of two kinds: 1) those whose predicate is made up of a nominal or a nominal phrase; 2) sentences made up of a predicate which is neither verbal nor nominal; they are more like sentence fragments in that they consist of an interjection. These sentences are all of exclamatory form.

7. NON-NEGATABLE SENTENCES WITH NOMINAL PREDICATES

This fifth sentence type is far less frequent than those mentioned so far; it most frequently expresses some quantity, such as a person's age, the price of something, time expressions and the like. One feature which such sentences have in common is that they can be expanded into verbal sentences, usually by inserting either of the verbs *shì* and *yǒu*. This expanded version, which is synonymous with the underlying sentence, is, of course, negatable in the ordinary way. Since sentences of this type have a nominal predicate, they may be called *nominal sentences*.

Examples are:

Jīntian$_1$ *xīngqījǐ*$_2$. "What day$_2$ [is] today$_1$?"

Yǐjing$_1$ *wǔtiān*$_2$ *le*$_3$. "[It is] already$_{1,3}$ five days$_2$ (e.g. since I came here)."

---

[1] Note that *méi you* can always replace *méi*, whereas the opposite is not true: one cannot say: **yǒu qián mei*.

Tā₁ èrshíwǔsuì₂ le₃. "He₁ [is] now₃ twenty-five years₂ [old]."
Zhèibĕn₁ shū₂ liǎngkuài₃ qián₄. "This₁ book₂ [costs] two₃ dollars₄."
Wǒ₁ fùqin₂ Běijīngrén₃. "My₁ father₂ [is] from Peking₃."
Jiār₁ jiǎr₂. "What date₂ [is it] today₁?"
Nín₁ nǎr₂. "Where₂ [are] you₁?"
Dìsānge₁ mén₂ a? "Door₂ No. 3₁?"
Duōshǎo₁ qián₂. "How much₁ (money₂) [does it cost]?"

In the expanded form, so as to form verbal sentences, they would be rephrased thus:

Jīntian shì xīngqījǐ.
Yǐjing yǒu wǔtiān le.
Tā yǒu èrshíwǔsuì le.
Zhèibĕn shū, (jiàqian) shì liǎngkuài qián.
Wǒ fùqin shì Běijīngrén.
Jiār shì jiǎr.
Nín zài nǎr.
Shì dìsānge mén a?

Although sentences like *Jīntian xīngqījǐ* ~ *Jīntian shì xīngqījǐ.* are, for practical purposes, synonymous, it should be clearly understood that they represent different sentence types. They should not, therefore, be considered as variants of the "same" sentence.[1]

8. OTHER NON-NEGATABLE SENTENCES

A non-negatable sentence which is not a nominal sentence, is typically a one-word sentence of exclamatory form. It consists of an interjection. Phonologically such a sentence is distinct from other sentences in that it has no tone, only intonation; in addition it sometimes has a unique form, i.e. it represents syllabic shapes not found outside this specific class. Such sentences differ from other non-verbal sentences in that they are not expandable, i.e. they cannot, by having a verb inserted, be transformed into verbal sentences.

Examples are:

Weiwei! "Hello!"
Aiya! "Oh, my goodness!"
E! "That's right! you got it!"

---

[1] A nominal sentence may well be considered as a sentence with *zero central* (see the following subsection).

Ng, or *M.* "Yes, I see; Hm."
Lh. (short, voiceless, "inverted" (i.e. sucking in air) type of l-articulation.) Sometimes used in lively speech to dramatize, attract attention, etc.

9. THE CENTRAL

In Chinese, verbal sentences are by far the most common type of sentence. The simplest form of verbal sentence consists of a verb. Sentences such as the following are quite frequent and normal, especially as responses to a preceding stimulus sentence:

Niànwánle. "[I] have finished reading [it]."
Shuìzhe. "[Someone] is sleeping."
Jìde. "[I] remember."
Chīguo. "He has (in the past) tasted [it]."
Kànbuqīngchu. "[I] cannot see [it] clearly."
Piányi. "[It] is cheap."

Of all word classes (except interjections) the verb is the only class which frequently forms a sentence alone, without being supplemented by other words (except by bound words like particles). Single nouns, although in principle syntactically free words, normally require some kind of modification or other supplement in order to form sentences. Sentences consisting of a noun, such as:

Rén. "People."
Kuàizi. "Chopsticks."
Shūjí. "Books."

occasionally occur, but only in special contexts, to which they are normally rather closely tied. Thus, *Rén.* as a sentence would hardly occur except, for example, in the case of a student reading aloud the Chinese character for "man, person"; *Kuàizi.* could be said as a sentence if meant to be the answer to the question, "What do you call 'chopsticks' in Chinese?"; *Shūjí.* could be heard in a situation where a teacher corrects a student's pronunciation: *shūjí* "books" (not *shūjì* "secretary"). Normally, the answer to a question, *Shì shéi zuò de.* "Who did it?" would not be, as in English, "I" (*wǒ*), but rather: *Shì wǒ.* In the same way, "A friend of mine." as an answer to the question, "Who has told you?" would normally be: *Shì wǒ yíge péngyou.*

The verb of the predicate is of fundamental importance in a Chinese sentence; everything else in the sentence ultimately depends on it. In any

sentence a predicate is required; it is a non-omissible part of it and thus
the center of the sentence taken as a whole. In the same way, in a verbal
predicate the verb is the center; the verb forms a non-omissible part
of it.

The term *non-omissible* as used here refers to an element or segment
of a sentence/a predicate which is an inexpendable constituent of and a
common factor in all possible derived variants of it. Derived variants are
here to be understood as all sentences which can be said to be *reduced*
versions of the original sentence, and are still felt to be sentences which
in each case are recognizable as a part of the original sentence. The
original sentence is taken to be the maximal variant; the shortest variant
is the sentence stripped to its barest minimum. As an example of such a
reduction, carried out step by step, let us look at the following sentence:

Subject	Predicate

Lánqiúchǎng$_1$ *de*$_2$ *zhōuwěi*$_3$, *yǐjing*$_4$ *dōu*$_5$ *jímǎnle*$_6$ *rén*$_7$ *le*$_8$.
"The whole area$_3$ of$_2$ the basketball field$_1$ is$_6$ already$_{4,8}$ completely$_5$
crowded$_6$ [with] people$_7$."

Reduced variants:

(1) *Nàr, yǐjing dōu jímǎnle rén le.* (subject reduced to a minimal
 word; predicate not reduced)
(2) *Yǐjing dōu jímǎnle rén le.* (zero subject; predicate not
 reduced).
(3) (4) *Nàr, yǐjing/dōu jímǎnle rén le.* (minimal subject, *yǐjing* or *dōu*
 deleted)
(5) (6) *Yǐjing/dōu jímǎnle rén le.* (zero subject; predicate
 reduced)
(7) *Nàr* *jímǎnle rén le.* (minimal subject; predicate
 further reduced)
(8) *Jímǎnle rén le.* (zero subject; predicate as in 7)
(9) *Nàr,* *jímǎn rén le.* (minimal subject; predicate
 further reduced)
(10) *Jímǎn rén le.* (zero subject; predicate as in 9)
(11) *Nàr,* *jímǎn le.* (minimal subject; predicate
 further reduced)
(12) *Jímǎn le.* (zero subject; minimal predicate)

Jímǎn le. is the minimal sentence variant. It is common to, and a
necessary part of, all variants. *Jímǎn* is the essential core of the predicate
as well as that of the sentence.

This is even more clearly brought out if we rephrase the original sentence, putting it into an interrogative form:

Lánqiúchǎng de zhōuwěi, yǐjing dōu jǐmǎnle rén le ma.

All reduced variants (1) through (12) would be possible answers. On the other hand, answers like: **Dōu.*; **Nàr yǐjing.*; **Nàr dōu.*; **Yǐjing rén le.*; **Nàr rén le.* would all be impossible or at least very unlikely, since they are not acceptable as meaningful sentences. No reduced variant in which *jǐmǎn* is omitted would be acceptable as a reduced variant of the original sentence.

Furthermore, if the sentence were to be negated, it would take the following form:

Lánqiúchǎng de zhōuwěi, hái méi jǐmǎn.

The negation is introduced before *jǐmǎn.*

A non-omissible verb in the predicate is a *central*. Since it occurs only in the predicate and never outside the predicate, it is in actual fact a predicate central. But since it is the virtual cornerstone of the whole sentence and may generally be a substitute for the whole of the sentence, we shall often refer to it as the sentence central.

In order to identify the central, it should be kept in mind that:

1) A verb which is part of the sentence topic subject is not a central:

Zhuǎnchéng$_1$ zhèngshì$_2$ xuésheng$_3$ de$_4$ shǒuxù$_5$, xiànzài$_6$ hěn$_7$ jiǎndān$_8$. "The formalities$_5$ of$_4$ becoming$_1$ a regular$_2$ student$_3$ are$_8$ now$_6$ quite$_7$ simple$_8$." *Zhuǎnchéng* is not the central. *Jiǎndān* is the central.

2) A verb which is part of a modifier, whether in the subject or the predicate, is not a central:

Wǒ$_1$ zhǎobudào$_2$ wǒ$_3$ zuótian$_4$ mǎi$_5$ de$_6$ kùzi$_7$. "I$_1$ cannot find$_2$ the trousers$_7$ (which$_6$) I$_3$ bought$_5$ yesterday$_4$." *Zhǎobudào*, not *mǎi*, is the central.

3) No coverb is a central.

Wǒ$_1$ yòng$_2$ kuàizi$_3$ chī fàn$_4$. "I$_1$ eat$_4$ with$_2$ chopsticks$_3$." *Chī* is the central.

If the predicate contains only one verb, that verb functions as a central. Some predicates contain more than one verb. The case of coverbs has already been mentioned. In verbal constructions in series the last verb is the central (*yuǎn* in *lí zhèr hěn yuǎn* "far from here", *fàng(zài)* in *Bǎ nèiben shū fàngzài zhuōshang.* "Put that book on the table."); in a modal phrase the modal verb is the central and the action verb is the "object" (*bù zhǔn* is a negated central in *Bù zhǔn chōu yān.* "Not permitted to smoke."). There are, however, sentences whose predicates contain more than one central. Such a compound predicate is made up of two or more predicate phrases in *coordination*; the relation may be explicitly indicated by markers or may be indicated by simple juxtaposition. A sentence whose predicate contains two or more centrals is a *multicentral* sentence. A multicentral sentence, with one predicate consisting of three verbal phrases, each with its own central, is the following:

$Wǒmen_1$ $chōu$ $yān_2$, $hē_3$ $jiǔ_4$, $dǎ_5$ $pái_6$. "We$_1$ smoke$_2$, drink$_3$ wine$_4$ [and] play$_5$ cards$_6$."

Sometimes two or more coordinated centrals (with their dependent words) are connected by a marker (usually *yě*):

$Hǎiguān_1$ $zhíyuán_2$, $huì_3$ $shuō_4$ $Yīngwén_5$, $yě_6$ $huì_7$ $shuō_8$ $Zhōngwén_9$. "The customs$_1$ official(s)$_2$ can$_3$ speak$_4$ English$_5$ and also$_6$ ([they] can$_7$ speak$_8$) Chinese$_9$."

In other cases there is no such marker:

$Tā_1$ $tiāntiān_2$ $xiě_3$ $xìn_4$ $huì_5$ $kè_6$. "He$_1$ writes$_3$ letters$_4$ [and] receives$_5$ callers$_6$ every day$_2$."

$Zhèiwèi_1$ $xiānsheng_2$, $bú_3$ $shì_4$ $yíwèi_5$ $xuésheng_6$, $shì_7$ $yíwèi_8$ $jiàoshòu_9$. "This$_1$ gentleman$_2$ is$_4$ not$_3$ a$_5$ student$_6$, [he] is$_7$ a$_8$ professor$_9$."

Note that the same construction can be used in sentences which are questions (coordinated question phrases):

$Nǐ_1$ $chī_2$ $fàn_3$ $chī_4$ $miàn_5$. "Are$_2$ you$_1$ going to eat$_2$ rice$_3$ [or] are [you] going to eat$_4$ noodles$_5$?"

Sometimes each constituent is marked by correlative markers: *yòu . . . yòu, yě . . . yě, yímiàn . . . yímiàn* ("both . . . and"):

Ta_1 $yòu_2$ $yóu_3$ $lǐmào_4$, $yòu_5$ $hěn_6$ $héǎi_7$. "He$_1$ is$_3$ both$_2$ polite$_4$ and$_5$ nice$_{6,7}$.

$Nǐ_1$ $yě_2$ $bú_3$ $qù_4$, $wó_5$ $yě_6$ $bù_7$ $lái_8$. "Neither$_{2,3}$ do$_4$ you$_1$ go$_4$, nor$_{6,7}$ do$_8$ I$_5$ come$_8$."

$Wǒ_1$ $yímiàn_2$ $kàn_3$ $zhàoxiàngjī_4$, $yímiàn_5$ $tīng_6$ $yīnyuè_7$. "Part$_2$ [of the time] I$_1$ was looking at$_3$ cameras$_4$ [and] part$_5$ [of the time] [I] was listening to$_6$ music$_7$."

A special case of juxtaposed centrals is the alternative question formula: non-negated verb + negated verb:

Nǐ$_1$ lái$_2$ bu$_3$ lái$_4$. "(Do$_2$ you$_1$ come$_2$ [or] do [you] not$_3$ come$_4$ =) are you coming?"

Nǐ$_1$ huì$_2$ shuō$_3$ Zhōngguo$_4$ huà$_5$ bu$_6$ huì$_7$. "Can$_{2,6,7}$ you$_1$ speak$_3$ Chinese$_{4,5}$?"

Tīngdejiàn$_1$ tingbujian$_2$. "Can$_1$ [you] hear$_1$ [it] ([or] not$_2$)?"

Tā$_1$ yǒu$_2$ qián$_3$ mei$_4$ you$_5$. "Does$_2$ he$_1$ have$_2$ money$_3$ ([or] does$_5$ [he] not$_4$ have$_5$)?"

Such sentences are called ambivalent sentences, as has already been pointed out. For practical purposes we consider such combinations as *huì bu hui, tīngdejiàn tingbujian* as single centrals. Such centrals may be called *ambivalent centrals*. A sentence is ambivalent when it has an ambivalent central.

In our discussion of sentence types we have so far only spoken of simple sentences, i.e. sentences consisting of only one clause. Many sentences, however, are compound sentences, containing several clauses, each with its own predicate, and consequently, with its own central. Thus, a multicentral sentence may be either a simple sentence with a multicentral predicate or a compound sentence with several independent centrals. Thus, in

Tā$_1$ zhēn$_2$ yònggōng$_3$; wó$_4$ hén$_5$ lǎn$_6$. "He$_1$ is$_3$ really$_2$ diligent$_3$, I$_4$ am$_6$ quite$_5$ lazy$_6$."

yònggōng and *lǎn* are two independent centrals. In the following example, which consists of three clauses combined into one sentence, the three centrals are respectively, *yǒu, zhùzai,* and *kéyi*; the clauses are in this case marked off by markers *kěshi* and *suóyi*:

Shìjièshang$_1$ hěn duō$_2$ difang$_3$ dōu$_4$ yǒu$_5$ shuō$_6$ Zhōngguo yǔyán$_7$ de$_8$ rén$_9$; kěshi$_{10}$ bǎifen-zhī-jiǔshíwǔ$_{11}$ yǐshàng$_{12}$ shuō$_{13}$ Zhōngguo yǔyán$_{14}$ de$_{15}$ rén$_{16}$ dōu$_{17}$ zhùzai$_{18}$ Zhōngguo$_{19}$; suóyi$_{20}$ wǒmen$_{21}$ kéyi$_{22}$ shuō$_{23}$ Zhōngguo yǔyán$_{24}$ shì$_{25}$ yìzhǒng$_{26}$ guójiā de$_{27}$ yǔyán$_{28}$. "[In] many$_2$ places$_3$ in the world$_1$ (everywhere$_4$) there are$_5$ people$_9$ who$_8$ speak$_6$ Chinese$_7$; but$_{10}$ more than$_{12}$ 95%$_{11}$ of the people$_{16}$ who$_{15}$ speak$_{13}$ Chinese$_{14}$ (all$_{17}$) live in$_{18}$ China$_{19}$; therefore$_{20}$ we$_{21}$ may$_{22}$ say$_{23}$ [that] Chinese$_{24}$ is$_{25}$ a$_{26}$ national$_{27}$ language$_{28}$."

In a compound multicentral sentence each central may be negatable, negated, or negative. It follows that in a given sentence all clauses may be negatable, as in the example just quoted; all clauses may be negated (*Wǒ₁ méi₂ yǒu₃ qián₄; nǐ₅ yě₆ méi₇ yǒu₈.* "I₁ have₃ no₂ money₄, nor₆,₇ dog₈ you₅ (have₈).") ; and all clauses may be negative (*Wǒ₁ méi₂ qián₃; tā₄ méi₅ gōngfu₆.* "I₁ have no₂ money₃ [and] he₄ has no₅ time₆."). Ambivalent sentences are almost always simple sentences. There remain a number of cases in which one or several constituent clauses are negatable, whereas others are negated or negatable.

We shall distinguish between the following *compound sentence types*:

a) A "pure" type in which all clauses are homogeneous in this respect: in such cases we say that a given sentence, taken as a whole, is a negatable sentence, a negated sentence, or a negative sentence. Thus,

Tā₁ bú₂ huì₃ shuō₄ Yīngwén₅; wǒ₆ bú₇ huì₈ shuō₉ Zhōngwén₁₀. "He₁ cannot₂,₃ speak₄ English₅ [and] I₆ cannot₇,₈ speak₉ Chinese₁₀."

is a negated compound sentence.

b) A "mixed" type in which the clauses are heterogeneous in this respect. Such clauses are often marked off from each other by means of markers such as *dànshi, kěshi, suóyi*; in addition, there are the usual pausal and accentual signals, which in the last analysis are decisive, since the question as to whether we have to do with one or two clauses in each individual case depends on these signals (the markers mentioned can also start off sentences). There are a large number of possibilities, especially if we remember that there is no definite limit to the number of clauses which may be included in one sentence. Since, however, the vast majority of compound sentences represent mixtures of only two of the contrastive types negatable/negated/negative, we can subsume the various possibilities under the following amalgamated types:

(1) mixed negatable/negated
(2) mixed negatable/negative
(3) mixed negated/negative.

Here are some examples:

Tā₁ zhīdao₂ guówáng₃ yào₄ shā₅ ta₆; dànshi₇ méi₈ fázi₉ táochu₁₀ guó₁₁ qu₁₂. "He₁ knew₂ [that] the king₃ wanted to₄ kill₅ him₆, but₇ [he] had no₈ way₉ [of] getting to flee₁₀,₁₂ the country₁₁." (type 2)

Cóng₁ dà₂ hé₃ de₄ zhèi₅ yìbiān₆ kàn₇ duìmiàn de₈ nèi₉ yìbiān₁₀; shémme₁₁ yě₁₂ qiáobujiàn₁₃. "From₁ this₅ side₆ of₄ the great₂ river₃ [we] look toward₇ the₉ opposite₈ side₁₀; [but] [we] cannot see₁₃ anything₁₁,₁₂." (type 1)

10. SENTENCE TYPES: SUMMARY

Bearing in mind that the type of central is decisive for the type of sentence in each case, we may set up altogether 13 sentence types, including three types of non-verbal sentences, which lack centrals. The various types can be arranged systematically as in the following list:

Sentence types

A. Verbal sentences

   I. Simple sentences

     a) negatable: *mǎi shū.*; *yǒu shū.* (1)

     b) negated: *bù/méi/bié mǎi shū.*; *méi yǒu shū.* (2)

     c) negative: *méi shū.* (3)

     d) ambivalent: *mǎi bu mai shū.*; *yǒu mei you shū.* (4)

   II. Compound sentences

     a) pure type:

       1) negatable: *wǒ qù*; *nǐ yě qù.* (5)

       2) negated: *wǒ bú qù*; *nǐ yě bú qù.* (6)

       3) negative: *wǒ méi qián*; *tā méi gōngfu.* (7)

     b) mixed type:

       1) negatable/negated: *wǒ qù*; *nǐ bú qù.*; *wǒ bú qù*; *nǐ qù.* (8)

       2) negatable/negative: *wǒ yǒu qián*; *nǐ méi qián.*; *wǒ méi qián*; *nǐ yǒu.* (9)

       3) negated/negative: *wǒ bú qù*; *méi gōngfu.*; *wǒ méi qián*; *suóyi wǒ bú qù.* (10)

B. Non-verbal sentences

   I. Simple sentences

     a) nominal predicate: *jiār jiǎr. chūsān.* (11)

     b) non-nominal predicate: *āiyā!* (12)

   II. Compound sentences

     nominal predicates: *wǒ zhèr*; *nǐ nǎr.* (13)

E. Sentence Forms

1. LIST OF SENTENCE FORMS

Sentences are classified not only according to type, but also according to *form*. Our use of the term *sentence form* in this book is based on the concept of *sentence value* as defined by Chao (1968, pp. 58–60).

Accordingly we shall distinguish between five sentence forms:
1) declarative, 2) interrogative, 3) imperative, 4) vocative, and
5) exclamatory.

2. DECLARATIVE SENTENCES

Sentences of this form typically have Intonation I; they are statements.
This form is extremely frequent, especially in narratives and in lectures,
articles, reports, etc.:

Wǒ₁ zài₂ xuéxiào₃ xuéle₄ yìnián₅ de₆ Zhōngguohuà₇. "I₁ have
studied₄ Chinese₇ for₆ one year₅ at₂ school₃."
*Wǒ₁ fùqin₂ hén₃ xǐhuan₄ zài₅ chīwán₆ wǎnfàn₇ de₈ shíhou₉, hé₁₀
wǒmen₁₁ zuòzai₁₂ kètīngli₁₃, géi₁₄ wǒmen₁₅ shuō₁₆ gùshì₁₇.*
"My₁ father₂ liked to₃,₄ sit₁₂ with₁₀ us₁₁ in the living-room₁₃
after₅,₈,₉ [we] had finished eating₆ dinner₇, telling₁₆ us₁₄,₁₅
stories₁₇."
*Suíran₁ fángzi₂ lǐmian₃ méi₄ yǒu₅ jiāju₆, dànshi₇ fángzū₈ hěn₉
dà₁₀.* "Even though₁ (there was₅ no₄ furniture₆ in₃ the house₂ =)
the house was unfurnished, (but₇) the rent₈ was₁₀ very₉ high₁₀."

3. INTERROGATIVE SENTENCES

Sentences of this form, which are all questions, comprise altogether five
patterns, which are dealt with below.

a) The sentence contains a *question word* or question word element.
The most important are: 1) substitutes such as *shéi* (more formal: *shuí*)
"who?", *shém(me)* "what?", *zěm(me)* "how?", *nǎr* (or *nǎli*) "where?",
duōshao "how many, how much?", *duōzan* "when?" 2) a few elements
occurring as demonstratives: *něi-* as in *něige* "which one?", *jǐ-* as in *jǐwèi*
"how many gentlemen?", and sometimes *hé-* as in *héshí* ("what time" =)
"when?". Common combinations are: *shémme shíhou* "when?", *wèi
shémme* "why?", *cóng nǎr* "where from?", *zěmmeyàng* "how is it? in
what way?"; somewhat less common are *hébì* and *hégù* "why?", and
hébù "why not?" Note also such expressions as *duó dà* "how big?" and
tā kě néng lái "can he come?" (here *kě* is a question word).

The following should be specially kept in mind: In order to have
interrogative function, question words must be fully stressed. If they
occur with zero stress, question words have indefinite meaning: *wǒ
gàosong ni shemme* "I'll tell you something"; *tīng shei shuō . . .* "I heard
someone say . . .". Whenever a fully stressed question word (especially, in
this case, *shéi, shémme, zěmme, nǎr*) is followed immediately by *dōu* or

yě, it does not function as a question word, but in the sense of "every-, any-", as is shown by the following examples: *Tā shémme yě bù dǒng.* "He doesn't understand anything."; *Shéi dōu zhīdao.* "(It is something which) everybody (or: anybody) knows."; *Nǎr dōu zhǎo le.* "I have looked everywhere." Finally, if the question word is dependent on a verb which is not the central, it is not translatable in the interrogative sense: *Wǒ bù zhīdào tā shì shéi.* "I don't know who he is."; *Gàosong wo yào duōshao.* "Tell me how much you want." None of these are interrogative sentences.

The following are examples of interrogative sentences containing question words:

Nǐ$_1$ *niànle*$_2$ *shémme*$_3$ *shū*$_4$. "What$_3$ books$_4$ have$_2$ you$_1$ read$_2$?"

Zhèijiàn$_1$ *dōngxi*$_2$, *Zhōngguohuà*$_3$ *jiào*$_4$ *shémme*$_5$. "What$_5$ is$_4$ this$_1$ thing$_2$ called$_4$ [in] Chinese$_3$?"

Nǐ$_1$ *wèi shémme*$_2$ *bú*$_3$ *xiàng*$_4$ *ta*$_5$ *dàoqiàn*$_6$. "Why$_2$ do$_3$ you$_1$ not$_3$ apologize$_6$ to$_4$ him$_5$?"

Zhè$_1$ *shì*$_2$ *shémme*$_3$ *yìsi*$_4$. "What$_3$ is$_2$ the$_1$ idea$_4$?; what does this mean?"

Nǐ$_1$ *shì*$_2$ *shéi*$_3$. "Who$_3$ are$_2$ you$_1$?"

Zhè$_1$ *shì*$_2$ *shéi*$_3$ *shuō*$_4$ *de*$_5$. "Who$_3$ (was$_2$ it (who$_5$)) said$_4$ this$_1$?"

Shì$_1$ *shéi*$_2$ *de*$_3$ *màozi*$_4$. "Whose$_{2,3}$ hat$_4$ is$_1$ [it]?"

Nǐ$_1$ *zěmme*$_2$ *huì*$_3$ *nèm(me)*$_4$ *shǎ*$_5$. "How$_2$ can$_3$ you$_1$ be$_5$ so$_4$ stupid$_5$?"

Nǐ$_1$ *zěmme*$_2$ *lái de*$_3$. "How$_2$ did$_3$ you$_1$ come$_3$?" (i.e. by train, by plane, or by boat?)

Nín nǎr. "Where are you?" (i.e. where are you calling from?)

Wǒ nǎr zhīdao. "How [should] I know?"

Nǐ$_1$ *jìnlái*$_2$ *zěmmeyàng*$_3$. "How$_3$ have$_3$ you$_1$ been$_3$ recently$_2$?" (= how have things been . . .)

Nǐ$_1$ *něitiān*$_2$ *lái de*$_3$. "What day$_2$ did$_3$ you$_1$ come$_3$?"

Děngle$_1$ *duó*$_2$ *dà*$_3$ *gōngfu*$_4$. "How$_2$ long$_3$ time$_4$ have$_1$ [you] been$_1$ waiting$_1$?"

Tā$_1$ *yào*$_2$ *jǐzhāng*$_3$. "How many sheets$_3$ does$_2$ he$_1$ want$_2$?"

Zhèige$_1$ *mài*$_2$ *duōshao*$_3$ *qián*$_4$. "How much$_3$ (money$_4$) do$_2$ [you] sell$_2$ this one$_1$ [for]?"

b) The sentence has an *ambivalent central*, but no question word (cp. Section D, subsection 4, p. 45). Questions formed on this pattern, which indicate an alternative choice between a verb and its negated form, do not necessarily anticipate an affirmative answer, but indicate a slightly higher probability of consent than questions expressed by the final particle *ma*. In alternative choice questions, the negators *bu* and *mei* may be in the neutral tone; the second (negated) verb may have the same feature.

Examples of interrogative sentences with alternative choice:

Dà bu da. "Is [it] big?"
Tā shízì bu shizi. "Can he read?"
Kànjian bu kanjian. "Do [you] see it?"
Kàndejiàn kanbujian. "Can [you] see it?"
Nǐ shì bu shi Wáng Guó-dào. "Are you Wang Kuo-tao?"
Wǒ de bìng, yàojǐn bu yaojin. "Is my sickness serious?"
Nǐmen₁ néng bu neng₂ bǎ₃ tā de₄ jiǎnghuà₅ fānchéng₆ Yīngwén₇. "Can₂ you₁ translate₆ his₄ lecture₅,₃ into₆ English₇?"
Nǐ₁ yǒu₂ yàofāngr₃ mei₄ you₅. "Do₂,₄,₅ you₁ have₂,₄,₅ a (medical) prescription₃?"
Hái₁ yóu₂ bǐ₃ zhège₄ piányi₅ de₆ mei₇ you₈. "Do [you] have₂,₇,₈ one which₆ is cheaper₁,₅ than₃ this one₄?"
Tā de₁ bóshì lùnwén₂ kāishí₃ xiě₄ le₅ meiyou₆. "Has₃,₆ he started₃ to write₄ his₁ doctoral thesis₂ yet₅?"

Sentences of this form are spoken with Intonation I, i.e. with the same intonation as declarative sentences.

As is seen from the examples, the negatable may be separated from the negated form by, for example, an object: *ní yǒu yàofāngr mei you*. Actually, such a sentence has three alternative forms, which are synonymous:

1. *Ní yǒu yàofāngr mei you.*
2. *Ní yǒu mei you yàofāngr.*
3. *Ní yǒu yàofāngr mei you yàofāngr.*

Alternative 3 is far less common than the other two. Similarly:

1. *Nǐ yào chī fàn bu yao.*
2. *Nǐ yào bu yao chī fàn.*
3. *Nǐ yào chī fàn bu yao chī fàn.*

Further, note the special — and very frequent — type of expression which consists of a sequence in the declarative form, with an alternative choice construction tagged on at the beginning, at the end, or inserted in the middle, in a way similar to the French expression *n'est-ce pas?*:

Wǒ₁ shuō₂ de₃ yóu₄ lǐ₅, shi-bu-shi₆. "What₃ I₁ said₂ was₄ right₅, wasn't it₆?"

*Nǐ*₁, *shi-bu-shi*₂, *qùguo*₃ *Běijīng*₄. "Isn't it so that₂ you₁ have been to₃ Peking₄?"

*Shànghǎi*₁ *bǐ*₂ *Běijīng*₃ *dà*₄, *shi-bu-shi*₅. "Shanghai₁ is bigger₄ than₂ Peking₃, isn't it₅?"

*Nǐ*₁ *kāi*₂ *chē*₃, *dui-bu-dui*₄. "You₁ can drive₂ (a car₃), (isn't it true₄ =) can't you?"

*Wǒmen*₁ *yíkuàr*₂ *qù*₃, *hao-bu-hao*₄. "We₁ go₃ together₂, OK₄?"

Other such expressions are *xíng-bu-xing*; *kéyi-bu-keyi*.

c) The sentence contains no question word, but two juxtaposed verb forms; they are different, however, from the arrangement described under **b)** in that 1) the verbs are often different verbs, 2) they may both be in the affirmative, or one may be in the affirmative, the other in the negative, and 3) they are very often separated by *háishi* "or" or *shì*, or each may be preceded by either *háishi* or *shì*. The effect is the meaning of "*or*"; the forms can shift position. Examples are:

*Zhāng xiansheng*₁ *chī*₂ *fàn*₃ *chī*₄ *miàn*₅. "Does₂ Mr. Chang₁ eat₂ rice₃ [or] does₄ [he] eat₄ noodles₅?" (or: *chī miàn chī fàn.*)

More commonly the disjunction is made explicit:

Tā chī fàn háishi chī miàn. or:
Tā háishi chī fàn háishi chī miàn. or:
Tā shì chī fàn chī miàn.

*Nǐ*₁ *péngyou*₂ *ài*₃ *wo*₄ *háishi*₅ *hèn*₆ *wo*₇. "Does₃ your₁ friend₂ love₃ me₄ or₅ hate₆ me₇?"

*Zhège*₁ *háizi*₂ *shì*₃ *nán de*₄ *shì*₅ *nǚ de*₆. "Is₃ this₁ child₂ a boy₄ or₅ a girl₆?"

*Chuānghu*₁ *xiànzài*₂ *kāizhe*₃ *háishi*₄ *guānzhe*₅. "Are₃,₅ the windows₁ now₂ open₃ or₄ closed₅?"

*Nǐ*₁ *qù*₂ *kàn*₃ *diànyǐngr*₄ *háishi*₅ *bú qù*₆. "Are₂ you₁ going to₂ (see₃) the movie₄ (or₅ not₆)?"

d) The sentence has a straightforward declarative form, except that at the very end one of a small number of final particles is added (interrogative particles). These are *ma* (or *me*), *a, ba, ne*. Questions formed by any of these particles are mostly of the type often called yes-or-no questions.

Interrogative sentences ending in *ma* (*me*), which often have a relatively high intonation level, are felt to anticipate a slightly higher probability of an answer in the negative than is the case for sentences with ambivalent centrals. In other words, a question ending in *ma* indicates a little more doubt: *Tā dǒng ma.*, whereas *Ta dǒng bu dong.* is more often felt to anticipate a higher probability of an affirmative answer. Otherwise the two forms are equivalent. But note that a question which in English has negative form ("doesn't he understand?") is translatable into Chinese only in the form of a question ending in a particle: *Tā bù dǒng ma.* (Consequently, *Tā dǒng bu dong.* cannot be translated into English as "Doesn't he understand?") A question which is phrased affirmatively in English can, on the other hand, be translated both ways: *Tā huì bu hui shuō Zhōngguohuà.* or *Tā huì shuō Zhōngguo-huà ma.*

The particle *a* has the effect of 1) softening the possible bluntness of the question, 2) seeking confirmation of something already heard, but not clearly or exactly understood, or 3) when making a suggestion, asking for approval. The particle *ba* usually corresponds to "I suppose", "isn't it so?". In the case of the particle *ne* a preceding question is often assumed; a question is asked in a context of other questions ("and now, what about . . ."); it sometimes has a slightly emphatic value ("and what about *me*, then").

In general each of these particles is added to verbal as well as non-verbal sentences, with the same effect. Particles *a* and *ne*, (but hardly *ma* and *ba*) can occur in sentences which contain a question word: *Shéi a.* "Who is it?"; *Tā shì nǎr lái de a.* "Where did he come from?"; *Nǐ yǒu mei you qiānbǐ ne.* "Do you have a pencil?"; *Tā lái bu lai ne.* "And is he actually coming, then?"

Examples of interrogative sentences with final particle:

Zhū xiansheng zài jiā ma. "Is Mr. Chu at home?"

Nǐ shì Gǔ xiansheng ma. "Are you Mr. Ku?"

Jīntian wǎnshang$_1$, nín$_2$ yǒu$_3$ gōngfu$_4$ lái$_5$ xiántán$_6$ ma. "Do$_3$ you$_2$ have$_3$ time$_4$ to come$_5$ [over] [and] have a chat$_6$ tonight$_1$?"

Tāmen$_1$ dào$_2$ gōngyuánli$_3$ liūdá$_4$ qu$_5$ le$_6$ ma. "Have$_{5,6}$ they$_1$ gone$_5$ to$_2$ the park$_3$ [for] a stroll$_4$?"

Bú shì$_1$ zhēn de$_2$ ma. "Isn't$_1$ [it] true$_2$?"

Nǐ$_1$ bú yào$_2$ gēn$_3$ ta$_4$ shuō huà$_5$ ma. "Don't$_2$ you$_1$ want to$_2$ talk$_5$ with$_3$ him$_4$?"

Shàng$_1$ xīngqīsān$_2$ a. "Last$_1$ Wednesday$_2$ (was that what you said (or meant))?"

Nǐ$_1$ hē$_2$ kāfēi$_3$ ne, hē$_4$ chá$_5$ ne. "Do$_2$ you$_1$ drink$_2$ coffee$_3$ [or] (do you drink$_4$) tea$_5$?"

Zhèi$_1$ liǎngjiàn$_2$ shì$_3$, shì$_4$ shémme$_5$ guānxi$_6$ ne$_7$. "And$_7$ what$_5$ connection$_6$ is there$_4$ [between] these$_1$ two$_2$ things$_3$?"

*Wǒ*₁ *tì*₂ *ni*₃ *ná*₄ *yíjiàn*₅ *ba.* "Shall₄ I₁ carry₄ one₅ (e.g. bag) for₂ you₃?"
*Zánmen*₁ *zǒu*₂ *ba.* "Shall₂ we₁ go₂?"
*Qiānbǐ*₁ *zài*₂ *nàr*₃ *ba.* "The pencils₁ are₂ there₃, I suppose?"
Nǐ bú qù a? "You aren't going (is·that what you mean, or: what you said)?"

Except for special expressions like *kě bú shì ma*! "(Yes,) isn't that so!" all sentences ending in *ma* are questions. But not *all* sentences ending in *ne, ba*, or *a* are questions. The reason is that these particles also have functions other than that of signalling a question. A sentence ending in *a* which is intended as a question is uttered with a somewhat low and breathy intonation, while the same sentence with ordinary Intonation I is not a question. Thus:

Ni zhǎobuzháo a. (Intonation I) "So you cannot find (or see) it."
Ní zhǎobuzháo a? "You cannot find it?" (low).

A detail worth keeping in mind is that a question ending in *ma* and containing a negation requires *shìde*, otherwise translatable by "yes", as an answer, if the negated assumption is confirmed. If the negated assumption in the question is not confirmed, *búshì* or *búshìde* "no" is used. For example:

Nǐ bù lái ma. "Aren't you coming?" Answer: *Shì(de), (wǒ bù lái).* (Yes, I am not coming =) "No, I am not coming."
Or: *Búshì(de), (wǒ lái).* (No, I am coming =) "Yes, I am coming."

An interesting historical sidelight which may throw some light on the origin and development of interrogative sentences in Chinese is the theory that the particles *ma* and *ba* are contractions of old negative adverbs and the particle *a*. The element *m-* may be what remains of an old negator (cp. Hakka *lôi m̄ lôi = lái bu lai*). If we assume the sentence *lái m- (lái) -a* to be the original form, the present form is easy to explain. Similarly: *lái bu (lai) a > lái bu'a > lái ba.* If this is so, questions of type **d)** have developed from type **b)**.

e) The sentence is a straightforward declarative sentence from the segmental point of view, but, instead of the final drop in intonation, there is a high intonation trend throughout the sentence, followed by a rising final contour:

Nǐ bù xǐhuan kàn xì?! "You don't like to go to the theater?"
Zhèi shì ǀtā shuō de?! "HE said this?"
Tā bú zànchéng?! "He is not in favor (of it)?"

4. IMPERATIVE SENTENCES

Sentences in the form of a command are usually spoken in a somewhat faster tempo, with an increased pitch range, and often with emphatic stress. Further, they often lack subjects. Examples are:

> *Qù!* "Go!"
> *Mǎshàng jiù qù!* "Go at once!"
> *Zài shuō!* "Say it once more!"
> *Gǔnchūqù!* "Get out of here!"
> *Bié* (or *bú yaò*) *nào!* "Stop that noise!"
> *Bié gēn wo dǎchà!* "Don't interrupt me!"
> *Xiǎoxin huǒchē!* "Look out, the train is coming!"
> *Xiàcì bié hē jiǔ!* "Next time, don't drink wine!"

Sometimes the particle *ba* is added:

> *Kuài diar zǒu ba!* "Walk a little faster!"

Verbs which occur in imperative sentences are naturally most often verbs expressing an action. Quality verbs, if used in this way, tend to be reduplicated (*Mànmārde!* "Take it easy!"), or are followed by *yidiar* (*Màn yidiar!* "Not so fast!"). Note also: *Zuò yizuo!* "Sit down!"; *Děng yideng!* "Wait a little!"

Sentences in the imperative form are rather brusque in tone, and are therefore not very common. A more frequent mode of expression is found in polite requests of the following type: *Qǐng ni kuài diar zǒu.* "Please walk a little faster."; or *Qǐng ni bié qù.* "Please don't go [there]." Sentences in this rephrased form are not imperative sentences; they are best classified as a subtype of declarative (minor) sentences: "I ask you to ..."

5. VOCATIVE SENTENCES

This sentence form has a reduced pitch range and a falling final contour. Thus, if, for example *Lǎo Wáng.* "Wang." is said as a sentence in answer to the question, *Shì shéi shuō de.* "Who was it who said it?", the sentence would be spoken as an ordinary declarative sentence with Intonation I. If, on the other hand, the sentence is spoken directly to the person in order to call his or her attention, it is a vocative sentence with its characteristic "squeezed" intonation. Thus, there is a contrast; *Lǎo Wáng.* ~ *Lǎo Wáng!*

In the same way:

Hé xiansheng! "Mr. Ho!"
Zhōu jínglǐ! "Manager Chou!"
Kēzhǎng! "Mr. dean!"; "Chairman!" (as said to the head or director
of a department or section leader).

6. EXCLAMATORY SENTENCES

Such sentences, typically consisting of one word, an interjection, contain
no tonal features, only intonation and stress (often emphatic stress).
Examples are such expressions as *Aiya*! "Oh"; *Wei(wei)*! "Hello" (also:
Wai!).

Sometimes a declarative sentence is started off by an interjection:

Wei, géi wo$_1$ bǎ zhèige$_2$ píbāo$_3$ dāng$_4$ xíngli$_5$ fāle$_6$ ba! "Hello there,
can I$_1$ have$_1$ this$_2$ bag$_3$ registered$_6$ (or: checked) as$_4$ baggage$_5$!"

In such a case we do not have an exclamatory sentence in the sense in
which the term is used here, but rather a declarative or perhaps,
depending on intonational features, an imperative sentence.

7. SENTENCE TYPE AND SENTENCE FORM

In this and the preceding section two classes of criteria for the
classification of sentences have been introduced, viz. type and form. We
have established 13 types and 5 forms. The 13 types were summarized at
the end of Section D (p. 54). The 5 forms were listed at the beginning of
this section (p. 55). By combining these two classes of criteria we can
now classify a sentence according to type *and* form in the following way:

Verbal simple negatable/declarative:
Tā xǐhuan huà huàr. "He likes to paint."

Verbal simple negated/interrogative:
Nǐ bú rènshi tā de fùqin ma. "Don't you know his father?"

Verbal simple ambivalent/interrogative:
Nǐ rènshi bu renshi tā de fùqin. "Do you know his father?"

Verbal compound pure negated/interrogative:
Shéi bù néng qù; shéi bú yào qù. "Who cannot go, and who does not
want to go?"

Verbal compound mixed negatable; negated/declarative:
Yŏu de yào qù; *yŏu de bú yào.* "Some (of them) want to go, some don't."
Etc.

In Table II the resulting combinations are marked by x. Only such combinations as actually occur are marked in this way. Altogether 31 patterns exist according to this system (the five subtypes of interrogative sentences are counted as one form). Some categories, such as ambivalent type and exclamatory form, are extremely limited as to possibilities of combination; among the various forms, the interrogative shows the greatest number of possible combinations (12). No type goes with every form; more than half of the types go with three forms.

TABLE II. Sentence types and sentence forms

TYPE	FORM				
	Declarative	Interrogative	Imperative	Vocative	Exclamatory
Verbal					
Simple					
Negatable	x	x	x		
Negated	x	x	x		
Negative	x	x			
Ambivalent		x			
Compound pure					
Negatable	x	x	x		
Negated	x	x	x		
Negative	x	x			
Compound mixed					
Negatable/negated	x	x	x		
Negatable/negative	x	x			
Negated/negative	x	x			
Non-verbal					
Simple					
Nominal	x	x		x	
Non-nominal					x
Compound					
Nominal	x	x		x	

F. Sentence Structure

1. THE SENTENCE: A HIERARCHY

Although a sentence is a chain of linguistic material which is grammatically independent of other chains and which forms an accentual and semantic whole, it is not simply a concatenation of elements in a certain order. Order is important, but the relations between the elements which occur in succession must also be taken into account. In the expression *zuì dà de* "the biggest one" *zuì* presupposes *dà*, and *de* presupposes (*zuì*) *dà*. In *bú shì zuì dà de* "it is not the biggest one" *zuì dà de* is dependent on *bú shì*, and *bú* in turn on *shì*. In other words, a sentence is a network of dependencies. These dependencies operate on various *levels*, and especially in sentences of a certain length, the number of such levels may be quite high. Each level has its constituents, and a given level taken as a whole enters into a direct structural relationship with at least one other level. The sentence can thus be seen as a *hierarchy* of levels and constituents. To define and describe this hierarchy is an important part of *syntax*.

2. IMMEDIATE CONSTITUENTS

One possible way of analyzing linguistic forms (i.e. sentences, clauses, phrases, expressions, words) is to assume that they and their parts can be successively divided into *binary* units. This means that a given form is broken down into two parts which balance each other, by making a cut at a certain point in the sequence. Each resultant partial is further divided into two parts, and this operation is continued until the possibilities are exhausted, i.e. the partials cannot be subjected to further division. In this way a sentence, or any other constitute, can be analyzed, step by step, into parts of smaller extent, so that each part consists of a constitute which forms a grammatical (and usually semantic) whole. In syntactic analysis the analysis is continued until one reaches the level of the *word*.

Each successive step brings the analysis to a lower *level*. The highest level is represented by the whole, undivided utterance; the lowest level contains only single words. All other levels consist of two constituents, which together form a construct, i.e. a grammatical form. An example will show the procedure.

Tā dào nàr qù. "He is going there."

The first cut is made between *Tā* and the rest of the sentence. Next, *dào nàr* is cut off from *qù*. Finally *dào* and *nàr* emerge as minimal syntactic units. Constructs identified in the process are *dào nàr qù* and *dào nàr*; *tā, qù, dào* and *nàr* are not constructs on the syntactic level, they are just words (words may turn out to be constructs from the point of view of morphology (*nà + r*), but this does not concern us here). If we put this into graphic form, we get the following result:

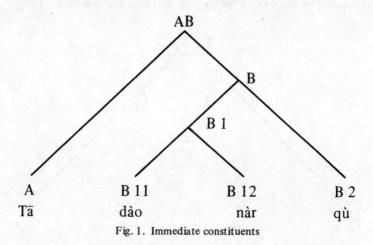

Fig. 1. Immediate constituents

Here AB stands for the complete sentence;

A = *tā*; B = *dào nàr qù*.
     B 1 = *dào nàr*; B 2 = *qù*
     B 11 = *dào*; B 12 = *nàr*.

A and B are the partials resulting from the first cut and are said to represent the second level. B 1 and B 2 form the third level, and B 11 and B 12 are partners on level 4, which is the last one in this sentence. The digital numbers are chosen so as to show consecutive steps in the analysis: B 1 is cut into two parts, which are given digits 11 and 12 respectively. B is divided into B 1 and B 2 respectively.

A and B, B 1 and B 2, B 11 and B 12 are partners; they balance each other. There is a close connection between the two partners on each level. Such partners are called *immediate constituents*. Each word is a constituent, but belongs directly only with its partner; thus we say that although *dào* and *qù* are both constituents, they are not constituents with one another, i.e. they do not belong together in this sentence, although they may do so in other sentences.

Our diagram shows what belongs together, but not the specific relationship between constituents. We realize that *tā* is omissible; *dào nàr qù*, taken as a whole, is not. Within the latter sequence, however, *dào nàr* is omissible, whereas *qù* is not. We say that *tā* presupposes *dào nàr qù*, but not vice versa; *dào nàr* presupposes *qù*, but not vice versa; *nàr* is dependent on *dào*. We can now draw another diagram in which these dependencies are indicated: > means that the item or sequence on the left depends on the one on the right; < indicates the opposite:

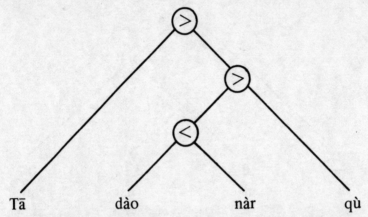

Fig. 2. Immediate constituents, with relationships between constituents.

Our analysis has shown that

1) *tā* is an immediate constituent with *dào nàr qù*; the latter is the center because it is presupposed by the former;
2) *dào nàr* is an immediate constituent with *qù*; the latter is the center because it is presupposed by the former;
3) *dào* is an immediate constituent with *nàr*; the former is the center because it is presupposed by the latter.

A construct in which one of the constituents is a center in this sense is an *endocentric construct* (endocentric = "center within"). A construct in which none of the constituents is a center, is an *exocentric construct* (exocentric = "center outside"). The three constructs *tā/dào nàr qù*, *dào nàr/qù*, and *dào/nàr* are all endocentric; the centers are *dào nàr qù*, *qù*, and *dào* respectively.

Examples of endocentric constructs are: *hǎo de duō* "much better" (center: *hǎo*; explicit marker: *de*; *de* "means" <); *ní xiě de zì* "the characters you have written" (center: *zì*; explicit marker: *de*; *de* "means" >); *xiǎng qù kànkan* "plans to go and take a look" (center: *xiǎng*; no explicit marker); *fùqin huílaile* "father is back" (center: *huílaile*); *dà yidiar* "a little better" (center: *dà*; no explicit marker); *yòng Tàiyǔ jiángyǎn* "give a lecture in Thai" (center: *jiángyǎn*; no explicit marker); *mǎi shū* "buy books" (center: *mǎi*; no specific marker); *bóshì lùnwén* "doctoral dissertation" (center: *lùnwén*; no explicit marker); *Shāndong zhī de chóuzi* "silk cloth made in Shantung" (center: *chóuzi*; marker *de*); *liǎngge rén* "two people" (center: *rén*; no explicit marker).

Exocentric constructs are less common; most of them are within the field of morphology. *Dǒngshi* "board member" (literally "to manage" + "affairs" → a noun); *yǒumíng* (literally "have" + "name" → quality verb "to be famous") are examples. Syntactic constructs with a nominalizing *de* may be regarded as exocentric (*mài shū de* "a bookseller"), since neither the marker *de* nor *mài shū* (whose center is *mài*) can be regarded as the center of the construct as a whole.

Although a construct can usually be divided into two parts, in some cases the number of constituents cannot reasonably be assumed to be just two. Thus, in *Máobǐ, qiānbǐ, gāngbǐ,/dōu hǎo.* "A brush, a pencil, [or] a (steel) pen/are (all of them) OK." we obviously have three constituents of the same category and on the same level. In other words, even though in most cases the structures are binary, in some exceptional cases they are not.

We shall now give a few examples of longer sentences, to illustrate the principle of immediate constituents. Fig. 3 gives an analysis, in the form of a diagram, of the sentence, *Nèige wàiguorén, huì shuō jiǎndān de huà, hái méi shuōguàn.* "That foreigner has some elementary language knowledge, [but] hasn't got sufficient speaking practice." In this example the immediate constituents form constitutes in the following manner:

	Immediate constituents	*Constitute*
Level II	A + B	AB Level I
	(*nèige w.*) + (*huì ... shuōguàn*)	whole sentence
Level III	A 1 + A 2	A Level II
	(*nèige*) + (*wàiguorén*)	*nèige wàiguorén*
Level III	B 1 + B 2	B Level II
	(*huì shuō ... huà*) + (*hái méi shuōguàn*)	*huì ... shuōguàn*
Level IV	B 11 + B 12	B 1 Level III
	(*huì*) + (*shuō jiǎndān de huà*)	*huì ... huà*
Level IV	B 21 + B 22	B 2 Level III
	(*hái*) + (*méi shuōguàn*)	*hái méi shuōguàn*

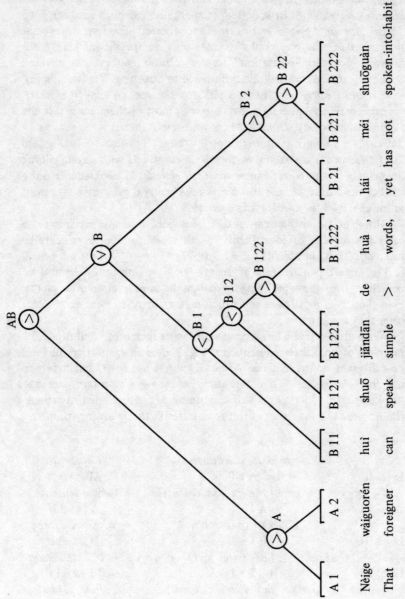

Fig. 3. Sentence analysis (immediate constituents).

Level V	B 121 + B 122	B 12 Level IV
	(*shuō*) + (*jiǎndān de huà*)	*shuō jiǎndān de huà*
Level V	B 221 + B 222	B 22 Level IV
	(*méi*) + (*shuōguàn*)	*méi shuōguàn*
Level VI	B 1221 + B1222	B 122 Level V
	>	
	(*jiǎndān*) (*de*) (*huà*)	*jiǎndān de huà*

In the diagram the constituents are assigned digits showing constituent relationships. Sentence immediate constituents are A and B; immediate constituents on lower levels have the same number of digits, and all digits except the last are identical. Thus B 21 and B 22 are immediate constituents on the same level; the same can be said of B 1221 and B 1222. The diagram also shows dependencies indicated by the signs already mentioned; in addition there is, on node B, a sign ∨ which indicates coordination (both > and < denote subordination, depending on the location of the center. We consider coordination to be endocentric; in this case one may speak of two centers, not one).

A *node* is a point where "branches" denoting constituents meet; these points are marked by circles. Note that the single words at the ends of "branches" are not nodes; they are not subject to further subdivisions and are thus *ultimate syntactic constituents*.

We can now rearrange the diagram so as to bring out more clearly not only the constituents, but also the various levels. In this way we can see the complexity of the sentence used as an example. Figure 4 shows the structure of the sentence, and gives an idea of the Chinese-box fashion in which the sentence components are joined together into a whole.

The sections into which a sentence is thus divided, step by step, in most cases coincide with those which a native speaker will arrive at on the basis of his own intuition. The method is not absolutely perfect, and is not in all cases equally easy to apply. There are cases where two alternative analyses may seem equally acceptable. But in most cases the method will work well enough for the purposes that concern us here.

The sentence just illustrated is "back-heavy" in the sense that its network of "branches" is more highly developed on the right-hand side, i.e. the second part of the sentence (or, put in a different way, there are more "boxes" at the end than at the beginning). This is by no means always so. To illustrate a "front-heavy" sentence, let us take as an example the following sentence:

Dài dà yǎnjìngr de nèige rén, shì shéi. "Who is the person who wears (those) big glasses?"

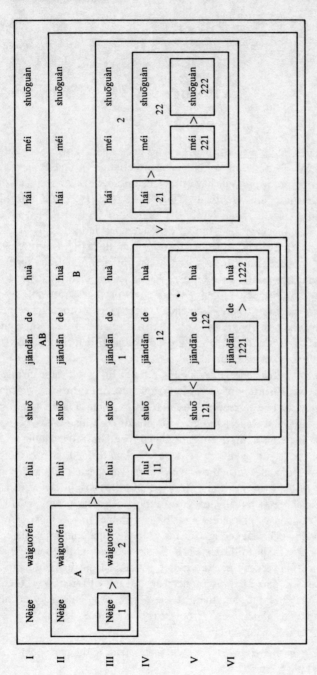

Fig. 4. Structural chart of constituents (in box form).

An immediate constituent analysis is shown in Fig. 5.

Fig. 6 gives the same analysis, in box form.

Finally, to indicate some of the complexities, let us look at the following sentence:

Tā₁ búdàn₂ shì₃ yíge₄ kēxuéjiā₅, érqiě₆ yě₇ shì₈ yíge₉ shīrén₁₀, nà₁₁ shì₁₂ hěn₁₃ míngxiǎn₁₄ de₁₅ shìqing₁₆. "[That] he₁ is₃ not only₂ a₄ scientist₅, but₆ [that], in addition₆, [he] is₈ also₇ a₉ poet₁₀, (that₁₁) is₁₂ something₁₆ which is₁₅ quite₁₃ obvious₁₄."

AB
{
A: *Tā . . . shīrén*
B: *nà . . . shìqing*
}

A
{
A 1: *Tā búdàn shì yíge kēxuéjiā*
A 2: *yě shì yíge shīrén*
}

B
{
B 1: *nà* (terminal)
B 2: *shì hěn míngxiǎn de shìqing*
}

A 1
{
A 11: *tā* (terminal)
A 12: *búdàn shì yíge kēxuéjiā*
}

A 2
{
A 21: *yě* (terminal)
A 22: *shì yíge shīrén*
}

B 2
{
B 21: *shì* (terminal)
B 22: *hěn míngxiǎn de shìqing*
}

A 12
{
A 121: *búdàn* (terminal)
A 122: *shì yíge kēxuéjiā*
}

A 22
{
A 221: *shì* (terminal)
A 222: *yíge shīrén*
}

B 22
{
B 221: *hěn míngxiǎn*
B 222: *shìqing* (terminal)
}

A 122
{
A 1221: *shì* (terminal)
A 1222: *yíge kēxuéjiā*
}

A 222
{
A 2221: *yige* (terminal)
A 2222: *shīrén* (terminal)
}

B 221
{
B 2211: *hěn* (terminal)
B 2212: *míngxiǎn* (terminal)
}

A 1222
{
A 12221: *yíge* (terminal)
A 12222: *kēxuéjiā* (terminal)
}

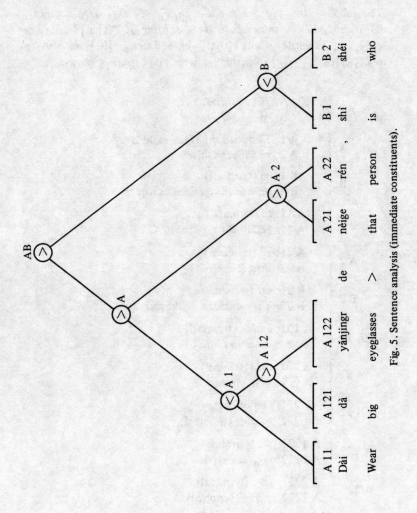

Fig. 5. Sentence analysis (immediate constituents).

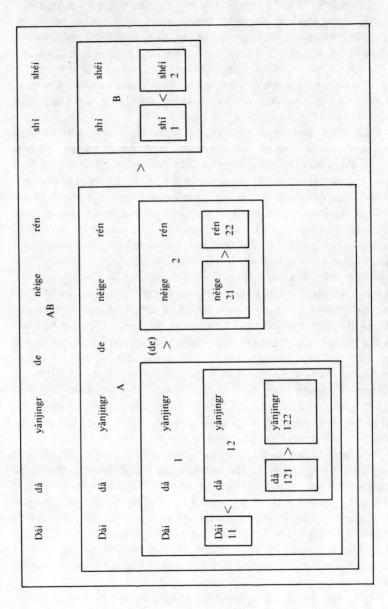

Fig. 6. Structural chart of constituents (in box form).

To illustrate the result of this analysis we combine the "branch" method and the "box" method into one diagram, with each constituent, and its index number, placed on the proper level. Terminal points, on which we find words only, are marked by a horizontal line; each node is indicated by a circle. The direction of the dependency is indicated by either >, <, or V. Note that *érqiě* and *de* are not constituents by themselves; they are markers and stand outside the constituent system. The former is a marker of coordination; the latter is a marker of subordination. Fig. 7 shows the relationships.

Each node represents a construct; all nodes except AB represent constructs which enter into other constructs. Although these constructs are, in this sentence, joined together into one structural whole, each of them can potentially occur independently (e.g. A 122 *shì yíge kēxuéjiā*, or B 22 *hěn míngxiǎn de shìqing*). Each construct, as it occurs in the analysis, represents a construction type; each construct and its constituents represent a *form class.* Thus, A 11 *tā* represents a class of nominal expressions, i.e. any nominal or nominal construct denoting a person can be substituted for it. *Dài dà yǎnjìngr nèige rén* "the gentleman who wears big glasses"; *zhèige yǒumíng de zhèngzhìjiā* "this famous politician"; *nǐ de péngyou* "your friend", are examples of possible substitutes. A 122 *shì yíge kēxuéjiā* is structurally parallel to constructs like *yǒu sānge xiǎoháizi* "has three small children", *mǎile hěn duō de shū* "bought many books", *zhǎobudào tā de xīn mǎi de màozi* "could not find his newly bought cap". This is the class of verb + object constructs. *Nà shì hěn míngxiǎn de shìqing* represents the class of predicative constructions, here in the form of a major clause; the construct consists of a subject + predicate construction (other examples: *Zhè shì rénren dōu zhīdao de.* "It's something which everybody knows."; *Ní xiǎng shì zhēn de ma.* "Do you think it is true?").

To a large extent the division of a construct into constituents depends on phonological signals. In the last example the division of the whole sequence AB into A and B depends on the fact that between *shīrén* and *nà* a major pause is possible; between B 1 *nà* and B 2 *shì hěn míngxiǎn de shìqing* another pause, dependent on the former, is possible. Within B 2, *shì* (B 21) is separable from B 22 *hěn míngxiǎn de shìqing*, and so on. Phonological signals are very important; they are not limited only to pauses. Pauses are closely tied to other essential features, viz. intonation and stress.

Up to this point, when discussing immediate constituents, we have only taken the segmental elements of the sentence into consideration. By segmental elements we mean those linguistic components which occur in

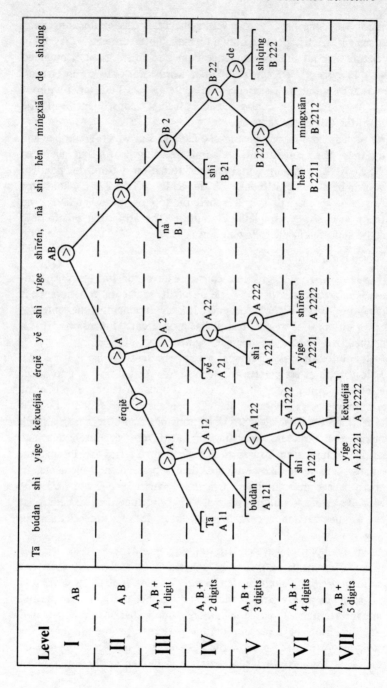

Fig. 7. Immediate constituents and levels of analysis

sequence, viz. consonants and vowels, syllables, words, expressions. Such a sequence is strictly speaking only a formula, not a sentence. It is merely a skeleton without life. No sentence comes to life until it is provided with suprasegmental elements. In other words, not only are intonation and stress essential to a sentence (no sentence can be uttered without them), they are to be considered as immediate constituents with the whole of the rest of the sentence.

We have spoken of sentence levels, i.e. levels at which we isolate and define immediate constituents. A complete analysis of a sentence must also include the suprasegmental levels. Intonation is from this point of view an immediate constituent with the sentence taken as a whole. In a sense, we might say that it is added on top of the other layers; no sentence analysis is complete without it. The structural relationship could be indicated in the following way:

Tā dào nàr qù/Intonation.

However, whereas segmental constituents occur *successively*, intonation is *simultaneous* with any and all of the segmental constituents; it is spread out over the whole sequence. It is a component of the sentence, but in a different sense, because it has a different "dimension". It is a component without actually being a segment.

Just as intonation is an integral part of the sentence, so is stress. We have dealt with stress patterns in Section C; we shall not go into detail here. Stress is primarily a phrase feature; if a clause/sentence consists of several phonological phrases, it will contain a succession of stress patterns, each with a nuclear stress. In principle, therefore, we speak of a suprasegmental structure consisting of two layers, viz. intonation and stress. As we have seen, pauses are closely tied to stress and intonation. But pauses are more like segmental than suprasegmental elements. In addition, pauses are sometimes "articulated pauses" (*nèige rén a, dào nàr qù ma*). Reverting to our box system, we now include the two additional layers. We then get a more complete and exact idea of sentence structure, as shown in Fig. 8.

As an example we have chosen one of the sentences we used in our discussion of immediate constituent analysis, in a slightly shorter version: *Nèige wàiguorén, huì shuō jiǎndān de huà*. We have limited ourselves to a simple sentence as an example; the chief difference between a simple and a compound sentence, apart from a more complicated box system, would be the inclusion of more intonation patterns. In the diagram, the abbreviation N is used to show the placement of nuclear stress in each phrase. It is assumed that the sentence is spoken as three phrases; a

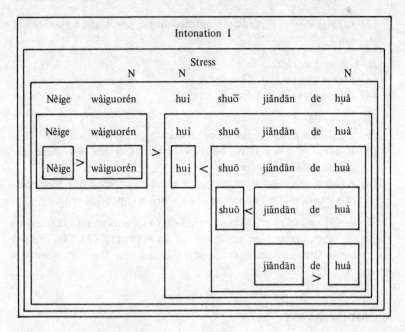

Fig. 8. Chart of sentence structure (in box form).

different (and equally valid) assumption would be that the sequence *huì shuō jiăndān de huà* is spoken as one phrase. In the latter case the whole sequence would have no more than two nuclear stresses, namely those on *rén* and on *huà*.

3. MAIN ENDOCENTRIC CONSTRUCTION TYPES

Among endocentric types there are two categories, usually referred to as *coordination* and *subordination.* Subordination is a pattern which includes a center and a satellite. Coordination is a pattern in which both constituents are centers.

Within this general framework, altogether seven construction types may be distinguished:

A. Satellite + center:
(1) attributive constructions (modifier + modified): *modification* (pp. 78 et seq.)

(2) topic subject + predicate constructions: *predication* (pp. 80 et seq.)

B. *Center + satellite*:
(3) verb + object: (pp. 85 et seq.)
(4) verb + complement (pp. 87 et seq.)

C. Center + *center*:
(5) nominal + nominal; reference identical: *apposition* (p. 88)
(6) nominal + nominal *or* verbal + verbal; reference *not* identical: *additive constructs* (p. 88)
(7) nominal + nominal *or* verbal + verbal; reference *not* identical; references mutually exclusive: *disjunction* (pp. 88 et seq.)

Types (3) and (5) are always unmarked; (4) is almost always marked; the other types are marked or unmarked. In types (1), (2), (3), and (4) the order is *fixed*; in the other types, the order of the components is *reversible*.

4. MODIFICATION

If the center is a verb, the construct is a *verbal expression*; if the center is a nominal, the construct is a *nominal expression*. In the former case the satellite constituent functions adverbially; in the second case it has a function similar to that of adjectives or relative clauses in other languages: it describes, classifies, or in some other way specifies the center. In both types of expression the relationship is marked by the marker *de*; in some subtypes the use of a marker is required, in other types it is not required or even excluded. The subtypes are the following:

a) *Nominal expressions*

(1) The first constituent is a nominal. *wǒ de shū* "my book"; *tā mǔqin* "his mother"; *fángzi de qiántou* "in front of the house"; *Xīnhài gémìng* "revolution of 1911"; *Xīnhài gémìng yǐqián* "before the revolution of 1911"; *bóshì lùnwén* "doctoral dissertation"; *nèi shíhou* "(at) that time". The use of the marker is not obligatory (in the case of such expressions as *tā mǔqin*, which indicates personal relations, the marker is usually omitted); sometimes the use or non-use of a marker makes a difference, thus: *Zhōngguo péngyou* "a Chinese friend" or "a friend in China" ~ *Zhōngguo de péngyou* usually: "friends of China".

(2) The first constituent is a verb or a verbal expression: *lái de₁ rén₂* "people₂ who come (or: came)₁"; *hěn gāo de₁ shān₂* "high₁ moun-

tains$_2$"; *bù$_1$ yuǎn de$_2$ dìfang$_3$* "a place$_3$ not$_1$ far off$_2$"; *chī de$_1$ dōngxi$_2$* "things$_2$ to eat$_1$"; *zǒuchulai$_1$ de$_2$ rén$_3$* "people$_3$ who$_2$ are coming out$_1$; people who have come out"; *xiěcuòle$_1$ de$_2$ zì$_3$* "characters$_3$ which$_2$ are written wrong$_1$"; *bù kě shōushi de$_1$ dìbù$_2$* "an irremediable$_1$ condition$_2$"; *zài$_1$ Zhōngguo$_2$ zuò$_3$ mǎimai$_4$, kāi$_5$ gōngchǎng$_6$ de$_7$ wàiguorén$_8$* "foreigners$_8$ who$_7$ carried on$_3$ trade$_4$ [and] built$_5$ factories$_6$ in$_1$ China$_2$".

(3) The first constituent has the segmental form of a major clause ("sentence modifier"): *nǐ$_1$ bú$_2$ rènshi$_3$ de$_4$ rén$_5$* "people$_5$ whom$_4$ you$_1$ do not$_2$ know$_3$"; *shōucheng$_1$ bù$_2$ hǎo$_3$ de$_4$ shíhou$_5$* "(at those times$_5$) when$_4$ harvests$_1$ were$_3$ no$_2$ good$_3$"; *dìyícì$_1$ shìjiè$_2$ dàzhàn$_3$ kāishǐ$_4$ yǐhòu$_5$* "after$_5$ the First$_1$ World$_2$ War$_3$ began$_4$"; *káogǔ xuéjiā$_1$ suǒ$_2$ fāxiàn$_3$ de$_4$ kèzai$_5$ gǔtoushang$_6$ de$_7$ jiágǔwén$_8$* "the Oracle Bone inscriptions$_8$ engraved on$_5$ bones$_6$ which$_7$ the archeologists$_1$ discovered$_{2,3,4}$". In this type of construct the marker *de* (or sometimes, mostly in clichés, the literary marker *zhi*) is used.

b) *Verbal expressions*

(1) The first constituent is an adverb: *bù hǎo* "is no good"; *hěn dà* "(very) big"; *gèng dà* "(still) bigger"; *zuì dà* "biggest"; *yě yǒu* "there are/is also"; *jiù lái* "comes right away"; *mànmārde zǒu* "walks slowly"; *fǎnzhèng bù néng qù* "I cannot go in any case"; *yǐjīng láile* "has already come".

(2) The first constituent is an adverbial phrase or a verbal expression functioning as an adverbial. Apart from such special expressions as *pīnzhe mìng (de) (nèmme) pǎo* "runs like mad", where the marker *de* and a resumptive *nèmme* may be used, the cases which fall into this category are subsumed under the designation *verbal expressions in series* (originally introduced by Chao, 1948). This is an extremely common type of construction. It usually consists of one or more *coverbs* followed by an object, and a primary verb which is often the central of the sentence. Semantically constructs of this type fall into a limited number of major categories (for details see pp. 150–159). Here we give only a few examples: *Nǐ$_1$ cóng$_2$ nǎr$_3$ lái$_4$.* "Where$_3$ do$_4$ you$_1$ come$_4$ from$_2$?"; *Tā$_1$ gēn$_2$ wo$_3$ yíyàng$_4$ gāo$_5$.* "He$_1$ is$_5$ as$_4$ tall$_5$ as$_2$ I$_3$."; *Yòng$_1$ máobǐ$_2$ xiě zì$_3$.* "Write$_3$ with$_1$ a brush$_2$."; *Tā$_1$ bá$_2$ suóyǒu de$_3$ qián$_4$ yòngwánles$_5$.* "He$_1$ has spent$_{2,5}$ all the$_3$ money$_4$." Note that the pretransitive construction with the coverb *bǎ* (as in *Bá$_1$ suóyǒu de$_2$ zì$_3$ dōu$_4$ xiěxialai$_5$.* "(Take$_1$ all the$_{2,4}$ characters$_3$ [and] write down$_5$ =) write all the characters down") is only a special case of verbal constructions in series.

5. PREDICATION

The Chinese sentence is endocentric. It consists either of a predicate alone or of a construct made up of a topic subject as the secondary partner, with a predicate as its primary partner or center. The predicate may be verbal or nominal. If the predicate has a verb as its center, the sentence is a verbal sentence; if the predicate has a nominal as its center, the sentence is a nominal sentence.

If the sentence consists of a predicate only, it is a *minor sentence*. If the sentence contains a topic subject as well as a predicate, it is a *major sentence*. The latter type is predominant, but minor sentences are by no means uncommon. Minor sentences may be said to have a *zero topic subject*. No sentence can have a zero predicate. In other words, if a sentence does not contain both a subject and a predicate, it contains at least a predicate.

The relationship between the topic subject and the predicate is logically and grammatically loose and hard to define in precise terms. The topic subject introduces a topic; the predicate adds a comment on the topic. The topic subject functions like a headline which may indicate time, place, acting person, or the general circumstances or framework in which the action expressed in the predicate takes place. It may indicate whether the state of affairs described in the predicate is present or non-present. In the context the topic subject can be compared with an "upstroke"; as such it is incomplete and thus felt to be "hanging in the air" unless it is followed by a "downstroke", which gives the comment or statement containing the new and essential information. Typically the topic subject is separated or separable from the predicate by a pause or by an "articulated pause" in the form of a particle a; thus the logical "looseness" has a formal parallel. Examples of such topic + comment sentences are:

Chūntian$_1$/qù$_2$; qiūtian$_3$/bú$_4$ qù$_5$. "In the spring$_1$ [we] go$_2$, [but] in the fall$_3$ [we] don't$_4$ go$_5$."
Bóshì lùnwén$_1$ (a)/hái$_2$ méi$_3$ kāishí$_4$ xiě$_5$. "(As far as) the doctoral dissertation$_1$ (is concerned) [he] hasn't$_3$ started$_4$ writing$_5$ [it] yet$_2$."
Bàoshang$_1$/yǒu$_2$ shémme$_3$ xīnwén$_4$. "What$_3$ news$_4$ is there$_2$ in the newspaper$_1$?"
Tā$_1$/jìxing$_2$ hén hǎo$_3$. "(He$_1$, the memory$_2$ is good$_3$ =) he has a (very) good memory."
Zhèr$_1$,/rén$_2$ duō$_3$. "There are many$_3$ people$_2$ here$_1$."

Nèijù$_1$ huà$_2$,/Zhōngguohuà$_3$ jiào$_4$ shémme$_5$. "What$_5$ do you call$_4$ this$_1$ word$_2$ in Chinese$_3$?"
Kànwán$_1$ diànyǐng$_2$,/tā$_3$ jiù$_4$ huí jiā$_5$ qù le$_6$. "After he had seen$_1$ the film$_2$, he$_3$ (then$_4$) went$_6$ home$_5$."

In a major sentence the topic subject and the predicate are the immediate sentence constituents; the order is almost invariably subject + predicate. In a few exceptional cases, subjects and predicates occur in inverted order; in such cases the subject is added as an afterthought, and always with zero stress (and neutral tone); predicates always carry full stress when they occur in the normal position. An example of inverted order predicate/subject is:

Lǎnduòjíle, neige ren! "He certainly is lazy, that man!"

Topic subjects as well as predicates may have a great variety of forms. Topic subjects or predicates which are immediate constituents of a sentence construct, and which are not further analyzable into sub-constituents on the word level are *simple* subjects and/or predicates; topic subjects and predicates which are themselves constructs are said to be *complex* topic subjects and/or predicates. In *Wǒ/méiyou nǐ nèmme hǎo*. "I am not as good as you." there is a complex predicate; the subject is simple. *Nèibiār shānshang de tǎ,/nǐ kàndejiàn ma*. "Can you see the pagoda on top of that hill?" has a complex subject as well as a complex predicate. In *Wǒ/nádeliǎo*. "I can carry [it]." we have a simple topic subject followed by a syntactically simple (but morphologically complex!) predicate.

The following possibilities exist:

A	B
Topic subjects	Predicates
1. a nominal	1. a nominal
a nominal expression	a nominal expression
2. a verb (simple or compound)	2. a verb (simple or compound)
a verbal expression	a verbal expression
3. (an embedded) major clause	3. (an embedded) major clause
(= a predication)	(= a predication)
4. zero	

It should be noted that in each case the predicate may end on a predicate particle (*le, ma, ba,* etc.). Note also that since a nominal expression as well as a major clause in the function of A or B may contain embedded minor or major clauses, each main type subsumes a great number of possible combinations. Here we can only suggest, by a few examples, the extraordinarily wide range covered by each category.

(a) *Nominal topic subject + nominal predicate*:
Jīntian/xīngqīsān. "Today [is] Wednesday."; *Mǔqin,$_1$/yǐjing$_2$ qīshísuì$_3$ le$_4$.* "Mother$_1$ [is] already$_2$ seventy years old$_3$ now$_4$."; *Zhèige$_1$ Zhōng-Yīng$_2$ cídiǎn$_3$,/shíwǔkuài$_4$ qián$_5$.* "This$_1$ Chinese–English$_2$ dictionary$_3$ [costs] fifteen$_4$ dollars$_5$."

(b) *Zero topic subject + nominal predicate*. These are all minor nominal sentences:
Sāndiǎn zhōng. "(At) three o'clock."; *Míngr jídiǎn zhōng.* "(At) what time tomorrow?"; *Dìsān kè.* "Third lesson."; *Dìyí mù.* "Act I."; *Xìng Wáng de.* "A person by the name of Wang."; *Zhēn de a?* "Is it true?"; *Nánfāng de nán.* "The character 'nan' ('South') as in 'South China'."; *Nǎr lái de rén.* "People (coming) from where?"; *Dài dà yǎnjìngr de nèiwèi wàiguórén.* "The foreigner who is wearing (those) big glasses."; *Shémme shíhou.* "(At) what time?"; *Běijīng Guǎngbó Diàntái!* "Peking Broadcasting Station!"; *Wáng xiansheng!* "Mr. Wang!". Vocative sentences, labels and other designations such as many book titles belong here.

(c) *Nominal topic subject + verbal predicate* is an extremely common form of a major sentence:
Tā/pǎole. "He has run away."; *Nǐ/pádeshàngqù ma.* "Can you climb up there?"; *Nèizuò shān,/hěn gāo.* "That mountain is quite high."; *Guóqìng$_1$ zhāodàihuì$_2$,/zài$_3$ yànhuìtīng$_4$ jǔxíng$_5$.* "The reception$_2$ in connection with the national celebration$_1$ takes place$_5$ in$_3$ the banquet hall$_4$."; *Tā$_1$ chàng de$_2$ Zhōngwén$_3$ gē$_4$,/hǎotīngjíle$_5$.* "The Chinese$_3$ song$_4$ she$_1$ is singing$_2$ is extremely beautiful$_5$."; *Zuótian wǎnshang$_1$,/xià yǔ$_2$.* "Last night$_1$ it rained$_2$."; *Fùqin$_1$/bù néng$_2$ lái$_3$.* "My father$_1$ cannot$_2$ come$_3$."; *Máobǐ$_1$ qiānbǐ$_2$,/dōu$_3$ hǎo$_4$.* "A brush$_1$ [or] a pencil$_2$ are$_4$ both$_3$ all right$_4$."; *Wó$_1$/bǐ$_2$ ni$_3$ gāo$_4$ yìdiar$_5$.* "I$_1$ am$_4$ a little$_5$ taller$_4$ than$_2$ you$_3$."; *Nǐ$_1$/shuō de$_2$ hěn$_3$ qīngchu$_4$.* "You$_1$ speak$_2$ very$_3$ distinctly$_4$."; *Wó$_1$/mǎile$_2$ sānben$_3$ shū$_4$.* "I$_1$ bought$_2$ three$_3$ books$_4$."; *Qián$_1$/dōu$_2$ yòngwánle$_3$ ba$_4$.* "Has$_3$ all$_2$ the money$_1$ been spent$_3$?$_4$"

(d) *Verbal topic subject + verbal predicate*:
Zhīdao/nán; zuò,/róngyi. "To know is difficult; to act is easy."; *Shuō$_1$ Zhōngguohuà$_2$,/hǎo de$_3$ duō$_4$.* "It is$_3$ far$_4$ better$_3$ to speak$_1$ Chinese$_2$ (= it would be a good idea (for you) to . . .)."; *Kàndedǒng$_1$ kànbudǒng$_2$,/méi$_3$ guānxi$_4$.* "Whether [you] can read [it]$_1$ [or] not$_2$ does not$_3$ matter$_4$."

(e) *Topic subject in major clause form + verbal predicate*:
Nǐ$_1$ shuō$_2$ Zhōngguohuà$_3$,/hén$_4$ hǎo$_5$. "It is a good thing$_4$,$_5$ that you$_1$

speak$_2$ Chinese$_3$.”; *Zhèliàng$_1$ qìchē$_2$ zuò$_3$ sìge$_4$ rén$_5$,/shì zhēn de$_6$.* “It is true$_6$ that this$_1$ car$_2$ can take$_3$ four$_4$ people$_5$.”; *Fùqin$_1$ xiěle$_2$ zhèifēng$_3$ xìn$_4$,/cái$_5$ guài$_6$ ne.* “It would be strange$_6$ if$_5$ father$_1$ had written$_2$ this$_3$ letter$_4$.”; *Jiānglái$_1$ dàodǐ$_2$ zěmme$_3$ fāzhǎn$_4$,/shízài$_5$ nánshuō$_6$.* “How$_3$ it will$_4$ actually$_2$ develop$_4$ in the future$_1$ is$_6$ really$_5$ hard to tell$_6$.”

(f) *Zero topic subject + verbal predicate:*
Bù zhīdào. “(I) don’t know.”; *Yòng kuàizi chī fàn.* “[One] eats with chopsticks.”; *Xià yǔ.* “It rains.”; *Niànwánle ma.* “Have you finished reading [it]?”; *Duìle.* “That’s right.”; *Bié dá wǒ de chà!* “Don’t interrupt me!”; *Qǐng zuò.* “Please sit down.”; *Kāi fàn le.* “The meal is served.”

(g) *Nominal topic subject + predicate in major clause form:*
Zhèi$_1$ píng$_2$ píjiǔ$_3$,/nǐ$_4$ hēdeliǎo hēbuliǎo$_5$. “Can$_5$ you$_4$ drink$_5$ this$_1$ glass$_2$ [of] beer$_3$?”; *Nèige rén$_1$,/jìxìng$_2$ hén$_3$ hǎo$_4$.* “He$_1$ has$_4$ a very$_3$ good$_4$ memory$_2$.”; *Tā$_1$/lìliang$_2$ hěn dà$_3$.* “(As far as he is concerned$_1$, the strength$_2$ is big$_3$ =) he is very strong.”; *Tā shuō de Zhōngwén$_1$,/wǒmen$_2$ dōu$_3$ néng tīngdǒng$_4$.* “We$_2$ all$_3$ understand$_4$ (the Chinese he speaks$_1$ =) his Chinese.”; *Zuótian wǎnshang$_1$,/wó$_2$ géi ni$_3$ dǎ diànhuà$_4$.* “I$_2$ called$_4$ you$_3$ on the telephone$_4$ last night$_1$.”

(h) *Verbal topic subject + predicate in major clause form:*
Zhēn$_1$ jiǎ$_2$,/wǒ$_3$ bù$_4$ zhīdào$_5$. “[Whether it] is true$_1$ or not$_2$, I$_3$ don’t$_4$ know$_5$.”

(i) *Topic subject as well as predicate in major clause form:*
Nǐ$_1$ qù$_2$,/wǒ$_3$ bú$_4$ qù$_5$. “If you$_1$ go$_2$, I$_3$ don’t$_4$ go$_5$.”; *Nǐ bú qù,/wó yě bú qù.* “If you don’t go, nor do I.”; *Nǐ qù,/wó yě qù.* “If you go, so do I.”

All topic subject + predicate constitutes introduced so far have been unmarked, i.e. no specific marker has indicated the function of the two sentence immediate constituents. In other words, relative position is of decisive importance. Topic subjects come first, predicates follow topic subjects. Topic subjects as well as predicates may, however, include specific markers. In addition to their function as markers, these markers also have another semantic content: they correspond to, and are translatable as, conjunctions in other languages. We distinguish between *subject markers* and *predicate markers*. In a given sentence only the topic subject may have a marker, or only the predicate may have a marker, or a marker may be included in both constituents. In some cases a given marker in the topic subject is paired with a given marker in the predicate. Semantically the subject markers fall into one of three categories: a) concessive, b) causal, or c) conditional.

(a) If the subject is *concessive*, the marker is *suírán* "although" or *gùrán* "(even though) it is true that"; the predicate in such cases includes one of the markers *dànshi* or *kěshi*:

Suírán₁ tā₂ de qián₃ hén₄ shǎo₅,/dànshi tā₆ lái de₇ shíhou₈ tā₉ zǒng₁₀ dài₁₁ yíjiàn₁₂ lǐwù₁₃. "Although₁ he₂ has₅ very₄ little₅ money₃, he₉ always₁₀ brings₁₁ a₁₂ present₁₃ when₈ he₆ comes₇."; *Tā₁ suírán₂ bìng de₃ hěn₄ lìhai₅,/dànshi bu₁ kěn₂ jìn₃ yīyuàn₄.* "Although₂ he₁ is₃ very₄,₅ sick₃, [he] does not₁ want₂ to enter₃ the hospital₄."

Suírán is placed either at the beginning of the sequence or (more commonly) after the nominal. *Dànshi* and *kěshi* appear at the beginning of the predicate.

(b) In topic subjects which indicate the *cause* or *reason*, the markers are *yīnwei . . . (suóyǐ)* or *jìrán . . . (jiù)* respectively:

Yīnwei₁ jīntian₂ xià yǔ₃,/suóyí₄ wǒ₅ méi₆ chūqu₇. "Since₁ it rained₃ today₂, I₅ (therefore₄) didn't₆ go out₇."; *Tā₁ jìrán₂ bù kěn₃,/wǒmen₄ bú₅ zài₆ qǐng₇ ta₈ le₉.* "Since₂ he₁ is unwilling₃, we₄ are not₅ going to₉ ask₇ him₈ again₆."

(c) In topic subjects indicating a *condition* a number of markers are possible; the predicate usually includes the marker *jiù*; the subject markers either precede or follow the nominal; the predicate marker follows the nominal of the predicate. The most common subject markers are *yào, yàoshi, jiǎrú, rúguǒ, ruòshi, tǎngruò, jiǎruò, jiáshǐ, tángshǐ*, all of which carry the meaning "if":

Nǐ₁ yàoshi₂ yǒu₃ yíwèn₄ de dìfangr₅,/qǐng₆ bú yào kèqi de₇ zhǐjiào₈ ba. "If₂ there is₃ anything₅ you₁ are in doubt about₄, please₆ don't hesitate₇ to seek information₈."; *Nǐ rúguǒ bú xìn,/kéyi wèn ta.* "In case you do not believe [it], you may ask him."

Often only the predicate is marked; the marker which is most common is *jiù* "then". Sometimes *cái* "then, and only then" is used: *Nǐ qù,/wǒ jiù bú qù.* "If you go, (then) I don't."; *Zuò₁ dì shíwǔhào de₂ chē₃,/jiù₄ kéyi₅ dào₆.* "If you take₁ bus₃ no. 15₂, (then₄) [you] can₅ get there₆."; *Nǐ₁ géi₂ wo₃ qián₄,/wǒ₅ cái₆ bāngzhu₇ ni₈.* "If you₁ give₂ me₃ money₄ (= pay me), only then₆ will₇ I₅ help₇ you₈."

A similar use involves *yě* as a marker in the predicate; in this case the topic subject is translatable as "even if": *Nǐ kū,/yě wúyòng.* "Even if you cry (cried), it is (would be) of no use."

When topic subjects and/or predicates have major clause form, each separate constituent has its own subject. In one sense a sentence may thus contain several "subjects". But it is important to realize that the various subjects are on different levels and thus enter into different constructs. In the sentence: *Tā₁/jìxing₂ hǎo₃.* "(As far as) he₁ (is concerned), (the memory$_2$ is good$_3$ =) has a good memory.", *tā* is the sentence topic subject, and is an immediate constituent with *jìxing hǎo*. Within the predicate *jìxing* is a subject, and is an immediate constituent of the (endocentric) predicate constitute, with *hǎo* as its partner. Such a subject is not a sentence topic subject, but a subject within the predicate. Such a secondary subject may be called a *small subject*. Examples: *nǐ* is a small subject within the predicate in: *Zhōngguohuà*$_1$,/*nǐ*$_2$ *xuéhǎole*$_3$ *ma.* "Are$_3$ you$_2$ proficient$_3$ [in] Chinese$_1$?". *Yìzhī yǎnjing* and *yìzhī* are small subjects in the predicate in: *Tā*$_1$/*yìzhī*$_2$ *yǎnjing*$_3$ *kàndejiàn*$_4$, *yìzhī*$_5$/*kànbujiàn*$_6$. "He$_1$ can see$_4$ on one$_2$ eye$_3$, [but he] cannot see$_6$ (on one$_5$ =) on the other." *Wǒ* is a small subject in *Nǐ*$_1$ *lái de*$_2$ *shíhou*$_3$,/*wǒ*$_4$ *hái*$_5$ *méi*$_6$ *xǐng*$_7$. "When$_3$ you$_1$ came$_2$, I$_4$ wasn't$_6$ awake$_7$ yet$_5$." Similarly, *rénmín* and *shēnghuo* in *Rénmín*$_1$ *yǒu*$_2$ *tián*$_3$ *kě zhòng*$_4$,/*shēnghuo*$_5$ *hén*$_6$ *hǎo*$_7$. "When the people$_1$ had$_2$ fields$_3$ to till$_4$, life$_5$ was$_7$ pretty$_6$ good$_7$."

6. VERB + OBJECT

A verb + object construct is a type of endocentric verbal expression which may enter into a topic subject construct or, more typically, form a predicate construct, or enter as a constituent into a predicate construct. Objects may be 1) nominal, 2) verbal, or 3) of a major clausal type. The kind of object selected depends on the class and function of the preceding verb.

In the majority of cases objects are nominals or nominal expressions; if the verb is a transitive verb, the object is very often a nominal. In such cases the general meaning of the construction is action + goal; the object in a verb + object phrase carries primary stress (unless the object is a personal pronoun: $_|$*kàn* $^|$*bào* "read a newspaper", but $^|$*kàn ta* "see him"). Furthermore, nominals in object position are of indefinite reference unless otherwise specified: *Náchuqule shū le.* "[He] has taken away (some) books."; *Shū náchuqu le.* "The books have been taken away." Examples of verb + object constructs: *hē jiǔ* "drink wine"; *shuō Zhōngwén* "speak Chinese"; *yǒu jīhui* "has an opportunity"; *dài màozi* "wear a cap"; *xià yǔ* "it is raining"; *zài jiāli* "to be at home"; *qùguo Zhōngguo* "has (some time in the past) been to China". Intransitive verbs are not excluded from taking objects, but the objects they can take are of rather limited kinds, i.e. they denote quantity, duration, destination, or extent: *bìngle sāntian* "was sick for three days"; *zhǎngle yícùn* "has grown one inch"; *fēi Lúndūn* "to fly to London"; *shuōle sāncì* "has said [it] three times". The verbs *zài* and *dào* take only place words or time words as objects: *dào wo zhèr* "(to my place =) to me". A few verbs take two objects, one for direct reference, one for indirect reference; the indirect object comes first: *gěi ta qián* "gives him money"; *Nı wèn ta shémme.* "What did you ask him about?"

Verbs and verbal expressions as objects occur after modal verbs: *néng lái* "can come"; *huì shuō Zhōngwén* "can speak Chinese"; *gǎn qù* "dares to go"; *děi huíqù* "has to return"; *kěn bāngzhu ta* "is willing to help him"; *kéyi chōu yān* "it is allowed to smoke".

Objects in clausal form are common after verbs of thought and perception:

$Wǒ_1$ $wàngle_2/nǐ_3$ $bú_4$ $huì_5$ $shuō_6$ $Zhōngwén_7$. "I_1 forgot$_2$ [that] you$_3$ cannot$_{4,5}$ speak$_6$ Chinese$_7$."; $Tā_1$ $juézhe_2/wǒ_3$ $bù_4$ $yīnggāi_5$ $qù_6$. "He$_1$ feels$_2$ I$_3$ should$_5$ not$_4$ go$_6$."; $Tāmen_1$ $shuō_2/nǐ_3$ $qí_4$ $xià_5$ de $bú$ $cuò_6$. "They$_1$ say$_2$ you$_3$ play$_5$ chess$_4$ very well$_6$."; $Wǒ_1$ $xiǎng_2/wǒ_3$ $zhèi_4$ $liǎngtian_5$ $méi$ $kòngr_6$. "I_1 think$_2$ I$_3$ shall be busy$_6$ these$_4$ next few days$_5$."

Other important verbs of this class are *zhīdao* "to know", *(kǒng)pà* "to be afraid that", *tīngshuō* "to have heard (someone say) that", *xīwang* "to hope", *jìde* "to remember".

A pivotal construction (the term was introduced by Chao, 1968, pp. 124–129) is a construction in which the object of a verb I serves the double function of also being the subject of a verb II; the object/subject is called a *pivot*, because the construction "turns" on it. The closest counterpart in English would be a construction like *He made me go*, in which *me* is an object of *made*, but also "the doer of the action" in respect to *go*. In Chinese the difference I/me is non-existent: *Wǒ qù.* "I go.", *Tā jiào wo qù.* "He makes me go." In the latter example *wo* has a dual function and is thus a pivot. A sentence with such a pivotal construction as its predicate (which is the most common case) is built according to the following formula:

(Topic subject) → Verb I ← Object
$$\text{Subject} \to \text{Verb II} \leftarrow \text{(Object)}$$

Predicate

Wó	*qíng*	*ni*	*chī*	*wǎnfàn*
I	ask	you	to eat	dinner

"I invite you for dinner."

If the object/subject is a personal pronoun, it has an optional neutral tone.

The class meaning of such constructions is "to act in order to have someone do something", and the verb I is thus a verb meaning "to ask", "to cause", "to help", "to recognize", "to send", etc. Examples:

Wo₁ bú₂ ràng₃ ta₄ jìnlai₅. "I₁ don't₂ let₃ him₄ enter₅."
Wŏmen₁ shĭ₂ rén₃ gāoxìng₄. "We₁ make₂ people₃ happy₄."
Fùqin₁ jiào₂ háizimen₃ tīng₄ yīnyuè₅. "Father₁ lets₂ (or: has) the children₃ listen to₄ music₅."
Xiānsheng₁ quàn₂ women₃ xuéxi₄. "The teacher₁ encourages₂ us₃ to study₄."

A special case within this category is the rather frequent use of *you* to introduce the logical subject. This usage is comparable with the introductory phrase "there is/are..." in English: *yŏu rén shuō...* "(there are) people (who) say..." Other examples: *Yŏu kèren láile.* "A guest has come."; *Yŏu rén zài lĭtou shuō huà.* "There is someone inside who is speaking." Notice that the same construction in negated form starts with *méi*: *Méi rén zhīdao.* "Nobody knows."

Notice also constructions such as: *Wŏ méi yŏu fàn chī.* "I have (no food =) nothing to eat."; *Wó géi ni jiŭ hē.* "I'll give you (some) wine to drink."

7. Verb + Complement

Forms like *náchulai* "take out", *cāgānjing* "wipe clean", *shuōbudìng* "cannot say for sure" are compounds with directional/resultative/potential complements as second constituents. Syntactic verb + complement constructs are different from these; they involve only free words as constituents and are almost always marked by the marker *de*. The type with which we are concerned here can be illustrated by the example *lái de zăo* "comes early", in which the primary constituent is usually regarded as being *lái*. The complement is consequently *zăo*. Such constructs are called *predicative complements*. Complements of this type may have the form of 1) a single (quality) verb, 2) a verbal expression, 3) an adverb (usually *hěn*), or 4) a sequence in major clause form. Examples:

Tā₁ zŏu de₂ kuài₃; wó₄ zŏu de₅ bù₆ hěn₇ kuài₈. "He₁ walks₂ fast₃, I₄ don't₆ walk₅ very₇ fast₈."; *Ní₁ xiě₂ zì₃, xiě de₄ hén₅ hăo₆.* "You₁ write₂,₄ (characters₃) very₅ beautifully₆." (notice that when the verb has an object, the verb, in this case *xiě*, is repeated); *Tā₁ jiāo de₂ hén₃ hăo₄, hěn₅ qīngchu₆.* "He₁ teaches₂ very₃ well₄ [and] very₅ clearly₆." (two coordinated complements); *Tāmen₁ gāoxìng de₂ hěn₃.* "They₁

really$_3$ are$_2$ very$_3$ happy$_2$."; *Mèimei$_1$ tiàowǔ de$_2$ hǎokàn bu haokan$_3$.*
"Does$_2$ your sister$_1$ dance$_2$ beautifully$_3$?"; *Tā$_1$ hè$_2$ de$_3$ shuōbuchū$_4$ huà$_5$ lái$_6$.* "He$_1$ got$_2$ so$_3$ scared$_2$ that$_3$ [he] could not utter$_{4,6}$ one word$_5$."; *Tāmen$_1$ nào$_2$ de$_3$ dàjiā$_4$ dōu$_5$ shuìbuzháo jiào$_6$.* "They$_1$ made$_2$ such$_3$ a noise$_2$ that$_3$ nobody$_{4,5}$ could get to sleep$_6$."

8. APPOSITION

Two nominal expressions with identical reference, with no pause between, and always without a marker, are said to be in apposition. They form a coordinative construct, and the order is reversible. Examples: *Wǒ péngyou Lǎosān.* "My friend Laosan."; *Zhè shì Běijīng Zhōngguo shǒudū.* "This is Peking, the capital of China."

9. ADDITIVE CONSTRUCTS

This is also a type of coordinative construct, but of a different kind from appositional constructs. One important formal difference is that additive constructs may be marked or unmarked, whereas appositional constructs are never marked; another (semantic) difference is that the component parts of additive constructs refer to different things, persons, or concepts. One feature they have in common is that the order of the items is not fixed, although idiomatic usage may prefer one particular order in specific cases. If no marker is present, each component of an additive construct has a slightly prolonged falling pitch at the end. Markers, if used, are most commonly *gēn*, *hé*, or *tóng*. In the case of coordinated verb constructs, each component may be introduced by *yòu*: *yòu . . . yòu.* Examples:
Māma gen bàba. "Mommy and daddy."; *Zhèiwèi he nèiwèi dōu shì Yīngguórén.* "This person as well as that person is English."; *Tā yòu cōngming yòu yònggōng.* "He is bright as well as diligent."; *Zhèixie$_1$ zìláishuǐ bǐ$_2$, shóubiǎo$_3$, bàndáotǐ shōuyīnjī$_4$, lùyīnjī$_5$, diànshìjī$_6$, zhàoxiàngjī$_7$, diànyǐng fàngyìngjī$_8$, diàn-xǐyījī$_9$, dōu$_{10}$ shì$_{11}$ Rìběn zhìzào$_{12}$ de chūpǐn$_{13}$.* "All$_{10}$ these$_1$ fountain pens$_2$, wrist watches$_3$, transistor radios$_4$, tape recorders$_5$, television sets$_6$, cameras$_7$, projectors$_8$, and electric washing machines$_9$ are$_{11}$ Japanese-made$_{12}$ products$_{13}$."

10. DISJUNCTIVE CONSTRUCTS

These are marked or unmarked. The most common markers are *huòzhe* and *háishi*. Disjunctive constructs express mutually exclusive alternatives.

Examples:

Tā chī fàn chī miàn. "Does he eat rice [or] noodles?"; *Nǐ yào dà de háishi xiǎo de.* "Do you want big or small ones?".

A special subtype of coordinative disjunctive construction is found in the so-called ambivalent sentence: *Dà bu da.* "Is it big?"; *Kàndejiàn kànbujiàn.* "Can you see [it]?"; *Nǐ kànle nèige diànyǐng meiyou.* "Have you seen that film?"

11. MAJOR AND MINOR SENTENCES

As was mentioned in subsection 5 (*Predication*) above (p. 80), a sentence which consists of a predicate only is a *minor sentence*. If the sentence contains a topic subject as well as a predicate, it is a *major sentence*. Examples of minor sentences were given under (b) and (f) on pages 82 and 83 respectively. In such sentences a subject must be supplied in the English translation. Minor sentences occur typically in answers to questions, in requests, and in commands. On the whole they are more common in informal conversation than in more formal speech. Care should be taken not to confuse a major sentence with a long sentence, or a minor sentence with a short sentence. A major sentence is often, but by no means always, longer than a minor sentence. The terms "major" and "minor" do not refer to length, only to structure. Compare the following sentences:

(1) *Tīngshuō$_1$ lí$_2$ zhèli$_3$ bù$_4$ yuǎn$_5$ yǒu$_6$ yíge$_7$ mài$_8$ qìyóu$_9$ de$_{10}$ dìfang$_{11}$.* "[I] have heard$_1$ [that] not$_4$ far$_5$ from$_2$ here$_3$ there is$_6$ a$_7$ place$_{11}$ where$_{10}$ [they] sell$_8$ gasoline$_9$."

(2) *Jīntian$_1$ tiānqi$_2$ hén$_3$ hǎo$_4$.* "The weather$_2$ is$_4$ really$_3$ nice$_4$ today$_1$."

(1) is a minor sentence, since it contains only a predicate. A possible topic subject might be *wǒ*, as suggested in the translation; other possibilities would be *wǒ péngyou, Mǎ xiansheng*, etc.

(2) is a major sentence, with *jīntian* as its topic subject. The minor sentence is longer than the major sentence.

Nor should a major sentence be confused with a *verbal* sentence. The only requirement for a sentence to be classified as a major sentence is that it must contain a topic subject as well as a predicate. Even if the sentence is non-verbal it may be a major sentence. For example:

Shíge zì, liùmáo qián. "Ten words, sixty cents." (as when sending a telegram); *Tā érzi bāsuì le.* "His son [is] now eight years old."

These are both major sentences, of the zero-central type.

12. SIMPLE AND COMPOUND SENTENCES

A sentence which contains only one clause is a *simple sentence*. A sentence which contains more than one clause is a *compound sentence*. For intonational and pausal signals in compound sentences, see section B of this chapter, Intonation (pp. 24–32), where examples of compound sentences were given. In a compound sentence, one or both clauses may be major or minor. The clauses stand in coordination with each other, and this relation may be marked or unmarked. Let us look at the following compound sentences (the clauses are separated by slashes):

(1) *Tā$_1$gànle$_2$ yíbèizi$_3$;/jiéguǒ$_4$ yě$_5$ méi$_6$ shémme$_7$ chéngjiù$_8$.* "He$_1$ worked$_2$ a whole lifetime$_3$, [but] in the end$_4$ achieved$_8$ nothing$_{5,6,7}$."

(2) *Kèren$_1$ dōu$_2$ dàolaile$_3$;/kuài cuī$_4$ kāi$_5$ fàn$_6$.* "All$_2$ the guests$_1$ have arrived$_3$, [so] let's hurry$_4$ [and] start$_5$ eating$_6$."

(3) *Měitian$_1$ záo$_2$ qǐ$_3$ wǎn$_4$ shuì$_5$;/yìtian$_6$ zuò$_7$ dào$_8$ wǎn$_9$.* "[They] get up$_3$ early$_2$ every day$_1$ [and] go to bed$_5$ late$_4$, working$_7$ all day long$_6$ (until$_8$ late$_9$)."

(4) *Dōngtian$_1$ zài$_2$ héshang$_3$ liū$_4$ bīng$_5$;/xiàtian$_6$ zài$_7$ héli$_8$ yóuyǒng$_9$.* "[We] go$_4$ skating$_5$ on$_2$ the river$_3$ in winter$_1$ [and] go swimming$_9$ in$_7$ the river$_8$ in summer$_6$."

(5) *Ānshān$_1$ zài$_2$ Zhōngguo$_3$ de$_4$ dōngběi$_5$ bù$_6$;/Fúzhōu$_7$ zài$_8$ Zhōngguo$_9$ de$_{10}$ dōngnán$_{11}$ bù$_{12}$.* "Anshan$_1$ is in$_2$ the north-eastern$_5$ part$_6$ of$_4$ China$_3$; Fuchow$_7$ is in$_8$ the south-eastern$_{11}$ part$_{12}$ of$_{10}$ China$_9$."

(6) *Tā$_1$ xīwang$_2$ míngnian$_3$ yǒu$_4$ jīhui$_5$ dào$_6$ Zhōngguo$_7$ qù$_8$;/kěxī$_9$, bú$_{10}$ huì$_{11}$ shuō$_{12}$ Zhōngguo huà$_{13}$.* "He$_1$ hopes$_2$ to have$_4$ a chance$_5$ to go$_8$ to$_6$ China$_7$ next year$_3$, [but] unfortunately$_9$ [he] cannot$_{10,11}$ speak$_{12}$ Chinese$_{13}$."

(7) *Wǒmen$_1$ gēn$_2$ ni$_3$ qù$_4$ kéyǐ$_5$;/dànshi$_6$ wǒmen$_7$ děi$_8$ zàodiar$_9$ huílai$_{10}$.* "It's all right$_5$ [that] we$_1$ go$_4$ with$_2$ you$_3$, but$_6$ we$_7$ have to$_8$ be back$_{10}$ somewhat early$_9$."

(8) *Zuótian$_1$ wǎnshang$_2$ xià yǔ$_3$;/suóyi$_4$ méi$_5$ chūqu$_6$.* "Yesterday$_1$ evening$_2$ it rained$_3$, so$_4$ [we] didn't$_5$ go out$_6$."

(9) *Wǒ$_1$ bù$_2$ dǒng$_3$ Zhōngwén$_4$;/wó$_5$ zhí$_6$ hǎo$_7$ qíng$_8$ ni$_9$ fānyifanyi$_{10}$.* "I$_1$ do not$_2$ understand$_3$ Chinese$_4$, [so] (the only$_6$ good thing$_7$ =) it is best [that] I$_5$ ask$_8$ you$_9$ to translate$_{10}$."

(10) *Rúguó$_1$ yǒu$_2$ shíjiān$_3$, wǒ$_4$ jiù$_5$ kànwán$_6$;/rúguǒ$_7$ shíjiān$_8$ bú$_9$ gòu le$_{10}$, wó$_{11}$ zhí hǎo$_{12}$ míngtian$_{13}$ zài$_{14}$ kànwán$_{15}$.* "If$_1$ [I] have$_2$ time$_3$, (then$_5$) I$_4$ will finish reading$_6$ [it]; if$_7$ there is$_{10}$ not$_9$

enough$_{10}$ time$_8$, I$_{11}$ had better$_{12}$ (again$_{14}$) finish it$_{15}$ tomorrow$_{13}$."

All these sentences contain more than one clause. In most of the examples the order of the clauses could in principle be reversed without difficulty. Some of the sentences (3, 4, 5, 7, 9, 10) contain only major clauses. Two sentences have identical topic subjects in each clause (*wǒ* 9, *wǒmen* 7); in (1) and (6) the two clauses have a common subject, which is expressed in the first clause but not repeated in the second. In two cases (7, 8) coordination is marked (by *dànshi* and *suóyi* respectively); in the other examples simple juxtaposition is used. The most common markers used to indicate coordination between clauses are *dànshi* "but", *búguò* "but", *érqiě* "in addition, moreoever", *yīnwei* "because", *suóyi* "therefore", *yīncǐ* "for this reason", *huòzhě* "or". Since some of these markers function as sentence connectors as well as subject or predicate markers they are ambiguous and do not provide sufficient evidence to prove that we are dealing with compound clauses. Only when such markers occur in conjunction with the appropriate accentual and pausal signals do they signal coordination of two clauses into one sentence. Each of the sentences could be divided into two by inserting a full pause accompanied by falling intonation between the clauses.

13. SENTENCE CLASSIFICATION

At the end of Section E of this chapter, subsection 7 (p. 63), it was shown that sentences may be classified according to type and form. A more complete method of classification would include criteria taken from this structural survey. If we limit ourselves to adopting four supplementary classes of criteria from our discussion of sentence structure (simple/compound; major/minor; type of topic subject and type of predicate) we get a total of seven categories of criteria. A sentence may then be classified by selecting one term from each category. The classes of criteria are based on type, form, and structure. The categories are listed below:

A. Type
1. Verbal/non-verbal (nominal/non-nominal)
2. Negatable/negated/ambivalent/negative

B. Form
3. Declarative/interrogative/imperative/vocative/exclamatory

C. Structure

4. Simple/compound (marked/unmarked)
5. Major/minor
6. Topic subject zero/nominal/verbal/major clause form (marked/unmarked)
7. Predicate nominal/verbal/major clause form (marked/unmarked)

CHAPTER III

THE CLAUSE

1. THE PLACE OF THE CLAUSE IN THE LINGUISTIC HIERARCHY

A clause is either a sentence or a component of a sentence. In other words, clauses form the material of which sentences are built. This means that whenever there is a sentence, at least one clause is involved. As has been pointed out already, a sentence which contains only one clause is a *simple* sentence, whereas a sentence which contains more than one clause is a *compound* sentence.

The clause thus occupies the highest level below the sentence level. In theory the two levels are distinct from one another, but in the case of the simple sentence they coincide. In the case of those simple sentences that consist of only a phrase, the sentence/clause/phrase levels coincide. *Yǒu cídiǎn ma.* "Do you have a dictionary?" is a sentence containing one clause; the clause consists of one (verbal) phrase. *Yìběn₁ Zhōngwén₂ cídiǎn₃, duōshao qián₄.* "How much₄ [does] a₁ Chinese₂ dictionary₃ [cost]?" is a sentence containing one clause; the clause consists of two (nominal) phrases. *Mǎnjiāng₁ dà₂ wù₃; shémme₄ dōu₅ kànbuqīng₆.* "All over the river₁ [there was] a (big₂ =) dense fog₃ [and] nothing₄,₅ could be clearly seen₆." is a sentence containing two clauses, the first of which is a nominal major clause, and the second a verbal major clause.

2. THE SENTENCE AND THE CLAUSE

Any given clause is potentially a sentence; whether or not a particular clause is a sentence depends on 1) whether or not it ends on a final sentence intonation (Intonation I), 2) whether or not it is followed by a major pause, or 3) whether or not it stands in grammatical construction with other linguistic elements. In the last example the first clause *Mǎnjiāng dà wù* does not end on the dropping pitch typical of

Intonation I, and it is not followed by the major pause which occurs between sentences. The two parts of the sentence form one grammatical whole; they are said to stand in *coordination*. If, on the other hand, the sequence were spoken differently: *Mǎnjiāng dà wù. Shémme dōu kànbuqīng.*, there would indeed be two sentences, each consisting of one clause.

In a compound sentence there is no definite limit to the number of clauses, nor is there any limitation as to type or form. Examples of compound sentences have been given in Chapter II F 12 (pp. 90–91). Very often, clauses in a compound sentence have parallel structures: *Yǐqián₁ zhèli₂ shì₃ yípiàn₄ huāng₅ shān₆; xiànzài₇ zhèli₈ kāikěnle₉ yíkuài₁₀ tītián₁₁.* "Earlier₁ there was₃ a stretch of₄ barren₅ hills₆ here₂, [but] now₇ [they] have opened up₉ a₁₀ terraced field₁₁ here₈."

However, a clause must at least contain a predicate. It follows that a clause may consist of only one word: *Xièxie.* "Thank you.", *Hǎo.* "OK". Such clauses are most common as responses to immediately preceding stimulus sentences, thus, *Bù.* "No." occurs occasionally alone as an answer. In such cases all levels coincide (sentence/clause/word; note that in our terminology *hǎo* or *bù* are words, or minimal expressions, not phrases, since a phrase must consist of more than one word). On the whole, words which are clauses/sentences are verbs or interjections. Nominals rarely function independently in this way. In response to a question, "What is that?" or "Who is he?" (*Nà shì shémme.* or *Tā shì shéi.*) one would probably say *Shì (yìběn) shū.* and *Shì xuésheng.* rather than *Shū.* and *Xuésheng.* respectively. But in response to a sentence/clause *Nǐ₁ wǎnshang₂ fùxí₃ ma.* "Do₃ you₁ review₃ your lessons₃ in the evening₂?" one might very well say: *Fùxí.*, which would here be translatable by "Yes (I do)".

3. "SUBORDINATE CLAUSES" AS TOPIC SUBJECTS

In most grammars a distinction is made between subordinate (or dependent) clauses and main (or independent) clauses. Let us look at some examples:

(1) *Nǐ qù, wǒ bú qù.*
(2) *Nǐ qù, wǒ jiù bú qù.*
(3) *Yàoshi nǐ qù, wǒ bú qù.*
(4) *Yàoshi nǐ qù, wǒ jiù bú qù.*

All these sentences mean: "If you go, I don't."

(5) *Tā₁ suīran₂ yǒu₃ gōngfu₄, kěshi₅ tā₆ bú₇ yuànyi₈ qù₉.* "Although₂ he₁ has₃ time₄, (but₅ =) still he₆ is₈ not₇ willing₈ to go₉."

(6) *Yīnwei₁ tā₂ méi₃ gōngfu₄, tā₅ bù néng₆ qù₇.* "Because₁ he₂ has no₃ time₄, he₅ cannot₆ go₇."

According to the traditional analysis, *Nǐ qù* in (1) and (2), *Yàoshi nǐ qù* in (3) and (4), *Tā suīran yǒu gōngfu* in (5), and *Yīnwei tā méi gōngfu* in (6) are dependent clauses. In (1) and (2) the relationship is *unmarked* (i.e. not marked by a grammatical word, e.g. a conjunction); the dependent status is marked only by position (pre-modification) and by the pause feature. In (3), (4), (5) and (6) the relationship is marked (by "subordinative conjunctions" *yàoshi, suīran,* and *yīnwei* respectively). In the same way, *wǒ bú qù* in (1) and (3), *wǒ jiù bú qù* in (2) and (4), *kěshi tā bú yuànyi qù* in (5), and *tā bù néng qù* in (6) are independent clauses; (1), (3), and (6) are unmarked, whereas the others are marked, (2) and (4) by *jiù,* and (5) by *kěshi.* In (1) none of the clauses are explicitly marked as to function; in (4) and (5) both are so marked; in (2), (3), and (6) one clause or the other is marked.

Although such an analysis is possible, and may for certain purposes, such as translation, be quite useful, the distinction between dependent and independent clauses is, from the point of view of grammatical structure, an unnecessary complication, as Chao has convincingly shown (1968, p. 113). Following Chao's analysis, in this book we treat "dependent clauses" as topic subjects, and "independent clauses" as predicates. *Yàoshi, suīran,* and *yīnwei* are thus topic subject markers; *jiù* and *kěshi* are predicate markers in this context. The situations or circumstances indicated by *nǐ qù* (1), (2), *yàoshi nǐ qù* (3), (4), *Tā suīran yǒu gōngfu* (5), *yīnwei tā méi gōngfu* (6), regarded as whole units, are thus taken as topics to be commented on. Each is a topic subject in clause form, with or without a marker. A sequence *Nǐ qù, wǒ bú qù.,* when spoken as one sentence, i.e. with no internal final intonation, with an optional pause after the first phrase, and with a sentence final intonation at the end, automatically takes on the meaning "*If* you go, (*then*) I don't go". The phonological signals, together with the feature of relative order (a selective element) are decisive for this interpretation. If the order of the constituents is reversed (*Wǒ bú qù, nǐ qù.*) the meaning changes: "If I don't go, you go". The former sentence states the circumstances under which the statement "I am not going" is true; the second sentence states under what circumstances "you are going" is true. But notice that if in (2) the order of the constituents is reversed, the marker *jiù* remains as a predicate marker: *Wǒ bú qù, nǐ jiù qù.* "If I don't go, then you go". In the same way, *yàoshi, suīran*, and *yīnwei* always remain tied to the topic subject phrase or clause-like sequence.

If, however, sentence (1) is *not* spoken as a simple sentence containing one clause, but as a sentence containing two coordinated clauses (the first phrase with Intonation II, followed by a pause; the second phrase with sentence-final intonation and pause): *Nǐ qù; wǒ bú qù.* the first part is no longer "conditional": "You go, (and *or* but) I don't go." Whereas in *Nǐ qù, wǒ bú qù.* the relative order of the constituents cannot be reversed without a change in meaning, *Nǐ qù; wǒ bú qù.* and *Wǒ bú qù; nǐ qù.* are, for practical purposes, synonymous: in both cases it is "you" who are going, and "I" who am not. Finally, the same segmental sequence may be spoken as two independent sentences, each ending on a sentence-final intonation: *Nǐ qù. Wǒ bú qù.* "You go. I don't". *Nǐ qù; wǒ bú qù.* and *Nǐ qù. Wǒ bú qù.* are synonymous. We thus have:

(7) *Nǐ qù, wǒ bú qù.* "If you go, . . ."
(8) *Nǐ qù; wǒ bú qù.* "You go, and (but) . . ."
(9) *Nǐ qù. Wǒ bú qù.* "You go. I don't".

If we insert markers, we get:

(10) *Nǐ qù, wǒ jiù bú qù.* Or:
     Yàoshi ni qù, wǒ jiù bu qu.
(11) *Nǐ qù; dànshi wǒ bú qù.*
(12) *Nǐ qù. Dànshi wǒ bú qù.*

The marker *jiù* clearly indicates a subject + predicate relation within a sentence; the marker *dànshi* has a dual function: 1) it is a *clause* connector (coordinator); 2) it is a sentence starter, i.e. it connects *sentences*. The two functions are associated with phonological signals: with a non-final intonation and pause preceding, it is a marker combining clauses into one sentence; with a sentence-final intonation and full pause preceding, it is macrosyntactic, i.e. it points beyond the borders of one sentence. As a marker it is thus ambiguous. The phonological signals are, in the end, conclusive for the analysis into one or two sentences.

4. CLAUSES WITH MULTIPLE TOPIC SUBJECTS
AND/OR PREDICATES

Whereas sentences may be simple or compound, all clauses are simple clauses, since the immediate constituents of a clause consist of only one predicate construct and one topic subject construction. The predicate is necessary and sufficient; the subject is neither obligatory nor sufficient.

Although within the clause the topic subject and the predicate are immediate constituents, the structure of either the subject or the predicate may show some complexity. We have dealt with most of the possibilities in Chapter II, Section F, Sentence structure, subsection 5, Predication, pp. 80–85. We shall here limit ourselves to the cases in which there are multiple topic subjects and multiple predicates. The term "multiple" here refers to a structural unit consisting of several co-ordinated parts, each of which has the same grammatical function. It is thus, strictly speaking, a question of multiple constituents *within* a subject or a predicate construct, as the case may be.

In the following examples each sentence contains one clause with a multiple topic subject:

Mǔqin$_1$, fùqin$_2$, jiějie$_3$, mèimei$_4$ a,/Guǎngdōnghuà$_5$, Běijīnghuà$_6$, dōu$_7$ shuō de$_8$ hěn liúlì$_9$. "My mother$_1$, my father$_2$, my older sisters$_3$ [and] my younger sisters$_4$, [they] speak$_8$ both$_7$ the Cantonese dialect$_5$ [and] the Peking dialect$_6$ fluently$_9$."

Zhōngguo$_1$ yǔyánli$_2$ de$_3$ shēngdiào$_4$ de$_5$ míngzi$_6$, píngshēng$_7$, shǎngshēng$_8$, qùshēng$_9$, rùshēng$_{10}$, yángshēng$_{11}$, yīnshēng$_{12}$, dìyī shēng$_{13}$, dìèr shēng$_{14}$, dìsān shēng$_{15}$, dìsì shēng$_{16}$ a,/zhēn$_{17}$ fùzá$_{18}$ de bùdéliǎo$_{19}$. "The names$_6$ of$_5$ the tones$_4$ in$_3$ the Chinese$_1$ language$_2$ − 'the even tone$_7$', 'the rising tone$_8$', 'the going tone$_9$', 'the entering tone$_{10}$', 'the lower register tone$_{11}$', 'the upper register tone$_{12}$', 'the first tone$_{13}$', 'the second tone$_{14}$', 'the third tone$_{15}$', 'the fourth tone$_{16}$' − (they are) really$_{17}$ unbelievably$_{19}$ complicated$_{18}$."

In each example the topic subject is divided from the predicate by a slash; at this point there is a slight pause. In the first example the coordinated constituents of the subject and the predicate are of the additive type ("mother and father", etc., "the Cantonese dialect and the Peking dialect"); in the latter example, the whole of the additive construction *píngshēng, shǎngshēng, .. dìsì shēng* is in apposition with the preceding part *Zhōngguo .. de míngzi.*

In the following examples, where each sentence also contains one clause, there are compound predicates; thus there is no sentence-final intonation between the constituents:

Běifāng$_1$ de$_2$ háizimen$_3$,/hěn ài$_4$ duī$_5$ xuěrén$_6$, yě$_7$ ài$_8$ dá xuězhàn$_9$. "The children$_3$ in$_2$ the North$_1$ like$_4$ to build$_5$ snowmen$_6$, and [they] also$_7$ like$_8$ to have snowball fights$_9$."

Zhōngguo$_1$/zài$_2$ Shāngcháo$_3$ de shíhou$_4$ yǐjing$_5$ zhīdao$_6$ yǎng$_7$ niú$_8$, *yǎng*$_9$ *zhū*$_{10}$, *érqiě*$_{11}$ *yǐjing*$_{12}$ *huì*$_{13}$ *zào*$_{14}$ *fángzi*$_{15}$, *zào*$_{16}$ *chē*$_{17}$, *zào*$_{18}$ *chuán*$_{19}$ *le*$_{20}$. "[In] China$_1$ [people] already$_5$ during$_{2,4}$ the Shang Dynasty$_3$ knew how to $_6$ raise$_7$ cattle$_8$ [and] raise$_9$ pigs$_{10}$, and besides$_{11}$, already$_{12,20}$ could$_{13}$ build$_{14}$ houses$_{15}$, make$_{16}$ chariots$_{17}$, [and] construct$_{18}$ ships$_{19}$."

In the first example the relation between the constituents of the predicate is marked by *yě*; in the second it is marked by *érqiě*; in the latter example the sub-constituents *yǎng niú*, *yǎng zhū*, and *zào fángzi, zào chē, zào chuán* stand in simple juxtaposition. Both clauses/sentences are major, simple, verbal, negatable, with compound predicates. They are not compound sentences, because the phonological signals determine otherwise. In the first example a final intonation on the sequence ending on *xuěrén*, and a pause after it, would establish two separate sentences. The same is true of the second example, if the appropriate phonological signals occurred on and after *yǎng zhū*.

The immediate constituents of a compound predicate may be unmarked:

Qíncháo$_1$ *bǎ Zhōngguo*$_2$ *tǒngyī*$_3$ *yǐhòu*$_4$,/*jiéshùle*$_5$ *fēngjiàn*$_6$ *zhìdu*$_7$, *jiànlìle*$_8$ *yíge*$_9$ *tǒngyī de*$_{10}$ *guójiā*$_{11}$. "After$_4$ the Ch'in Dynasty$_1$ had united$_3$ China$_2$, [it] abolished$_5$ the feudal$_6$ system$_7$, [and] established$_8$ a$_9$ unified$_{10}$ state$_{11}$."

5. THE FUNCTIONS OF CLAUSE-LIKE SEQUENCES

As has already been pointed out, a sequence in the form of a major clause (i.e. a construct consisting of a topic subject and a predicate), is potentially a sentence in its own right, or, in the case of a compound sentence, an immediate constituent of a sentence. But in many cases such clause-like sequences are embedded in larger constructions and thus occupy a lower status in the syntactic hierarchy. Before we conclude this chapter we shall sum up the most important functions of clause-like elements which are not in fact clauses.

a) Topic subjects: *Tā bú xìn ni, shì bú duì de*. "It is not true that he does not believe you."

b) Predicates: *Wǒ, jìxing hǎo*. "I have a good memory."

c) Modifiers in nominal expressions: *Wǒ cóng nàr lái de dìfang*. "The place I come from."

d) Objects: *Wǒ zhīdao tā bú huì shuō Zhōngwén*. "I know that he cannot speak Chinese."

e) Incorporated into a subject as a part of it: *Nǐ wàngle tā bú huì shuō Zhōngwén, zhēn qíguài.* "It is strange that you should forget that he cannot speak Chinese."

f) Incorporated into a predicate as an object: *Wǒmen xīwang nǐmen jiānglái kaīshǐ xué Zhōngwén.* "We hope that you will in the future start learning Chinese."

CHAPTER IV

THE PHRASE

1. THE PHRASE AS A PHONOLOGICAL UNIT

A phrase is a stress group, i.e. a group of words which belong together grammatically and which are dominated by one nuclear stress (cp. Chapter II, section C, subsection 6, p. 40). A phrase is also, at least potentially, a pause group. In the hierarchical order a phrase occupies, in principle, a lower rank than a clause, although in the case of a clause consisting of just one phrase, the two levels coincide. It follows that a phrase is either a clause in its own right (a phrase/clause) and in that case a potential sentence, or a constituent of a clause, and in that case, if the clause is a simple clause, potentially an immediate sentence constituent.

2. TYPES OF PHRASES

As was pointed out in Chapter I, C 1.3. (p. 9) phrases are *verbal* or *nominal*, depending on whether the nucleus of the phrase is a verb or a nominal. Verbal phrases will be dealt with in more detail in Chapter VIII pp. 176 et seq.; nominal phrases will be described further in Chapter XII (pp. 263 et seq.). Both types of phrases are endocentric. The immediate constituents of a phrase may stand in coordination with or in subordination to one another; in the same way the relation of two phrases to one another may be one of coordination or subordination. The various possibilities have been outlined in Chapter I.

3. THE PHRASE AND THE EXPRESSION

Whether a certain sequence is a phrase in the sense in which the term is used in this book, depends on whether it contains one or more than one nuclear stress. Very often a group of words which make up one grammatical construction turn out to contain more than one stress group. For example:

Gěi$_1$ tā$_2$ péngyou$_3$ dǎ$_4$ diànhuà$_5$. "To make$_4$ a telephone call$_5$ to$_1$ his$_2$ friend$_3$."; *Dài$_1$ dà$_2$ yǎnjingr$_3$ de$_4$ nèige$_5$ wàiguorén$_6$.* "The$_5$ foreigner$_6$ who$_4$ is wearing$_1$ big$_2$ glasses$_3$." Both sequences are likely to be spoken as two phrases, since primary stress is likely to fall on *péngyou* as well as on *diànhuà*, and on *yǎnjingr* as well as on *wàiguorén*. Both sequences form regular grammatical constructions (verbal expressions in series in the first case; a nominal modified by a clause-like sequence in the second case). To deal with such cases we use the term *syntáctic expressions*. We shall use this term rather loosely, so as to describe grammatical constructs regardless of whether they consist of one or more than one stress group. We thus distinguish between single-phrase expressions and multi-phrase expressions. Since in endocentric constructs the distribution of the construct as a whole is in most respects identical with the distribution of the nucleus, i.e. the nucleus alone has in the main the same grammatical functions as the whole construct, we may extend the use of the term *expression* to cover a single nuclear word in a construct. Such a word is then a *minimal expression*. As an operational term *expression* is thus the same as a form class; it is useful because it refers to single words as well as to longer sequences. Expressions of the same type belong to the same form class; in an endocentric construction the whole construct is said to belong to the same form class as the nuclear word.

4. THE FUNCTION OF PHRASES

Phrases fulfil a great variety of functions. Most of these have been pointed out in Chapter II, and will be further elaborated in Chapters VIII and XII, so we need not go into detail here. We shall just give a brief summary.

a) Phrases which function as predicates:

xìng shémme in: *Nèige$_1$ rén$_2$ xìng$_3$ shémme$_4$.* "What$_4$ is the name$_3$ [of] that$_1$ man$_2$?"; *hē chá* in: *Báixiānsheng hē chá.* "Mr. Pai is drinking tea."; *jiù shèng wǔmáo qián* in: *Wó$_1$ liǎngge$_2$ péngyou$_3$, jiù$_4$ shèng$_5$ wǔmáo qián$_6$.* "My$_1$ two$_2$ friends$_3$ have$_5$ only$_4$ fifty cents$_6$ left$_5$."; *wó hén tǎoyàn* in: *Tā$_1$ shuō huà$_2$, wǒ$_3$ hen$_4$ tǎoyàn$_5$.* "[When] he$_1$ talks$_2$, I$_3$ am$_5$ quite$_4$ bored$_5$."

b) Phrases functioning as topic subjects:

Wǒ xiān shuō de in: *Wǒ$_1$ xiān$_2$ shuō$_3$ de$_4$, tāmen$_5$ dōu$_6$ míngbai$_7$.* "What$_4$ I$_1$ said$_3$ at first$_2$, they$_5$ understood$_7$ completely$_6$."; *Zhōngguo* *gǔdài yúfǎ* in: *Zhōngguo$_1$ gǔdài$_2$ yúfǎ$_3$, nánxué$_4$ ma.* "Is$_4$ (Chinese$_1$ ancient$_2$ grammar$_3$ =) Chinese classical grammar difficult to learn$_4$?"; *Wángxiansheng de jiā* in: *Wángxiansheng de jiā, zài chénglitou.* "Mr. Wang's home is inside the city."; *nǐ géi wo dǎ diànhuà de shíhou* in: *Nǐ$_1$ géi wo$_2$ dǎ diànhuà$_3$ de shíhou$_4$, wǒ$_5$ zhèng$_6$ gēn$_7$ jǐge$_8$ péngyou$_9$ liáo tiār$_{10}$ laizhe$_{11}$.* "When$_4$ you$_1$ called$_3$ me$_2$ up$_3$ on the telephone$_3$, I$_5$ was just$_{6,11}$ chatting$_{10}$ with$_7$ some$_8$ friends$_9$."

c) Phrases functioning as adverbial modifiers:

yòng lùyīnjī in: *Wǒmen$_1$ yòng$_2$ lùyīnjī$_3$ xué$_4$ yǔyán$_5$.* "We$_1$ use$_2$ tape recorders$_3$ [when] learning$_4$ languages$_5$."; *zài xuéxiàoli* in: *Zài$_1$ xuéxiàoli$_2$ yǒu$_3$ xuésheng$_4$.* "In$_1$ the school$_2$ there are$_3$ students$_4$."; *jīngguo Éguo cóng Xībólìyǎ tiělù zuò huǒchē* in: *Tāmen$_1$ jīngguo$_2$ Éguo$_3$ cóng$_4$ Xībólìyǎ$_5$ tiělù$_6$ zuò$_7$ huǒchē$_8$ huílai le$_9$.* "They$_1$ returned$_9$ by$_4$ the Siberian$_5$ railway$_6$ via$_2$ Russia$_3$, by$_7$ train$_8$."

d) Verbal phrases functioning as nominal phrases by the use of the nominalizing phrase marker *de*:

yóngyuǎn bú miè de in: *Zài wùlǐxuéshang shuō, wùzhì shì yóngyuǎn bú miè de.* "In physics it is said that matter is something which can never be destroyed." This type of phrase is dealt with in more detail in Chapter XII F.

CHAPTER V

THE WORD AND
THE MORPHEME

1. WORDS AND "WORDS"

A *word* contains at least one segmental *morpheme* (cp. Chapter I A 2.6, p. 2); many words contain more than one (compound and complex words, cp. Chapter I D 1.4 and 1.5 (p. 14)). But a morpheme is not necessarily a word (bound morphemes, cp. Chapter I A 2.6). The distinction between words and morphemes is therefore an essential one. But in traditional usage all monosyllabic units tend to be called "words", whether they are actually syntactic sentence constituents or not (cp. Mullie 1932, vol. I, p. XXVII: "The Chinese language is monosyllabic in the broad sense of the word, i.e. the words consist of one syllable."). This was so because the Chinese term *zì* could be interpreted as "character" (= graphic representation of a monosyllabic unit) as well as in the sense of "word". Thus, what we today call morphemes were previously simply regarded as words. For example, bound forms like *yīn* in *yīnwei* "because", and *shì* in *shìjiè* "world" were, in this sense, termed "words"; forms like *yīnggāi* "ought to", *míngbai* "understand", *shítou* "stone", *xiànzài* "now", and *dōngxi* "a thing" were, by the same token, regarded as "two words" (*liǎngge zì*).

This terminology was all the more understandable because in Chinese almost all syllables carry meaning. Thus, *shì* in *shìjiè* generally means "world" or "generation", and *jiè* "realm" or "boundary". Exceptions to this general trend are such forms as *méigui* "rose", *kāfēi* "coffee", *gánlán* "olive". Forms like these are best regarded as bisyllabic morphemes; the former category (*shì, jiè, yīn, wèi, míng, bái,* etc.) are monosyllabic morphemes.

2. SYNTACTIC WORDS

In Chinese, as in other languages, there is a need for recognizing a type of linguistic unit which is intermediate between the morpheme as such and the phrase or the sentence. Such a unit is the *word*.

However, the borderline between words and other segments is by no means always clearcut. Since overt phonological and morphological signals on the whole yield few criteria for the definition of the word, a solution must be sought in other directions. The lack of an established tradition in Chinese as to what constitutes a word eliminates the conventional dictionary as a resource in this regard. Although dictionaries like *Mathews' Chinese-English Dictionary*, or the *Chinesisch-Deutsches Wörterbuch* (published in Peking, 1959), certainly contain words, they make no overt distinction between morphemes, words, phrases, and other syntactic constructions. In this respect, Chao and Yang's *A Concise Dictionary of Spoken Chinese* (1947) is unique in giving a great deal of information about words and their grammatical functions.

A general definition of the word is in fact next to impossible at the present stage of the language, and such a definition will not be attempted here. But in spite of the fact that a theoretical approach to the problem is apt to lead to all sorts of complications, the assumption of the existence of the word in Chinese is, for practical purposes, a necessity for a discussion of syntax. We shall proceed to suggest some possible ways of establishing segments which can serve as operational units in sentence construction.

In spite of the difficulties on the theoretical level, it is in practice usually possible to reach fairly unanimous agreement as to how many words a *given* sentence contains. Thus, in a sentence like

$T\bar{a}_1$ *gàosong*$_2$ *wo*$_3$ *nǐ*$_4$ *péngyou*$_5$ *zài*$_6$ *Běijīng*$_7$. "He$_1$ tells$_2$ me$_3$ [that] your$_4$ friend$_5$ is in$_6$ Peking$_7$."

most people would readily accept that it consists of seven words (i.e. segments which speakers consciously and freely operate with in many contexts when making sentences).

In practical terms the problem is to decide where a word begins and where it ends, in other words, to determine word boundaries in a given sentence. To begin with, all minimal segments which may potentially occur independently as sentences are obviously words, since a speaker, if speaking, is hardly going to utter less than what he or she consciously takes to be a minimal utterance. Thus, conceivable answers to the question, "When?" might be, *Xiànzài*. "Now." or *Míngtian*. "Tomorrow." Partials, such as **Xiàn.*, **Tiān.*, **Míng.*, or **Zài.*, would not, in this case, be sufficient. *Xiànzài* and *míngtian* occur and recur as fixed units; they are obviously the kind of items that would qualify as words in this respect. Other such segments are, *shì* ("it is so =) yes"; *yǒu* "there is/are"; *tīng* "listen"; *péngyou* "friend"; *píngjù* "evidence"; *mùtou* "wood (as material)"; *zhànzhēng* "war".

If such items occur bounded by pauses, they are miniature sentences. Most sentences, however, are more extended. As Chao has pointed out (1968, pp. 151–155), one way of establishing word boundaries in such larger sequences is to look for potential pauses. A speaker is not likely to make a break in the middle of such words as *xiǎoxin* "to be careful", *yònggōng* "to be diligent", *fúshuǐ* "to swim", *jīhui* "opportunity", *zhíwù* "a plant", *dìfang* "place". If interrupted, the speaker is likely to start over again from the beginning of the word. On the whole, pauses between words more often occur in slow speech than in fast or normal speech tempo. Hesitating speech is revealing in this respect.

According to Chao (1968, p. 151), a sentence like *Jīntian₁ wǒ₂ yào₃ shàng₄ lǐfàpù₅ qù₆ lǐfà₇*. "Today₁ I₂ want to₃ go to₄,₆ the barbershop₅ to have a haircut₇." could, in a case of extreme hesitancy, be spoken in the following way: *Jīntian a, wǒ ya, yào – shàng – negenege – lǐfa–, lǐfàpù–, qù lǐ– lǐ– lǐfà.* If spoken in this way, with pause particles, with prolongation of the end tone-pitches at the points indicated by dashes, and with a filler word (*negenege*), the words of which the sentence consists are clearly brought out. *Lǐfà* as a segment admits of no internal break; in the same way, *pù* is not separable from *lǐfà* and cannot occur alone (unless followed by *–zi*), but the whole sequence must be repeated: *lǐfà–, lǐfà–, lǐfàpù.* Taking these factors into consideration, the sentence consists of seven relatively independent units which are words: *Jīntian, wǒ, yào, shàng, lǐfàpù, qù, lǐfà.*

In a given sentence we shall recognize such potential pausal units as syntactically free words.

Another very useful approach to the question of deciding what is a word and what is not a word is suggested by Kratochvil (1968, p. 93). He takes the sentence *Jīntian tiānqi hén hǎo*. "The weather is (very) nice today." as a *maximal* utterance, i.e. an utterance which contains all other possible utterances in the same context. In the example just quoted, *Hǎo*. would be a *minimal* utterance. Limited by these two extremes, a definite number of *intermediate* utterances (in this case five) would be possible (we are dealing here only with segmental morphemes):

(1) *Jīntian*   *hén hǎo.*
(2) *Jīntian*   *hǎo.*
(3)   *Tiānqi hén hǎo.*
(4)   *Tiānqi*   *hǎo.*
(5)   *Hén hǎo.*

The seven sentences, including the maximal and the minimal utterances, form an utterance group; all other combinations are excluded. All sentences share the unit *hǎo*; the units *jīntian*, *tiānqi*, and *hěn* are the only members which are used to differentiate between member sentences. In other words, these three segments, plus *hǎo*, represent the four minimal units with which a speaker of Chinese consciously operates in this case. Consequently, these segments are the smallest units which can serve as constituents of Chinese syntactic constructions, i.e. they are words.

By and large both tests, when applied to *specific* sentences, lead to the establishment of the same kind of free syntactic segment: the word. But the identification of, for example, *tiānqi* as a word in this *context* does not exclude the possibility of recognizing the partial *tiān* "the sky", in *tiānqi* as a word in other contexts, as for example in *Tiān hēi le*. "The sky became dark.", and of the other partial *qì* "the air", as in *Qì hén hǎo*. "The air is (very) nice."

3. BOUND WORDS

There are, however, some units which are not readily identifiable as words by means of Kratochvil's method. Nor are these units capable of occurring as an independent sentence. The units in question, in other words, never occur alone, but presuppose the presence of other units, i.e. they are bound to other units recognized in the context as words, or to phrases, or to clauses/sentences as a whole. Thus, in an expression like *Nǐ gen wǒ*. "You and me.", the unit *gen* is separable from *nǐ* and *wǒ* by a potential pause in Chao's sense, but whereas *nǐ* as well as *wǒ* can potentially occur alone, in answers like "I" or "you", this is not the case with *gen*. Utterances like *Nǐ gen*. and *Gen wǒ*. are both unlikely to occur; in other words, *gen* presupposes *nǐ* as well as *wǒ*, in much the same way as "and" does in English between two nominals. *Gen* is a *marker*; its "meaning" is to establish coordination between *nǐ* and *wǒ*. We shall recognize it as a word. It is, however, not a syntactically free word in the same sense as *tiānqi*, *hǎo*, or *tāmen*. It is a type of *bound word*.

Similarly, in: *Suírán$_1$ yǐjing$_2$ wǎnle$_3$, (kěshi)$_4$ wǒ$_5$ ràng$_6$ ni$_7$ qù$_8$.* "Although$_1$ it is$_3$ already$_2$ late$_3$, (but)$_4$ I$_5$'ll let$_5$ you$_7$ go$_8$.", *suírán* is bound to the whole topic subject phrase, and marks it as such; *kěshi*, if included in the sentence, is bound to the predicate as a whole. In: *Zuótian lái de rén.* "The man who came yesterday.", *de* marks subordination of the preceding expression to the following word, establishing the whole sequence as a nominal phrase. Taken as a subordinating particle, *de* is a word bound to the preceding expression. *Ma* in: *Nǐ bú qù ma.* "Aren't you going?" is bound to the predicate phrase as a whole, transforming it into a question. *Ma* is a bound word; it never forms a pause group by itself. Like *gen* and *de*, *ma* is atonic. No free syntactic word is atonic; among bound words, some have this feature.

4. WORD STRUCTURE

George Kennedy estimates (1964, p. 113) that "at least sixty-three percent of the vocabulary [of a collection of material extending to over 900,000 syllables] was in polysyllabic form." A rough survey of 20 pages, chosen at random in the *Concise Dictionary of Spoken Chinese* by Chao and Yang (1947), containing altogether 430 character entries, shows that entries designated F (= free words) make up 27.5%, and entries marked B (= bound morphemes) make up 33.9% of the total. The rest, 38.6%, consists of items which are free as well as bound. John DeFrancis (1950, p. 153, footnote), reports the result of a similar count, in which F was 29%, B 22%, and "semi-bound" 49%.

It seems to be beyond doubt that only a minority of Chinese syntactic words are monosyllabic. That this is true, not only in the lexical sense, but also in a given running text, is further confirmed by even a perfunctory glance at the transcribed text pages of, for example, *Twenty Lectures on Chinese Culture*, by Parker Po-fei Huang et al. (1967), or at the entries in the alphabetically arranged *Chūgokugo jiten* by Kuraishi Takeshirō (1968).

Among polysyllabic words, the bisyllabic type seems to be the most common. It is probably safe to say that the bisyllabic type is the predominant word type in the language as a whole.

Bisyllabic words contain, as a rule, but by no means always, two morphemes. Words like *dìfangr* "place", *zhèyàngr* "in this manner", although bisyllabic, contain three morphemes.

A bisyllabic word is either a compound or a complex word, or a reduplicated form. As has been mentioned in Chapter I D 1.4 and 1.5, a complex word always contains an *affix* (usually a suffix): *shùr* "a small tree", *màozi* "hat", which means that it is derived from some underlying word or morpheme, whereas a compound word is made up of at least two root morphemes, each of which may be free or bound. Both types are extremely numerous and productive. We shall not go into details here, since these types will be dealt with elsewhere, especially in Chapters VI (Verbal structure, p. 116) and X (Nominal structure, p. 205).

Although suffixed forms occur in large numbers in a given text, the actual number of *suffixes* in the language is very small. Only about five noun-forming suffixes can be said to be common. About half a dozen suffixes serve to form place and time words. Four or five suffixes can be added to verbs in order to express aspectual relations. In addition there are a few *prefixes*, and two *infixes*. Suffixes occur in nominals as well as verbs. Prefixes are limited to nominals; infixes are found in verbal forms. In the following we give a list of the most important affixes:

(1) In nominals: the suffixes *-zi*, *-r*, *-tou*, *-ba*, and *-men*, which mostly form nouns; suffixes like *-shang* "on", *-xia* "under", *-li* and *-nèi* "inside", *-wài* "outside", *-qián* "in front of", *-hòu* "behind", etc., which form place words (note also compound suffixes like *-shangtou* as in *qiáng-shangtou* "on the wall", and *wūzilitou* "in the room"). The suffix *-r* sometimes, but by no means always, carries a diminutive meaning; the suffix *-zi* is simply a nominalizer. Thus, *shùr* usually means "a small tree" (*shù* "a tree"); *gàr* or *gàizi* both mean "lid". The suffix *-r* is rather versatile in that it also forms time words (*jiār* "today", *míngr* "tomorrow"). In connection with the suffix *-r* certain modifications of a morphophonemic kind take place in the preceding root. Thus, if the last sound in the root is *-i* or *-n*, (*e*)*r* replaces these: *zì* "a (written) character", cp. *zèr* (same meaning); *wèi* (bound morpheme) "a taste", cp. *wèr* "taste, odor"; *gài* "to cover", cp. *gàr* "a lid"; *gān* "to be dry", cp. *-gār* "something which is dry or dried", e.g. *pútaogār* "raisin". If the last sound of the root is *-ng*, the vowel of the root is retroflexed and nasalized simultaneously: *liàng* "to be bright", cp. *liàngr* [liã̃ᵣ] "illumination". On the whole, the suffix *-r* tends to color the syllable as a whole. Note that this suffix is non-syllabic, i.e. it joins with the root into one syllable, and the unit contains only one toneme.

(2) In verbs: the suffixes *-le*, *-zhe*, *-qilai*, *-guo*. These all express aspectual relations, and are discussed in detail in Chapter VI A (pp. 117–133). Suffice it to say here that *-le*, which expresses the perfective aspect, is on the whole by far the most common in conversational and narrative speech. The suffix *-le*, which is always part of a word, should be kept distinct from the particle *le*, which is not

bound to a word as such, but to a whole phrase or a larger construction, most commonly a predicate. A verb-forming suffix is -*de*, which is found in a few verbs which have potential meaning: *rènde* "can recognize = knows"; *jìde* "(can) remember".

Prefixes in the strict sense of the word are few: *dì*- in ordinal numbers (*dìsān* "No. 3, the third"); *chū*- especially when giving dates up to the tenth (of the month): *chūsān* "the third (of the month)"; *lăo*- in such forms as *láoshu* "rat", and *lăoèr* "number two (among brothers and sisters)", etc.

Infixes are limited to -*de*- and -*bu*- in certain verbal compounds; they are constituents in potential forms: *kàndejiàn* "can see" is a potential resultative compound; *nábushànglái* "cannot bring up" is a potential directional compound.

Reduplicated forms (most common types: A + A, AA + BB, or AB + AB) are by nature polysyllabic; we treat them here as a class apart; they are thus neither compounds nor complex words. Reduplication always has a grammatical function; details are given elsewhere (Chapters VI and X). Note, however, such "irregular" types of reduplication as *húlihútū* "confused(ly)", *rèhūhū* "piping hot".

By way of summary, we give below a classification of free words according to monosyllabicity/polysyllabicity, and according to internal structure. Only the most important categories are included, and only a few examples are given.

A. Monosyllabic

(1) Simple:
   Verbs: *zŏu* "to walk", *dà* "to be big"
   Nominals: *rén* "man", *nĭ* "you".
   Adverbs: *zuì* "most", *xiān* "first", *yě* "also"
   Interjections: *wei!* "hello!"
(2) Compound: (non-existent)
(3) Complex:
   Verbs: *wár* "to play"
   Nominals: *zhèr* "here", *wèr* "taste, odor", *wār* "bend, turn (e.g. in a road)", *shùr* "a number"
   Adverbs: *năr* "how?"

B. Polysyllabic

(1) Simple:
   Verbs: *chóuchu* "to hesitate"
   Nominals: *pútao* "grapes", *luóji* "logic"

(2) Compound:

Verbs: *xiǎoxin* "to be careful", *míngbai* "to understand", *fèichú* "to abolish", *tóuténg* "to have a headache", *hǎokàn* "to be good-looking", *gǎiliáng* "to improve", *kànjian* "to see", *tīngbudǒng* "(listens but) cannot understand", *náchulai* "take out".

Nominals: *xīnlǐ* "psychology", *mǎimai* "trade", *guǎnggào* "advertisement", *zhèige* "this one", *sānkuài* "three pieces", *zuótian* "yesterday", *zhuōshang* "on the table".

Adverbs: *fǎnzhèng* "anyway", *gēnběn* "basically", *gāngcái* "just now".

(3) Complex:

Verbs: *xiěle* "wrote/has written (something to completion)", *xiězhe* "is writing", *jìde* "remember".

Nominals: *pùzi* "shop, store", *qiántou* "front (side)", *líba* "fence", *nǐmen* "you (pl.)".

Adverbs: *hūrán* "suddenly".

(4) Reduplications:

Nominals: *mèimei* "younger sister", *gēge* "elder brother", *bǎobao* "baby", *māma* "mama", *rénrén* "everyman", *chùchùr* "every place", *xīngxing* "star", *xīngxing(r)* "orangutan".

Verbs: *xiángxiang* "just think", *zhùyizhuyi* "pay a little attention", *tǎoluntaolun* "discuss", *qīngqīngchǔchū* "to be perfectly clear".

Adverbs: *chángcháng* "regularly, ordinarily", *jiànjiàn* "gradually", *mànmārde* "very slowly".

Onomatopoetic and miscellaneous forms: *dǎhāha(r)* "to joke, make fun of", *luōliluōsuō* "to be wordy and fussy", *dinglangdanglang!* "ting-a-ling" (like a bell)

5. WORD CLASSES

A given word, in a given syntactic context, has a grammatical value, i.e. it is a verb, a nominal, an adverb, etc. Thus, as we have seen, words like *lái* "come", *hǎo* "good", and *chī* "eat" have been assigned to the class of verbs, whereas other items, like *rén* "man", "people", *shū* "book(s)", and *zhuōzi* "table(s)" are said to be nominals. Translation forms do not yield dependable criteria for the class membership of a word in Chinese, although the translation of a word does in many cases indicate such a membership. Note, however, that a word like *shíhou* in the sequence *tā lái de shíhou* "when he comes" is translated by means of a conjunction "when" only because of the requirements of English syntax. In Chinese it is a nominal.

Words which have the same grammatical value are said to belong to the same word class. The question is how to determine the grammatical value of a given word. A number of words, like *zhuōzi* "table", and *shítou* "stone", are marked as nouns by means of a suffix, and words like *děng* "to wait", and *mài* "to sell" may in a given text occur with suffixes attached (*-zhe, -le*, etc.), something which singles them out as verbs. But words like *căiyòng, jìngzhēng, săo* or *bàng*, as isolated forms, contain no overt indication as to whether they may be used as verbs or nouns or both. No clue is given by syllabic structure, "ending", stress, or tone. Except for words which contain characteristic suffixes, therefore, the grammatical value is inherent and potential. Thus, if *căiyòng* is found to be usable only as a verb, with the meaning of "apply; select for use", and if *jìngzhēng* is found to be usable as a noun ("competition") as well as a verb ("compete"), whereas *bàng* ("stick") only functions as a nominal, these facts are due to arbitrary selection. In those cases where criteria for the determination of class membership are not available within the word, one has to look beyond the word. This means that syntactical, rather than morphological criteria, must be used in such cases. On the whole, therefore, grammatical *function* is the key to the question of grammatical *value*. In other words, although the value is assumed to be inherent, it can be determined only by observing how the given unit functions in syntactical patterns: with which other units can the item be combined or not combined; and if combined with other units, which relative position can it occupy?

Syntactically free words which are *negatable* by *bù* and/or *méi*, and which have the privilege of occurrence as sentence centrals, are termed *verbs*. This large, open class can be further divided into a number of major and minor sub-categories, depending on supplementary criteria. Since the whole of Chapter VII is devoted to this sub-classification, there is no reason to go into detail here. Suffice it to say that the feature of negatability as defined above applies to all members of the overall verb class, with a single exception: the verb *méi*, which is the negative existential verb ("there is/are not"), is not modifiable by negators, for logical rather than grammatical reasons. Since, however, it shares most syntactic functions with other verbs, we class it with this group rather than assigning it to a class all of its own.

All words other than verbs share the basic feature of being *non-negatable*. We thus have a great cleavage of the whole vocabulary into negatable and non-negatable words. Within the latter group five major classes can be established: 1) nominals, 2) adverbs, 3) interjections, 4) particles, and 5) markers.

Nominals form a large, open class of words, most of which are modifiable by other nominals, by verbs, and by larger syntactic constructions in the segmental form of phrases or clauses. Nominals typically occur precentrally as topic subjects, and as objects of verbs they occur precentrally (if occurring after coverbs and verbs functioning as such) and postcentrally. Nominals are further divided into a number of major and minor sub-categories (see Chapter XI for details).

Adverbs are non-modifiable words which modify verbs and verbal expressions. They express manner, degree, etc. Note that the negators (*bù* and *méi*) are adverbs. Adverbs are dealt with in some detail in Chapter IX (pp. 198–203).

Interjections are typically sentence-words, i.e. they usually make up full sentences, and have intonation, but no tone. Occasionally they occur as part of a longer sentence: *Mm, bú-yàojǐn*! "Oh no, that's all right!" Such a sentence is in the exclamatory form.

The two remaining word classes, particles and markers, are bound, atonic words which form closed classes. Their functions are largely grammatical.

Particles are bound to phrases or larger expressions, such as topic subjects or predicates. They do not occur at the beginning of a sentence, but are quite common in final position in a sentence. The most common final particles are *ma* (question), *le* (new situation), *a/ya* (question, exclamation, vocative, etc.), *ne* (certain questions, etc.), *ba* (advice and supposition), and *zhene* (intensity). Most particles which are not final particles are pause particles; these sometimes separate topic subject from predicate and even (in slow or hesitant speech) word from word.

The question particle *ma* has been dealt with in Chapter II E 3, Interrogative sentences, subsection d (pp. 55–59). Only a few supplementary points need be added here. If several final particles occur, *ma* occupies the ultimate final position: *Nǐ chī fàn le ma*. "Have you eaten?" Some questions with *ma* are of the rhetorical kind; this is always the case if the sentence is of the negated type: *Nǐ₁ bù₂ zhīdao₃ nèizhǒng₄ yào₅ hěn₆ wēixiǎn₇ ma₈*. "Don't₂ you₁ know₃ [that] the₄ medicine₅ is₇ very₆ dangerous₇ (you should know)?₈"

The particle *le* has a number of functions, but they can nearly all be subsumed under the class meaning, "such and such a situation has (now) come into being; from the present point of view it must be realized that . . .". Consider the following: *Tā hē shuǐ*. "He drinks water." ∼ *Tā hē shuǐ le*. "(The situation that he drinks water has come into being =) he drinks water now (he has *begun* to = he didn't or couldn't do so up to now)." *Tā bù lái*. "He doesn't come (or: isn't coming)." ∼ *Tā bù lái le*. "(The situation that he doesn't come has become a reality =) he doesn't come (or: isn't coming) any more." Similarly: *Tā₁ cóngqián₂ shì₃ gōngrén₄, xiànzài₅ shì₆ dàxuéshēng₇ le₈.* "He₁ was₃ a worker₄ before₂, [but] now₅ (his being₆ a student₇ has come about₈ =) he has become a university student." *Tā₁ dào₂ nàr₃ qù₄ xiūxi₅, tā₆ shēntí₇ hǎo₈ le₉.* "He₁ went₂,₄ there₃ to rest₅, and (his₆ body's₇ being good₈ has come about₉ =) now he has recovered." Note that in such cases *le* occurs after verbs as well as after members of other word classes; *le* is added after the word which happens to come last in the preceding sequence.

In some cases the idea of "new situation" has the connotation of "extent of some quality or state of affairs not realized before": *Zhèige dōngxi guì le.* "This thing is (really) too expensive." *Yīngguo zài Ōuzhōu de běibiar le.* "England is in the northern part of Europe (that distant!)."

In many cases sentences with *le* refer to past time, but this is by no means always so. *Nà wǒ jiù bù zǒu le.* "In that case (my not going has now become a reality =) I (then) won't go." refers to future time rather than to the present. The same applies to the example already given: *Tā bù lái le.* "He's not coming any more." A very important part of the basic idea conveyed by *le* is that something is beginning to be so or so, a state of affairs has begun to exist. The realization that a situation is new is assumed to take place at the moment of speaking: *Xià yǔ le.* "(As of now, I realize the fact that it rains; it may have been raining for quite some time, and others may have noticed it, but *now* my awareness of it is part of my experience =) it is raining now, I see."

From one point of view, therefore, *le* may be said to relate some event or condition, or the relevance or importance of it, to the present moment, or rather to the moment of speaking. This is seen even more clearly in cases where the verb of the sentence has an aspect suffix -*le* attached ("action completed"), at the same time as a sentence-final *le* is present: *Tā zài Běijīng zhùle sānnián le.* "(His having completed three years' stay in Peking is a fact which has now come into being =) he has stayed (or: has been staying) in Peking for three years (and is still there)."; cp. *Tā zài Běijīng zhùle sānnián.* "He stayed in Peking for three years." (completed action of the past, not related or relatable to the present moment, because he is not there any more). Similarly: *Chīle fàn le.* "I have eaten." Sentences with a suffix -*le* as well as a final particle *le* are therefore usually translatable by the perfect tense, whereas a sentence like *Wó mǎile sānběn shū.* "I bought three books." may be translated by the simple preterite.

The particle *a/ya* actually has a number of different forms, depending on the last sound of the word it follows, thus *lái ya*, *zhēn na*, *hǎo wa*, etc. (except that *ya* is the form occuring after the single or main vowels a, e, and o); but, despite the variant forms, we are dealing with the same particle. It is used in exclamations (*Jīntian tiānqi zhēn lěng* (*ng*)*a*! "It is really very cold (weather) today!"), in vocatives (*Láo Lǐ ya*! "Oh, Lao Li!"), in commands and impatient statements (*Shuō ya*! "Say it!"; *Wǒ méi gōngfu wa*. "I don't have time, don't you see!"), and in a few other cases.

The particle *ne* occurs in questions posed in a context (*Yuàn shéi ne*. "Well then, whom shall we blame?"; *Nà zěmme bàn ne*. "And how should we do that?"). In addition to being a final particle, *ne* (as well as *a*) is also used as a phrase particle to separate a topic subject from its predicate (*Nèige₁ rén₂ ne₃, tā₄ yi-tiān-dào-wǎn₅, lǎo zai nar₆ shuō huà₇*. "As for₃ that₁ man₂, he₄ keeps₆ talking₇ from morning to night₅.").

The particle *ba* is mostly used to indicate advice or exhortation (*Wǒmen zǒu ba*. "We had better go now.") or to express the idea "I suppose that . . ." (*Jīntian shì xīngqīliù ba*. "It must be Saturday today, I suppose?").

The particle *zhene* expresses intensity (*Kě duō zhene*! "There are awfully many!").

Markers have been dealt with in Chapter I D 8 (pp. 20—21), and further in connection with the specific constructions in which they occur. There is thus no need to go into detail here. It should, however, be noted that these words are among the most fundamental in the language because they are signals of structural meaning. Since they are characterized by a high degree of grammatical formalization, they may seem to be of a somewhat vague and abstract nature. They are, however, important clues to a deeper and more exact understanding of how the language works, and therefore contribute in a very basic way toward a total grasp of the language.

Although a given word may belong to a certain word class, it does not necessarily follow that all words belong only to one class. There is a great deal of *class overlap* in Chinese. A number of such cases are mentioned in various chapters of this book, but a few more examples are included here of one category which is very common, viz. the case where a given word has a dual membership: it belongs to the verb class as well as to the class of nominals. Examples are *suǒ* "a lock, to lock", *xìng* "a surname, to have a surname", *gǎigé* "a reform, to reform", *fāyīn* "pronunciation, to pronounce", *xiūxi* "a rest, to rest", *yùfáng* "precaution, to take precautions".

In Chinese, nouns are derived from verbs, not vice versa, cp. *lóng* "to be deaf", *lóngzi* "a deaf person". It would thus be possible to consider cases like *xiūxi* as having a basic verbal form, and the homophonous nominal as being derived from the verb by means of a zero suffix.

6. THE MORPHEME AND ITS ROLE

In the last analysis a sentence is a product of its morphemes and their arrangements. As was pointed out in Chapter I A 2.6, a morpheme is a minimal unit which carries form as well as meaning. It is irreducible in the sense that if further subdivided, the resulting items (phonemes) have only form, but no meaning. Consonants, vowels, and tones are components of morphemes. But since grammar deals with the arrangements and uses of meaningful forms, the smaller units fall outside the scope of grammar in the proper sense.

The morphemes of Chinese are, with few exceptions, monosyllabic. This is one of the characteristic features of the Chinese language. The cultural importance of this feature is seen in the fact that the Chinese, in their analytic work on their own language, have to such a large extent concentrated on the study of the meaningful syllable. They developed, and – alone among the nations of the world – have exclusively kept to a writing system based on the syllable as a meaningful unit. The script is thus both syllabic and – in an approximate, not a strictly scientific sense – morphemographic.

Morphemes have certain shapes. In languages with a more or less highly complex inflectional and derivational morphology, each given morpheme may take on a large number of different shapes. We then speak of alternating shapes, and since each shape is made up of phonemes, the alternations involve the shifting of phonemes. Thus in English the morpheme of the plural of nouns has a number of shapes: *-s* as in *girls*, *-es* as in *matches*, *-en* as in *oxen*, *zero* as in *fish*, to mention only a few. Such alternations are called *morphophonemic alternations*.

In Chinese, morphophonemic alternations are few and relatively unimportant. Some are connected with tones (an example is *hén hǎo* "very good", cp. *hǎo de hěn*; the third tone of a morpheme changes into the second tone if the morpheme is followed by another third-tone morpheme); others concern the suffix *-r* (cp. above, 4. Word structure, *suffixes*).

Finally it should be pointed out that morphemes may be segmental or suprasegmental. Morphemes which consist of vowels, consonants, and tones, are said to be segmental; others, which are of a different nature, cover larger stretches of speech. Thus, Intonations I, II, and III, described in Chapter II B (pp. 24–32), are of morphemic nature. The same applies to the stress patterns described in Chapter II C.

CHAPTER VI

VERBAL STRUCTURE

In this chapter the structure of *words* will be analyzed. This is called *morphological analysis*, since we analyze words into their morphemic parts. The morpheme is the smallest unit of meaning in the language. Here, then, the smallest independent verbal units of a sentence — verbs — will be analyzed into their further component parts.

A. Verbal Suffixes

1. GENERAL

There are a small number of frequently occurring verbal suffixes in modern Chinese which indicate the aspects of the verbs they are attached to.

A verb can only take one suffix at a time, in other words, suffixes are mutually exclusive. This rule can sometimes help distinguish suffixes from homophonous morphemes in doubtful cases. Compare the example containing *zŏuguole* on p. 129, where it follows from *-le* being a suffix that *-guo* here must be a directional complement, rather than a suffix.

In many cases no aspect suffix is present; the aspect is indicated in other ways. In this sense it may be said that the use of suffixes is sometimes optional or facultative. Therefore one cannot give hard and fast rules for the *normative* use of suffixes, but only *explain* their use in given instances.

The verb in its basic or minimal form, without any aspect suffixes, expresses *habitual action* or *near-future action*. Examples of the former are:

Wŏ xué Zhōngwén. "I study Chinese."
Tā₁ zài₂ Běijīng₃ Huàgōngchǎng₄ gōngzuò₅. "He₁ works₅ at₂ the Peking₃ Chemical Factory₄."

Sometimes time words or adverbs emphasize the habitual aspect, as in

Tā$_1$ měitian$_2$ jiāo$_3$ liǎngge$_4$ zhōngtóu$_5$ de$_6$ shū$_7$. "He$_1$ teaches$_3$ two$_4$ hours$_5$ (worth of$_6$ books$_7$) every day$_2$."

Wǒmen$_1$ chángcháng$_2$ zài$_3$ lǐtáng$_4$ kàn$_5$ diànyǐng$_6$. "We$_1$ often$_2$ watch$_5$ movies$_6$ in$_3$ the auditorium$_4$."

Examples of near-future action are:

Wó$_1$ mǎi$_2$ yìběn$_3$ Zhōngwén$_4$ shū$_5$. "I$_1$ am buying/going to buy$_2$ a$_3$ Chinese$_4$ book$_5$."

Nǐ$_1$ shémmo$_2$ shíhou$_3$ huí$_4$ jiā$_5$. "(What$_2$ time$_3$ =) When are you$_1$ returning$_4$ home$_5$?"

Wǒ$_1$ gēn$_2$ ni$_3$ yìqǐ$_4$ qù$_5$. "I$_1$ will go$_5$ (together$_4$) with$_2$ you$_3$."

Just as *měitian* and *chángcháng* may be extra clues to indicate habitual action, so there are also ways to make explicit near future action. A time word may be included, such as *míngtian* "tomorrow"; or the special pattern with *kuài* or *yào* before the verb and the sentence particle *le* at the end of the phrase, may be used.

2. THE PERFECTIVE ASPECT SUFFIX -LE

The suffix *-le* for the perfective aspect indicates the completed action of the verb to which it is attached. *Le* itself does not indicate a specific time relation. The context or other elements in the sentence indicate whether a given sentence containing a suffix *-le* refers to the past or the future, as will be seen from the following examples:

Wǒ$_1$ péngyou$_2$ mǎi$_3$le$_4$ yìběn$_5$ Rénmín huàbào$_6$. "My$_1$ friend$_2$ has$_4$ bought$_3$ a copy$_5$ of *Renmin Huabao$_6$*."

Tāmen$_1$ tǎolùn$_2$le$_3$ liǎngge$_4$ wèntí$_5$. "They$_1$ have$_3$ discussed$_2$ two$_4$ problems$_5$."

Nǐmen$_1$ xià$_2$le$_3$ kè$_4$ gàn$_5$ shémmo$_6$. "What$_6$ (are) you$_1$ going to do$_5$ after$_{2,3}$ class$_4$?"

Wǒmen$_1$ xià$_2$le$_3$ kè$_4$ qù$_5$ duànliàn$_6$. "After$_{2,3}$ class$_4$ we$_1$ are going to$_5$ exercise$_6$ (do gymnastics)."

Tā$_1$ měitian$_2$ xiàle$_3$ kè$_4$ jiù$_5$ qù$_6$ duànliàn$_7$. "He$_1$ goes$_6$ to exercise$_7$ right$_5$ after$_3$ class$_4$ every day$_2$."

Nǐmen$_1$ zuótian$_2$ kàn$_3$le$_4$ diànyǐng$_5$ meiyou$_6$. "Did$_4$ you$_1$ see$_3$ the movie$_5$ yesterday$_2$ or not$_6$?"

Liànxí$_1$ li$_2$ de$_3$ jùzi$_4$, nǐmen$_5$ fānyi$_6$le$_7$ ma$_8$. "Have$_7$ you$_5$ translated$_6$ the sentences$_4$ in$_{2,3}$ the exercise$_1$?$_8$"

Tā₁ fānyi₂le₃, wǒ₄ méiyou₅ fānyi₆. "She₁ has₃ translated₂ (them), (but) I₄ haven't₅ (translated₆)."

In the last example we are introduced to the negated form of a verb with suffix *-le*, which is *méiyou* or only *méi* + the verb without *-le*.

What often makes *le* something of a problem for students of Chinese, is the difficulty of distinguishing between the suffix illustrated above and the homophonous *phrase particle le* which indicates 1) *new situation*, as in:

Xià₁ yǔ₂ le₃. "It is raining₁,₂ (now₃)."
Shémmo₁ shíhou₂ le₃. "What₁ time₂ is it (now₃)?"

or 2) *that an event happened in the past*, as in:

Tā₁ zǎoshang₂ gàosong₃ wo₄ le₅. "He₁ told₃,₅ me₄ this morning₂."
Wǒ₁ zuótian₂ dào₃ Zhāng₄ jiā₅ chī₆ fàn₇ le₈. "I₁ went₃,₈ to₃ the Changs₄,₅ for dinner₆,₇ yesterday₂."

Even though it is difficult to distinguish the suffix from the particle, there are, in addition to the differences in function, also fairly clear formal criteria by which to decide whether we have before us the one or the other in a given example.

First of all, the suffix comes directly after the verb, whereas the particle comes at the end of a phrase or a sentence. However, where a verb is the last word in the phrase or sentence, we need further criteria on which to decide. We have to take the semantic function of *le* into account. The suffix expresses completed action, therefore the suffix *-le* normally follows verbs which express an action that can be completed, and not just a state or a quality. One major function of the particle *le*, on the other hand, is to express a change to a new situation, and therefore it naturally follows verbs expressing quality or a state of being. An exception to this otherwise fairly general rule is the case where the quality verbs change their function and resemble action verbs in that they express a process, as in:

Tā₁ gāo₂le₃ sān₄ cùn₅. "He₁ has₃ grown₂ three₄ inches₅."
Tā₁ fùqin₂ bìng₃le₄ sān₅ nián₆. "His₁ father₂ was₄ sick₃ for three₅ years₆."

In cases like this we would still have no problem in deciding that the *-le* is a suffix, since it comes between the verb and the object, whereas the particle would be placed after the object, or at the end of the phrase.

There is still a problem, however, in cases where the verb is an action verb followed by *-le*, and comes at the end of the sentence, as in:

$W\check{o}_1$ $ch\bar{\imath}_2le_3$ $f\grave{a}n_4$ $ji\grave{u}_5$ $z\check{o}u_6$ le_7. "After$_3$ eating$_{2,4}$ I$_1$ (then$_5$) left$_{6,7}$."

The final *le* is here a particle expressing a past event rather than a suffix expressing completed action. In such cases we have to use semantic criteria to decide. But it is possible to test our decision by, for example, substituting for the final action verb another action verb with an object. Then, if *le* comes after the object, we know by formal criteria that *le* is a particle, otherwise *-le* would come between the verb and its object.

$T\bar{a}_1$ $ch\bar{\imath}_2le_3$ $f\grave{a}n_6$, $ji\grave{u}_5$ $k\grave{a}n_6$ $b\grave{a}o_7$ le_8. "After$_3$ eating$_{2,4}$ (then$_5$) he$_1$ read$_{6,8}$ the newspaper$_7$."
$T\bar{a}$ *mǎile zìdiǎn, jiù huí jiā le.* "After buying the dictionary, he returned home."

Since in these two sentences the final *le* is established as being a particle by formal criteria, we can deduce that *le* above after *zǒu* must also be a particle, since the pattern of all these sentences is the same.

From a structural point of view the particle *le* is in construction with the whole of the preceding phrase, and if we divide a sentence with a particle into immediate constituents, the particle will be one immediate constituent and the rest of the sentence the other constituent. However, with the suffix *-le* the opposite is true: only when the immediate constituents (IC) analysis is carried into the structure of the words do we split the suffix *-le* from the verb it is attached to.

The verb to which the suffix *-le* is attached may be a compound verb, for example a verb with a resultative complement:

$T\bar{a}_1$ $k\grave{a}n_2w\acute{a}nle_3$ $li\acute{a}ngb\check{e}n_4$ $sh\bar{u}_5$. "He$_1$ finished$_3$ reading$_2$ two$_4$ books$_5$."

If the verb has a resultative complement, the idea of completed action is already present, and therefore the suffix *-le* is very common after such compounds.

The compound verb may also be one which etymologically consists of verb and object. Still *-le* comes after the compound and cannot split it. Example:

$Sh\acute{e}i_1$ $ch\bar{u}b\check{a}n_2le_3$ $zh\grave{e}ib\check{e}n_4$ $sh\bar{u}_5$. "Who$_1$ has$_3$ published$_2$ this$_4$ book$_5$?"

The form **chūle bǎn* does not occur.

Just as the suffix *-le* for the perfective aspect is very frequently attached to verbs with resultative complements, it also readily combines with certain verbs, such as *wàng* "forget" or *sǐ* "die", as in:

Wǒ₁ wàng₂le₃ dài₄ biǎo₅le₆. "I₁ forgot₂,₃,₆ to put₄ on (my) wrist watch₅."
Tā fùqin sǐle. "His father has died."

The negated form of a verb with suffix *-le* is *méiyou* (or only *méi*) + the verb (occurring without *-le*), for example:

Tā méiyou kàn bào/Tā méi kàn bào. "He has not read the newspaper."

Corresponding to the alternative question pattern verb + *bu* + verb, there is a pattern where *méiyou* or *méi* + verb expresses the second alternative. Thus a question containing a verb with suffix *-le* can take several forms:

Tā kànle bào ma. "Has he read the paper?"
Tā kànle bào meiyou. (most common)
Tā kànle bào mei kan. (rare)

However, this use of *méiyou* to form an alternative question is not limited to sentences with the suffix *-le*. It may occur in a sentence in which there might have been a suffix *-le*, as in:

Tā₁ duì₂ ni₃ shuō₄ zhèijiàn₅ shì₆ meiyou₇. — Shuōle. "Did₇ he₁ discuss₄ this₅ matter₆ with₂ you₃ or not₇? — Yes, he did."

Further, the *méiyou* pattern may actually occur in sentences that have the particle *le* rather than the suffix *-le*:

Nǐ mǎi shū le meiyou. "Did you buy books?"
Nǐ yǐjīng niàn dàxué le meiyou. "Have you already attended college?"
Nǐ kànjian Ālǐ le meiyou. "Have you seen Ali?"

Negative answers to these questions are expressed by *méi(you)* + the verb. But the normal negation of a sentence with the particle *le* is simply *bu* before the verb (while retaining the particle at the end), as in:

Wǒ₁ bù₂ chī₃ le₄. "I₁'m not₂ eating₃ any more₄."
Bú xià le. "It is not raining (or snowing) any more."

To explain the use of *méiyou* as the negation of a predicate followed by the particle *le*, one must assume some kind of overlap of function between the particle and the suffix. Such overlap occurs when there is completed action in the verb (the requirement for the use of the suffix *-le*) and when it refers to some past occurrence (one of the functions of the particle *le*). The clue can be said to lie in the words "any more" in the English translation of the examples with *bu* and the particle *le*. For when the particle *le* is used in a clear-cut case of "new situation", the verb must be negated by *bu*, even if the sentence refers to the past. An example is

Hòulái$_1$ *bàba*$_2$ *bú*$_3$ *fàng*$_4$ *yáng*$_5$ *le*$_6$. "Afterwards$_1$ papa$_2$ did$_6$n't$_3$ herd$_4$ sheep$_5$ any more$_6$."

To further illustrate this difference between the two functions of the particle *le*, let us consider the sentence *Xià yǔ le*. "It's raining now." We can ask the question: "Is it raining now?"

Xià yǔ le ma.

But another possible question is:

Xià yǔ le meiyou.

To make the difference clear, we must translate the latter as: "Had it started to rain?" where the particle *le* indicates a new situation (it did not rain before), but also that this has happened in the past, which is made explicit by *méiyou*. If, on the other hand, we take the negative *Bú xià le* "It is not raining any more", and turn it into a question, the only possibility would be: *Bú xià le ma*. This would also be the question corresponding to the second question above referring to the past (there cannot be a **Bú xià le meiyou*.), and then it would mean: "Didn't it rain any more?"

Finally, in the case of new situation with quality verbs, the same conditions apply. Consider the following:

Tā fùqin bìngle sānnián. Tā xiànzài hǎo le. "His father was sick for three years. Now he is well again."

Asking about the father's present condition, we have two possibilities:

Tā xiànzài hǎo le meiyou.
Tā xiànzài hǎo le ma.

Since both refer to the present (*xiànzài* = now), the difference must be contained in the possible different functions of *hǎo*. In addition to being a normal quality verb "be well", it may tend towards being an action verb "recover". Thus the preferred translations are: "Has he recovered now?" and "Is he well now?" respectively. This leads us back to the first sentence: *Tā xiànzài hǎo le.* in which the use of *le* as particle for new situation was taken for granted. Now we see that it can be very close in function to the suffix *-le* for the perfective aspect.

An expression consisting of a verb + *-le* followed by a simple object is an incomplete utterance; something else is expected to follow. Consider for example: *wǒ chīle fàn* "after eating". For the sequence to be complete, the particle *le* is a minimum supplement:

Wǒ chīle fàn le. "I have eaten."

Similarly

Wǒ zuótian jièle shū, "After I borrowed books yesterday, . . ."

creates an expectation of something to follow. If, however, the object is modified by a sequence indicating a quantity, the case is different:

Wǒ zuótian jièle liǎngběn shū. "Yesterday I borrowed two books."

This makes a complete sentence, so the expectation that something will follow exists only when the object is *simple*, with no quantitative modifications.

Whenever a sentence expressing past time relation has an object that is quantified − as in the example above − the verb almost without exception requires the suffix *-le*:

Hǎiwá fàngle liù nián yáng. "Haiwa herded sheep for six years."

where "six years" is a quantitative modification of *yáng* "sheep". If this sentence had the particle *le* at the end, the meaning would be "Haiwa has been herding sheep for six years now."
Other examples:

Tā niànle sānnián Zhōngwén. "He studied Chinese for three years."
Tā niànle sānnián Zhōngwén le. "He has been studying Chinese for three years."

The suffix *-le* expresses the perfective aspect of the verb. But sometimes the fact that the action expressed by a verb is completed will be obvious for other reasons, even in the absence of the suffix. Thus, for example, if a time word indicating past time, such as *zuótian* "yesterday" or *qùnian* "last year", is included, *-le* is not necessary and is less likely to occur than in a sentence without such a time reference.

Wǒ zuótian yùjian ta le. "I met him yesterday."

Here there is no suffix, but instead the particle *le* for a past event. Similarly:

Tā jīntian zǎochen shàng fēijī le. "He took the plane this morning."

In both of these examples it is worth noting that the object is simple and unmodified. If the object in the first example is quantified, we get instead:

Wǒ zuótian yùjianle hěn duō péngyou. "I met a lot of friends yesterday."

Here the quantified object requires that the suffix *-le* follow the verb, and the specific time reference *zuótian* renders superfluous the use of the particle *le* at the end of the sentence, as this use of the particle – after verb + *le* + *quantified object*, as we saw above, usually indicates the continuance of some action or state of affairs.

One can already see how many different types of considerations determine the use or non-use of both the suffix and the particle *le*. There are considerations of time relation or completion of action which are further influenced by the use or non-use of specific time reference. Further, there is the consideration of the *form* of the object (quantified or not). In addition to these and other factors, there are the more subtle nuances of meaning, as can be seen, for instance, in the following examples:

Nǐ chī fàn le ma.
Nǐ chīle fàn le ma.

The former means "Have you eaten?", and is often used as a greeting. The latter could, in addition, mean "Have you already eaten? (if not, would you join us?)". Similarly we have nuances in

Nǐ kàn bào le meiyou.
Nǐ kànle bào le meiyou.

The former translates as: "Did you see the paper (it is really interesting today)?". The latter could be translated the same way, but also as "Have you finished reading the paper (can I have it now)?".

The negative imperative in Chinese with *bié* "don't" similarly operates with both the suffix and the particle *le* to express differing meanings. Thus we have:

Bié kǎn shù le! "Don't cut trees (any longer) (= stop cutting!)."
Bié kǎnle nèikē shù! "Don't cut that tree."

Bié hē shuǐ le! "Don't drink water (any longer)."
Bié hēle shuǐ! "Don't choke on water (now that you are swimming)."
Qiántou yóu gǒu, kànjian le meiyou. Bié pèngle gǒu. "Further ahead is a dog, do you see it? Don't hit it!"

The negative imperative with the particle *le* refers to an ongoing action which the agent is told to break off, but the use of the suffix puts emphasis on the object: one is told not to perform a given action upon a certain object. In other words, in the latter case the object is specific, whereas in the former case it is not; the main concern is with the action itself.

In a sentence referring to the future, like

Wǒ jīnnian bìyè le. "I'll graduate this year."

it may seem reasonable to take *le* to be a suffix, indicating completed action in the future: "I will have graduated", but examples with verb and object show that *le* comes after the object, as in

Wǒ jiù yào chī fàn le. "I'm about to eat."
Wǒmen kuài yào shàng kè le. "We're going to class."

This shows that the particle *le* is used to indicate imminent future action, usually combined with *jiù, yào* or *kuài*.

It has been shown that there are cases in which an intransitive action verb appears at the end of the sentence with a *le*, and that it seems difficult to determine whether the *le* is a suffix or a particle. Sometimes it is both, in that one *le* represents a sequence of the suffix *and* the particle. In:

Tā yǐjīng zǒu le. "He has already left."

le may be, depending on the context, both the suffix expressing completed action and the particle indicating that the event is in the past. Logically the sentence should therefore read

*Tā yǐjīng zǒule le.

but there is a resistance to having two consecutive forms *le*, and they are combined into one *le* by *haplology*.

To summarize some of the basic points made in this section, the most common functions of *le* are listed below. (V = verb, O = object, mod. = modification or quantification, -le = suffix, le = particle).

V le	new situation (p. 118)
V O le	indefinite past (p. 118)
V-le O le	completed action in the past (p. 122)
V-le O, V	completed action before some future action (p. 117)
V-le O, V le	completed action in the past (p. 119)
V-le mod. O	completed action some time in past (p. 122), or in the present (p. 122).
V-le mod. O le	completed action and continued action (p. 122)
Kuài V le	imminent future action (p. 124)
Bié V O le	imperative stressing *action* itself (p. 123)
Bié V-le O	imperative stressing *object* of action (p. 123)

3. DURATIVE ASPECT SUFFIX *-ZHE*

Zhe is the verbal suffix for non-perfective or durative aspect. It is often translated as the *-ing* form of English, as in

> $Tā_1$ $zài_2$ $wǒ_3$ $qiánbian_4$ $zuò_5zhe_6$. "He$_1$ is$_6$ sitting$_{5,6}$ in$_2$ front$_4$ of me$_3$."
> $Tā_1$ $ná_2zhe_3$ $yìběn_4$ $huà_5bào_6$. "He$_1$ is$_3$ hold$_2$ing$_3$ an$_4$ illustrated$_5$ magazine$_6$."

Frequently a sentence with verb + *-zhe* has a particle *ne* at the end, which reinforces the idea of an action that continues or is progressive:

> *Wǒ tīngzhe lùyīn ne.* "I am listening to a recording."
> *Wǒ chīzhe fàn ne.* "I am eating."

Zhe is less frequent than *-le*, and is often facultative. Durative action may be expressed by means other than suffixation by *-zhe*. Adverbs like *zhèngzài, zhèng* or *zài* may be placed in front of the verb:

> *Wǒmen zhèngzài shàng kè.* "We are attending a class."
> *Nǐ zài gàn shémmo.* "What are you doing?"
> *Wǒ jìnqu de shíhou, tā zhèng gěi háizimen jiǎng gùshi ne.* "When I went in, she was telling the children a story."

The last example has the particle *ne* at the end, to stress the durative aspect. Sometimes ongoing action is expressed merely by the use of the particle *ne*:

> *Tāmen láodòng ne.* "They are working."

In the case of two concomitant actions expressed by two different verbs, the first verb, with *-zhe*, denotes the ongoing action, while the second verb, without *-zhe*, indicates the action that occurs during the course of the first action:

Wǒ$_1$ chī$_2$zhe$_3$ fàn$_4$ niàn shū$_5$. "I$_1$ study$_5$ while$_3$ eat$_{2,4}$ing$_3$."
Hǎiwá yímiàn chuānzhe yīfu, yímiàn shuō. "While putting on his clothes, Haiwa spoke (said)."

Another pattern involving two verbs, one with *-zhe*, the other without *-zhe*, is the case where the first verb, with *-zhe*, gives the condition under which the action of the main verb occurs. The verb with *-zhe* thus functions subordinatively in relation to the central, as in:

Zhèige$_1$ shì$_2$, kànzhe$_3$ hǎo$_4$ zuò$_5$. "This$_1$ job$_2$, when you look at it$_3$, is easy$_4$ to do$_5$."
Nǐmen$_1$ dōu$_2$ kànzhe$_3$ bù$_4$ guǎn$_5$. "You$_1$ all$_2$ see$_3$ (what's the matter) but don't$_4$ do$_5$ anything (about it)!"

Zhe may be used to indicate a *state* or *condition* which is the remaining result of the action indicated in the verb:

Nèiběn$_1$ zìdiǎn$_2$shàng$_3$ xiě$_4$zhe$_5$ tā de$_6$ míngzi$_7$. "On$_3$ that$_1$ dictionary$_2$ is$_5$ written$_4$ his$_6$ name$_7$."
Chénglóu$_1$shàng$_2$ gāo$_3$ xuán$_4$zhe$_5$ guó$_6$huī$_7$. "High$_3$ on$_2$ the rostrum$_1$ is$_5$ hang$_4$ing$_5$ the national$_6$ emblem$_7$."
Chuānghu kāizhe, mén méi kāizhe. "The windows are open, but the door is not."

The last example introduces the negated form of a verb with *-zhe*. Like a verb with suffix *-le*, a verb with suffix *-zhe* is negated by *méi*, but unlike the former, the negated verb retains the attached durative suffix.

Tā$_1$ shǒu$_2$li$_3$ méi$_4$ názhe$_5$ dōngxi$_6$. "He$_1$ is not$_4$ holding$_5$ anything$_6$ in$_3$ his hand$_2$."

Zhe is often used, as is the *-ing* form in English, when the verbal action itself is the topic of discussion, i.e. when the verb forms part of the sentence subject:

Zǒuzhe lù shuōzhe huà, hén yǒu yìsi. "Walking and talking are very interesting."

All examples so far have shown *-zhe* after action verbs, but occasionally it is used after verbs expressing a quality or state of being, as in:

Wŏ bìngzhe ne hái déi kǎoshì. "I'm sick but still have to take the exam."
Tā zài jiā mángzhe zuò fàn ne. "She's busy cooking at home."

In the first example, too, the idea of continuance is clearly important, although here it is the state of being sick, rather than the performance of some action, which is emphasized.

Tā₁ máng₂zhe₃ dào₄ huŏchēzhàn₅ qù₆. "He₁ is₃ in a hurry₂ to go₆ to₄ the railway station₅."
Tā jízhe xūyào yìběn Zhōng-Yīng zìdiǎn. "He urgently needs a Chinese-English dictionary."

In these two examples the quality verbs with *-zhe* function adverbially in the sentence, and therefore in a sense resemble the cases mentioned above: *Nǐmen dōu kànzhe bù guān.*, etc.

There are many cases involving the pattern: quality-verb + *-zhe* + *ne*:

Zhèige duō zhene. "There is an awful lot of this!"
Xié hēi zhene. "The shoes are really black."
Jīntian de cér kě duō zhene. "There sure are a lot of (new) words today."

These appear to be similar cases of *-zhe* following quality verbs as suffix. But here the function of *zhe* is different; in construction with *ne* it *intensifies* the meaning of the verb. The difference becomes clear in the following examples:

Wó xiǎngzhe ni ne. "I'm thinking of you."
Wó xiǎng ni zhene. "I miss you terribly."

In the second example the *zhe* comes after the object and cannot, therefore, be a suffix, as it is in the first example. The constellation *zhene*, with an intensifying function, is a phrase *particle*. Like the particle *le* it comes at the end of the phrase or sentence. The same is also true of the three examples above with quality verbs, i.e. intensifying function, and *zhene* at the end of the sentence; therefore we have a particle rather than the suffix *-zhe* in those examples.

The last example involved a transitive verb with an object. In the case of a quality verb followed by *zhene*, it is harder to decide whether it is the particle or the suffix unless the meaning of the sentence is known. Consider this sentence:

Tāng rè zhe ne. "The soup is awfully hot."

If the context or the facultative pause gives this meaning, then *zhene* is a sentence particle. But it could also mean "The soup is being heated.", where *rè* functions causatively rather than as a quality verb. In this latter case, *-zhe* is the suffix followed by the phrase particle *ne*.

Finally, *-zhe* often follows verbs in the imperative, both in the positive, as in:

Názhe. "Hold on to it!"
Dàizhe màozi. "Wear a hat!"
Mànzhe. "Slow!"

and in the negative:

Bié lǎo zhànzhe. "Don't stand there all the time!"

Certain verbs are almost always followed by *-zhe*: *jìzhe* "remember", *xiàngzhe* "be on the side of". Some have a different meaning when they are followed by *-zhe* as compared with the zero-suffix form. Examples: *xiězhe* "is written", *xuánzhe* (or *guàzhe*) "is hanging", *kāizhe* "is open", used with a non-personal subject. A rather special case is *yìwèizhe* "mean, have the meaning of", which has recently been formed from the noun *yìwèi*, and which always occurs with the suffix *-zhe*.

4. INDEFINITE PAST ASPECT SUFFIX *-GUO*

The verbal suffix *-guo* has been called the "experiential suffix" because its main function is to indicate that the action expressed by the verb has been experienced some time in the past:

Tā yǐqián qùguo Zhōngguó. "He has been to China."
Nǐ chīguo Rìběn fàn ma. "Have you (ever) eaten Japanese food?"

This function is also referred to as the suffix for the indefinite past aspect,

$Tā_1$ $fānyi_2guo_3$ $yìběn_4$ $shū_5$. "He_1 has_3 $translated_2$ a_4 $book_5$ (some time in the $past_3$)."

The difference between this suffix for the *indefinite* past and the suffix *-le* for completed action, is seen in these examples:

Wó mǎile yìben yǒumíng de xiǎoshuō. "I have bought a famous novel."
Wó mǎiguo yìben yǒumíng de xiǎoshuō. "I (once) bought a famous novel."

Wǒ shuāiduànguo tuǐ. "I broke my leg (once)."
Wǒ shuāiduànle tuǐ le. "I have broken my leg (and it is still broken)."

The same difference comes out in negated examples,

Tā méi lái. "He hasn't come.", versus:
Tā méi láiguo. "He hasn't been here."

As in the case of the suffix *-zhe*, the negated form in connection with *-guo* is *méi* + the verb + *-guo*.

> *Tā méi chīguo Zhōngguó fàn.* "He has never eaten Chinese food."
> *Tā zhǐ xuéguo Yīngwén, méi xuéguo Zhōngwén.* "He has only studied English, not Chinese."

This suffix *-guo* is, semantically and historically, a reduced form, etymologically evolved from the action verb *guò* "to pass", as in:

> *Nǐ xiān guò sānge lùkǒur.* "First, you pass three intersections."

In an intermediate position between the semantically "full" verb and the semantically "empty" suffix, there is the directional complement *guo*, which in certain cases of extended use is hard to distinguish from the suffix. But whereas the suffix *always* has neutral tone, the complement has *facultative* neutral tone. Sometimes the difference is clear according to the formal criteria of position:

> *Wó dǎbuguò tā.* "I cannot beat him (in this game)."

This example contains the potential form of the resultative complement.

> *Nǐ₁ yǐjīng₂ zǒu₃guo₄le₅ túshūguǎn₆.* "You₁ have₅ already₂ walked₃ past₄ the library₆."

Here it is evident from its position before the object (*túshūguǎn*) that *-le* is a suffix and not a sentence particle. From this it can be deduced that *guo* cannot be the suffix: Suffixes are mutually exclusive (p. 116). Therefore, *guo* is here to be taken as a directional complement, a conclusion which also fits the semantic relationship well.

The hardest cases are those where *guo* as a complement follows verbs which one does not expect to take *directional* complements, that is, verbs which are not verbs of motion (see p. 182). In such cases, of course, *guo* is not strictly a *directional* complement, but is used rather to indicate the "passing" of time, or the completion or *result* of some action, but going further than the suffix *-le* in emphasizing the completed result. So although the *function* of this *guo* is closer to that of a suffix the formal criteria of optional zero stress and position in the sentence place it in the category of complements. To illustrate the difference between this last kind of complement and the suffix *-guo*:

> *Nǐ chīguo lǐyú meiyou./Chīguo.* "Have you ever eaten carp?/Yes, I have."
> *Nǐ chīguole lǐyú meiyou./Chīguole.* "Have you finished eating your carp (yet)?/Yes, I have (and I am ready for the next course)."

These two examples, the former with the suffix *-guo* and the latter with the complement *guo* followed by the suffix *-le*, have different meanings. The same holds for the answers to the questions. Its position (verb + *guo* + *le* + object) shows that *guo* could not be a suffix, since *-le* must be the suffix appearing before the object, and since there cannot be two consecutive suffixes. But sentences such as the following may present a problem:

> *Wǒ jīntian dàoguo túshūguǎn le.* "I have been to the library today."
> *Nǐ zuótian zhǎoguo Máo xiānsheng le ma./Wǒ méi zhǎoguo ta.* "Did you visit Mr. Mao yesterday?/I didn't visit him."

A positional analysis (verb + *guo* + object + *le*) leaves us with two possibilities: *guo* is either suffix or complement in the extended usage. It has been pointed out that the suffix *-guo* indicates the *indefinite* past aspect of the verb. The two examples above, however, have definite time references (*jīntian, zuótian*).[1]

It seems most consistent to assume that *guo* is, in this case, the same kind of complement as that which occurred in the previous examples, although clearly there is a transitional category between a very weakened complement and a suffix. This is a reflection of the etymological relationship between the verb (*guò*), the directional complement (*guo*), the weakened form of this complement, and the suffix (*-guo*).

There are certain restrictions on the use of the suffix. It is most frequent with action verbs; it is rare after quality verbs. An example of the latter is:

> *Cónglái méiyou zhèmmo hǎoguo.* "It has never been so good before."

Here *hǎo*, if it is a quality verb, takes on another feature typical of action verbs, i.e. the use of *méiyou* for negation in the past.

---

[1] This use of time reference may, however, also be seen as the framework in which something may happen at an *unspecified* point in time, as in: *Jīnnian cǎoméi hái méi shàngguo shì ne.* "Strawberries have not yet been on the market *this year*."

In the sentence *Nèige háizi, gāo guò tā mǔqin le*. "That child is taller than her mother." *guò* is not a suffix, nor a complement, but the full verb *guò*. This is brought out in a more literal translation: "That child, when it comes to height (*gāo*), surpasses (*guò*) her mother."

Like the suffix *-le*, *-guo* also occurs after verbal complement compounds:

Nǐ kànjianguo tā huà de huàr ma. "Have you ever seen the painting he has done?"
Wǒ shuāiduànguo tuǐ. "I broke my leg (once)."

5. INCHOATIVE ASPECT SUFFIX *-QILAI*

The suffix *-qilai* for inchoative aspect indicates that the action of the verb, or the state expressed by it, is beginning to take place:

Tāmen$_1$ wár$_2$zhe$_3$ wár$_2$zhe$_3$ hūrán$_4$ kū$_5$qilai$_6$ le$_7$. "They$_1$ were$_3$ play$_2$ing$_3$ and play$_2$ing$_3$ and suddenly$_4$ start$_6$ed$_7$ to cry$_5$".
Liǎngge háizi dǎqilai le. "The two children began to fight."

In these two examples *-qilai* combines with intransitive action verbs, but it is also very common after quality verbs:

Tiānqi mànmārde nuǎnhuoqilai le. "The weather has slowly started to get mild."
Tā pàngqilai le. "He has begun to get fat."

When the verbs taking *-qilai* are transitive, there is a strong tendency for the logical "object" to appear in a preverbal position, as a topic for the sentence, rather than as an object after the verb. Probably the length of the verbal expression, with a verb + a compound suffix, accounts for this phenomenon, which is illustrated in:

Nèihuí shìqing, nǐ yī tíqilai wǒ jiù shēng qì. "Every time you (start to) mention that incident, I get angry."
Yǔyánxué, yánjiuqilai hén yǒu yìsi. "Studying linguistics is very interesting."

But there are exceptions to this avoidance of an object in the post-central position:

Nǐ tíqilai nèige rén, wó yě rènshi. "As you (start to) mention that man, I also know him."

The example above about "studying linguistics" illustrates a special and frequent function of -*qilai*, which was also found in the suffix -*zhe* (p. 126): it is used when the verb to which it is attached is the topic of a sentence:

Zuò chē hěn jìn. Zǒuqilai hén yuǎn. "It's close if you go by car, but quite far if you walk."
Zuò Zhōngguo fàn, xuéqilai hěn róngyi. "Learning how to cook Chinese food is very easy."

Also like the suffix -*zhe* (p. 126) the suffix -*qilai* often serves to subordinate the verb it follows to another verb (central) in the sentence, and in so doing states the condition under which the action indicated by the central verb is valid or not valid:

Tuánjiéqilai, wǒmen yídìng néng qǔdé gèng dà de shènglì. "By uniting together we shall certainly be able to reach even greater victories."
Kànqilai, zhèijiàn shìqing hěn máfan. "On examination this matter is quite a nuisance."
Zèmmo xuéqilai, ní hěn kuài jiù huì le. "By studying in this way you will master it very quickly."

As is the case with *guo*, *qilai* can also overlap as both a full verb and a directional complement in addition to being a suffix. The full verb *qǐlai* means "get up, rise", as in:

Ní zǎochen shémmo shíhou qǐlai. "When do you get up in the morning?"

The directional complement *qilai* as a rule follows a verb of motion and indicates upward movement, as in:

Wǒmen yíkuàr náqilai ba. "Let's lift it together."

The problems appear when the directional complement takes on functions one would expect to see expressed by the suffix, but retains the various relational characteristics of a complement. A rather intriguing example is:

Zhèi₁ jǐtian₂ suóyǒude₃ dōngxi₄ dōu₅ guì₆qilai₇ le₈. Dàgài₉ jiù shì₁₀ chī de dōngxi₁₁ guì₁₂buqǐlai₁₃. "All₃,₅ things₄ have been₈ getting₇ expensive₆ these₁ days₂. Probably₉ only₁₀ food₁₁ can't get₁₃ expensive₁₂."

The first sentence clearly contains the suffix, since the construction of a quality verb + *qilai* is quite common. But the expression *guìbuqǐlai* has the form of a potential complement compound with *qǐlai* as complement even though the semantic function seems to be the same as in the first sentence.[1]

There are more instances of such "suffix-like" functions and "complement-like" shapes:

Yí kànwán diànyǐng, dàjiā jiù tánqi kàn diànyǐng de gánxiǎng lai le. "As soon as we had seen the film, we began to talk about what we thought of it."

The splitting of *qilai* by an object (verb + *qi* + object + *lai*) is a typical complement pattern, and is excluded in the case of a suffix. But the inchoative function — typical of the suffix *-qilai* — is present here.

The lack of clear-cut distinctions in every single case between suffix and complement is — as was pointed out earlier in connection with *guo* — a result of the continuous development of a living language. Logically and historically speaking, the starting point is the *verb*, which is "full" of semantic meaning. The next step is the *complement*, where this "fullness" is gradually reduced. The grammatically formalized function is ever more present in the extended, suffix-like uses of the complement. The end result is the "pure" suffix.

B. Reduplication

Reduplication of verbs consists in repetition of the verb, usually with tonal modification. If the original verb is of more than one syllable, the reduplication can take various forms.

There are two different kinds of verbal reduplication: one which occurs with action verbs and another which occurs with quality verbs.

1. REDUPLICATION OF ACTION VERBS

This kind of reduplication has been treated as an aspect suffix for the *tentative* aspect, but it differs from other suffixes in that each verb has its own form, namely the same form as the verb it is attached to, whereas with the other verbal suffixes there is a single suffix for each aspect, which is attached to all types of verbs.

---

[1] One can easily imagine, however, that the idea of "rising" prices here has caused *qilai* to function as a complement, and turned *guì* into something more of an action verb expressing the process of "getting expensive".

Examples of reduplication as the tentative aspect suffix:

Wŏ shuōshuo, nĭ kàn duì buduì. "I'll try to say it, you see if it is correct or not."
Nĭ yídìng néng huídá zhèige wèntí, zài xiángxiang. "You certainly can answer this question, (try and) think again."

Here the tentative aspect function is clearly present. But often reduplication seems simply to imply repetition of the action expressed by the verb:

Jīntian de kèwén bĭjiào nán, wŏ yào duō fùxifuxi. "Today's lesson is relatively hard, I have to review it a bit more."

The morphological process of reduplication of action verbs should not be confused with the syntactic construction of verb + cognate object, where the cognate object contains a form which is identical with the verb. Examples:

Nèikè yúfă wŏ méi tīngdŏng, lǎoshī yòu géi wó jiăngle jiăng. "I didn't understand that grammar lesson so the teacher explained it to me a little more."
Wŏmen zài zhèr zuò yizuo, hăo bu hăo. "Let's sit here a while, OK?"

Cognate objects, which are discussed elsewhere (see p. 194), are clearly differentiated from reduplication, either by means of the verbal suffix -*le* or by use of the numeral *yi*. Reduplication, being a morphological process, does not permit any such insertion. However, although the structural differences are thus clear enough, it is interesting to note that the function of this type of cognate object frequently overlaps with that of reduplication. Compare the following example, which contains both reduplication and verb + cognate object:

Jīntian wănshang qĭng nín dào wŏ jiā lái zuò yizuo tántan. "Please come to my home tonight to sit and chat for a while."

2. Reduplication of Quality Verbs

When quality verbs are reduplicated, an intensification of the quality is implied. Thus, reduplication is used in the exhortation:

Hǎohāo xuéxí. "Study well!"

A common feature of reduplication of quality verbs is that the tone of the reduplicate is changed to first tone, if it is not already first tone.

Whereas reduplicated action verbs retain their functions as action verbs, reduplicated quality verbs are *usually* transformed into adverbials, most commonly with the adverbial marker *-de*. If the quality verb is a monosyllable, it very often takes the form: verb + verb + suffix *-r*. Compare, for instance, the above example with the following:

Ní déi hǎohārde niàn shū. "You must study really well."

When dissyllabic quality verbs are reduplicated, however, such phonetic modification does not usually take place. For example:

Háizimen gāogāoxìngxìngde dào xuéxiào qù le. "The children went happily to school."

Notice also that first the initial syllable is repeated, and then the second. Earlier it was shown that *fùxi* "to review" was reduplicated differently: *fùxifuxi*.

Tā yào qù chēzhàn jiē yíge péngyou, zǎozāorde jiù zǒule. "He had to go to the station to meet a friend, so he left very early/a long time ago already."
Wó₁ yuǎnyuārde₂ jiù₃ kànjian₄ ta₅ wàng₆ zhèr₇ lái₈ le₉. "From far off₂ I₁ saw₄,₉ him₅ coming₈ this way₆,₇."

In these two examples we see the reduplicated form functioning more as a verb than as an adverbial, although it is subordinate in relation to the central verb after *jiù*. It functions here as a quality verb, giving the condition or state of affairs under which the agent performs the action of the main verb: "it was early" when he left; and "I was far away" when I saw him.

A reduplicated quality verb can also occur as the central of a sentence, as in

Ní zěmmo lǎo nèmmo húlihútūde. "How come you are always so muddleheaded?"

Húlihútūde, which is the reduplicated form of *hútū* "muddled", shows a pattern of partial reduplication, sometimes used with onomatopoetic function. In *Kuàikuārde!* "Hurry up!" and in *Hǎohāorde!* "Be good!" the reduplicated verb is the central verb of the imperative sentence.

C. Verbal Compounds

1. GENERAL

As a rule the component parts of a verbal compound are not separable by other morphemes, just as verbal suffixes are not separable from the verbs. However, many verbal compounds are formed from verb + object constructions, which on occasion may function as regular verb + object *phrases*, which means that the verb may take a suffix or a complement, while the object may take various modifiers. In cases where this happens, we deal with *actual* verb + object *phrases*, even though we still refer to the verb + object as a compound when, for example, we give its meaning. Thus we say that the compound *fānshēn* means "to emancipate", literally "to turn the body", but in the clause *tā fānle shēn yǐhòu* "after he was emancipated", we are dealing with a verb in the completed action aspect, which takes an object *shēn*.

The important point here is that *fānshēn* has a somewhat special meaning: one does not think in terms of literally "turning over one's body", as one would literally think of "buying books" in the case of *mǎi shū*. Further, the object of *mǎi* can take an appropriate modifier. But that is not true of *shēn* in *fānshēn*.

2. VERB + OBJECT COMPOUNDS

It is mostly with verbal compounds of verb + object form, which are themselves – *as* compound verbs – *action verbs*, that separation of the components is regular. As soon as the verbal verb + object compound takes on the function of a *quality* verb, the components will not normally be separated. Take, for example, *dǒngshì*, literally "to understand things", a quality verb "to be sensible":

> *Zhèige háizi jiǎnjiār dǒngshìqilai le.* "This child is gradually becoming sensible."
> *Nǐ zěmmo zhèmmo bù dǒngshì a.* "How can you be so senseless?"

Similarly with *àiguó*, literally "love country", a quality verb "to be patriotic", as in:

> *Nèige rén hěn àiguó.* "That person is very patriotic."

But in the sentence *Nǐ bú ài nǐ de guójiā ma.* "Don't you love your country?", *ài* is a transitive quality verb taking an object.

Huáiyí, literally "harbor doubt", i.e. "be skeptical about, to doubt", can be used both transitively and intransitively:

Wó hěn huáiyí ní nèige shuōfǎ. "I very much doubt your theory."
Wǒ duìyú ní nèige shuōfǎ hěn huáiyí. "About your theory I am very doubtful."

The same applies to *zhùyì*, literally "fix attention", i.e. "pay attention to, watch", as in:

Qíng ní zhùyì nèige háizi! "Please watch that child!"

The components of *zhùyì*, however, can be separated to form a verb + object phrase: *zhù yìdiǎr yì* "pay a little attention", where the object is modified.

3. SUBORDINATIVE COMPOUNDS

The compound *xiàohuà*, literally "laugh + words", is *not* a V-O compound meaning "to laugh words, laugh". The components of this compound stand in a relation of *subordination*, the first modifying the second. As a verb this compound means "to laugh at".

Verbal compounds of this structure are usually exocentric. Further, unlike V-O compounds, the components cannot be separated by other morphemes.[1]

Whereas a V-O compound always consists of a verb and an object, when analyzed morphologically, a subordinative compound can consist of different combinations. *Xiàohuà* is action verb + noun, which is rare in this category, *xiǎobiàn* is quality verb + noun, which is very frequent. Both of these compounds are action verbs, while *xiǎoxin* — literally "small mind/heart", i.e. "careful", also quality verb + noun — is a quality verb.

The form *guīdìng*, literally "rule-determine", i.e. "regulate, fix," etc., is analyzed as noun + action verb, and the resulting compound is itself an action verb. Similarly with *yóuzhá*, "oil fry", i.e. "deep fry".

---

[1] This difference becomes very natural when one considers the respective structures of *verb + object* and *subordination*. A V-O compound lends itself to separation by suffix or modification of the object to such an extent that sometimes compounds that are not even V-O in structure are split as if they were! Thus for instance, the *subordinative* compound *xiǎobiàn*, literally "minor convenience", i.e. "to urinate", has been rendered as *xiǎo yìdiǎr biàn* meaning "urinate a bit" (reported by Chao 1968).

The most common subordinative verbal compounds are those in which the last component is a verb. Example: *qīngshì* literally "light-regard", i.e. "regard lightly, despise", which consists of quality verb + action verb.

4. COORDINATIVE COMPOUNDS

Coordinative verbal compounds usually consist of morphemes which are themselves verbs: *qíguài*, lit. "strange + strange", where both parts as well as the compound are quality verbs. *Shībài*, lit. "lose and be defeated", i.e. "to fail", consists of two action verbs, and the compound is also an action verb. In both of these examples we notice that the components have such closely related meanings that they can be said to be synonymous or near-synonymous compounds. *Báoshǒu*, lit. "protect and defend" is also a synonym compound of action verbs, but the compound can be either a quality verb, "to be conservative", or an action verb, "keep, preserve, conserve".

Most *verbal* coordinative compounds consist of synonymous parts, or parts which at least resemble each other in meaning, such as *gānjing*, lit. "dry and clean", which means "clean". An example of a verbal *antonym* compound may be *máodùn*, which literally means "spear and shield", and as an exocentric compound verb means "to be contradictory, inconsistent". *Máodùn* is relatively rare in that two component nouns make up one compound verb. Another example of this is *jiānghú* lit. "rivers and lakes", which is an exocentric verb meaning "to be venturesome, world-wise".

5. SUBJECT + PREDICATE COMPOUNDS

Verbal subject + predicate compounds – like V-O compounds – consist of morphemes that are themselves nouns and verbs, only here the noun comes before the verb. For example, the verb *tóuténg* consists of the noun *tóu* "head" + the verb *téng* "aches", both of which are free words, as illustrated in:

Wǒ tóu hěn téng. "My head aches a lot (or: I have a headache)."

But *tóuténg* is a compound quality verb " to have a headache". It also functions as a transitive quality verb, as in:

Wǒ shízài tóuténg zhèijiàn shì. "I find this thing a real headache."

Another common S-P compound which forms a quality verb is *niánqīng*, lit. "years are light", i.e. "young, youthful", as in

Zhèige rén hěn niánqīng. "This person is very young."

Lùguò, lit. "the road passes, i.e. "go by way of", is a transitive action verb, as in

Wǒ lùguòle Shànghǎi. "I have gone by way of Shanghai."
Ní dǎsuàn lùguò něixiē chéng. "Which cities are you planning to pass on the way?"

6. VERBAL COMPLEMENT COMPOUNDS

Very important types of verbal compounds are the resultative and directional compounds, which contain (resultative and directional) complements. The extent to which the component morphemes of complement compounds can form syntactical relationships in other contexts varies greatly. Some can never occur otherwise than in compounds, others commonly occur in freer syntactical phrases. An example of the former kind is *gǎiliáng*, lit. "change (to) good", i.e. "improve", as in

Gōngrén de shēnghuó hái méi gǎiliáng. "The life of workers still has not improved."

An example of the latter is *chībǎo* "eat (with the result that one is) full", as in

Wó yǐjīng chībǎole. "I'm full already."

But the same morphemes occur in:

Zhèige háizi chī de tài bǎo. "This child eats too much."

Between these two categories of complement compounds there is a third intermediate type in which only the infixes *bu* or *de* may be inserted to make potential complements, such as

tīngbudǒng "(listen but) cannot understand"
tīngbujiàn "(listen but) cannot hear"
chīdexià "(in eating) can get (it) down".

The great majority of resultative verbal complement compounds, when analyzed into their component parts, consist of action verb + quality verb/action verb: *chībǎo* "eat (oneself) full". Directional compounds consist of action verb + action verb: *jìnqu* "go in".

There is still another type of verbal complement compound in which the first morpheme is a quality verb and the second is one of a small group of elements of various origins used as complements. These complements are intensifying rather than resultative, since one cannot think of the *result* of a quality verb. Examples: *hǎojíle* "very good, extremely good", *Wǒ lèsǐle*. "I am thrilled to death.", where *sǐle* functions in the same way as *jíle*. Although these types of verbal complement are *compounds*, they will be treated in detail under Verbal Complements (Chapter VIII, A) together with complement constructions that are not compounds.

CHAPTER VII

VERBAL CLASSES AND FUNCTIONS

A. Classification of Verbs

There are two major classes of *negatables*, or *verbs: description verbs* and *relation verbs*. The former class is open, i.e. it has unlimited membership (the inventory can be listed only in a comprehensive and up-to-date dictionary). Examples: *lái* "come", *mǎi* "buy", *dǎ* "hit", *dà* "be big", *cōngming* "be intelligent", *ài* "love, be fond of".

Relation verbs, on the contrary, form a closed class, with listable membership. Examples: *shì* "to be", *xìng* "be surnamed", *zài* "be at, in, on", *duìyú* "concerning", *néng* "be able to". However, the term "closed" here must not be taken in an absolute sense. There is some movement into this class from the class of description verbs. Example: *dàibiǎo* "representing", which may be a coverb (from the action verb "to represent" or the noun "a delegate"). Similarly there is movement into the class of description verbs from non-verbal classes. Examples: *máodùn* "to be contradictory" (from noun "contradiction"), *guānxi* "to have a vital bearing on" (from noun "relation(ship), importance").

One major function of description verbs is to form predicates or centrals in predicates. They carry full semantic weight, in contradistinction to relation verbs, for which the *grammatical* function takes on an essential importance. Although some of the relation verbs may be, and even usually are, centrals in predicates, they are different from description verbs in that only under certain specific conditions do they form a predicate alone. An exception to this is the case where a relation verb appears as an answer to a question, where what would normally follow is understood from the context. Example: *Nǐ huì bú huì kāi chē. – Bú huì.* "Can you drive? –No, I can't."

The function of relation verbs is to indicate relationships between parts of the sentence in which they occur: 1) the relationship of existence or non-existence (*yǒu* and *méi*), 2) the relationship between the subject and the object (classificatory verbs), 3) the relationship of time, place, etc. that has a bearing upon the action of the main verb of the predicate (coverbs), or 4) modal relationships between the agent/subject and the action/main verb (modal verbs).

Another feature which bears out this difference between description verbs, which carry lexical meaning, and the grammatically significant relation verbs, is that the former can take verbal complements – which serve to elaborate further on certain aspects of the semantic content of the verb, such as the degree of a quality or the result of an action – whereas the relation verbs never take verbal complements, and, further, they rarely take verbal suffixes.

Description verbs often occur as modifiers of nominals. The relationship is either unmarked or marked by the subordinative *-de*.[1] They thus describe the nominal by means of some attributive quality or action. The relation verbs, whose major function is grammatical, cannot generally modify nouns in this manner. Apparent exceptions to this are certain idiomatic phrases with specialized function, such as *suóyǒude* "all", and *shìde* "yes", as an affirmative answer to questions.

There is a great deal of class overlap between the different verb classes. Thus, many relation verbs (especially coverbs) can also function as description verbs. The most important of these will be noted in the following.

B. Relation Verbs

All relation verbs are transitive. As has already been pointed out, a major characteristic of these verbs is that they nearly always occur with objects. Relation verbs are subdivided into four classes according to their specific functions.

1. EXISTENTIAL VERBS *YǑU* AND *MÉI*

The verb *yǒu* is different from all other Chinese verbs in that it is not negatable by *bu*, but instead by the negator *méi*.

---

[1] Examples: *lái de rén* "a person who has arrived", *hǎo rén* "good people".

This negator *méi* must not be confused with the homophonous verb *méi*, which is the *negative verb*, and which therefore cannot itself be negated.

Yǒu expresses existence and *méi* expresses non-existence. Thus the verb *méi* is functionally equivalent to *méi yǒu*.

The relation between the existential verbs *yǒu* and *méi* is shown by the following examples:

Tā yǒu qián. "He has money."
Tā méi qián. "He does not have money."
Tā méi yǒu qián. "He does not have money."

Yǒu and *méi* translate naturally as "has, have" and "has/have not" respectively. To capture the basic existential relationship expressed by *yǒu*, the subject would have to be singled out:

"As for him, there is money."

An extended use of *yǒu* is found in a pattern of comparison:

Ní yé yǒu tā nèmmo hǎo. "You are (also) as good as he is."

This can be negated:

Nǐ méi yǒu tā nèmmo hǎo. "You are not as good as he is."

Nèmmo can be left out, and *méi* can be substituted for *méi yǒu*:

Nǐ méi tā hǎo.

Usually the quality being compared, such as *hǎo* above, is expressed by an intransitive quality verb. But it may consist of longer phrases as well:

Wǒ méi yǒu tā nèmmo xǐhuan kàn shū. "I am not as fond of reading (books) as he is."

Yǒu is also used in a special pattern to emphasize the object in a verb + object phrase, where *chī fàn* "eat (rice =) food", becomes inverted and preceded by *yǒu*:

Tā méi yǒu fàn chī. "He has no food to eat."

Similarly

Wǒ méi yǒu shì zuò. "I have no work to do."
Wó yǐjīng gēn ta shuōle hěn duō huà. Xiànzài méi yǒu huà shuō le.
"I've already talked a lot with him. Now I don't have anything more to say."

But consider the following two examples:

Tā méi yǒu yíge dìfang méi qùguo. "There isn't a place he hasn't been to."

Tā₁ méi₂ yǒu₃ yìtiān₄ bu₅ gēn₆ biérén₇ tǎolùn₈ shèhuìzhǔyì₉ de. "There is₃ not₂ a day₄ when he₁ does not₅ discuss₈ socialism₉ with₆ other people₇."

Although the pattern is similar to the examples above, here we have double negation and verb + object phrases that are not as closely knit as *chī fàn* and *zuò shì.*

A common pattern with *yǒu* is to have a subject indicating place or time, then *yǒu*, and finally the object expressing whatever exists:

Zhètiáo jiēshang yóu hěn duō shāngdiàn. "There are many shops in this street."

Gōngyuánli yǒu shān, yóu shuǐ, yé yǒu shù. "In the park there are hills, water and trees."

Jīntian wǎnshang yǒu kè. "There will be guests tonight."

But often there is no subject:

Yǒu wù. "There is a fog."

Yǒu rén. "There is somebody." or "Occupied."

Méi fázi. "There is no way."/"Nothing can be done (about it)."

Existence is expressed by a different pattern, in which the thing existing appears as the subject of *yǒu*, and there is no object. In this respect *yǒu* is unique among relation verbs, which otherwise always take objects. Still, this use of *yǒu* is restricted to two cases. In the first, several items are listed, e.g.:

Hǎorén yé yǒu, huàirén yé yǒu, shémmo yàng de rén dōu yǒu. "There are good people, there are bad people, there are all sorts of people."

In the second case, *yǒu* has a more specialized function, in the idiomatic use with the particle *le*, where *yǒu le* means "to have appeared", and *méi (yǒu) le* means "to have disappeared, to be finished":

Qìyóu wánquán méi yǒu le. "The gasoline is entirely gone", i.e. "We're out of gas."

Yǒu le. "I've got it!"

Yǒu can also mean "exist" in the more concrete sense of "occur, happen", etc. In such cases *yǒu* is perhaps closer to the class of description verbs. Examples are:

Zhōngguo₁ zàozhǐ₂ cóng₃ Hàn₄cháo₅ jiù₆ yǒu₇ le₈. "Papermaking₂

has₈ existed₇ in China₁ (as early as₆) from₃ the Han₄ dynasty₅ ."
Zhèizhòng shì shì cháng yǒu de. "This kind of thing is something that often exists/happens."
Nèizhòng cuòwu shì hěn huì yǒu de. "That kind of error is something that can very well be – (it is quite a possibility)."

There are also other cases of *yǒu* taking no object. In these cases the "logical object" is placed first in the sentence, as a topic or "big subject":

Shū wó yǒu. "Books, I have."

This pattern is common with transitive description verbs, but is impossible with any other relation verbs. This again shows that *yǒu* is a very versatile verb.

Yǒu without a subject commonly introduces the pivot of a pivotal construction, i.e. the object of *you* is a subject in its turn:

Yǒu rén zài lóuxià zháo ni. "There is someone downstairs looking for you."
Méi yǒu rén bu xǐhuan chī Zhōngguo fàn. "There is no one who does not like (to eat) Chinese food."

In such cases *you* may also have a time or place word as a subject:

Túshūguǎn jīntian méi yǒu rén kàn shū. "There is nobody in the library today reading."

The phrase *you yìdiǎr*, which in form is verb + cognate object, occurs in a pattern followed by quality verbs:

Wǒ zhèi jǐtian yǒu yìdiǎr máng. "I've been a bit busy these past days."
Tā yǒu yìdiǎr xiàng tā muqin. "He looks a bit like his mother."

Yǒu is sometimes added after action verbs which take cognate time objects, as in:

Tā zǒule yǒu sāntian mei you. "Has it been three days since he left?"
Tā zuótian jiáng yǒu sānge zhōngtou. "Yesterday he lectured for three hours."

2. CLASSIFICATORY VERBS

The specific role of classificatory verbs is to express relations between subject and object. There are not many members of this class, but it contains the very common verb *shì* "is, are", which will be discussed in some detail.

a. Shì. *Shì* establishes identity between the (usually) nominal elements between which it occurs:

Sān jiā liù shì jiŭ. "3 plus 6 equals 9."
Míngtian shì xīngqīrì. "Tomorrow is Sunday."
Tā shì shéi. "Who is he?"
Zhè shì shémmo. "What is this?"

Shì is similar to English "is" in another important function, that of specifying the class to which the subject belongs:

Tā shì Zhōngguorén. "He is (a) Chinese."
Wŏmen dōu shì xuésheng. "We are all students."
Zhèibĕn shū shì xīn de. "This book is a new one."
Zhèzhī qiānbĭ búshì hóng de. "This pencil is not a red one."

Another function related to these two is where *shì* merely expresses some vague relation between the subject and the object. Translating *shì* by "is" in these cases will often be misleading. Examples are:

Wŏmen shì liăngge nán háizi yíge nŭ háizi. "We have two boys and one girl."
Nín dōu shì Zhōngwén shū a! "All you have are Chinese books! (i.e. none are English)."
A: *Nín shì dìyícì shàng zhèr lái ma.* B. *Búshì, wŏ shì dièrcì le.* "Is this the first time you have come here?" "No, this is the second time."

In the first two examples *shì* could well be replaced by *yŏu* "there is; has, have", since the relation is one regularly expressed by *yŏu*. This is not the only function of *yŏu* which *shì* sometimes takes over. Consider this passage:

Nèige gōngyuán hén hăo. Dōngbian shì shān, xībian shì shuĭ, nánbian hé bĕibian yóu hĕn duō shù. "That park is nice. To the east there is a mountain, to the west a lake, and to the south and north many trees."

Here *shì* expresses existence, which is normally the function of *yŏu* — as in the last part of the sequence.

Sometimes *shì* is used in both of two minor sentences, almost as correlative conjunctions:

Bú shì wŏ bú yào lái, shì tā bú ràng wo lái. "Not that I didn't want to come, but (it was that) he didn't let me come."
Tā bú shi méi qián, tā shi bù xĭhuan măi dōngxi. "It isn't that he doesn't have any money, he doesn't like to buy things."

Wǒ bú shi shuō Chuāncài bu hǎo chī, wǒ shi shuō wǒ gèrén bu xǐhuan chī. "I didn't say Szechwan dishes aren't good, what I said was that I personally don't like them."

The force of *bú shi* here can be brought out in the translations: "it is not that . . .", etc.

In most of the examples so far (except for the ones just above), *shì* is the main verb of the predicate. But *shì* has also several much more specialized grammatical functions, of which the most important is the specifying *shì . . . de* pattern.

Tā shì zuò fēijī lái de. "He came by plane."

A translation that would bring out the force of *shì* would be: "It was by plane that he came." *Shì* specifies the means of transportation. It can also specify time and place,

Tā shì qùnian lái de. "It was last year that he came."
Tā shì cóng dàxué lái de. "It was from the university that he came."

This use of *shì* should be distinguished from the simpler classifying use that was explained above, where one example was: *Zhèiběn shū shì xīn de.* "This book is a new one." where *xīn de* is, logically speaking, short for *xīn de shū* "a new book". One could perhaps imagine that similarly a final nominal was left out in the *shì . . . de* cases as well, so that one could logically change the above example into: *Tā shì qùnian lái de rén.* However, this would mean "He is the (or: a) person who arrived last year.", instead of "It was last year that he came.". Again there is a difference between *shì* as the verb of the predicate and *shì* as part of the grammatical *shì . . . de* pattern. This pattern is actually limited to specifying and emphasizing the time, place, or some further circumstance of the action of the main verb, such as:

Tāmen shì zěmmo dào Shànghǎi qù de. "How did they go to Shanghai?"
Tā bú shi gēn gōngren dàibiǎotuán yìqǐ dào Zhōngguo qù de. "She did not go to China together with the workers' delegation."

The pattern of *zhèiběn shū shì xīn de*, where we have: subject + *shì* + a quality verb + *de*, is also very common; and even though in principle one should be able to add a nominal after *de*, this would in most cases just be a repetition of the subject and would sound rather awkward. Further examples of this pattern are:

Huìbào shì gēnběn cuòwu de. "The report is fundamentally wrong."

Zhèi shì shì yǒuzhe tā de zhòngyàoxìng de. "This matter has its importance."

In the last example the phrase starting with *yǒuzhe* is grammatically a verb + object phrase, but it functions as, and can be transformed into a quality verb (i.e. *zhòngyào* "is important") without change of meaning.

In the *shì . . . de* pattern, *shì* is optional, as in:

Wǒ (shì) jīntian zǎoshang kànjian ta de. "It was this morning that I saw him."

However, in the negated pattern, *bú shì* cannot be omitted:

Wǒ bú shì jīntian zǎoshang kànjian ta de.
Tā bú shì qùnian bìyè de. "It was not last year that he graduated."

When the central verb of the predicate has an object, *de* may be placed between the verb and its object, as in:

Wǒ shì cóng túshūguǎn jiè de zìdiǎn. "It was from the library that I borrowed the dictionary."
Wǒmen shì xīngqīliù kàn de diànyǐng. "It was on Saturday that we saw the movie."

De in this case is not analyzable as the subordinative particle[1] ("I am the dictionary that was borrowed from the library."). But if *shì* is omitted, (cp. above) we get *wǒ cóng túshūguǎn jiè de zìdiǎn*, which certainly *can* mean "the dictionary that I borrowed from the library"; here the context, or the pronunciation (proper pauses and intonation), will tell us whether we have a sentence or merely a modified noun.

Consider the following sequence:

Wǒ zuótian mǎi de Zhōngguo shū.

There are actually three possible meanings.

1. "the Chinese books that I bought yesterday", which is a nominal *phrase.*
2. "It was yesterday that I bought Chinese books.", which is the specifying pattern with *shì* omitted.
3. "What I bought yesterday was Chinese books."

The last possibility is a reduced form of *Wǒ zuótian mǎi de shì Zhōngguo shū*, where *shì* expresses the relation of identity. Without *shì*, *Zhōngguo*

---

[1]Chao classifies the *de* of *shì . . . de* as a subtype of nominalizing *de* (1968, pp. 296–7).

shū becomes a nominal predicate. In actual speech, phonological features will indicate which of these three meanings we actually have.

There is often an option between a nominal predicate and predicate with *shì*, in time expressions,

> *Xiànzài (shì) shémmo shíhou.* "What time is it now?"
> *Xiànzài (shì) liángdian bàn.* "It's 2:30."
> *Jīntian (shì) xīngqījǐ.* "What day of the week is it today?"

The same holds for indication of prices:

> *Zhèizhī bǐ yìmáo qián.* "This pen is (costs) a dime."
> *Liángběn zìdiǎn shì liǎngkuài qián.* "Two dictionaries cost two dollars."

Another important function of *shì* is to stress and emphasize various parts of a sentence:

> *Wǒ shì bú qù.* "As for *me* it is (a case of) not going (i.e. *I* am not going)."
> *Tā shì lèi, bú shì kùn.* "He is *tired*, not *sleepy*."

b. Other classificatory verbs. Other typical classificatory verbs are *xìng* "to be surnamed (so and so)", and *jiào* "to call, be called (so and so)". *Xìng* is used only for giving family names:

> *Tā xìng Wáng.* "His name is Wang."

Jiào can be used either for given names of persons (*not* family names) or names of things:

> *Tā xìng Wáng, jiào Shǒu-rén.* "His name is Wang Shou-ren (lit. He is surnamed Wang, and named Shou-ren)."
> *Zhèige jiào shémmo.* "What is this called?"
> *Zhèige jiào shémmo míngzi.* "What is the name of this?"

Jiào can also be an *action verb* meaning "call for (someone), ask or order (someone to do something)"; further it can be a *coverb* commonly used in passive constructions.

Dāng and *zuò* are both used with jobs or other functions people might have, as in:

> *Tā gēge zài fànguǎr dāng chuīshiyuán.* "His elder brother serves as cook in a restaurant."
> *Nǐ$_1$ dāng$_2$ lǎoshī$_3$ yǐjīng$_4$ hěn$_5$ duō$_6$ nián$_7$ le$_8$ ba$_9$.* "You$_1$ have$_8$ already$_4$ been$_2$ a teacher$_3$ for many$_{5,6}$ years$_7$, I suppose$_9$?"

Tā méi yǒu zuò jiàoyuán de běnshi. "He does not have the ability to be a teacher."

Note especially expressions like: *zuò guān* "be an official"; *dāng bīng* "serve as a soldier"; *dāng quán* "be in a position of power or authority", i.e. "to be in power, or office".

By extension *dāng* and *zuò* can be used putatively: "consider (something) to be":

Tāmen ná Sìshū zuò kèběn. "They consider the *Four Books* to be/as a textbook."
Tā₁ shícháng₂ ná₃ jiǔ₄ dāngzuò₅ shuǐ₆ hē₇. "He₁ often₂ takes₃ wine₄ and drinks₇ (it) as₅ (if he considered it to be) water₆."

Dāng can also be a *coverb* of location, and *zuò* can be an action verb "do, make".

Some *coverbs* of location can function as the central of a sentence and are then classificatory verbs. Examples are:

Tā zài jiā. "He is at home."
Tā zài shémmo xuéxiào. "What school is he at?"
Zhèige chuānghu cháo běi. "This window faces north."

Děngyu expresses equivalence and thus covers one of the functions of *shì*:

Sān jiā sì děngyu qī. "3 plus 4 equals 7."
Gàosongle ta méi tīngqīngchu jiù děngyu méi gàosong. "To have told him and not to be heard clearly is as good as not to have told him."

3. COVERBS

a. **General.** Coverbs share the characteristics that relation verbs in general possess. They form a closed class, which is the largest subclass among relation verbs. They cannot take verbal complements, nor can they modify nominals. They are transitive, and with very few exceptions occur with objects.

Coverbal phrases (i.e. coverbs + their objects) generally form subordinate parts of the predicate, and together with the central they form a syntactic construction called *verbal expressions in series*. Verbal expressions in series, in turn, are in most cases made up of coverbal phrases and centrals. The coverb is never the central.

Coverbal phrases indicate the circumstances under which the action of the central occurs. It may express "place where", "means whereby", etc. Coverbs are usually translated by prepositions in English.

Many coverbs overlap with other verbal classes. Some can also function as *description verbs*; of these most are *action verbs*, and a few are *quality verbs*. A few can serve as *classificatory verbs*, and some tend towards being pure *markers* with only grammatical meaning.

Coverbs can be further classified into groups according to the specific manner in which they modify the action of the predicate as a whole. This will often limit the possible types of centrals of the same predicate, in such a way that certain coverbs allow only action verbs, and others only quality verbs.

b. Coverbs of spatial and temporal relationships. A very important group of coverbs indicate *spatial* relationships. These exclude quality verbs from being centrals of the predicate. *Zài* indicates the place *at, on* or *in* which something takes place. Examples are:

Tāmen zài Běijīng Dàxué xuéxí Zhōngwén. "They are studying Chinese at Peking University."
Dàjiā zài huìshang yǐjīng tǎolùnle zhèige wèntí. "We've already discussed this question at the meeting."

Zài takes only a place word as its object. In the last example the addition of the place word suffix *-shang* is necessary to produce a place word.

Up to this point the common pattern has been: subject + coverbal phrase + central verb. But it is not uncommon to have coverbal phrases in the subject position, as in:

Zài gōngzuòshang, wǒmen hùxiāng xuéxí, hùxiāng bāngzhu, jīngcháng jiāoliú jīngyàn. "At work we learn from each other, help each other and constantly exchange experiences."

We sometimes have a variant of the same pattern with *yǒu* expressing existence, as in:

Zài Shāndōng méi yǒu dà hú. "In Shantung there aren't any big lakes."

In such cases the coverb can be omitted:

Shāndōng méi yǒu dà hú.

The coverb *zài* is likewise optional if a noun designating a person or a thing is modified by a place word. Thus we can have either: *zài wàitou de rén* or: *wàitou de rén*, both meaning "the person(s) who is (are) outside". Similarly: (*zài*) *Měiguo de dà hú* "the great lakes in America".

As a general rule coverbs — indeed all relation verbs — cannot modify nominals. In the above cases, coverbal *phrases* modify the nominals, and the coverbs themselves are actually omissible.

When coverbs occur in verbal expressions in series, the negator *bu*, other adverbs, or modal verbs as a rule come before the coverbal phrase:

Tā yě bú yào zài jiā chī fàn. "He too will not eat at home."

Zài and a few other coverbs sometimes appear *after* the main verb but *before* the object:

Tā zhùzài Shànghǎi. "He lives in Shanghai."

But since this happens only with a few specific verbs, we shall consider it a special kind of verbal complement, and discuss it in the next chapter under complements (p. 186).

Other spatial coverbs are *dào* and *cóng*, translated by "to" and "from", respectively.

Nǐ cóng nǎr lái. "Where do you come from?"
Wǒ cóng bàngōngshì lái. "I come from the office."
Tā dào nèr qù. "He is going there."
Cóng$_1$ zhèr$_2$ dào$_3$ nèr$_4$ zěmmo$_5$ zǒu$_6$. "How$_5$ does one go$_6$ from$_1$ here$_2$ to$_3$ there$_4$?"

In the last example the whole coverbal phrase complex functions as subject to *zǒu*.

Cóng and *dào* also express *temporal* relations, like "from" and "to" in English:

Wǒmen shàngwǔ cóng bādiǎn dào shíyīdiǎn bàn shàng kè. "We attend classes from 8 to 11:30 in the morning."

The compound coverb *zìcóng* is used exclusively for time relations:

Zìcóng tā zǒule yǐhòu, wǒ yìzhí lǎo bú fàngxīn. "Ever since he left, I've been worried all the time."

Whereas *cóng* and *dào* can also be action verbs, meaning "follow" and "arrive at" respectively, *zìcóng* is limited to its function as a coverb. It resembles a marker in that it usually introduces what is translatable as a time clause, coming first in the sentence.

A number of coverbs are translated by "toward". *Wàng* and *cháo* are used for directions:

Wŏmen cháo nán zŏu ba. "Let's go south!"

Cóng shūdiàn wàng yòu guăi. "Turn right from the bookstore."

Xiàng and *duì* are also translatable by "toward", but are normally used in the sense of "vis-à-vis, facing":

Tā duì wo shuō tā bù lái le. "He said to me that he wasn't coming."

Tā duì wénxué hén yŏu xìngqu. "He is very interested in literature."

Semantically there is a gradual transition from concrete direction to abstract mental attitude: "toward". In *Tā duì ta péngyou shuō tā duì wénxué méi xìngqu.* "He said to his friend that he was not interested in literature." both meanings of *duì* occur in the same sentence. Similar shades of meaning can be seen in the following examples with *xiàng*:

Cóng wŏmen xuéxiào xiàng nánbiar zŏu, jiù dào nèige gōngchăng le. "Walk toward the south from our school, and there you'll find that factory."

Wŏ xiàng wo péngyou jièshàole Běijīng hěn duō yŏumíng de dìfang. "I introduced my friend to a lot of well-known places in Peking."

Tā gōngzuò rènzhēn nŭlì, wŏmen yīnggāi xiàng ta xuéxí. "He works conscientiously and puts in a great effort, we ought to learn from him."

The coverb *lí* is special among spatial coverbs in that it restricts the following verb to the quality verbs *jìn* ("near, close") and *yuăn* ("far, distant") or *yŏu* + an expression denoting distance. *Lí* indicates the point of departure when judging distance. Examples:

Wŏ jiā lí túshūguăn hěn jìn (yuăn). "My home is very close to (far from) the library."

Dàxué lí wŏ jiā yŏu sānlĭ lù. "The university is 3 *li* from my home."

c. Instrumental coverbs. The *instrumental* coverbs explain the means by which something happens or is done. *Zuò*, which can also be an action verb: "sit", expresses the means by which one travels:

Tāmen zuò qìchē jìn chéng le. "They entered the city by car."

Tā cóng zhèr zuò fēijī dào Zhōngguo qù le. "He went from here to China by plane."

Yòng translates as "with, using, by means of":

Tā néng yòng máobĭ xiě zì. "He can write with a brush."

Lăoshī yòng Zhōngwén wèn wŏmen wèntí, wŏmen yĕ yòng Zhōngwén huídá. "The teacher asks us questions in Chinese, and we answer in Chinese."

Ná resembles *yòng*; both are also common as action verbs, meaning respectively "take, hold" and "use". *Ná* as instrumental coverb:

Ní děi ná hǎo huà mànmārde quàn ta. "You have to persuade him gradually with kind words."

d. Pretransitive coverbs
Qíng nǐ ná yàoshi bǎ zhèige mén kāikai. "Please open the door with the key."

The second coverb in this sentence, *bǎ*, is the so-called *pretransitive* coverb, which is very important. Its basic function is to transform a verb + object phrase into the verbal expression in series pattern according to the following basic formula: verb + object > *bǎ* + object + verb (*kāi mén* > *bǎ* (*zhèige*) *mén kāikai*). The main verb cannot be a simple monosyllabic form, and the object must either be in the form: determiner + noun or have specific reference. In the example above we have such an object: *zhèige mén*, and the main verb is reduplicated (*kāikai*), which is a required minimum addition to the monosyllable *kāi*. The addition to the main transitive verb usually consists of a suffix or any kind of complement:

Tā bǎ nèiběn shū huánle. "He has returned the book."
Wó bǎ jīntian de liànxí zuòwánle. "I've finished today's exercises."
Wǒmen yīnggāi bǎ shēngcí jìzhù. "We should remember the new words."
Tā bǎ kèwén niàn de hěn shú. "He studied the lesson till he knew it well."

The second verb may take an object of some kind, including a cognate object:

Zámen bǎ nèixiē wèntí tǎolùn yíxiàr ba. "Let's discuss those questions a bit!"

or objects following a bound verb + object complement:

Wó bǎ tā de xìn fàngzài zhuōzishang le. "I put his letter on the table."
Wǒmen yào bǎ fāngbian rànggěi biéren, bǎ kùnnan liúgěi zìjǐ. "We must make things convenient for others while taking on the difficulties ourselves."

The pretransitive may also be used with compound verbs without anything added, or with verbs modified by adverbials or adverbs:

Wǒmen yídìng yào bǎ zhèixiē kùnnan kèfú. "We shall certainly overcome these difficulties."
Tā bá jiǔ bùtíng de hē. "He drinks wine continually."

This is less frequent than *Tā bùtíng de hē jiǔ.*

To summarize: The basic requirement is that the *central verb phrase* must have no less than two syllables. Thus, the possibilities are as follows:

bǎ + O + V + suffix
bǎ + O + V + reduplication
bǎ + O + V + object
bǎ + O + V + verb−object complement
bǎ + O + V + complement
bǎ + O + compound verb
bǎ + O + adverbial + V.

A sentence with a pretransitive coverbal phrase can usually be translated into a verb + object sentence:

Tā zuótian bǎ nèijià lùyīnjī mǎilaile. "He bought the tape recorder yesterday."
vs *Tā zuótian mǎilai yíjià lùyīnjī.* "He bought a tape recorder yesterday."
Tā bǎ shū géi wo. "He gave me the book."
vs *Tā géi wo yìběn shū.* "He gave me a book."

Beside *bǎ*, which is by far the most frequent pretransitive, there are a few others, among them *gěi*, which in addition has other coverbal functions. The following example with *gěi* also illustrates the rather infrequent case of omission of object after a coverb:

Xìn xiěwánle, qíng ní gěi chāole jìzǒu ba. "The letter is finished, please copy (it) and mail it."

The object that is omitted after *gěi* is the noun *xìn* at the beginning of the sentence.

e. Coverbs of benefit and purpose. *Gěi* also belongs to a group of coverbs which expresses for whom, or for whose benefit, something is done:

Lǎoshī géi wǒmen fēnxi yúfǎ. "The teacher analyzed the grammar for us."
Wǒ péngyou géi wó mǎile yìběn huàbaò. "My friend bought an illustrated magazine for me."

Tì functions in the same way:

> *Qíng nǐ tì wǒ shuō jǐjù hǎo huà.* "Please say a few good words on my behalf/for me."

Wèi or *wèile* has a similar function, as in:

> *Wèile nǐ, wǒ cái dào zhèr lái.* "For your sake I have come here."

However, the transition from this use to that translatable as "in order to" or "because of" is not very long, and usually *wèile* functions like a marker at the beginning of expressions that indicate cause or purpose, where *wèile* takes sentence objects:

> *Wèile bāngzhu wǒmen kèfú xuéxíshang de kùnnan, lǎoshī jīngcháng liáojiě women de xuéxí qíngkuàng.* "In order to help us overcome our study difficulties, the teacher constantly looks into our studying conditions."

Yīnwei as a coverb usually indicates a cause:

> *Tā yīnwei shémmo yuángu bu néng lái.* "For what reason couldn't he come?"

But more often it is a pure topic subject marker, usually in correlation with *suóyǐ* "therefore".

f. Coverbs and markers of coordination. Another important group of coverbs often overlaps with markers of coordination. Frequently used are *gēn, hé* and *tóng*, while *yú* and *jí*, which are borrowed from the classical language, are not infrequent in writing. When these words are coverbs, they are translatable by "with", "together with", but when they are markers, they are translatable by "and". Consider the following two sentences:

> *Wǒ gēn ni qù.* "I am going with you."
> *Shū gēn bǐ dōu shì wǒ de.* "The books and the pens are all mine."

In the first case we have the coverb; notice that there can be a negator *bu* in front of *gēn*. In the second case there cannot be a *bu* before *gēn*, because *gēn* is a pure marker.

The coverb *gēn* is often used in a pattern with *yìqǐ* or *yíkuàr* to mean "together with":

> *Wǒ gēn wo de tóngxué yìqǐ liànxí xiě Hànzì.* "I practice writing characters together with my schoolmates."

Tā gēn fùmǔ yíkuàr zhùzài Shànghǎi. "He lives together with his parents in Shanghai."

g. Coverbs of comparison. *Gēn* is also used in a pattern of *comparison:*

Wǒ de liànxí běnzi gēn tā de bù yíyàng. "My exercise book is different from his."

In this pattern *gēn* + object is regularly followed by the quality verb *yíyàng* "to be the same", and the subject of the sentence is compared with the object of the coverb.

Another coverb of comparison, *xiàng*, is also used in connection with *yíyàng:*

Nǐ$_1$ bú$_2$ yào$_3$ xiàng$_4$ xuéfá$_5$ yíyàng$_6$ wúduān$_7$ yǐ$_8$ shǐ$_9$ yà$_{10}$ rén$_{11}$. "You$_1$ must$_3$ not$_2$ arbitrarily$_7$ use$_8$ force$_9$ and suppress$_{10}$ people$_{11}$ like$_{4,6}$ a scholar-tyrant$_5$."

The most important coverb of comparison is *bǐ:*

Zhèige bǐ nèige hǎo. "This is better than that."
Wǒ péngyou shuō Zhōngwén bǐ wo liúlì de duō. "My friend speaks Chinese much more fluently than I."
Tā jīntian lái de bǐ zuótian wǎn yìdiǎr. "Today he came a bit later than yesterday."

h. Coverbs of inclusion and exclusion. The coverbs of inclusion and exclusion occur in patterns with optional second elements. *Lián ... yě/dōu* means "even, including", whereas *chúle ... yǐwài* means "except for, besides":

Jīntian rèjíle; lián diǎr fēng yě méi yǒu. "Today it is extremely hot, there isn't even a breath of wind."
Chúle nǐ yǐwài méi rén huì. "Besides you nobody can."

These coverbs are unique with regard to the kind of objects they can take. In the first example above the coverb takes the subject of the central verb as its object.[1] It could be the logical[2] object, as in:

Nǐ ràng ta fānyi nèige gùshi; tā lián zìdiǎn yě méi chá, jiù fānyihǎole. "You asked him to translate that story, and he finished it without even using the dictionary."

---

[1] Other coverbs can also introduce the subject of a sentence. This use of coverbs should not be confused with *pivotal constructions*, see p. 196.
[2] Grammatically speaking, *zìdiǎn* is of course the object of the coverb *lián*.

Tā chúle xiǎoshuō yǐwài, shémmo shū dōu bú kàn. "Except for novels he doesn't read any books."

Or it could be a repeated predicate central:

Zuótian de diànyǐng, tā lián kàn yě méi kàn; zěmmo zhīdao hǎo bu hao ne. "He didn't even see the movie yesterday, how could he have known whether it was good or not?"

i. Coverbs indicating the agent. One important group of coverbs is used to indicate the agent in sentences which are translatable with passive meaning:

Dìshang de xuě bèi fēng guā de yìdiǎr yě méi yǒu le. "The snow on the ground was completely blown off by the wind."

Bèi often occurs without an object and thus tends to become a marker of the passive:

Qīnlüèjūn dōu bèi gǎnchuqule. "The invading troops were all driven out."

Other coverbs with the same function are *jiào* and *ràng*:

Nèige$_1$ shòu$_2$ zhòng$_3$ shāng$_4$ de zhànshì$_5$, jiào$_6$ Báiqiúēn$_7$ dàifu$_8$ jiùhuó$_9$le$_{10}$. "That$_1$ seriously$_3$ wounded$_{2,4}$ soldier$_5$ was$_{10}$ saved$_9$ by$_6$ Dr.$_8$ Bethune$_7$."
Wǒmen shuō de huà, ràng tā tīngjianle. "What we said was heard by him."

Sometimes there is both a coverb of the logical agent and a marker of the passive before the verb:

Tā ràng wo géi dǎ le. "He was beaten by me."

j. Coverbs of reference. Finally there is a group of coverbs used for reference to a state of affairs or a topic under discussion, etc. ("with regard to"). We saw earlier that *duì* could have this function:

Wǒ duì lìshǐ hén yǒu xìngqu. "I'm very much interested in history."

The compound coverbs *duìyú* and *guānyú* are used in the same way:

Wǒ duìyú zhèli de qíngxing bù shóuxi. "I'm not familiar with the situation here."
Guānyú nèige wèntí, wǒ hái méi dǎdìng zhǔyi ne. "With regard to that problem I have not yet made up my mind."

Only the most important coverbs have been dealt with, since a complete list cannot be given here. But most of those not mentioned are synonymous with those we have discussed, or have similar functions. There is a wide variety of types: some resemble and overlap with the category of description verbs, others tend towards pure markers with specialized functions.

4. MODAL VERBS

a. General. The third subclass of relation verbs, *modal* verbs, share the distinguishing properties of relation verbs: they do not take verbal complements or verbal suffixes, and are not used as modifiers before nominals. Usually they occur with their objects, but are freer, syntactically speaking, than coverbs in that they can stand without an object in short answers to questions, if the modal verb with its object occurs in the near context.

Modal verbs are different from other relation verbs in that they only take other verbs as their "objects". Various types of action verbs also take verbal objects, but they are clearly distinguished from modal verbs in that they do take complements, suffixes etc., and in that they do not perform the specific function of modal verbs, which is to express a relation of modality between the agent (or the subject) and the central verb. This modal relationship can be one of possibility, desirability, necessity, and so on.

The modal verb can be separated from the verb it is directed towards, by adverbs or adverbials, including coverbal phrases. Modal verbs can be directed towards almost all classes of verbs, but are quite rare before other relation verbs and quality verbs. In other words, they usually express the modality of action verbs.

b. Types of modality. *Néng, huì* and *kéyi* all express capability:

Tā huì shuō Zhōngguo huà. "He can speak Chinese."
Néng lái, jiù qǐng lái. "Please come if you can."
Nèige gōngchǎng kéyi zhìzào hěn duō dàjīqi. "That factory can produce much heavy machinery."

Huì usually expresses an acquired capability, although *néng* and *kéyi* also have a similar meaning:

Tā huì huá bīng, wǒ bú huì. "He knows how to skate, but I don't."
Tā néng kàn Zhōngwén bào. "He is able to read Chinese newspapers."

Normally modal verbs cannot be used in the imperative, but there are exceptions, as in this instruction regarding language exercises:

Niànshú kèwén, bìng néng liúlì de jìnxíng huìhuà. "Read aloud the text until fluent, and be able to carry on a conversation on it fluently."

Néng and *kéyi* also express permission or prohibition:

Zhèli néng (or: *kéyi*) *chōu yān.* "Smoking is permitted here."

When *néng* and *kéyi* express capability, the negated verb can only be *bù néng*, whereas to express prohibition both *bù kéyi* and *bù néng* can be used. An example expressing capability:

Běijīng de dōngtian kéyi huá bīng, bù néng huá xuě. "During the winter in Peking one can go skating, but one cannot go skiing."

An example expressing prohibition:

Zhèli bù kéyi chōu yān. "Smoking is not permitted here."

Huì also expresses possibility, usually in relation to some future occurrence, as in:

Bú huì xià yǔ, nǐ qù ba. "It can't (possibly) rain, you go ahead!"
Tā huì lái bāngzhu nǐ. "He may come to help you."
Wó xiǎng zhèmmo jiǎngjiu de lǚguǎn bú huì tài piányi de. "I should think such an elegant hotel can't be too inexpensive."

The last sentence also illustrates the rather infrequent use of a modal verb before a quality verb.

Yào expresses the future likelihood of some happening, as in:

Yào xià yǔ le. "It is going to rain".
Wǒ yào qù túshūguǎn. "I'll be going to the library."

The last sentence could also mean "I want to go to the library", since *yào* also expresses will, wish or "wanting to". A third meaning is *necessity*:

Niàn shēngcí, yào zhùyi shēngdiào. "Reading the new words aloud one must pay attention to the tones."

The negative counterpart of *yào* meaning "to wish" is *bù xiǎng*; in the case of *yào* implying necessity, the negative counterpart is *bú yòng*:

Wǒ bù xiǎng qù túshūguǎn. "I don't want to go to the library."

Nǐ bú yòng jì zhèige shēngcí. "You don't have to remember this new word."

Bú yào is used for negative imperatives, meaning "don't (do that)!"

Nǐ bú yào lái! "Don't come!"

Xiǎng expresses desire, and *xǐhuan* inclination or preference:

Tā láo xiǎng dào nèr qù. "He always wanted to go there."
Háizimen xǐhuan wár. "The children like to play."

Both of these modal verbs can also be quality verbs, and *xiǎng* can be an action verb as well.

Yuànyi and *kěn* both express willingness, but *yuànyi* also means "to wish to":

Wǒ yuànyi cānjiā yóuxíng. "I wish to participate in the parade."
Wǒ bú yuànyi dāndú yíge rén qu chī fànguǎr. "I don't like to go to eat in a restaurant all by myself."
Shéi kěn zuò nèige shì. "Who is willing to do that?"
Tā bú shì bù néng lái, jiù shì bù kěn lái. "It isn't that he can't come, he is unwilling to."

Yīnggāi, gāi, and *yīngdāng* all mean "should, ought to":

Wǒmen yīnggāi nǔlì xuéxí, yě yào chángcháng duànliàn shēntǐ. "We should study very hard, and must also do physical exercise."
Nǐ bù yīngdāng nèmmo shuō. "You shouldn't talk like that."
Wǒ xiànzài gāi zǒu le. "I ought to go now."

Beside *yào* there are a number of other modal verbs expressing necessity. The most commonly used are *děi, bìděi,* and *bìxū*; their negative counterparts are *bú yòng, bú bì* and *bù xūyào.* Examples are:

Wǒ děi zǒu le. "I must go."
Wǒ jīntian bìděi kànwan nèiběn shū. "I must finish reading this book today."
Zhǐ niàn, bú bì xiě. "Just read, you don't have to write."
Quán Dǎng bìxū zūnzhào Máo Zédōng tóngzhì de zhǐshì. "The whole Party must follow comrade Mao Tsetung's instructions."

The form *méiyou* is a modal verb that negates verbs that in the positive form are followed by the suffixes *-le, -zhe,* and *-guo.* The negator *méi* performs the same function. The form *méiyou* should be distinguished from the negated form of the transitive verb *yǒu: Méi yǒu shū.* "There are no books."

When the modal verb *méiyou* is used, the suffix *-le* is not retained after the verb, whereas *-zhe* and *-guo* are retained in the negated forms:

Tā méiyou kàn bào. "He hasn't read the newspaper."

Examples with the negator *méi*:

Tā shǒuli méi názhe dōngxi. "He isn't holding anything in his hand."
Tā méi chīguo Zhōngguo fàn. "He has never eaten Chinese food."

This modal verb is also used in alternative questions, and it may occur without the "object" at the end of the sentence, something the negator *méi* cannot do:

Nǐ kànle bào meiyou. "Have you read the newspaper?"
Nǐ kànle bào mei kan.

Gǎn means "to dare to", and *pà* "to be afraid of". The latter can take a nominal as its object as well as a verb, but *gǎn* is a modal verb only:

Zhèige dǎzìjī néng yòng jǐnián wó kě bù gǎn shuō. "I don't dare say for sure how many years this typewriter can be used for."
Zhèige háizi hěn pà jiàn shēngrén. "This child is very much afraid of meeting strangers."

Bù hǎo yìsi is a quality verb expression meaning "to be embarrassed". But there is also a modal verb *hǎoyìsi*:

Tā jūrán hǎoyìsi chīle yě bù gěi qián. "He actually had the nerve to eat without paying for it."
Tā bù hǎoyìsi yào. "He is too shy to ask for it."

There are other less frequently used modal verbs, and now and then new members of this class appear, such as *qǐtú* "attempt to", which is of fairly recent origin.

C. Description Verbs

1. GENERAL

The great majority of verbs are *description verbs*, which in contradistinction to *relation verbs* form an open class, the members of which cannot be listed except in a comprehensive and up-to-date dictionary. The main function of description verbs is to serve as nuclei in predicates and/or centrals in sentences. Some of these verbs are *intransitive* (i.e.

they can only take very special kinds of objects) and some are *transitive* (i.e. they can take a wide variety of objects, the choice being limited only lexically, not grammatically). In this respect description verbs differ from relation verbs, which are all transitive, and which only in very rare and special cases occur without their objects. Even *transitive* description verbs can relatively freely occur without an object.

In contrast to relation verbs, description verbs can take verbal complements, and they can singly modify nominals, whereas relation verbs cannot modify nominals except *with* their objects. Finally, description verbs can take the various verbal suffixes.

Some description verbs describe or express some action or event. These verbs can be either transitive or intransitive. They are called *action verbs*.

Other description verbs differ from action verbs in that they describe some quality or state of being. These are also either transitive or intransitive. They are called *quality verbs*.

These two subclasses of description verbs differ from one another in a number of ways: as to what type of complements they take, as to what kind of adverbial modifications they can have, as to how they can modify nominals (marked or unmarked), etc. These differences will be discussed in detail in the next two subsections.

2. ACTION VERBS

Action verbs cannot be modified by adverbs of degree, such as *hěn* "very". Nor can action verbs modify nominals directly. Modification of nominals by action verbs must be marked by *de*, as in: *mǎi de shū* "the books that were bought", *lái de rén* "the people who came".

Forms which are apparent exceptions to this rule, such as *láirén* "messenger", are usually to be interpreted as compounds.

Although some individual action verbs are limited as to what kind of complements they can take — for semantical reasons — the class as a whole can take all kinds of complements except the intensifying complements of degree. *Xiě* "write" can take

1) predicative complements:

> *Tā xiě Hànzì, xiě de hén hǎo.* "She writes Chinese characters very well."

2) resultative complements:

> *Wó xiěwánle xìn.* "I finished writing the letter."

3) directional complements:

Bǎ tā de jīngyàn xiěchulai. "(She) wrote out her experiences."

4) bound verb + object complements:

Bǎ tā de míngzi xiězài shūshang. "(He) wrote his name in the book."

   a. **Intransitive action verbs.** Among *intransitive* action verbs there is a great deal of variety as to what kind of special objects they can take. Some are limited to taking *cognate objects*, indicating, for example, the duration of an action, or the quantification of an action, i.e. how many times an action occurred:

Nín$_1$ zài$_2$ zhèige$_3$ gōngchǎng$_4$ gōngzuò$_5$ le$_6$ hěn$_7$ duō$_8$ nián$_9$ le$_{10}$ ba$_{11}$. "You$_1$ have$_{6,10}$ probably$_{11}$ worked$_5$ for many$_{7,8}$ years$_9$ in$_2$ this$_3$ factory$_4$?"

The verb *gōngzuò*, which can overlap as a noun: "work", does not take any other kind of object. Notice that "place of work" is expressed by means of a coverbal phrase.

   In the following example we have a cognate object of time:

Wó děi xiūxi yìhuǐr le. "Now I must rest a bit."

   b. **Verbs lai and qu.** One important group of intransitive action verbs is formed by *verbs of motion*, which usually take as objects place words that express whither or whence a move takes place:

Tā qùnian jiù qù Zhōngguo le. "He went to China last year."
Tā zuò fēijī lái Běijīng le. "He came to Peking by plane."

The "whither" of these two examples can also be expressed by a coverbal phrase occurring before the verb of motion:

Tā qùnian jiù dào Zhōngguo qù le.
Tā zuò fēijī dào Běijīng lái le.

Lai and *qu* are very frequently used as simple directional complements indicating movement towards or away from the speaker:

Tā yǐjīng huíqule. "He already returned (back there)".
Tā yǐjīng huílaile. "He has already come back."
Qǐng dàjiā jìnlai ba. "Ask everyone to come in."
Tā fùqin chūqule. "His father has gone out."

A special function of *lai* and *qu* is to express a combination of motion and purpose: "to go (in order) to" or "to come (in order) to":

Wǒ qù kàn péngyou. "I'm going to see some friends."
Tā lái mǎi shémmo. "What has he come to buy?"
Tā jīntian lái jiè shū ma. "Is he coming today to borrow the books?"

Related to the purposive function of the verbs *qu* and *lai* is their function as *particles of purpose*. As particles they occur at the end of the phrase or sentence with neutral tone and zero stress, whereas in other functions tone and stress are facultative.

Wǒ míngtian jiè shū lai. "I'll (come) tomorrow (to) borrow books."
Tā jīntian bú kàn shū qu. "He's not going (there) today to read."

Lai and *qu* as particles of purpose still indicate movement towards or away from a speaker.

In the following examples *lai* and *qu* occupy different positions in the sequences; but as far as meaning is concerned, the sentences are synonymous or near-synonymous:

Tā lái jiè shū. "He is coming to borrow some books."
Tā jiè shū lai.
Tā lái jiè shū lai.

Note that one may have either the *action verbs lái/qù* indicating purpose, or the *particles* of purpose, or both, in the same sentence.

As a particle, *lai* (or *qu*) comes before any other final particles that may occur in the same sentence:

Xīnlái de tóngxué cānguān gōngchǎng qu le. "The newly arrived schoolmates went to visit the factory."
Nǐ xiūxi qu ba! "You go to rest, OK!"

We have seen that aside from a different position in the sentence (and sometimes a difference with regard to tone, in that the particle always has neutral tone, whereas the verbs *lai* or *qu* indicating purpose sometimes have full tones, sometimes not) the particles of purpose function very much like the verbs of purpose.

Lai and *qu* can also occur at the end of a sentence *without* being particles of purpose. This happens when the verb takes a compound directional complement with an object and the object splits the complement, as in:

Qǐng nín bǎ zìdiǎn sònghui túshūguǎn qu ba! "Please send the dictionary back to the library!"

For practical purposes *qu* may here be taken to be part of the compound verbal complement *huiqu* "back to (there)". But even the directional complement *lai*, split away from the rest of the complement, may seem to retain something of the idea of purpose in the following example (although this sentence could also be taken as two coordinated verbal phrases):

> *Dàjiā dōu pǎochu jiàoshì lai huānyíng xīn tóngxué.* "Everybody has come running out of the classroom to welcome the new students."

In addition to these related functions of *lai/qu* as 1) verb of motion, 2) verb of purpose, 3) simple directional complement, 4) part of a compound directional complement, possibly split from the other part of the complement by an object, and 5) particle of purpose, *lái* and *qù* can by class overlap function as (causative) transitive verbs:

> *Lái yìhú chá ba.* "Bring a pot of tea."

Here *lái* is used causatively: "cause to come", i.e. "bring".

Sometimes *lái* takes as object its own agent, also called "the logical subject":

> *Wǒmen xuéxiào xīn láile liǎngge jiāo Zhōngwén de laòshī.* "Recently there came two teachers of Chinese to our school."
> *Wǒmen jīntian wǎnshang lái kèrén.* "We're having guests tonight."

Finally, *lái* and *qù* can have specialized, idiomatic meanings:

> *Wǒ zìjǐ lái ba!* "Let me do it!"
> *Bǎ zhèige zì qù le.* "Take out this word."
> *Tā fùqin shì qùnian qù de shì.* "His father passed away last year."

Qù de shì is derived from the underlying expression *qù shì* which means to "leave the world" or "die".

c. Other intransitive action verbs. The other important intransitive verbs of motion also overlap the class of transitive verbs, but as transitive verbs they are rather more limited than the regular transitive verbs. *Zǒu* means "to go, leave", as in:

> *Zámen zǒu ba!* "Let's go!"

It can function transitively like *lái*:

> *Wǒmen bān zǒule sānge tóngxué, tāmen dào Zhōngguo qù xuéxi le.* "Three of our classmates have left us, they have gone to China to study."

Jìn and *chū* means "to go in, enter" and "to go out", respectively. They are normally limited to taking place words as objects:

Wǒ gāng jìn chéng, jiù xiàqi yǔ lai le. "I had just entered town when it started to rain."
Tā chūle yuàn, yìtiān dōu méi xiūxi, jiù lái shàng kè le. "After he was out of the hospital, he came to class without a single day's rest."

Jìn and *chū* often take *lai* or *qu* as directional complements, or combine with them to form compound directional complements.

Qǐng dàjiā dōu jìnlai ba. "Ask everyone to come in."
Tā fùqin chūqule. "His father has gone out."
bānchulai "move out"
pǎojinqu "run inside"

In addition, there is a transitive use, as in:

Chū tàiyang le. "The sun is up."
Chūle shémmo shì le. "What went wrong?" (from *chū shì* "have an accident")
Nǐ yíge yuè jìn duōshao qián. "How much money do you make in a month?"

There is a similar class overlap to transitive verbs with *shàng* "go to, go up, ascend", *xià* "go down, descend", *huí* "go back, return", *guò* "cross, go over, go through", *qǐ* "come up, arise". These also regularly take *lai* and *qu* as complements, and form compound complements with *lai* and *qu*. Some examples are:

shàng shān "ascend a mountain"
shàng xué (or: *kè*) "go to school (or: class)"
zǒushanglai "to come up here"
náxiaqu "to take (something) down"

Used transitively and idiomatically:

Xiān shàng tāng. "Serve the soup first."
xià dàn "lay eggs"; *xià gǒu* "have puppies"
xià xuě (or: *yǔ*) "to snow (or: rain)"
xià yù "send (someone) to prison"

Similarly with *huí*, as verb of motion:

Xiàle kè, tā huí jiā qu le. "After class he returned home."
Wǒ xiànzài děi huí xuéxiaò le. "I have to go back to school now."

Transitively, with other kinds of objects:

huí xìn "answer a letter"
huí shǒu "return a blow"

With *guò*, we have:

Wómen yǐjīng guòle Shànghǎi le. "We've already passed Shanghai."
Jīntian lùshang guòlai guòqu de rén hěn dūo. "Today there are a lot of people going back and forth on the road."

Guò can also take objects of temporal as well as spatial meaning, as in *guò nián* "celebrate New Year", or "spend a night" *guò yè.* The various uses of *guo* as directional complement and suffix have been discussed already (p. 128).

Qǐ, or more often *qǐlai*, is used intransitively to express motion:

Tā qǐ de bù zǎo. "He doesn't get up early."
Nǐ zǎoshang shémmo shíhou qǐlai. "When do you get up in the morning?"

Qilai used as an inchoative suffix, and as a directional complement, has already been discussed (p. 131). *Qǐ* is used transitively, as in:

Tā liǎnshang qǐle yíge bāo. "A boil has developed on his face."

Other intransitive verbs are *sǐ* "to die", *shēng* "to be born", *shēnghuo* "to live", *xiūxi* "to rest", *bìyè* "to graduate", *děng* "to wait". Examples are:

Nǐmen shēnghuo de zěmmoyàng. "How do you live?"
Tā bìyè liǎngnián le. "He graduated two years ago."
Qǐng nǐ děng yìhuǐr. "Please wait a moment."

d. **Transitive action verbs.** *Transitive action verbs* can, in principle, take a great variety of objects, although many are restricted lexically. Transitive action verbs are quite free to occur without objects. Compare:

Nǐ yǐjīng chī fàn le ma. "Have you eaten?"
Chīle. "Yes (I have eaten)."
Nǐ yīnggāi mǎi zhèiběn shū, hén yǒu yìsi. "You ought to buy this book, it's very interesting."
Wó yǐjīng mǎile. "I've already bought it."

Most, but not all, transitive action verbs may occur with their logical objects in a coverbal phrase before the action verb itself. Most commonly the pretransitive coverb *bǎ* (see p. 154 for this and other pretransitive coverbs) is used. Compare:

1) *Wǒmen yídìng yào kèfú xuéxíshang de kùnnan.* "We certainly must overcome difficulties in studying."

With *bǎ*:
Wǒmen yídìng yào bǎ zhèixiē kùnnan kèfú.

2) *Lǎoshī fēnxi yúfǎ.* "The teacher analyzes the grammar."
With *bǎ*:
Qǐng nǐ bǎ zhèige jùzi fēnxifenxi. "Please try and analyze this sentence."

Examples of verbs that never take the pretransitive construction:

Xià yǔ le. "It's raining now."
Wǒ fā shāo. "I have a fever."
huá bīng (or: *xuě*) "go skating (or: skiing)"
guā fēng "Blows wind", i.e. "The wind blows."

Transitive action verbs differ as to what types of objects they can take. Some can take two objects, one indirect object and one direct object:

Wó géi nǐ yìběn Rénmín Huàbào, hǎo bu hao. "I'll give you a copy of Renmin Huabao, OK?"
Xuéshēng wèn lǎoshī wèntí. "The students ask the teacher questions."
Tā jiāo wǒmen lìshǐ. "He teaches us history."

Two or more coordinated direct objects are common:

Wǒmen₁ huì₂ shuō₃ Yīngwén₄ hé₅ Fǎwén₆. "We₁ can₂ speak₃ English₄ and₅ French₆."
Wó měitian fùxí jiù kè, yě yùxí xīn kè, wǒ yùxí xīn kè de shēngcí, kèwén hé yúfǎ. "Every day I review the old lesson and prepare the new lesson, I prepare the new words, and the text and grammar of the new lesson."

Many verbs can take another verb or a verb + object phrase as object:

Wǒmen liànxí tīng, yě liànxí shuō. "We practice listening as well as speaking."
Wǒ gēn wo de péngyou yìqǐ liànxí xiě Hànzì. "I practice writing Chinese characters together with my friend."
Tīngle jièshào, wǒmen jiù kāishǐ cānguān le. "After having heard the introduction we started on the tour."

Certain transitive action verbs — especially "think" and "link" verbs —

take objects which in turn are subjects of a following verb. Such objects are called *pivots*:

> *Wó qǐng ta gēn wo yìqǐ qù cānguān zhánlǎnhuì.* "I asked him to go with me to visit the exhibition."
> *Tā jiào wo gěi ta jièshaojieshao nèige diànyǐng.* "He asked me to tell him something about that movie."

These *pivotal constructions* should be distinguished from constructions where a transitive verb takes a whole clause as its object. *Qǐng* and *jiào* merely take the pivot as object, not what follows the pivot. Examples of verbs taking *clause objects*:

> *Wó xiǎng, tā yídìng lái.* "I think he will certainly come."
> *Tā shuō tā yídìng yào huí jiā.* "He says that he must go home."

Other common transitive action verbs are *mǎi*, *mài* (buy, sell), *jiè* (borrow), *chǎo* (fry), *dǎ* (hit), *dài* (wear), etc., which are all very versatile with regard to the objects they can take.

3. QUALITY VERBS

a. General. Quality verbs are distinguished from action verbs in that they can be modified by adverbs of degree:

> *Zhèiběn shū hén hǎo.* "This book is very good."
> *Tā fēicháng zhùyì yúfǎ.* "He especially pays attention to grammar."

Further, quality verbs may modify nominals directly (without *de*) to form nominal *phrases*. Action verbs require *de*, otherwise they form *compounds* (cp. *láirén*, p. 163). Thus, we have *hǎo shū* "good book", *hóng mòshuǐ* "red ink", etc. But polysyllabic quality verbs modifying nominals are marked by *de*: *fùzá de wèntí* "complicated questions". The same applies to monosyllabic quality verbs that are themselves modified by adverbs: *hén hǎo de péngyou* "very good friends".

Since quality verbs, in contrast to action verbs, denote some quality or state of affairs, they cannot take resultative or directional complements, which typically express the result of an action verb or the direction of an action verb expressing motion. The only kinds of complements that quality verbs can take are those which typically give the *degree* or the *extent* of the quality expressed by the verb. Such complements are intensifying complements of degree, as in:

> *Nà hǎojíle.* "That's really good!"
> *Wǒ lèisǐle.* "I'm dead tired!"

Zhèibĕn shū bĭ nèibĕn qiănduōle. "This book is much easier than that."

Zhèixiē shù yìnián bĭ yìnián gāo, yĭjīng bĭ zhèizuò lóu gāohăoduō le. "These trees are getting taller every year, they are already much taller than this building."

The other kind of complement that quality verbs can take is a variant of the predicative complements. These complements can take several different forms, even full phrases:

Nèige hăo de duō. "That one is much better."
Tā₁ màn₂ de₃ jí₄ rén₅. "He₁ is so slow₂ that₃ he makes₄ people₅ impatient₅."
Dàxué yuăn de kànbujiàn le. "The university is so far away that it cannot be seen."
Wŏ lèi de chībuxià fàn. "I'm too tired to eat."

Transitive quality verbs too can take this kind of complement, but they occur more often with modifying adverbs of degree, as in:

Tā zhēn pà guĭ. "He's really scared of ghosts."

It is possible to say: *Tā pà guĭ pà de shuìbuzháo le.* "He is so scared of ghosts that he can't go to sleep.", where the central verb is repeated with the complement. With the intensifying complements, one can say: *Wŏ xiăng ni xiăngsĭle.* "I miss you terribly.", but not **tā pàjíle guĭ* with the object after the verb + complement, as one can say *chībuxià fàn.*

b. **Intransitive quality verbs.** *Intransitive* quality verbs, which regularly translate as English adjectives, can only take cognate objects:

Tā bìngle sānnián. "He was sick for three years."
Mèimei bĭ wo xiăo liăngsuì. "My little sister is two years younger than me."
Dìyī bān de xuéshēng, bĭ dìèr bān shăo sānge. "Class I has three students fewer than Class II."
Nèizuò lóu bĭ zhèizuò lóu gāo sānmĭ. "That building is three meters higher than this one."

A variant of this comparative pattern with cognate object is the pattern where the quality verb functions adverbially, and what would logically have been the cognate object of the quality verb comes after the central verb, as in:

Tā bĭ women duō xuéle liăngnián Zhōngwén. "He has studied Chinese two years more than us."

Wómen bǐ tamen shǎo xué yíkè. "We have studied one lesson less than they."

Wó bí ni zǎo láile shífēnzhōng. "I came ten minutes earlier than you."

Even though the objects in these three cases belong grammatically to the whole verbal *phrase* (adverb + verb), semantically they refer back to the quality verb which functions as an adverb.

As mentioned above, a distinguishing feature of quality verbs is that they can be modified by adverbs of degree. Actually, most intransitive quality verbs, when used predicatively in declarative sentences, tend to occur with such an adverb, usually *hěn*, which is very much reduced semantically:

Zhèibě̌n shū hěn xīn. "This book is new."

If there is no such adverb of degree, the implication is usually that two qualities or things are being contrasted:

Zhèibě̌n shū xīn, nèibě̌n shū jiù. "This book is new, that one is old."

Instead of using an intransitive quality verb predicatively, one sometimes uses a nominal expression consisting of a quality verb + *de*, preceded by the central verb *shì*, as in:

Zhèibě̌n shū shì xīn de. "This book is new." (Literally: "This book is a new one.")
Zhèi shì lán de shì hóng de. "Is this blue or red?"

Intransitive quality verbs regularly modify nominals:

Duǎn kèwén róngyi, cháng kèwén yě bù nán. "The short lesson is easy and the long lesson isn't difficult either."

Functioning adverbially, they also regularly modify action verbs as adverbs, which we saw examples of above. Other examples are:

Zhèijian shì hǎo zuò. "This job is easy to do."
Zhōngguo zì, bù háo xiě. "Chinese characters are not easy to write."
Zhǐ$_1$, gòu$_2$ xiě$_3$ ma$_4$. "Is there enough$_2$ paper$_1$ to write on$_3$?$_4$"

Gòu "enough", differs from other quality verbs in that it cannot modify nominals. It can be used only predicatively, or as an adverb or a complement:

Qián gòu ma. "Is there enough money?"
Nǐ kàngòu zhèizhāng huàr le ma. "Have you looked enough at this picture?"

A quality verb modifying a verb can take (*yì*) *diǎr* "a bit, a little", which is a cognate object often used to indicate the comparative degree:

> *Kuài yìdiǎr huí jiā!* "Hurry up and get home!"
> *Màn yìdiǎr zǒu.* "Go a bit slower."

Polysyllabic quality verbs that function as adverbs usually take *de*:

> *Tā hěn zhùyì de tīng.* "He listens very attentively."

Just as a quality verb modifies a central verb as an adverb, it can also modify a central as a complement. In fact, quality verbs are the forms most commonly used as complements. Thus most resultative complements and intensifying complements are formed from quality verbs. Further, all regular predicative complements contain at least a quality verb as a nucleus. Examples of quality verbs as resultative complements:

> *Nèige wèntí, wǒ huídáduì le.* "I answered that question correctly."
> *Zhèige zì, wó xiěcuòle.* "I have written this character incorrectly."
> *Wǒ méi tīngqīngchu.* "I didn't hear (it) clearly."

As predicative complements:

> *Tā lái de hén zǎo.* "He comes very early."
> *Tā niàn kèwén, niàn de hěn shú.* "He reads the lesson very smoothly."
> *Tā shuō Zhōngwén shuō de bù liúlì.* "He does not speak Chinese fluently."

We notice, in summing up, that quality verbs typically describe the quality of a thing or an action. A thing is described predicatively: *Zhèibén shū hén hǎo.* "This book is good.", or attributively, i.e. it is modified: *hǎo shū* "good book". An action is described adverbially: *màn zǒu* "go slowly", or by a complement: *zǒu de màn* "walk slowly".

Intransitive quality verbs can occur in a large number of patterns indicating comparative degree. The coverb *bǐ* "compared with" has already been discussed (p. 157). It occurs with a quality verb as the second verb in verbal expressions in series:

> *Tā bí wo gāo.* "He is taller than me."

Comparison can also occur in an expanded predicative complement:

> *Wǒ péngyou shuō Zhōngwén, shuō de bí wo liúlì de duō.* "My friend speaks Chinese much more fluently than me."

This is a complex complement in that the quality verb *liúlì* in its turn takes the complement *de duō*.

The use of certain simple adverbs of degree also has a comparative effect. *Gèng* and *zuì* are especially common:

> *Zhèizuò shān hěn gāo, nèizuò gèng gāo.* "This mountain is high, but that one is still higher."
> *Zhèi sìge rén lǐtou, tā shì zuì gāo de.* "Of these four men he is the tallest."

c. Transitive quality verbs. The *transitive quality verbs* — like transitive *action verbs* — can take a wide variety of objects. As was shown before, they can also take complements, but more frequently they are modified by adverbs of degree. They can function adverbially, but in such cases are usually marked by *de*:

> *Xièlì fēicháng zhùyì yúfǎ. Lǎoshī fēnxi yúfǎ, tā hěn zhùyì de tīng.* "Hsieli especially pays attention to grammar. When the teacher analyzes the grammar, he listens attentively."

Transitive quality verbs function in various comparative patterns:

> *Tāmen bǐ wo liáojiě xuéxiào de qíngkuàng.* "They understand the conditions at the school better than I."
> *Tā zuì ài xiǎo érzi.* "He loves his youngest son most."

Transitive quality verbs occur in a pattern with *yǒu yìdiǎr* functioning adverbially:

> *Tā yǒu yìdiǎr xiàng tā mǔqin.* "He looks a bit like his mother."

Like other transitive verbs, transitive quality verbs usually take nominals as objects:

> *Wáng Māma zuò de cài, hěn hé wǒ de kǒuwèi.* "Wang Mama's cooking suits my taste."
> *Wǒ de péngyou, fēicháng guānxīn wǒ de shēnghuó.* "My friend is especially concerned about my livelihood."

But many also take verbs as objects:

> *Lǎoshī shuō Zhōngwén, wǒmen zhùyì tīng.* "When the teacher speaks Chinese, we make sure to listen."
> *Wǒ bù gǎnjué è.* "I don't feel hungry."

Further, the object may be a clause or a phrase:

> *Wǒ xīwàng, nǐ yǐhòu chángcháng lái wár.* "I hope you will come here often to visit us."

But consider the following:

Wó hěn gāoxìng jiàndao ni. "I'm very happy to meet you."

Here *gāoxìng* is not a quality verb but a modal verb. But *gāoxìng* can also be a quality verb, intransitive as well as transitive. In the following example it is transitive and takes a clause object:

Wó hěn gāoxìng nín néng lái. "I am very happy that you can come."

Other modal verbs also function as transitive quality verbs:

Tā hén xǐhuan Zhōngwén. "He likes Chinese."

Certain idiomatic verb + object phrases function as quality verbs, even though the verb by itself cannot take adverbs of degree; e.g. *shòu huānyíng* in:

Zhèzhǒng xīn chánpǐn, fēicháng shòu huānyíng. "This new variety of product was much welcomed (by the public)."

Shòu "to receive", is an action verb, but the phrase *shòu huānyíng* "receive welcome", takes the adverb of degree *fēicháng*.

CHAPTER VIII

SYNTACTICAL VERBAL CONSTRUCTIONS

Previously the internal structure of verbs has been examined. In this chapter we shall examine the structure of constructions that have a verb as a nucleus. Such constructions are called *verbal phrases*. In the following section, however, certain types of verbal compounds will also be discussed, since they have functions similar to those of the syntactical construction types dealt with in this chapter.

A. Verbal Complements

1. GENERAL

The modification of verbs is of two kinds, depending on position: either pre- or post-modification. A very frequent and versatile kind of post-modification is the verbal complement.

Verbal complements are either *free* or *bound*. Nuclear verbs form verbal *phrases* with free complements, whereas verbs + bound complements can be considered as *compound verbs*. Among the types of verbal complements to be discussed here, *predicative* and *verb + object complements* form verbal phrases, i.e. they are free complements, whereas *resultative, directional, potential* and *intensifying complements* are bound; the latter form verbal compounds with the verbal stem as a base.

A semantic or functional classification of complements cuts across the classification of free and bound complements. Both the predicative and the intensifying complements are typically descriptive of some quality of the nuclear or stem verb. Both resultative and potential complements express a (potential or actual) result of the action indicated in the stem verb. Directional complements indicate direction of movement of motion verbs, but are often used idiomatically with verbs other than those of motion to express result. The verb + object complements indicate direction, place, change, etc.

Finally, verbal complements differ according to whether or not they are followed by objects. Predicative and intensifying complements are *never* followed by objects, whereas verb + object complements are *always* followed by objects. Resultative, potential, and directional complements may or may not be followed by objects.

2. PREDICATIVE COMPLEMENTS

It has already been pointed out that action verbs cannot be modified by adverbs of degree. But the predicative complement following an action verb may contain an adverb of degree:

> *Tā zuótian lái de hén zǎo.* "He arrived late yesterday."
> *Ní xiě de fēicháng hǎo.* "You write particularly well."

A predicative complement normally follows an action verb, and is linked to the verb by the special marker *de.* The predicative complement is free; it always contains a verbal nucleus, which may be modified by adverbs or adverbials or may itself take a complement.

> *Wǒmen shēnghuó de hén hǎo, zǎoshang qǐ de hén zǎo, wǎnshang shuì de yě bú tài wǎn.* "We live very well, get up early in the morning, and go to bed not too late in the evening."

In the last part of this example, the nucleus *wǎn* of the complement is preceded by three adverbs.

> *Ní xiě Hànzì, xiě de bǐ ta hǎo de duō.* "You write Chinese characters much better than him."

In this example *hǎo*, the nucleus of the complement, is preceded by the coverbal phrase *bǐ ta* and is itself followed by the predicative complement *duō*. Different patterns of comparison also appear as parts of a predicative complement. Thus:

> *Ní xiě de gēn tā yíyàng hǎo.* "You write as well as he does."
> *Ní xiě zì, xiě de méi yǒu tā nèmmo hǎo.* "You don't write characters as well as she does."

The predicative complement may also consist of coordinated verbs:

> *Tā niàn kèwén, niàn de shú bu shu.* "Does he read the lesson smoothly or not?"

Nĭ shuō Yīngwén, shuō de yòu zhŭn yòu liúlì. "You speak English both correctly and fluently."
Tā xiĕ Hànzì, xiĕ de hĕn kuài, yé hĕn qīngchu. "He writes Chinese characters fast and also very distinctly."

There are cases where the predicative complement appears without the marker *de.* In such cases the verb which takes the complement often occurs with the perfective suffix *-le*:

Jīnnian zhèige gōngchăng de shēngchăn shuĭpíng bĭ qùnian tígāole hĕn duō. "This year the production level of the factory has increased very much as compared with last year."

In this, as in the following examples, there can either be the marker *de* or the suffix *-le*, but not both at the same time, since *-le* and *de* are mutually exclusive.

Zhèige dìfang găibiànle bù shăo. "This place has changed quite a bit."
Chē măile duō jiŭ le. "How long is it since (you) bought the car?"

Since *de* may be substituted for *-le* in these sentences, it seems reasonable to take them as cases of unmarked predicative complements. But it is also possible to analyze these sentences into a sentence subject (*chē măile*) + predicate (*duō jiŭ le*). The decision would depend on where the pause would be placed in actual speech.

Sometimes it is difficult to distinguish between predicative complements and potential complements. One can say: *Wŏ tīng de hĕn qīngchu.* "I hear it (very) clearly.", which obviously contains a predicative complement. *Wŏ tīng de qīngchu.* however, may contain either a simple predicative complement meaning "hear (it) clearly", or a potential complement, meaning "can hear (it) clearly". The negated form clarifies the situation, since the form containing the predicative complement will then be: *tīng de bù qīngchu* "does not hear clearly", and the potential: *tīng bu qīngchu* "cannot hear clearly". However, the sentence *Wŏ tīng bú dà qīngchu.* presents a problem. It can be taken as containing an *unmarked* predicative complement: "I don't hear too clearly." But it might seem possible also to take it as containing a potential complement: "I cannot hear too clearly." This, however, would be an exception to the rule that potential complements are bound compounds which do not allow for the insertion of other elements, since *dà* is inserted. Similarly with:

Tóngzhì, ní xiĕ de zì wŏ kàn bu dà qīngchu. "Comrade, I cannot see (very clearly) the characters you have written."

Phonological features would clarify these cases. A pause, in actual speech, before *bu* in the two examples above, would make it a predicative complement.

A special type of predicative complement occurs after quality verbs and expresses the *extent* of the quality. Such complements can take quite a variety of forms, from the simpler kinds, like *zāng de bùdéliǎo* "dirty no end", *hǎochī de duō* "even more delicious", to sequences which have sentence form, for example:

*See Basic
Chinese p 167/8*

> *Báiqiúēn dàifu gěi Bālùjūn kàn bìng, yǒu shíhou máng de lián fàn yě wàngle chī.* "When Dr. Bethune treated patients of the 8th Route Army, he was at times so busy that he even forgot to eat."
> *Wǒ lèi de chībuxià fàn.* "I am so tired that I cannot eat."
> *Nǐ xiě de xiǎo de wǒ kànbujiàn.* "You write so small that I cannot read it."

In the example about Dr. Bethune the complement consists of a coverbal phrase followed by a verb + verbal object. In the second example it is a potential complement + object, and the last example contains a predicative complement following an action verb. The nucleus of the complement (*xiǎo*) takes a complement of extent consisting of a subject (*wǒ*) and a predicate which in its turn is a potential complement construction (*kànbujiàn*).

3. INTENSIFYING COMPLEMENTS

Intensifying complements are used only after quality verbs. They are bound, and form verbal compounds with the verbs they follow. There are only a small number of these complements.

A form like *hǎojíle* "extremely good", in which *jíle* is an intensifying complement, carries a considerably stronger meaning than, for example, *zhēn hǎo* "very good" (premodification by an adverb) or *hén hǎo* "good", where *hén* is hardly more than a colorless epithet.

Further examples with -*jíle*, the most common intensifying complement: *piàoliangjíle* "extremely beautiful", *bènjíle* "extremely stupid". Other complements are *duōle*, *tòule* and *sǐle*, as in:

> *Nà hǎoduōle.* "That would be much better!"
> *Nèige rén huàitòule.* "That person is bad through and through."
> *Wǒ lèsǐle.* "I'm thrilled to death."

The complement parts of some of these compounds can also function as complements of other types, for instance as free predicative complements:

> *hǎo de duō* "very good"
> *Wó lěng de yào sǐ.* "I'm so cold that I'm dying (i.e. terribly cold)."

An intensifying complement (*-jíle*) can occur within a predicative complement. Compare:

> *Tā de Zhōngguohuà hǎojíle.* "His Chinese is excellent."
> *Tā Zhōngguohuà shuō de hǎojíle.* "He speaks Chinese extremely well."
> *Xuě xià de dàjíle.* "It is snowing extremely heavily."

From a syntactical point of view, the difference between free predicative complements and intensifying complements is that the first is free and the second bound. The difference between intensifying and resultative complements is primarily semantic. Further, a resultative complement may be followed by an object, whereas this is not the case with an intensifying complement:

> *Wǒ xiáng ni xiángsǐle.* "I miss you terribly."

4. RESULTATIVE COMPLEMENTS

A resultative complement compound consists of a stem verb, which is an action verb, and a complement, which is often a quality verb, expressing the result of the action of the stem verb.

> *Wǒ xiěcuòle zhèige zì.* "I have written this character incorrectly."
> *Nèige wèntí, tā huídáduìle.* "That question he answered correctly."

As can be seen from this, the complement may be followed by an object.

Since the result of the action logically follows the completion of the action, a resultative complement is regularly followed by the perfective suffix *-le*, and a verb with resultative complement is usually negated by *méi(you)*:

> *Nèige wèntí wǒ méi huídáduì.* "I did not answer that question correctly."
> *Zhèiběn huàbaò tā méiyou kànwán.* "He has not finished reading that illustrated magazine."

Of course, a sentence with a resultative complement can also refer to a situation in which the result has not yet been achieved. In such a case the sentence is negated by *bu*:

Zhōngwén bào wǒmen xiànzài hái bù néng kàndǒng. "We still cannot read (and understand) Chinese newspapers."

When the sentence refers to future time or is in the imperative form, the suffix *-le* is not normally used:

Wǒmen yídìng yào xuéhǎo Zhōngwén. "We certainly must study Chinese well."
Niàn₁ shú₂ kèwén₃. "Read aloud₁ the text₃ until (you read) smoothly₂."

If the resultative complement is a quality verb, it can sometimes be used adverbially to express the same idea as when it is used as a complement. Compare:

Tā wǎn láile. "He came late."
Wǒ láiwǎnle ma. "Am I late?"

A predicative complement can also be used to express (approximately) the same meaning:

Wǒ lái de wǎn ma.

Certain complements express the (successful) completion of an action; among these, we have seen examples of *hǎo* and *wǎn* ("to complete") above. Another is *dé*, as in:

Tā zuòdéle yíjiàn yīshang. "She has finished making a garment."

Guò is common as a directional complement, but can also function as a resultative complement to indicate completion, as in:

Wǒmen chīguole fàn jiù zǒu. "After eating we'll leave."

Other complements of direction can function as resultative complements. An example is *shàng*, "direction upwards", which can indicate the achievement of some goal:

Nèibù₁ jiāoxiǎngyuè₂, wǒmen₃ zhōngyú₄ tīng₅shang₆le. "We₃ finally₄ got a chance₆ to listen₅ to that₁ symphony₂."
Yào kàn zhèige diànyǐng de rén, fēicháng duō, wǒ hái méi kànshang ne. "There are an awful lot of people who want to see this movie, I still haven't got to see it."

Similarly *dào*, which indicates "direction towards", can function resultatively:

> *Ní mǎidào nèiběn shū meiyou.* "Did you get to buy that book or not?"

Jiàn "to perceive", is commonly used with various verbs of perception to indicate result:

> *Wǒ kànle, dànshi méi kànjian.* "I looked but didn't see (it)."
> *Wǒ tīngjian wàibiar xià yǔ le.* "I hear it has started to rain outside."

Another common resultative complement is *zhù*, which indicates firmness or determination:

> *Xuéguo de shēngcí, nǐ dōu jìzhùle ma.* "Do you remember all the new words you have studied?"
> *Wó jínjǐn de wòzhù ta de shǒu shuō: 'Xièxie nǐ'.* "I held his hand tightly and said: 'Thank you'."

Other complements expressing fixedness are *dìng, jǐn* and *sǐ*:

> *Zhèijiàn shì, wǒ zuòdìng le.* "I shall certainly do this."
> *Zhèi mén méi guānjǐn.* "This door was not shut tight."
> *Tā bǎ wèntí xiángsǐle.* "He thinks of the problem in a (too) fixed way."

Certain complements (such as *wán* "to complete") can follow a very large number of action verbs, others are limited to one or two lexical cases. Most fall between these two extremes. Thus one can say *sǎogānjing* "sweep clean" and *zhǎngdà* "grow big/up", where the limitations both for first verbs and complements are clear, but with *qīngchu* "clear" one can have *wènqīngchu* "ask clearly" as well as *shuōqīngchu* and *tīngqīngchu* "speak clearly" and "hear clearly", respectively.

5. DIRECTIONAL COMPLEMENTS

Both intransitive action verbs of motion and transitive action verbs indicating the handling of objects commonly take directional complements:

> *Fēijī luòxialaile.* "The plane has landed."
> *Tā zuótian nálaile hěn duō zhàopiàn.* "He brought a lot of photos with him yesterday."

Directional complements are either 1) simple or 2) compound. Simple directional complements consist of a single (directional) morpheme (e.g. *lai*). Compound directional complements consist of two (directional) morphemes (e.g. *shanglai, xiaqu*). In the latter case, the second element is either *lai* or *qu* (in this respect, these are unique). Only a small group of the most common simple directional complements form compound directional complements with *lai* or *qu* as the second element. These are: *shang, xia, jin, chu, qi, hui, guo, kai*, some of which occur in the following examples as simple directional complements:

Bié làxia dōngxi. "Don't leave anything behind."
Qíng nǐmen zài běnzishang xiěshang zìjǐ de míngzi. "Please write your names on your notebooks."
Huǒchē tōngguo nèige cūnzi. "The railroad goes through the village."
Tā náqi píbāo, jiù zǒule. "She picked up her purse and left."
sònghui Běijīng "send back to Peking"
pǎochu fángzi "run out of the house"

These complements occur more commonly, however, in the compound form with *lai/qu*.

Nèibiar fēiguolai yíge fēijī. "There is a plane flying over this way."
Tā zhànqilai gēn péngyoumen dǎ zhāohu. "He stood up to greet the friends."
Tāmen cóng wàibiar zǒujinlaile. "They came in from the outside."
Tā cóng túshūguǎn jièhuilai yìběn zìdiǎn. "He borrowed a dictionary from the library."
Wǒmen bǎ dàjiā de yìjiàn jìxialaile. "We recorded everyone's opinions."
Háizimen dōu pǎochuqu wár le ma. "Did the children all run out to play?"

In a number of the above examples we see that directional complements are followed by objects. But often the object comes between the verb and the complement — if the complement is simple (*shàng lóu lai*, see below), or the object splits the compound complement (*pǎochu jiàoshì lai*, see below). In these cases *lai* and *qu* invariably come after the object. At this point it is important to keep in mind the multiple functions of *lai/qu* discussed on pp. 164–166, especially their function as particles of purpose, which is often difficult to distinguish from their function as complements split from the rest of the verb by an object. Examples:

Tā shàng lóu laile. "He came upstairs."

Xiàle kè, tā huí jiā qu le. "After school was over, he went home."
Dàjiā dōu pǎochu jiàoshì lai huānyíng xīn tóngxué. "All have come running out of the classroom to welcome the new students."

If the object is a place word, it *must* come before *lai/qu*, as in the three examples above; in other cases the object may either come before *lai/qu*, or it may come after the full verbal complement form:

Wǒ yào qù sùshè, ná yìzhī gāngbǐ lai. "I want to go to the dorm to fetch a pen."
Tā cóng zhuōzishang náqi yìzhāng bào lai, zuòxialai kàn. "He picked up a newspaper from the table and sat down to read it."
Tā cóng zhuōzishang náqilai yìzhāng bào. "He picked up a newspaper from the table."

Other directional complements are, for example, *dào, zǒu, diào*: *Dǎdào diguózhǔyì.* "Down with imperialism!" where *dǎdào* literally means "to knock down". *Zǒu* and *diào* both indicate direction "away":

sòngzǒule "has sent away"
pǎodiàole "has run away"
Màozi gěi fēng guāzǒule. "My hat has been blown away by the wind."
Túshūguǎn de xīn huàbào yìběn yě méi yǒu le, dōu jièzǒule. "There is not even one new illustrated magazine in the library, they have all been lent out."

These latter and similar directional complements cannot form compound complements with *lai* and *qu*.

6. POTENTIAL COMPLEMENTS

Almost all resultative and directional complements can be changed into potential complements by the insertion of infixes *de* or *bu*:

kànbudǒng "cannot understand (when reading)"
tīngdejiàn "can hear (when listening)"

The potential form is semantically practically equivalent to a construction consisting of the modal verb *néng* + a verb with a resultative or directional complement.

Potential complements function as regular verbal compounds. They can take objects:

Tā yíge rén bānbudòng nèizhāng zhuōzi. "He cannot move that table by himself."

Nǐ tīngdedǒng Zhōngwén guǎngbō ma. "Can you understand broadcasts in Chinese?"

There are actually many more possible potential verbal compounds than those that can be formed from resultative and directional complements. Some are exclusively potential in form, others may occur in non-potential forms such as predicative complements. An example of the latter:

Xué wàiwén bù cháng shuō, jiù shuōbuliúlì. "When studying a foreign language, if one doesn't speak it often, one won't be able to speak it fluently."

The non-potential form would be *shuō de (bu) liúlì* "(does not) speak fluently". The complement *liǎo*, which indicates ability (to do something), is much more common in the potential form than in the resultative form:

Míngtian qù cānguān gōngchǎng, nǐ qùdeliǎo qùbuliǎo. "We are going to visit a factory tomorrow, will you be able to go or not?"

Wǒmen zuò liànxí, yòngbuliǎo zhèmmo duō zhǐ. "We won't use this much paper to do our exercises."

Jīntian wǎnshang de jīngyàn jiāoliúhuì, nǐ cānjiādeliǎo ma. "Will you be able to participate in tonight's meeting for exchange of experience?"

As shown in the first of the examples above, the alternative question form includes both the negative and the positive potential complement. Another example:

Wǒ zhèiyàng shuō, nǐmen tīngdeqīngchǔ tīngbuqīngchǔ. "If I talk like this, can you hear me clearly or not?"

It may sometimes be difficult to distinguish between the positive potential complement and the predicative complement, such as with the form *tīng-de-qīngchǔ* (discussed on p. 178). The possibility of a mixup, however, exists only where the predicative complement is minimal, i.e. consists only of one word, and where there is nothing else determining the case to be one of potential complement, such as a following object.

Potential complements are compounds that cannot as a rule be further expanded. But we saw earlier (p. 178) a possible exception to this rule: *Wǒ tīngbudàqīngchǔ.* "I cannot hear too clearly." where the potential meaning is clear from the context.

Directional complements can also take the potential form, as in:

Nèiliàng qìchē zuòdexià sìshíge rén. "That bus can seat 40 people."

Shūjiàshang fàngdexià zhèmmo duō shū ma. "Can one put down this many books on the bookshelf?"

But commonly a potential complement which consists of one of the more typical directional verbs has lost the directional meaning and acquired a specialized idiomatic meaning such as "attain a result", "finish", and so forth. Some examples:

Zhèijiān sùshè, zhùdexià zhùbuxià sānge rén. "Is this room big enough for three people?"

Nǐ zhèmmo shuō, jiào ta liǎnshang xiàbulái. "When you talk this way, you will embarrass him."

Zhège dìfang, nǐ guòdelái guòbulái. "Can you get used to living here?"

Tā xìng shémmo, wǒ yìshí shuōbushànglái le. "I can't recall at the moment what his name was."

Nǐ chīdelái wǒ zuò de fàn ma. "Do you like the food I have prepared?"

A kind of reduced or minimal potential complement consists of the stem verb + *de*: *yàode* "desirable", *chīde* "eatable − taste good", *zuòde* "can be done − feasible", *dǒngde* "understand", *jìde* "remember".

7. Verb + Object Complements

The distinguishing feature of this final category of verbal complements is that there must always be an object following the complement (e.g. *zhùzai Běijīng* "lives in Peking"). These complements form a small listable group, the most important members of which are: *zai, dao, cheng, gei, yu, xiang.* With the exception of *cheng* these can all function as coverbs, and a verb + object complement construction can in principle be translated into a construction consisting of coverb + object + verb. Compare:

Wǒ zhùzai Běijīng zhùle yìnián. "I lived one year in Peking." (complement)

Wǒ zài Běijīng zhùle yìnián. (coverb)

Wǒ jìgei ta yìfēng xìn. "I mailed him a letter." (complement)

Wó gěi ta jìle yìfēng xìn. (coverb)

Zhōnghuá Rénmín Gònghéguó yú yìjiǔsìjiǔnián shíyuè yírì chénglì. "The People's Republic of China was established on October 1, 1949." (coverb)

Lǐ Shí-zhēn shēngyu yìwǔyìbānián. "Li Shih-chen was born in 1518." (complement)

Of course this kind of change from a coverb to a complement construction cannot be done mechanically; in principle the two alternatives are semantically equivalent constructions. But, as will be shown, the complement construction is becoming more and more prevalent, especially in writing.

Cheng cannot function as a coverb, and thus differs from the other complements in this group. It expresses change or transformation:

Zhèiben shū, yǐjīng fānyicheng Yīngwén le. "This book has already been translated into English."
Tā bǎ sāndiǎn bàn xiěcheng sìdiǎn bàn le. "He wrote 4:30 for 3:30."

Zai, dao, and *yu* all take objects of location:

Shàng kè de shíhou, tā zuòzai wǒ qiánbian. "He sits in front of me in class."
Zhèige fēijī, luòzai něige fēijīchǎng. "At what airport is this plane landing?"
Wómen zǒudao xuéxiào. "We are going to school."
Zhèizhǒng fēizifěn bú yào shǐyòngzai háizi shēnshang. "Do not use this kind of talcum powder on children."
Tiānānmén wèiyu Běijīng de zhōngxīn. "Tien-an Men is located in the center of Peking."

These complements also indicate time, and more abstract relationships:

Měitian wǎnshang wǒ dōu xuéxídao shídiǎn bàn. "I study till half past ten every evening."
fāshēngzai guòqù de mǒu yícì shìjiàn "an event that happened sometime in the past"
guānxidao shèhuìzhǔyì gémìng "has an important bearing on the socialist revolution"
Tǎolùn bú yào júxiànyu zhèngzhì wèntí. "The discussion must not be limited to political questions."

There is a special use of *yu* after quality verbs, or verbal phrases that function as quality verbs, like *yǒuyìyu* ("be of benefit to") in:

Wǒmen yào quánxīn quányì wèi rénmín fúwù, zuò yíge yǒuyìyu rénmín de rén. "We must serve the people wholeheartedly and become persons beneficial to the people."

The same idea can be expressed in a coverb construction using *yú*:

> *Jīngcháng duànliàn yú shēntǐ yǒu yì.* "Constant exercise is beneficial to one's health."

This *yú* is becoming ever more frequent, and is used regularly after certain verbs, like *gǎn*:

> *Shǐ rénmín gǎnyu shuō huà, gǎnyu pīpíng, gǎnyu zhēnglùn.* "Let the people dare to speak out, dare to criticize, dare to debate."

B. Verbal Expressions in Series

1. DEFINITION

The term "verbal expressions in series", originally introduced by Chao (1948, pp. 38–39), refers to a specific type of syntactical construction in which the first verb(s) stand(s) in a relation of subordination to the last. It is the relationship between these two or more verbs/verbal phrases that distinguishes verbal expressions in series from other kinds of construction that also consist of two or more verbs.

Verbal expressions in series make up only one predicate, and there is therefore only one subject (simple or complex) for the different verbs of the series. Thus verbal expressions in series are different from a succession of clauses, which must each have its own predicate.[1]
Examples of clauses in succession:

> *Wǒmen chī fàn, yě hē jiǔ.* "We eat food and (we) also drink wine."
> *Tā zài kàn bào, wǒ zài xiě xìn.* "He is reading the paper, I'm writing a letter."

Examples of verbal expressions in series:

> *Wǒ qù shàng kè.* "I am going to attend class."
> *Tā yòng kuàizi chī fàn.* "He eats with chopsticks (uses chopsticks to eat)."

Verbal expressions in series should also be distinguished from coor-

---

[1] Even though the subject of the first clause may be common to several clauses, it is possible to repeat this subject for each clause, and in this respect clauses in succession differ from verbal expressions in series.

dinated verbs or verbal phrases. The order of the latter is reversible without any change in meaning:

Tā yòu yònggōng yòu piàoliang. "She is both diligent and beautiful."

Finally, verbal expressions in series should not be confused with various kinds of verb + object constructions, where the object is a verb or a verbal phrase, e.g. *Wǒ míngtian bù néng lái.* "I cannot come tomorrow.", where we have a modal verb *néng* taking *lái* as an "object". This is by far the most common type, but non-modal verbs can also take verbal objects:

Wǒmen liànxí xiě Hànzi. "We practice writing Chinese characters."
Nǐ zhīdao bu zhidao tā zài nǎr. "Do you know where he is?"

In the last example the object of *zhīdao bu zhidao* has a clause-like segmental form. But all these cases differ from verbal expressions in series, where the relationship is not one of a verb directed towards an object.

It is important to note that the relation between the verbs in the series is one of subordination, with the last (usually the second) verb as the center, modified by the preceding verb(s) or verbal expression(s). This is what is common to all verbal expressions in series, but there are minor variations from case to case. These will be illustrated below.

2. FORMAL TYPES OF VERBAL EXPRESSIONS IN SERIES

By far the most frequent type consists of a coverb with an object, followed by a second verb, which may or may not have an object; the last verb is the center.

yòng Yīngwén xiě yìfēng xìn "write a letter in English"
bèi rén piànle "has been fooled by someone"

The section on *coverbs* (pp. 150–159) has numerous illustrations of verbal series. One other variant is the type where the coverb has no object:

Qīnlüèjūn dōu bèi gǎnchuqule. "The invading troops were all chased out."
Wǒ bèi piànle. "I was fooled."
Wǒ bù dǒng wàiguohuà, qǐng nǐ gěi fānyi. "I don't understand any foreign language, please translate for (me)."

A somewhat more complex type consists of more than two verbs or verbal phrases. The occurrence of two or even three coverbal phrases before the central verb is not unusual:

> *ná yàoshi bǎ zhèige mén kāikai* "try and open this door with a key"
> *yòng dǎzìjī bǎ zhèixiē jùzi dǎchulai* "type these sentences out with a typewriter"

In the following example one of the coverbs lacks an object:

> *Bié bǎ bēizi géi dǎpòle.* "Don't break the cup for (me)."

An example with three coverbal phrases and a central verb is:

> *Tā cóng Shànghǎi zuò huǒchē dào Běijīng lái de.* "He came from Shanghai to Peking by train."

The examples used so far have contained one or more coverbs, but a first verb in a verbal expression in series construction is not necessarily a coverb. Description verbs may also be used, in which case there may or may not be an object. Some examples are: *lái wár* "come to play", *kūzhe chūqule* "went out crying", *shuìwánle qǐlai* "get up after having slept", *Hǎiwá tīngle gāoxìngjíle.* "Haiwa listened and became extremely happy." In the second example given here, the first verb takes the suffix *-zhe*, which is quite common for first verbs in verbal series which are not coverbs. In the third example the first verb takes a resultative complement and a suffix.

Some examples where the first verb has an object:

> *Děng yìhuǐr qù!* "Wait a while before you go!"
> *mǎile piào jìnqu* "bought the ticket and went in"
> *kāi huì tǎolùn* "hold a meeting to discuss"
> *guāngzhe tóu chūqu* "go out bare-headed"

A variant of this type is the case in which a verb is followed by an object, and then is repeated with a predicative complement; a verb + predicative complement cannot be followed by an object: *xiě Hànzì xiě de hén hǎo* "write Chinese characters very well". This case is somewhat special, as identical verb forms occupy first and second verb positions.

Only the second verb has an object in the following examples:

> *Wǒ qù shàng kè.* "I am going to attend class."
> *zuòzhe kàn bào* "read the newspaper sitting"

Both verbs have objects:

> *Wǎnshang wǒmen qù túshūguǎn kàn shū.* "In the evening we go to the library to read books."

There can be more than two verbs in the series: *dào wǎn chá lái hē* "pour a cup of tea to drink", *dá shuǐ qù xízǎo* "bring water to (go to) take a bath".

Further, numerous combinations of the types described above are possible, for example:

Tā zài jiā mángzhe zuò fàn ne. "She is busy at home making food."
xiě$_1$ *xìn*$_2$ *gěi*$_3$ *tā*$_4$ *dào*$_5$ *hè*$_6$ "write$_1$ a letter$_2$ to give$_5$ congratulations$_6$ to$_3$ him$_4$".

In the last example we have a case of a coverbal phrase *following* a verbal phrase. This somewhat unusual constellation can be explained by means of an analysis into immediate constituents (ICs), which would give *xiě xìn* as the first IC and *gěi tā dào hè* as the second. Thus the relationship between *gěi tā* and *dào hè* is the same as that of all other coverbal phrases to a central verb, and the relationship between *xiě xìn* and the second IC is the same as that commonly found between two predicative verbs in a verbal series: *purpose*. The letter is written *in order to* give congratulations. Thus the order of the two ICs is *not* reversible. In this respect the construction is different from that of a coordinate construction.

By way of summary, we present a list of the types that have been illustrated here (in order of occurrence), which will give an idea of the versatility of verbal series:
 (1) coverb + object/verb (+ object)
 (2) coverb/verb
 (3) coverb + object/coverb + object/verb
 (4) coverb + object/coverb/verb
 (5) coverb + obj./coverb + obj./coverb + obj./verb
 (6) verb/verb
 (7) verb + *zhe* (or: resultative compl.)/verb
 (8) verb + object/verb
 (9) verb + object/verb + predicative compl.
(10) verb/verb + object
(11) verb + object/verb + object
(12) verb + object/verb/verb
(13) coverb + object/verb + *zhe*/verb + object
(14) verb + object/coverb + object/verb + object

3. SEMANTIC CATEGORIES OF VERBAL SERIES

The meaning of verbal expressions in series is always modification (specification of manner, instrumentality, etc.) of the action indicated by the last verb. This relation of modification is most obvious when the first verbs are coverbs. Coverbal phrases are often said to function *adverbially*. The more specific meaning of a given verbal series with coverbs depends on the lexical meaning and function of the given coverb. Earlier these were discussed in categories depending on what kind of relations they expressed, such as: spatial and temporal relations (p. 151), instrumental (p. 153), pretransitive (p. 154), benefit (p. 155), causal (p. 156), association or coordination (p. 156), comparison (p. 157), inclusion and exclusion (p. 157), passive (p. 158), and reference to topic (p. 158).

In the case of verbal series that contain no coverb, the relation indicated is usually one of sequence in time, the action of the first verb occurring before that of the second. Alternatively, the first verb gives the manner in which, or the circumstances under which, the action of the second (last) verb takes place, such as in *zuòzhe kàn bào* "read the paper sitting".

Another important relation expressed in this way is that of purpose, e.g. the translation *"in order to"* of *xiě xìn gěi tā dào hè* "write a letter in order to give congratulations to him". This function tends to overlap with that of time sequence. Thus in *Wǒ qù shàng kè.* "I am going to attend class.", there is something of purpose as well as time sequence. Similarly in the following example: *Wǒ mǎi yìfèn lǐ sòng rén.* "I buy a gift to give to someone.", although the purpose-relation is dominant here.

C. Verb + Object Constructions

1. DEFINITION

The center in a verb + object construction is the verb, i.e. the first immediate constituent. In this respect the construction resembles the verbal complement constructions and, by the same token, differs from verbal expressions in series, where the center is the last constituent.

The first constituent is always a verb, whereas the second element — the object — can be a verb, a noun, or a clause-like sequence, as will be seen from the examples below. The fact that the object of a verb + object construction can sometimes be transformed into the subject of a subject + predicate construction — or vice versa — should not be allowed to confuse the concept of verb + object. It is the relative position of the verb and its object — that the verb *precedes* its object — that determines that we have a verb + object construction. We are not here concerned with the so-called "logical" object, i.e. the thing really acted upon. Thus

Láile yíge kèrén. "A guest has come."

is a verb + object construction, actually a predicate with no subject, whereas

Kèrén láile. "The guest has come."

is a subject + predicate construction. The same applies to common idioms like

Xià$_1$ yŭ$_2$ le$_3$. "It is raining (lit. (There is) coming down$_1$ rain$_2$ now$_3$)."
Qĭ$_1$ wù$_2$ le$_3$. "Fog$_2$ has$_3$ come up$_1$". i.e. "It is foggy now."

In a verb + object construction the verb may take a suffix, and the object may consist of a modifier + head.

2. TYPES OF OBJECTS

a. Nominal objects. Most objects are simply nouns or pronouns:

yòng kuàizi chī fàn "eat food with chopsticks (lit. use chopsticks eat rice)"
bă nèibĕn shū gĕi ta "give him that book (lit. take that book give him)".

It is above all coverbs, classificatory verbs, and transitive description verbs that take ordinary nominal objects of this kind.

Included in this category are also objects which from a logical or semantic viewpoint would seem to be subjects, such as in the following examples:

Chū tàiyang le. "The sun is out."
Xiàzhe yŭ ne. "It is raining."
Yào guā fēng le. "It is going to be windy."
Tā sĭle xífu. "He suffered the unexpected death of his wife."
Wŏ liú xuè le. "I am bleeding."

b. Double objects. A number of verbs take one indirect and one direct object, in that order. The first is often a pronoun and the second usually a noun, as in:

Lăoshī jiāo women Zhōngwén. "The teacher teaches us Chinese."
sòng ta yífèr lĭ "send him a gift"

gěi ta yìdiǎr qián "give him some money"
piànle wo xǔduō qián "swindled me out of a lot of money"

Sometimes the direct object is in the segmental form of a clause; in this case too the indirect object comes first:

Tā₁ gàosu₂ wo₃ diànyǐng₄ de₅ nèiróng₆ hén₇ hǎo₈. "He₁ told₂ me₃ the content₆ of₅ the movie₄ was very₇ good₈."
Lǎoshī gàosu wo wǒmen míngtian qu cānguān gōngchǎng. "The teacher told me that tomorrow we are going to visit a factory."

c. **Cognate objects.** These are objects which are *not* goals of an action (in the same way as a book that is bought, or a person who is being taught a language). The cognate object expresses something supplementary to the action of the verb itself, such as length of time, number of occurrences, or some other quantitative concept. Examples are:

Tā zài gōngchǎng yǐjīng gōngzuòle sānnián le. "He has already worked three years at the factory."
Yǔ xiàle yíge duō xiǎoshí. "It rained for more than an hour."

Notice that here *yǔ* is the subject, whereas in *xià yǔ* ("it is raining"), it is the object.

Nǐmen xué Zhōngwén xuéle bànnián duō le ba. "You have studied Chinese for over half a year, I suppose?"
děng yìhuǐr "to wait a while".

Cognate objects can further express the number of times the action occurred, as in:

Nǐ gēn ta jiànguo jǐcì jiù shóu le. "After you have met him a few times, you'll be better acquainted."
dá liǎng xiàr "strike a couple of strikes"
kànle liáng yǎn "gave two glances".

Similar to this is the case where the cognate object contains the verb itself repeated. This usage is also very similar to the verbal reduplication discussed under *verbal structure* (p. 133), and the meaning lies somewhere between that of reduplication (the tentative aspect) and that of a cognate object indicating the number of times the action has occurred ("once"): *kàn yíkàn* "take a look", *jiǎng yìjiǎng* "explain a little", *xiào yíxiào* "smile a smile".

A cognate object may also be used after an intransitive quality verb; it expresses quantity. Examples are:

Ní hǎoxiang shòule yìdiǎr. "You seem a little thinner."
Tā chángle sāncùn. "He is taller by three inches."

d. Place words. Certain verbs are limited to taking place words as objects, and are considered intransitive verbs because of this limitation. Examples of intransitive verbs of motion with place words as objects, are: *lái Zhōngguo* "come to China", *dàoguo Xīhú* "has been to the West Lake", *qù Běijīng* "go to Peking", *shàng/xià kè* "go to/leave class (lit. go up to/go down from class)". More examples are given in the section on intransitive action verbs (p. 167).

e. Verbal objects. Modal verbs take only verbs or verbal expressions as their objects:[1] *bú huì shuō wàiguohuà* "cannot speak any foreign language", *yīnggāi xuéxi* "ought to study", *yào qù túshūguǎn* "wants to go to the library", *pà shuō huà* "be afraid to talk", *xǐhuan kuài* "like to be fast".

Often action verbs take verbal objects[2] in such a manner that one can say that the verbal object is the goal of the action of the central verb, for instance:

jìnzhǐ chōu yān "prohibit smoking"
kāishǐ gōngzuò "begin to work"
Wǒ gēn wo de tóngxué yìqǐ liànxí xiě Hànzì. "I practice writing Chinese characters together with my schoolmates."
Zhōngyāng juédìng chèxiao huìbào tígāng. "The Central (Committee) has decided to revoke the outline report."

In some cases a "verbal object" seems to take on a nominal value, especially if preceded by a measure: *gǎn ge zǎo* "makes a try at being early" *tú ge kuàihuó* "attempt to be happy". In other cases of the same type, no measure is included: *chīguo xiāng* "has eaten (what is) fragrant" (i.e. "has been in favor"), *bāng wo de máng* "help my being busy (i.e. help me)".

f. Clause objects. These are objects in the form of a clause containing a subject. Typically the so-called "think" verbs take such objects:

Wǒ xīwàng nǐ gēn wo yìqǐ qù. "I hope you'll go with me."
Wǒ juéde tā shuō Zhōngwén shuō de fēicháng hǎo. "I feel he speaks Chinese exceptionally well."
Wó xiǎng tā bù lái le. "I guess he's not coming after all."

---

[1] In *bú huì Zhōngwén* "do not know Chinese", *huì* is not a modal verb but a regular transitive action verb.
[2] Or objects in the form of a verbal expression, e.g. verb + (nominal) object.

Verbs expressing knowledge or perception also take clause objects:

Nǐ zhīdao bu zhidao tā zài nǎr. "Do you know where he is?"
Wǒ kànjian tā cóng gōngchǎng huíláile. "I saw he came back from the factory."

Similarly verbs of indirect reported speech:

Wǒ shuō qián de shì bú yàojǐn. "I say the matter of money is not important."
Zuótian guǎngbō shuō jīntian huì xià yǔ. "Yesterday it was said on the radio that it would rain today."

In most cases of indirect reported speech, double objects are used. The first object is usually a pronoun or a noun; the second a clause object. Examples of this kind were given above (p. 194).

g. **Pivots.** A common construction type is one in which the object of one verb is at the same time the subject of a following verb. This has been called (by Chao 1968) a pivotal construction, and the nominal which performs the double function is called a pivot. The verbs that take a pivot as an object are limited in number and are often called "link" verbs. Examples:

Tā qǐng wo tīng yīnyuè. "He asked me to listen to music."
Tā bāngzhu wo xué Zhōngwén. "He helped me to study Chinese."
Tā shǐ wó hén gǎndòng. "He caused me to feel very moved."
Tā jiào wo tántan gōngzuò jīngyàn. "He told me to talk about my work experience."
Gǔ shíhou yǒu ge lǎo rén jiào Yú Gōng. "In ancient times there was an old man named Yü Kung."

Often a "link" verb starts the sentence without itself having a subject:

Qǐng nín děng yìhuǐr. "Please wait a while (lit. (we) ask you to wait a while)."
Yǒu rén qiāo mén. "There is someone knocking at the door."

3. WHAT VERBS TAKE WHAT OBJECTS

From what has been said about the different types of objects it is clear that there are many limitations as to what kinds of objects given types of verbs may take. By way of summary the following outline may be useful:

1) *Classificatory* verbs normally take regular nominal objects; specifically, *zài* takes place words and *yǒu* takes pivots.

2) *Coverbs* primarily take nominal objects; some take place words.
3) *Modal* verbs are limited to taking verbs as objects.
4) *Transitive action* verbs are most versatile in regard to the kinds of objects they take. They can take nominal objects, or cognate objects. Those verbs that usually take double objects, verbal objects (aside from *modal* verbs), clause objects, and pivots are also transitive action verbs.
5) *Intransitive action* verbs are usually limited to taking place words and cognate objects. However, these verbs may be used causatively, and in that case are transitive, e.g. *lái*, as in: *lái yìwǎn tāng* "bring (lit. cause to come) a bowl of soup".
6) *Transitive quality* verbs take nominal objects.
7) *Intransitive quality* verbs are usually limited to cognate objects.

Something remains to be said about combinations of verbal complements with objects.

1) *Predicative* complements cannot be followed by objects. Instead, the verb is repeated with the complement after the object: *shuō Zhōngwén, shuō de fēicháng hǎo* "speaks Chinese exceptionally well".
2) The same is true of *intensifying* complements: *pà guǐ pàjíle* "is extremely afraid of ghosts". This is, however, a relatively rare construction type.
3) Verb + object complements pose no problem since they are always followed by objects. It should be noted that if, in addition, one wants to use a cognate object of time, the *verb + object* construction is transformed into a verbal series construction, as in: *zài Běijīng zhùle sānnián* "lived three years in Peking".
4) *Potential* complements. Since the pretransitive construction is excluded in the case of potential complements, if there is an object it is necessarily and invariably placed after the complement.
5) *Resultative* complements may take objects, but are usually also combined with the pretransitive construction.
6) This holds for *directional* complements as well, but these are special in that their objects can be placed *within* the complement itself, as well as after it. Actually, what happens is that *lai* or *qu* – either as a simple directional complement or as the last element of a compound directional complement – regularly comes *after* the object: *huí sùshè qu le* "returned to the dormitory", *pǎochu jiàoshì lai le* "ran out of the classroom".
7) The same holds for compound directional complements in the *potential* form: *bānbujìn wūzi qu* "cannot move (it) into the room".

CHAPTER IX

ADVERBS AND THEIR FUNCTIONS

A. Adverbs as a Word Class

Adverbs are limited to occurring as modifiers of verbs or verbal expressions.

1. "PURE" ADVERBS

A relatively large number of words can function only as adverbs. Many of these are words that occur very frequently, such as *dōu, hěn, yě, jiù* in:

> *Wǒmen dōu lái.* "We are all coming."
> *Zhèběn shū hén hǎo.* "This book is very good."
> *Nèibén yé hǎo.* "That one is also good."
> *Wǒ jiù yǒu yìzhī gāngbǐ.* "I only have one pen."

Others are *gèng, zuì, hùxiāng,* and *chángcháng* as in:

> *Tā bǐ wo gèng liáojiě Běijīng de qíngkuàng.* "He knows even more about Peking than I."
> *zuì zhòngyào de shì* . . . "the most important is . . ."
> *Zài gōngzuòshang, wǒmen hùxiāng xuéxí, hùxiāng bāngzhu, jīngcháng jiāoliú jīngyàn.* "At work we study together, help each other, and constantly exchange experiences."
> *Tā chángcháng qu kàn diànyǐng.* "He often goes to see movies."

The most frequent adverb is the negator *bu*:

> *Wǒ bu dǒng.* "I don't understand."

2. QUALITY VERBS AS ADVERBS

As was mentioned in the discussion of intransitive quality verbs, one of their more important functions is to serve as adverbs. This is not true of all such verbs, but a large number of intransitive quality verbs frequently occur adverbially, e.g. *jīngcháng* "constant(ly)" in one of the examples above.

Zhēn "real, really," etc. rarely, if ever, functions predicatively as a verb, but takes on many of the other functions of quality verbs, such as modifying nominals: *zhēn zuànshí* "real diamond", or occurring nominalized with *de*, as in: *Shì zhēn de ma.* "Is it true?" Thus it is rather defective as a verb, but is frequent as an adverb. At any rate, *zhēn* is an illustration of the close relationship between the two classes.

Other examples of quality verbs as adverbs: *màn/kuài zǒu* "walk slowly/rapidly", *dà kū* "cry greatly", *duō liànxí* "practice a lot", *zǎo qǐlai* "get up early".

Hǎo functions as an adverb to a quality verb (almost synonymous with *hěn*) as in the greeting:

Hǎo jiǔ bú jiàn. "I haven't seen you for a long time."

It may also modify a group measure or a quantifier: *hǎo xiē rén* "quite a few persons", *hǎo jǐ nián* "several years". In the latter case *hǎo* does not modify the nominal expression as a whole, and it expresses a quantity rather than a quality. Here it seems to be closer to the adverbial function than to its function as a quality verb modifying a nominal.

3. ADVERBS AND MODAL VERBS

Adverbs and modal verbs share the property of appearing before other verbs and of being separable from the following verb only by other adverbs. Examples: *Néng lái* "is able to come", *bù lái* "(does) not come". But the two constructions are different in that a modal verb is actually the center of the predicate in which it occurs, whereas adverbs are subordinate to the verbs.

One way of showing this difference is to turn the verbal phrases containing the modal verb and adverb respectively into alternative questions. Then one gets: *Nǐ huì shuō Zhōngguohuà.* "You know how to speak Chinese.", which becomes: *Nǐ huì bu huì shuō Zhōngguohuà.*, whereas *Tā chángcháng shuō Zhōngguohuà.* "He often speaks Chinese." can be turned into a question only by means of the interrogative particle *ma.* There is no form **chángcháng bù chángcháng*.

4. ADVERBS AND MARKERS

It is not always easy to distinguish between markers and adverbs. Some markers are clearly not adverbs in that they can precede other kinds of words than verbs or adverbs. But since many markers *do* precede only verbs or adverbs, positional criteria are not sufficient to determine whether a given word is a marker or an adverb. Semantic criteria therefore become decisive. A (pure) marker has grammatical meaning only, whereas an adverb possesses lexical meaning. Thus *jiù* is a marker in:

Nǐ bù chūqu, jiù bǎ zìxíngchē jiè wó qǐ yíxiàr. "If you are not going out, then let me ride your bike a bit."

It indicates the beginning of the predicate. However, in:

Wǒ jiù yǒu yìzhī gāngbǐ. "I only have one pen."

jiù is an adverb. The borderline between impure markers and adverbs is, however, not always completely clearcut.

B. Phrases with Adverbial Functions (Adverbials)

1. UNMARKED ADVERBIALS

The first verb(s) in verbal expressions in series constructions may be said to function adverbially. Thus all coverbal phrases function in this way: *yòng kuàizi chī fàn* "eat with chopsticks", *Bié chòngzhe rén dǎ tì!* "Don't sneeze facing people!"

Similarly a first verb with suffix *-zhe* often functions adverbially: *mángzhe zuò fàn* "be busy cooking", *zuòzhe kàn bào* "read the newspaper sitting", *guāngzhe tóu chūqu* "go out bare-headed". In the last example we have V-*zhe* + O as a phrase which functions adverbially. Another example is: *zhāngzhe zuǐ dàxiào* "laugh greatly with the mouth open."

A little more special is: *yòng xīn zuò* "work carefully (lit.: use mind do)." which is a coverbal phrase. But *yòngxīn* can also function as a quality verb, and if such a verb is used adverbially we get: *yòngxīnzhe zuò* "work carefully".

2. MARKED ADVERBIALS

The most common form of marked adverbial is the reduplicated quality verb. A quality verb like *yòngxīn* occurs adverbially, as in: *yòngyòngxīn-xīnde zuò* "do it very carefully."

Other examples of this kind of reduplication, which gives an impression of liveliness:

gāogāoxìngxìngde qù le "went happily"
mànmārde zǒu "walk slowly"
hǎohāorde xuéxí "study well"
Zhuōzi₁ shang₂ zhéngzhěngqíqíde₃ fàng₄zhe₅ jǐběn₆ shū₇. "On₂ the table₁ some₆ books₇ were₅ ly₄ing₅ very neatly₃."
zǎozāorde zǒu leave early".

These examples show that *de* is a marker of adverbial modification. Its function is not, however, limited to reduplicated forms: *bù tíng de kū* "cry without stopping", *bú zhù de hài bìng* "constantly troubled by sickness".

The modifier can also be a repeated numeral + measure construction: *yíjù yíjù de jiěshì* "explain sentence by sentence", *yícì yícì de lái* "come time and again", *yígè yígè de náqilai* "pick up one by one".

In *pīnzhe mìng pǎo* "run like mad" no marker is included (zero marker). But in this and similar cases, a resumptive marker *nèmmo* may be inserted before the main verb as if to emphasize the adverbial nature: *pīnzhe mìng nèmmo pǎo* "run as if to save one's life", *dèngzhe yǎnjing nèmmo kàn* "look with staring eyes", *yìzhī jiǎo nèmmo zhànzhe* "stand on one foot".

This *nèmmo* can be replaced by *de* or occur together with *de*: *pīn mìng de pǎo* "run like mad", or *pīn mìng de nèmmo pǎo*.

C. Functions of Adverbs

1. MODIFICATION OF PREDICATE NUCLEI

This is the most common function of adverbs, and is illustrated in most of the examples given so far. These predicate nuclei have in all cases so far been verbs. Adverbs may, however, occasionally modify nominal predicates as well:

Zhèige rén gòu péngyou. "This man (is) enough of a friend."
Nà yídìng hǎo xiāoxi! "That certainly (is) good news!"
Nǐ jiǎnzhí shǎzi me! "You (are) just a fool!"

2. MODIFICATION OF ADVERB + VERB PHRASES

A first adverb modifies a verbal phrase consisting of adverb + verb: *hěn bù hǎo* "very bad". Here *hěn* modifies *bù hǎo*, not *bu* alone. This is also true of the following examples. If there are more than two adverbs in a row, the first adverb always modifies the whole of the following verbal expression. Examples are: *bù hén hǎo* "not very good", *Tāmen dōu fēicháng gāoxìng.* "They are all very happy." *yě dōu hěn bù hǎo* "are also all very bad".

Since the first adverb modifies the rest of the following verbal phrase, the order of the adverbs will often be crucial to the meaning of the verbal phrase. Consider the following:

> *Wǒmen dōu bú shàng kè.* "None of us are going to class (lit. we are *all not* going to class)."
> *Wǒmen bù dōu shàng kè.* "We are not all going to class."

3. ADVERBS AS INTENSIFYING COMPLEMENTS

Hěn and *jíle* (cp. p. 179) are adverbs[1] functioning as predicative, intensifying complements: *hǎo de hěn* "*very* good", *piàoliangjíle* "extremely pretty". These adverbs can also precede the verb (*hén hǎo, jí piàoliang*) with almost the same meaning.

4. MODIFICATION OF NUCLEI OF PREDICATIVE COMPLEMENTS

Since the predicative complement nuclei (*hǎo* and *liúlì* in the examples below) in practically all cases are verbal, they can be modified by adverbs – as can predicate nuclei of the same verbs. Thus we have:

> *Tā xiě de hén hǎo.* "He writes very well."
> *Tā shuō de fēicháng liúlì.* "He speaks exceptionally fluently."

5. MODIFICATION OF VERBS FUNCTIONING ATTRIBUTIVELY

Verbs used in attributive positions are also modified by adverbs, as are verbs in other positions: *kuài zǒu de rén* "the person who walks rapidly", *zuì piányi de shū* "cheapest books".

In the discussion of intransitive quality verbs it was said that these verbs could modify nominals directly if they were monosyllables. If,

---

[1] Strictly speaking *jí* is an adverb, while *jíle* is *always* an intensifying complement.

however, this attributive monosyllabic quality verb is modified by an adverb, a marker of modification (*de*) must come between the modifier phrase and the modified noun: *hǎo rén* "good man", *but*: *hén hǎo de rén*.

D. Semantic Categories of Adverbs

Adverbs as well as adverbials can be categorized into a number of classes according to their semantic functions. The coverbal phrases have already been so classified under the discussion of coverbs (pp. 151—159). Adverbials (or first verbs in verbal series) which consist of a verb followed by the suffix *-zhe*, usually express *manner*, and so do the reduplicated quality verbs: *zuòzhe kàn bào* "read the paper sitting", *mànmārde zǒu* "walk slowly".

Many adverbs also express manner. This is true of most of the quality verbs functioning as adverbs discussed above (p. 199).

Another important class of adverbs expresses *degree*. Adverbs of degree are important in that they are used to define quality verbs, which are the only verbs they can precede. We have already seen examples of *hěn* "very", *fēicháng* "exceptionally", *zuì* "most", *gèng* "still more". There are many others.

The adverbs of *negation* are very important, although very few. The most frequent are *bu* (which negates all verbs except *yǒu*) and *méi*, which negates *yǒu*, as well as action verbs with aspect suffixes *-le* (in non-negated form), *-zhe*, and *-guo*. This *méi* must not be confused with the negative transitive verb *méi*. A third adverb of negation is *bié* "don't", used in commands.

Adverbs of *time* make up a fairly large class of such frequent adverbs as *xiān* "first", *jiù* "right away", *cái* "just now", *zài* "once more", *hái* "still", and many others.

Adverbs of *interrogation* are also few but important, such as *duōmo* "how, to what degree", *zěmmo* "how, in what manner".

There are still more categories, but those mentioned above are the most important.

CHAPTER X

NOMINAL
STRUCTURE

A. Introduction

1. GENERAL

Nominals are non-negatable words which can occur before and after verbal nuclei. With the exception of pronouns, they are generally modifiable by determinative compounds, by verbs, and by sequences which have the segmental form of clauses.

Examples of nominals: *píngzi* (noun) "bottle"; *gōngchǎng* (noun) "factory"; *zì* (noun) "character"; *Zhōngguó* (place name) "China"; *shàngtou* (place word) "top (of something)"; *míngtian* (time word) "tomorrow"; *tā* (pronoun) "he, she, it".

Examples of modification of nominals: *wǒ jiā* "my family", where the nominal *wǒ* modifies another nominal *jiā*; *tā shuō de huà* "the words he says", where a nominal *huà* is being modified, with the marker *de*, by a sentence-like sequence consisting of a subject *tā*, which is a nominal, and a predicate, the verb *shuō*.

For a detailed analysis of nominals, their distinctive properties and their different classes, the reader is referred to Chapter XI, pp. 221–262. The syntactical properties are dealt with in Chapter XII, pp. 263–274. The present chapter concentrates on the morphology or structure of nominals in general. We shall give an analysis of nominals in order to identify the elements of which they consist, to show the relationship between the components, and to point out how and to what extent different classes of nominals can be established by means of morphological criteria.

2. STRUCTURE OF NOMINALS

From a structural point of view, a nominal is a simple (i.e. monomorphemic) word, a complex word, or a compound (i.e. polymorphemic) word. Nominals are primary or, in the case of compound or complex words, secondary words. Most nominals are free words, but some are bound (cp. p. 106).

A *simple* nominal consists of a root morpheme, which is either monosyllabic or polysyllabic. *Rén* "person" is a simple nominal consisting of one monosyllabic root morpheme; *dōngxi* "things" and *bōli* "glass (the material)" are simple bisyllabic nominals.

A *complex* nominal consists of one or several root morphemes and an affix, usually a suffix: *bàngzi* "a club, a stick" is a complex nominal consisting of a root morpheme *bàng* "club, stick", and a nominal suffix *-zi; shítou* "stone" is a nominal in which *shí* is the bound root, and *-tou* is a nominal suffix. As these examples show, the root morpheme may be bound or free; e.g. *shí-* "stone" is a bound root morpheme, while *bàng* in *bàngzi* is a free root morpheme. A complex noun is a so-called derived word (cp. p. 14). Thus, *shítou* is said to be derived from *shí*, and *bàngzi* from *bàng*. If the root morpheme is an otherwise free morpheme, the complex nominal is a secondary derived word: *lóngzi* "a deaf person" is derived from the free morpheme *lóng* "to be deaf". A primary derived complex nominal contains a bound root morpheme, e.g. *jìngzi* "mirror", based on the bound morpheme *jìng* "mirror".

A *compound* nominal is a word containing more than one root morpheme, usually two or three. The compound word is either an endocentric or an exocentric construction. An endocentric compound nominal is *jīdàn* "egg", where *dàn* is the center, while *mǎimai* "trade" is an exocentric compound nominal (two verbal roots form a noun). The root morphemes may be free or bound morphemes. In *jīdàn* "hen's egg", *jī* "chicken, fowl" and *dàn* "egg" are both free morphemes. In *quánshuǐ* "a spring", *quán* "spring" is a bound morpheme while *shuǐ* "water" is a free morpheme. Compound nominals are further discussed below, on p. 213.

B. Nominal Suffixes

1. GENERAL

Suffixes are start-bound morphemes with a purely grammatical function. They occur only as word constituents. The present chapter deals with nominal suffixes only; for verbal suffixes, see p. 116. Nominal suffixes form a listable class. They are attached to nominal or verbal root morphemes to form complex words, and, as a rule, receive zero stress.

Their principal function lies in word formation (they are morphological markers). Some nominal suffixes form complex words belonging to the class of nominals called "nouns", while other nominal suffixes form place words or time words. The nominal suffixes thus mark a word as a nominal, and they also define the class membership of the nominal.

We shall distinguish between three kinds of nominal suffixes: noun suffixes, place word suffixes, and time word suffixes.

2. NOUN SUFFIXES

The noun suffixes form a closed class of five suffixes: *-r*, *-zi*, *-tou*, *-ba* and *-men*. These suffixes may be affixed to nominal root morphemes, like *xìngr* "an apricot", *wǎngzi* "a small net", *háizi* "a child"; or to verbal root morphemes like *gǔnzi* "a roller" (*gǔn* "to roll"). The resulting nominal word is always a noun (cp. pp. 222–225).

Historically, these suffixes are reduced forms of free words. Forms with *-zi* and *-r* often show modification of meaning as compared to the root morpheme, like *hào* "to waste" and *hàozi* "rat, mouse".

Suffixed nouns are numerous; no attempt will be made here at a comprehensive listing (Chao (1968, pp. 228–244) gives a fairly exhaustive inventory).

a. The suffix *-r*. This suffix occurs in a large number of words. It forms nouns from nominal and verbal morphemes, bound or free morphemes. If the root morpheme is a bound morpheme, the resulting noun is a primary derived noun: *huār* "flower" (*huā* "flower", bound form); *zǐr* "a seed" (*zǐ* "child", bound form); *liàngr* "light, illumination" (*liàng* "to be bright", bound form); *páir* "a trade mark" (*pái* "a signboard", bound form); *yǎr* "eye, small hole" (*yǎn* "eye", bound form).

If the root morpheme is a free word, the resulting complex noun is a secondary derived noun: *shìr* "business, event" (*shì* "matter", free word); *chàngr* "a song" (*chàng* "to sing", free word); *huàr* "a picture" (*huà* "to draw", free word); *gàr* "a lid" (*gài* "to cover", free word); *qiúr* "a small ball" (*qiú* "ball", free word).

An individual measure can also form complex nouns with the suffix *-r*. The nouns so formed are usually nouns denoting the shape or size of the thing referred to, e.g. *tiáor* "thickness of a strip", *gèr* "stature of a person" and *zhāngr* "thickness of a sheet".

In a few cases it is possible to form a complex measure, i.e. a measure consisting of a measure + suffix *-r*: *bĕr* "volume of books" and *duìr* "pair of something"; *sānduìr gēzi* "three pairs of pigeons".

It should be noted that *-r* can be attached to action verbs as well as to quality verbs: *gàr* "lid" and *chàngr* "song" (both have action verbs as root morpheme, cp. above); *kōngr* "leisure" (*kōng* "empty", quality verb); *gāngr* "square" (*gāng* "square", quality verb); *huángr* "yolk" (*huáng* "yellow", quality verb).

There are several complex nouns in Chinese consisting of two root morphemes and the suffix *-r*. Very frequently, the complex noun is formed from a quality verb as a first root morpheme modifying a noun as the second root morpheme, e.g. *lăotóur* "old man", *xiăoháir* "child", *lăopór* "old woman". Another common construction is a complex noun consisting of two nouns as root morphemes, either of which may be free or bound. The relation between the two elements is usually that of subordination, e.g. *ménkŏur* "doorway", *miáotour* "sign, mark", *fànguăr* "restaurant", *yănjìngr* "eyeglasses". Examples of root morphemes in coordination: *miànpángr* "face, countenance" from *miàn* (bound) and *páng* (bound) both meaning "face"; *wèizhìr* "position" from *wèi* "position" (bound) and *zhì* "to establish" (free). Some suffixed nouns are also formed from a base consisting of a verb of action as the first root morpheme and a noun as the second. The relation between the verb and the noun is often that of verb + object. The meaning is usually specialized and not immediately deducible from the parts. Examples: *dīngzhir* "needle" from "to push a needle", *qŭhuŏr* "lighter" from "to get light".

We have mentioned that *-r* serves as a suffix whose function is to mark the complex word as a noun. Additionally, it sometimes implies the idea of smallness or lightness in style and tone, e.g. *shéngr* "a cord or small rope" (*shéng* "a rope"), *qiúr* "a small ball" (*qiú* "a ball"). The meaning of the suffixed form can sometimes be predicted from the meaning of the constituent morphemes, as in *miànpángr* "face". In other cases the suffixed form acquires a specialized meaning: *tiār* "weather" from *tiān* "sky, heaven" and *xìr* "message" from *xìn* "letter".

b. The suffix *-zi*. This suffix has a function similar to *-r*, in that it marks the complex word as a noun. There are actually a number of nouns which are formed from the same root morpheme but with alternating *-zi* or *-r* with no change of meaning, e.g. *dāor* or *dāozi*, "knife" and *háir* or *háizi* "child". The complex nouns formed with *-zi* can be analyzed according to the kind of root morphemes they have.

Primary derived nouns with *-zi*: *háizi* "child" (*hái* "child", bound form); *kuàizi* "chopsticks" (*kuài* "chopsticks", bound form); *shēnzi* "body" (*shēn* "body", bound form).

Secondary derived nouns with *-zi*: *dāozi* "knife" (*dāo* "knife", free word); *shūzi* "comb" (*shū* "to comb", free word); *wānzi* "a turn, a bend" (*wān* "to bend, to turn", free word); *pàngzi* "a fat person" (*pàng* "to be fat", free word).

A measure functioning as a root morpheme joins with the suffix *-zi* to produce complex nouns denoting some quality, for instance size or shape, e.g. *gèzi* "stature of a person", *fènzi* "gift".

Suffixed forms with *-zi* may be based on action verbs as well as quality verbs (cp. above). With a verb of action the resulting noun usually denotes the action, the agent or the goal of the action expressed in the verb: *shuāzi* "brush", from the verb *shuā* "to brush"; *yìnzi* "imprint", from the verb *yìn* "to print"; *lòuzi* "tract", from the verb *lòu* "to leak".

With a verb of quality as root morpheme the suffixed form with *-zi* is a noun denoting a thing or person, and at the same time some quality of this thing or person, like *shǎzi* "fool", from the verb *shǎ* "to be foolish"; *jiānzi* "a point", from the verb *jiān* "to be sharp"; *lóngzi* "a deaf person", from the verb *lóng* "to be deaf".

A very large number of complex words with suffix *-zi* have the form of a nominal preceded by a verb of quality which modifies the nominal: *lǎomāzi* "maid-servant", from the verb *lǎo* "to be old" and the noun *mā* "mother".

Complex suffixed nouns are also formed with a verb of action as the first root morpheme and a nominal, usually a noun, as the second morpheme, but this construction is not very common. Examples: *yáshuāzi* "tooth-brush", from the verb *shuā* "to brush" and *yá* "tooth"; *wéizuǐzi* "a bib" from the verb *wéi* "to surround" and *zuǐ* "mouth"; *xīnniángzi* "a bride", from *xīn* "new"; and *niángzi* "young woman."

More numerous, however, are suffixed forms consisting of a nominal, usually a noun, followed by another nominal, e.g. *shūjiàzi* "bookshelf" (*shū* "book" + *jiàzi* "a stand, a frame"), and *xiébázi* "shoehorn" (*xié* "shoe" + *bázi* "a puller").

Finally, a complex noun may be formed with a determinative compound as root morpheme. The determinative compound must consist of the numeral *yī* "one" and a measure. Examples of this kind of noun are *yíbèizi* "(one's) whole life", *yíyuànzi* "the whole courtyard", and *yíjiāzi* "the whole household". Nouns can be formed in this way provided that the measure can be followed by *-zi*, as with the measures *-jiā* "house" and *-yuàn* "courtyard" above.

c. **The suffix** *-tou*. This suffix does not have the same versatility as *-zi* and *-r*. The number of complex nouns with *-tou* is, however, consider-able. Most of these suffixed forms have a noun or a bound morpheme as root morpheme. Examples: *nǎitou* "nipple" with *nǎi* "breast, milk" (free word); *páitou* "the first in a row" with *pái* "row" (measure); *shétou* "tongue" with *shé* "tongue" (bound form); *shítou* "stone" with *shí* "stone" (bound form).

The suffix *-tou* is affixed to a verb of quality or action. With the quality verbs *zhǔn* "to be exact or true" and *shǎo* "to be short" the nouns *zhǔntou* "certainty" and *shǎotou* "shortage" are formed.

A special idiomatic construction with complex nouns of this kind, i.e. with a verb of action as root morpheme, is made with the verb *yǒu* "to have" and its negation *méi yǒu* "not to have", e.g. *méi yǒu chītou* "is not worth eating" and *yǒu kàntou* "is worth seeing".

d. The suffix *-ba*. This suffix is much less common than those previously listed. It is in fact only found in a few complex nouns, like *wěiba* "tail", *níba* "mud", and *líba* "fence".

e. The suffix *-men*. This suffix may be called a "pluralizing" suffix. Its main function is to produce explicit collective forms of nouns and pronouns. These forms are often translatable as plurals in English.

Nouns are generally to be taken in a collective sense by implication (*rén* "people"). The suffix *-men* makes this implicit sense explicit. It can only be used, however, with proper nouns and with personal pronouns. It is never used if a numeral is included in the modifier. Examples: *háizimen* "children", *lǜshīmen* "lawyers", *tóngzhìmen* "comrades". Note that there is no **sānge háizimen*, only *sānge háizi* "three children" is possible. With pronouns: *wǒmen* "we, us" (= he, she, and I); *zámen* "we, us" (= you and I); *nǐmen* "you" (plural); *tāmen* "they".

3. PLACE WORD SUFFIXES

Place word suffixes form a listable group of monosyllabic and bisyllabic start-bound morphemes. The suffixes generally have zero tone and no stress, and they have a very high degree of versatility. The place word suffixes occur with preceding nominal root morphemes in complex words. The root morpheme is very frequently a noun, a pronoun or a place name. The function of the place word suffix is to mark the word as a place word. The resulting word is called a complex place word. Examples: *chéngli* "in the city", consisting of the noun *chéng* "city, town" and the place suffix *-li* "inside"; *shānxia* "below the mountain", with the suffix *-xia* "below" and the noun *shān* "mountain", as root morpheme; in *nǐnar* "(over) there where you are", a pronoun *nǐ* "you" serves as the root morpheme, and *-nar* "there" is the place word suffix.

In other cases, however, the root morpheme is a locator stem (cp. p. 252). Locator stems form a listable group of end-bound nominal morphemes denoting a relative position in space, e.g. *lǐ-* "inside", *hòu-* "behind" and *xī-* "west". A list of locator stems is given in Chapter XI, p. 253. The locator stems occur as root morphemes in complex words with certain place word suffixes; *-bian/-biar* "side", *-mian/-miar* "side", *-tou* "end", *-r* and *-li* "inside". The resulting secondary derived words are called complex relative place words. Examples: *lǐtou* "inside" with locator stem *lǐ-* and the suffix *-tou* "end"; *nàr* or *nàli* "there" consisting of the locator stem *nà-* "there" and the suffixes *-r* "inside" and *-li* "inside."

The complex place words and the complex relative place words function as ordinary place words (cp. p. 250), e.g.

> *Wǒmen zhùzai chéngli.* "We live in the city."
> *Shānxia yǒu yìtiáo cháng de hé.* "There is a long river below the mountain."
> *Lǐtou méi yǒu rén.* "There is no one inside."[²]
> *Nàli de bǎihuògōngsī hěn dà.* "The store over there is very big."

In the first sentence, a complex place word, *chéngli*, functions as an object to the verb *zhùzai*. In the two succeeding sentences, *shānxia* and *lǐtou*, a complex place word and a complex relative place word respectively, serve as sentence subjects. The last sentence illustrates the position of a complex relative place word in the attribute position of a subordinative construct.

The place word suffixes are listed below: *-bei* "north", *-bian/-biar* "side", *-dong* "east", *-hou* "behind", *-jian* "between", *-li* "inside", *-nan* "south", *-mian/-miar* "side", *-nàr/-nèr* "there", *-nǎr/-nèr* "where?", *-nei* "inside", *-pang* "side", *-qian* "front, before", *-qianhou* "thereabouts", *-r* "inside", *-shang* "above", *-shangxia* "thereabouts", *-tou* "end", *-wai* "outside", *-xi* "west", *-xia* "below", *-you* "right", *-zher* "here", *-zhong* "between", *-zuo* "left", *-zuoyou* "thereabouts."

4. TIME WORD SUFFIXES

Time word suffixes form a listable group of monosyllabic and bisyllabic start-bound morphemes. The suffixes generally have zero tone and no stress, and they have a very high degree of versatility. They form complex words with preceding nominal root morphemes. The root morpheme is commonly a noun or a time name (cp. p. 257), and the function of the suffix is to mark the resulting word as a time word. The complex word is called a complex time word, e.g. *wǎnshang* "in the evening" with a noun *wǎn* "evening" and the time suffix *-shang* "in, on"; *chūntianli* "during, in the spring" with the time suffix *-li* "in" and the time name *chūntian* "spring" as root morpheme. In *Sòngcháochu* "at the beginning of the Sung dynasty", the time suffix *-chu* "beginning" is part of the complex word which has the time name *Sòngcháo* "the Sung dynasty" as a root morpheme.

In other cases, however, the root morpheme is a time stem. Time stems (cp. p. 260) form a small listable group of end-bound nominal morphemes denoting a relative position in time, e.g. *qián-* "before last", *hòu-* "after next", *zuó-* "yesterday", *míng-* "tomorrow", and *jīn-* "today". The time stems form complex relative time words with the time suffix *-r* "day", e.g. *míngr* "tomorrow", *qiár* "the day before last".

Both the complex time words and the complex relative time words function as ordinary time words. Examples:

> *Míngr wǎnshang wǒ niàn shū.* "Tomorrow evening I am (going to) study."
>
> *Chūntianli de tiānqi hěn huài le.* "The weather during the spring was very bad."

In the first sentence the sentence topic consists of two time words, the complex relative time word *míngr* and the complex time word *wǎnshang*. In the second sentence, the sentence subject is a subordinate construct with a complex time word, *chūntianli*, as the attribute.

The time suffixes are listed below: *-chu* "beginning", *-di* "end", *-hou* "after", *-li* "in, on", *-mo* "end", *-nei* "in, during" (rare), *-qian* "before", *-qianhou* "thereabouts", *-r* "day", *-shang* "in, on, before", *-shangxia* "thereabouts", *-wai* "outside" (rare), *-xia* "in, on, after", *-xian* "before", *-zhong* "between", *-zuoyou* "thereabouts".

C. Nominal Prefixes

1. INTRODUCTION

The nominal prefixes form a small class of bound morphemes which, in combination with other elements, form complex nominals. A prefix is affixed to a bound morpheme, forming a primary derived nominal, or to a free root morpheme, forming a secondary derived nominal. Examples of primary derived nominals are *dìmò* "the last" (consisting of the ordinal prefix *dì*- and the bound morpheme *mò* "last"), *chūyī* "the first of the month" (prefix *chū*-, and a numeral *yī* "one"), *Lǎo Wáng* "Wang" (prefix *lǎo*-, which is common before a surname). It should be noted that both numerals and monosyllabic surnames are bound morphemes; they thus form *primary* derived nominals. Examples with free root morphemes: *lǎoyīng* "eagle" (the prefix *lǎo*-, and *yīng* "eagle"), *lǎodà* "the eldest" (of a group of children).

Of the prefixes listed below, *lǎo*- and *chū*- should be distinguished from the homophonous free word *lǎo* meaning "old" and the bound morpheme *chū* meaning "beginning".

2. THE PREFIX LǍO-

As already shown in the examples above, *lǎo*- occurs in names of animals, e.g. *lǎoyīng* "eagle", in terms of informal address before monosyllabic surnames, e.g. *Lǎo Wáng*, and in kinship terms to indicate an order of age or status, e.g. *lǎodà*. Further examples are *láoshǔ* "mouse", *lǎoyā* "a crow", *láohǔ* "tiger", *lǎosān* "number three" (among a group of children in a family), *Lǎo Qián* "Ch'ien" (surname).

The use of *lǎo*- with surnames indicates familiarity. It is used when addressing or mentioning another person in an informal way. Examples: *lǎobó* "uncle" (who may be a genuine brother or merely a friend of the father's), *lǎodiē* "uncle" (informal way of addressing an old man), *lǎogē* "my friend".

3. THE PREFIX DÌ-

This is the general ordinal prefix in Chinese. It occurs affixed to numerals, forming complex nominals like *dìyī* "number one" or "the first", *dìwǔ* "number five" or "the fifth", *dìsānshísì* "number 34" or "the thirty-fourth", *dìyìbǎi* "number 100" or "the one-hundredth", and so forth. *Dì*- is not put directly in front of *-bǎi* "a hundred", *-qiān* "a thousand" and *-wàn* "ten thousand" because these are group measures (cp. p. 246).

4. THE PREFIX CHŪ-

This prefix functions in much the same way as *dì*-, but its use is more restricted. It is affixed to a numeral to denote the first ten days of a month, e.g. *chūyī* "the first" (day of the month), *chūèr* "the second" (day of the month), and so forth.

D. Compound Nominals

1. GENERAL

An exhaustive classification of compound nominals is beyond the scope of this book. For a detailed treatment of such forms the reader is referred to Chao (1968, pp. 359–495).

For our purposes a survey of the most common types will have to be sufficient. Our discussion will be based on two criteria. A c̓ompound is analyzed primarily with regard to the freedom of the parts and secondarily with regard to the grammatical relations between the parts (in other words, in terms of the internal structure). A subsidiary criterion is endocentricity versus exocentricity.

An endocentric compound "has its center within", i.e. the function of the whole is in the main identical with the center (head) of the construction. A non-endocentric compound is called exocentric, i.e. it "has its center without".

Examples of exocentric compounds are *tiānliàng* (noun "heaven" + verb "brighten" = verb) "dawn"; *mǎimai* (verb "buy" + verb "sell" = noun) "trade"; *lǐngshì* (verb "lead" + noun "affairs" = noun) "consul"; *dāngjú* (verb "to be in charge of" + noun "office" = noun) "authorities".

Examples of endocentric compounds are *dàmén* (quality verb + noun = noun) "front door"; *jīdàn* (noun + noun = noun) "egg"; *niúròu* (noun + noun = noun) "beef"; *dòngwù* (verb + noun = noun) "animal". The centers of these compounds are *mén*, *dàn*, *ròu*, and *wù*, respectively.

2. FREEDOM OF THE PARTS

The root morphemes of a compound nominal are either bound morphemes, or free words in other contexts.

A compound may consist of only nominal constituents, only verbal constituents, or it may be a combination of a nominal and a verbal constituent: *fēijī* (verb + noun) "air-plane", *yìsi* (noun + noun) "meaning", *fùmǔ* (noun + noun) "parents", and *biānji* (verb + verb) "editor".

Many compounds carry a specialized lexical meaning, e.g. *dàyī* ("big" + "coat") "overcoat" and *cháfang* ("tea" + "room") "waiter". Very often, however, the meaning of the compound is directly deducible from its parts, e.g. *cūhuà* ("coarse" + "words") "coarse language"; *jiānnán* ("hardships" + "difficulties") "hardships"; *yánse* "color"; *shēngyīn* "sound"; *zhíjiǎ* "fingernail"; *liánhuā* "lotus"; *yìsi* "meaning", "intention"; *guójìyuàn* "international institution" (*guójì* is bound).

(a) Both root morphemes are bound morphemes, as in *qìyuē* "contract, agreement"; *yīnghái* "an infant"; *zīwèi* "taste"; *xìngqu* "interest"; *fùqin* "father"; *fùmǔ* "parents".

(b) The first part of the compound is a bound morpheme and the second is a free word, as in: *jiézuò* "masterpiece", *méimao* "eyebrows", *guójìhuì* "international meeting", *jìnéng* "skill", *yúncai* "clouds", *diànhuà* "telephone", *jūnrén* "soldier".

(c) The first part of the compound is a free word and the second part is a bound morpheme, as in: *yǎnlèi* "tears", *yínqì* "silverware", *cháyè* "tea leaves", *qīngtái* "moss", *tiàowǔ* "a dance", *xīnzàng* "the heart".

(d) Both or all parts of the compound are free words, as in: *háidǎo* "island", *mǎimai* "trade, business", *pūgai* "bedding", *huójiǔ* "alcohol", *dàyáng* "ocean".

3. INTERNAL STRUCTURE

a. **General.** The internal structure of a compound nominal refers to the grammatical relations between the constituent morphemes. In the case of syntactically free constituents, as in *dàyáng* "ocean" (*dà* "big" and *yáng* "ocean" are both free morphemes), this relationship is usually easy to determine. If one or both constituents are bound forms, the relationship is not always clear, at least not from a descriptive point of view.

We shall, for our purposes, distinguish between four classes of compounds with regard to internal structure.

(1) If the first constituent modifies the second, as in *huǒchē* "train", and *zhèige* "this (one)", the form is a subordinative compound of type I.
(2) If the second constituent is historically the object of the first constituent, i.e. a verb—object construction, as in *lǐngshì* "consul", the form is a subordinative compound of type II.
(3) If none of the constituents is a modifier of the other, i.e. if both constituents are centers, as in *shēngyīn* "sound", the form is a coordinative compound.
(4) If the second constituent is historically a predicate attached to the first constituent, which is a subject, as in *tiānliàng* "dawn", the form is a subject + predicate compound.

b. **Subordinative compounds. Type I.** The center of the compound is most frequently a noun; the attribute is another noun or a verb.

Examples: *cháfáng* ("tea" + "room") "waiter"; *dōngtian* ("winter" + "time") "winter"; *huǒchē* ("fire" + "vehicle") "train"; *dàrén* ("big" + "person") "adult"; *měirén* ("beautiful" + "person") "beautiful woman"; *bāogōng* ("to hold" + "work") "contracted work"; *fēiyú* ("to fly" + "fish") "flying fish"; *huángyóu* ("yellow" + "oil") "butter"; *wòchē* ("to sleep" + "vehicle") "sleeping-car".

This class of compounds forms an open class, and several compounds have a meaning which is directly deducible from the meaning of the constituent parts. However, many subordinative compounds of type I carry a specialized meaning as seen in the examples above.

Determinative compounds form a subtype of this class of subordinative compounds. In a compound of this subtype, the center is a measure (cp. p. 243) which is modified either by a demonstrative (cp. p. 234) or by a numeral (cp. p. 239). Determinative compounds form a large class of transient words which have the modification of nouns as one of their main functions (cp. p. 232). Determinative compounds consisting of a demonstrative and a measure: *měige* ("each" + "piece") "each"; *biélèi* ("another" + "type") "another type"; *nèiwèi* ("which" + "person") "which person?"; *jǐcì* ("a few" + "a turn") "a few times". Determinative compounds consisting of a numeral and a measure: *sānbǎi* ("three" + "a hundred") "three hundred"; *liùbēi* ("six" + "cup") "six cups"; *liǎngge* ("two" + "piece") "two pieces of".

Demonstratives and measures are bound morphemes, but numerals include both bound morphemes and free words.

c. Subordinative compounds. Type II. This class of compounds consists of a number of exocentric compounds with a verb or a morpheme functioning as a verb as the first immediate constituent, and a noun or a morpheme with nominal function as the second constituent. The meaning of such a compound is frequently somewhat specialized, and can only in a few cases be directly deduced from the meaning of the separate parts. Examples: *lǐngshì* ("lead" + "affairs") "consul"; *zhījǐ* ("to know" + "oneself") "friend"; *diǎnxīn* ("to dot" + "the heart") "refreshments"; *dàishù* ("to substitute" + "numbers") "algebra".

d. Coordinative compounds. The immediate constituents of these compounds are free words or bound morphemes. Each constituent is a center, in contrast to the subordinative compounds discussed above. The order of the parts is irreversible. Thus *shūbào* means "reading matter", and there is no *bàoshū* in this sense. The constituents frequently belong to the same form class or word class, as will be evident from the examples:

(a) Both constituents are nouns, e.g. *shūbào* ("books" + "periodicals") "reading matter"; *chēmǎ* ("vehicles" + "horses") "traffic"; *shēngyīn* ("sound" + "sound") "sound"; *yǔyán* ("words" + "speech") "language"; *shānshuǐ* ("mountains" + "waters") "landscape"; *fùmǔ* ("father" + "mother") "parents". Some words of this category, like *shēngyīn* "sound" and *yǔyán* "language" represent a coordination of synonyms or near-synonyms. In other cases the constituents are antonyms. Coordination of antonyms is mostly used in forming compounds consisting of two intransitive quality verbs denoting opposite qualities, cp. below.

(b) Both constituents are verbs of quality: *fánnǎo* ("vexed" + "angry") "vexation"; *chángduǎn* ("long" + "short") "length"; *gāodī* ("tall" + "low") "height"; the last two compounds show the coordination of two antonyms.

(c) Both constituents are verbs of action, e.g. *fēnxī* ("divide" + "separate") "analysis"; *cáiféng* ("cut" + "sew") "tailor"; *jiàoshòu* ("teach" + "transmit") "professor"; *kāiguān* ("to open" + "to close") "switch".

(d) Both constituents are measures, which are bound morphemes, e.g. *jīnliǎng* ("catty" + "tael") "weight" and *hángliè* ("columns" + "rows") "formation".

(e) The first constituent is a noun, and the second is its ordinary measure; the result is often a noun with collective meaning. Examples: *zhǐzhāng* ("paper" + "sheet") "stationery" (cp. *yìzhāng zhǐ* "a sheet of paper"); *chēliàng* ("car" + "wheel") "cars" (cp. *yíliàng chē* "a car"). Note that such compounds cannot be formed freely; only certain combinations are allowed.

e. Subject + predicate compounds. The first constituent is usually a noun or a morpheme with nominal function, and the second a verb or a morpheme with verbal function. Examples: *tóuténg* ("head" + "painful") "headache"; *tiānliàng* ("day" + "brightens") "dawn"; *zhèngbiàn* ("government" + "changes") "coup d'état".

4. COMPLEX COMPOUNDS

The term "complex compound" as used here, means a compound consisting of more than two (usually three) constituents, e.g. *fēijīchǎng* "airport". Very often the first immediate constituent, in this case *fēijī*, which is a bimorphemic compound (*fēi* "to fly", modifies *jī* "machine"), modifies the second immediate constituent (here *chǎng* "field"). In other cases the first immediate constituent is a single morpheme, whereas the second is a compound. In *báipízhǐ* ("white" + "leather (like) paper") *bái* modifies the compound *pízhǐ* in which *pí* in turn modifies *zhǐ*.

Further examples: *huǒchē/zhàn* ("train"/ + "stand") "station"; *lùyīn/jī* ("record-sound"/ + "machine") "tape-recorder"; *jīnyú/chí* ("goldfish"/ + "pond") "goldfish pond".

The constituents of complex compounds can include both nouns and verbs in a great number of forms. A case of two verbs in the form of a coordinate compound modifying a noun, is *shēngjiàng/jī* "elevator" ("rise" + "descend"/ + "machine"). *Huǒchē/zhàn* "railway station" and *jīnyú/chí* "goldfish pond" contain only nouns, but in *qǐzhòng/jī* ("raise + weight"/ + "machine") "a crane" and in *lùyīn/jī* "tape-recorder", a verb-object compound modifies the final constituent.

Forms consisting of four root morphemes are on the borderline between words and phrases. Whether or not they are taken to be compounds, they mostly consist of two bimorphemic constituents in a subordinate construction. Each compound constituent may belong to any of the compound types discussed above. Common examples are *gōnggòngqìchē* ("public-together" + "steam-vehicle") "bus", *bǎihuògōngsī* ("hundred-goods" + "public-store") "department store".

5. USEFUL MORPHEMES IN WORD FORMATION

In English some morphemes, like -*er*, -*tion*, etc., occur as endings in a large number of nominal forms. Chinese also has a number of such end morphemes. Although they have some of the characteristics of suffixes, we shall deal with them here as components of compounds. Only a few of the most common morphemes can be dealt with. In addition to those which occur as end morphemes we shall also mention a few whose position is at the beginning of a compound word.

a. End morphemes.

1) -*dān* "document", e.g. *huòdān* "invoice", *shōudān* "a receipt".
2) -*fǎ* "method"; *fēnxifǎ* "method of analysis".
3) -*fǎ* "law", "method", e.g. *mínfǎ* "civil law", *xíngfǎ* "criminal law".
4) -*fū* "man", *e.g. pǐfu* "common man", *nóngfu* "farmer", *dàifu* "doctor", *zhàngfu* "husband".
5) -*guān* "point of view", e.g. *zhǔguān* "subjectivity", *luòguān* "optimism", *bēiguān* "pessimism".

6) *-jiā* "-ist", e.g. *kēxuéjiā* "scientist", *huàxuéjiā* "chemist", *xiǎoshuōjiā* "novelist".

7) *-lùn* "theory", e.g. *fāngfǎlùn* "methodology", *wéixīnlùn* "idealism".

8) *-qì* "air, essence", e.g. *qīngqì* "hydrogen" ("light air"), *yǎngqì* "oxygen", *píqi* "temperament", *yǒngqì* "courage".

9) *-rén* "man", e.g. *gōngren* "worker", *dàren* "adult", *láiren* "messenger".

10) *-shì* "scholar", "one who belongs to a profession", e.g. *hùshi* "nurse", *xuéshi* "Bachelor (of Arts)", *jiàoshi* "minister".

11) *-shī* "master, teacher"; *jiàoshī* "teacher", *lǜshī* "lawyer".

12) *-xīn* "heart", e.g. *cúnxin* "one's frame of mind", *nàixin* "patience", *zìxìnxīn* "self-confidence" ("self-confident-heart"), *liángxin* "conscience".

13) *-xìng* "nature, temperament", e.g. *tiānxing* "natural gifts", *tèxing* "specific properties", *jìxing* "memory".

14) *-xué* "a branch of study", e.g. *zhéxué* "philosophy", *dòngwùxué* "zoology", *xīnlǐxué* "psychology".

15) *-yuán* "member of a group", e.g. *guānyuán* "official", *hǎiyuán* "seaman", *fēixíngyuán* "pilot".

b. First morphemes. These are fewer in number than the end morphemes above, but they are quite common.

1) *dān-* "mono-, single", e.g. *dāntǐ* "a simple substance", *dānrén* "a single person", *dānwèi* "a standard".

2) *duō-* "many, poly-", e.g. *duōyì* "ambiguity", *duōshù* "majority", *duōyuánlùn* "polymorphism".

3) *fǎn-* "anti-, against", e.g. *fǎnluàn* "rebellion", *fǎndòng* "reaction", *fǎnguāng* "reflection".

4) *zì-* "self", e.g. *zìyóu* "liberty", *zìzhuàn* "autobiography", *zìzhì* "self-government".

E. Reduplication

1. GENERAL

Nominals in reduplicated form are based on roots which are free words or bound forms. The root *dì* in *dìdi* "younger brother" is a bound form; on the other hand, *rénrén* "everybody" is based on the free word *rén*.

Reduplication consists in repetition or partial repetition of a given morpheme, and it has a grammatical function. Reduplicated nominal forms are found 1) in certain terms of address denoting kinship (*dìdi* "younger brother"), 2) in a number of miscellaneous nouns (*zhūzhu* "spider"), and 3) in words which have a distributive meaning (*rénrén* "everybody"). As a rule, the repeated form has zero tone and no stress.

Reduplicated measures form a special category. These forms have distributive meaning (*zhāngzhāng* "every sheet"), and normally occur with stress and tone.

2. REDUPLICATED NOMINAL FORMS

The reduplication of nouns is most commonly seen in connection with terms of address denoting a person of kinship. The word being reduplicated is either a free word, e.g. *māma* "mom" and *bàba* "dad", or a bound morpheme, e.g. *dìdi* "younger brother" and *năinai* "grandmother". Further examples: *jiějie* "older sister", *mèimei* "younger sister", *gēge* "older brother". Note also *băobao* "baby" and *tàitai* "Mrs." or "wife".

Some nouns are followed by the nominal suffix *-r* (cp. p. 206) when they occur in reduplicated form, e.g. *xīngxingr* "monkey", and *zhūzhur* "spider". The repeated syllable has zero tone and no stress. The number of nouns which can be reduplicated is, however, limited.

Nouns do not generally form distributive reduplicates in the same way as measures. There are only a few nouns which can occur with the distributive sense. Examples are: *shānshān* "every mountain", *shìshì* "every affair" and *rénrén* "everyone".

3. REDUPLICATION OF MEASURES

The reduplication of measures results in free words with a distributive meaning, usually translatable as "every", e.g. *gègèr* "every one", *liàngliàng* "every vehicle", *huíhuír* "every time". The suffix *-r* is very frequently used after the second morpheme, and the resulting form is a complex nominal.

The reduplication of measures is limited to monosyllabic measures. Group measures, container measures, and temporary measures do not form distributive reduplicates. In contrast to reduplicated forms of nouns, the reduplicated measures retain normal stress on the last syllable as shown in the examples above.

The resulting distributive reduplicated form of a measure is a free nominal behaving according to the general properties of this word class (cp. p. 221). A reduplicated measure has definite reference, i.e. it refers to a definite class of objects. Consequently, a distributive reduplicate never occurs at the end of a sentence, but is always put in the first part of a clause or a sentence.

Rénrén dōu rènshi ni. "Everybody knows you."
Tā bá bénběn náqilai. "He takes every volume with him."

These sentences also illustrate the use of distributive reduplicates as free nominals. Likewise, the reduplicated measure can serve as the modifier of a noun. Thus:

Tiáotiáo gǒu jiù pǎodao zhèr láile. "Each dog is running hither."
Dùndùn fàn hén hǎo. "Each meal is very good."

CHAPTER XI

CLASSES OF NOMINALS

A. Introduction

Nominals have certain syntactic properties in common. They are all non-negatable words. They are especially common in subject position; in predicates they frequently occupy the position of objects of verbs. Examples:

Zhèiliàng qìchē dà. "This car is big."
Wŏmen chī yú. "We eat fish."

In the first sentence above, a nominal is found in a precentral position, while in the second sentence both the precentral and the postcentral positions are occupied by nominals.

Some nominals (but not pronouns and proper nouns) are modifiable by quality verbs, without an intervening *de*. The result is a nominal phrase, *tián júzi* "sweet oranges".

Most nominals are also modifiable by action verbs. In this case *de* is used: *xiě de xìn* "the letters that were written".

Nominals freely modify other nominals or nominal phrases. In the following phrase a nominal, *wŏ*, modifies a nominal phrase, with *de* as a marker: *wŏ de guì dáhuŏjī* "my expensive cigarette-lighter".

Nominals function as nominal predicates, in which case they can even be preceded by adverbs. Examples of nominals in predicate position are:

Zhèiwèi jiàoshòu Yīngguorén. "This professor is an Englishman."
Tā zhēn shăzi. "He is really a fool."

We shall distinguish between the following classes of nominals: *nouns* (including proper nouns, i.e. personal names), *pronouns* (including demonstratives), *determinative compounds, place words* and *time words*.

B. Nouns

1. GENERAL

Nouns form an open class of nominals. Except for proper nouns they can be modified by a determinative compound, e.g. *sānzhī mǎfēng* "three wasps"; *zhèiwèi xiānsheng* "this gentleman". A non-modified noun is generally to be taken in a neutral or collective sense: *fēijī* "airplanes"; *rén* "a person, people".

If a noun is modified by a determinative compound, the function of the modifier is to specify the noun as to definiteness, identity or number: *zhèizhāng zhǐ* "this sheet of paper", *něizhāng zhǐ* "which sheet of paper?", *sānzhāng zhǐ* "three sheets of paper", *yìzhāng zhǐ* "one/a sheet of paper".

The last example illustrates a common method of *singularization.* Compare: *mǎi shū* "to buy books", *mǎi yìběn shū* "to buy a book", *rén lái le* "the people/man have/has come", *yíge rén lái le* "one/a person has come".

Some nouns can be reduplicated, and in this case take on a distributive meaning: *tiāntiān* "every day", *rénrén* "everyone".

Certain suffixes have the function of forming nouns. Two very common suffixes with this function are *-zi* and *-r* (cp. p. 206): *màozi* "hats", *huār* "flowers". To this class belongs the suffix *-men*, which is used after nouns for persons (and pronouns) to form collective nouns. They are translatable as plurals: *lǜshīmen* "lawyers" (cp. *lǜshī* "lawyer" or "lawyers"), *xiānshengmen* "gentlemen" (cp. *xiānsheng* "gentleman" or "gentlemen"). Note that a form like **liǎngge xiānshengmen* never occurs.

2. CLASSES OF NOUNS

Depending on the type of determinative compound by which they are modifiable, nouns are classified into a number of subclasses.

a. **Individual nouns.** Nouns which are combined with a particular measure are grouped together as individual nouns. Each individual noun has a specific measure which is used in all determinative compounds that modify this noun. Examples of individual nouns are *xìn* "letter" and *shǒujuàr* "handkerchief" in: *sānfēng xìn* "three letters", *zhèitiáo shǒujuàr* "this handkerchief". In these examples the individual nouns *xìn* and *shǒujuàr* are each modified by the determinative compound containing the measures specific to the nouns, viz. *-fēng* and *-tiáo*.

Some measures combine with several nouns, e.g. *-zhāng* is a specific measure for *chuáng* "beds", *zhuōzi* "tables", *zhǐ* "paper" and *dèngzi* "stool".

On the other hand, some nouns are combinable with more than one specific measure. The use of an alternative measure results in a different meaning: *yídào mén* "a doorway", *yíshàn mén* "a door (as physical object)".

The measure *-ge* is a general measure. It can serve as a substitute for almost any individual measure, *zhèifēng xìn* or *zhèige xìn*, "this letter", *zhèizhāng chuáng* or *zhèige chuáng* "this bed". An indiscriminate use of *-ge* should, however, be avoided wherever a more specific measure is available.

It must be emphasized that a subordinating *de* is never inserted between an individual noun and a determinative compound. Thus an expression like **wǔtiáo de gǒu* "five dogs" does not occur.

b. Mass nouns. Mass nouns do not combine with specific measures, nor can they be modified by determinative compounds containing the general classifier *-ge*. Instead, mass nouns are accompanied by standard measures (cp. p. 243), temporary measures (cp. p. 247), container measures (cp. p. 247), or partitive measures (cp. p. 247).

Examples of mass nouns modified by standard measures: *wǔbàng chá* "five pounds of tea" (*chá*), *sānmǔ tián* "three mu of farmland" (*tián*).

Examples of mass nouns modified by temporary measures: *yìwǎn fàn* "a bowl of rice" (*fàn*), *zhèipíng huār* "this jar of flowers" (*huār*).

Examples of mass nouns modified by container measures: *yìxiázi shǒushi* "a box of jewelry", *sānlánzi lǐ* "three baskets of pears".

Examples of mass nouns with partitive measures: *yíkuài bù* "a piece of cloth", *sāncéng lóu* "a three-story building".

The subordinating *de* is freely used between the determinative compound and the mass noun, and accordingly, in all the examples above, *de* may be inserted without change of meaning.

c. Collective nouns. Nouns which are only combined with temporary and partitive measures are called collective nouns. This class includes nouns with the suffix *-men*, e.g. *háizimen*, "children", and nouns consisting of an enumeration of the members of a class or a collection of things, e.g. *fùmǔ*, "father and mother", i.e. "parents". Collective nouns are not modifiable by a determinative compound containing a numeral other than *yī* "one".

Examples of collective nouns with temporary measures: *yíyuànzi háizimen* "a courtyard of children", *yìtīngtáng zhuōyǐ* "a hall of tables and chairs".

Examples of collective nouns with partitive measures: *zhèixiē xuéshengmen* "these students", *yìkǒu qì* "a breath of air".

d. Abstract nouns. Abstract nouns are associated with a very limited number of measures: verbal measures, group measures, and partitive measures. To this class belong, for instance, nouns such as *xīwàng* "hope", *bìng* "sickness", *ēn* "kindness", *lǐ* "propriety". The following sentences illustrate the use of abstract nouns, both with and without measures.

> *Tā zhēn yǒu lǐmào.* "He certainly has propriety."
> *Wǒ hái yǒu yìxiē xīwàng.* "I still have some hope."
> *Zhèizhǒng bìng wǒ zhìbuliǎo.* "As for this disease, I cannot cure it."

3. PROPER NOUNS

Proper nouns are proper names of animate beings, mostly of persons. Among nouns they are unique in that they are not modifiable by determinative compounds. Although they thus form, strictly speaking, a separate class of nominals, we shall treat them as nouns. The class of proper nouns is an open class.

A proper noun refers to a specific individual or item, and therefore needs no further specification by means of a determinative compound. The presence of other modifiers (with the marker *de*) is possible, but rare.

Proper nouns include reference not only to beings actually living but also to beings imagined or remembered:

> *Wǒ jìde, Lǎo Wáng huài píqi.* "I remember, old Wang has a bad temper."

In this sentence, the proper noun, *Lǎo Wáng*, indicates a specific person who may, however, exist only in the speaker's mind.

Proper names include surnames, given or "first" names, courtesy names and nicknames. Surnames generally consist of one bound morpheme. In order to function as free words they are combined with nouns denoting a title or status, e.g. *Hán xiānsheng* "Mr. Han", *Zhāo dàshǐ* "Ambassador Chao", *Zhāng xiáojie* "Miss Chang", *Lǎo Wáng* "Old Wang".

Some surnames are made up of two morphemes, either of which is free or bound. The result is a free word:

Ōuyáng zǒu lù zǒu de hěn kuài. "Ou-yang walks very fast".

Ōuyáng is a bisyllabic surname.

First names (i.e. "last" names in Chinese) commonly contain two morphemes, either of which is bound or free. The combination functions as a free word:

Dìshān, nǐ míngtian zài nǎr chī fàn. "Ti-shan, where are you going to eat tomorrow?"
Wǒmen gěi Zǐpíng yìzhī biǎo. "We are giving Tzu-p'ing a watch."

First names consisting of only one morpheme are considered to be bound words regardless of whether the morpheme as such is free or bound. *Sōng*, "pine tree" is a free morpheme, but when serving as a first name it is a bound word: *Fàn Sōng.* Here *Fàn* is another bound word, a surname.

As in *Fàn Sōng*, surnames always precede first names. Further examples of this usage are *Yè Shàojūn* and *Chén Dúxiù.*

Courtesy names are invariably made up of two morphemes, bound or free, and together they form free words. *Qīngshān* means literally "green mountains" and contains two free morphemes. In *Wèidào* however, "Protector of the Way", both morphemes are bound.

Informal names or nicknames have a varying number of morphemes. A present-day nickname in Chinese literature is *Yíjǐ* (*Kǒng Yíjǐ*),[1] consisting of two bound morphemes. Bisyllabic nicknames are always free words, regardless of whether their constituent morphemes are bound or free morphemes. Monosyllabic nicknames are very rare, and they are invariably bound words.

C. Pronouns

1. GENERAL

Pronouns function as substitutes for other units, usually for other nominals, but sometimes even for sentences. They form a small, listable class of free words, e.g. *tā* "he, she or it", *wǒmen* "we", *zhèi* "this", *shéi*

---

[1] A story written by Lu Hsün.

"who?". *Tā bu xǐhuan wo, zhè nǐ zhīdào.* "He does not like me. This you know."

As nominals, pronouns are frequently found in the position of subject or object:

Wǒ bu xǐhuan ta. "I do not like him."
Nín xìng Chén ma. "Is your name Ch'en?"

Pronouns are not ordinarily modifiable by determinative compounds or by verbal expressions. On the other hand, pronouns can modify other nominals with or without the use of the intervening marker of subordination *de*: *wǒ de lùyīnjī* "my tape recorder", *Zhè shi shéi de zérèn.* "Whose responsibility is this?"

If the center of the subordinative construction is a word of personal relationship or spatial relations, *de* is usually omitted, e.g. *wǒ fùmǔ* "my parents", *tā bófù* "his uncle", *nǐ hòutou* "behind you".

When the personal pronouns (see below) *wǒ, nín, nǐ, tā,* and the corresponding plural forms with suffix *-men* occur in object position after verbs, they are usually pronounced with zero stress (and thus with neutral tone):

Wǒmen kànjian ta. "We see him."
Lǐ xiānsheng dìgei women sānkuài qián. "Mr. Li gives us three dollars."

If a contrastive effect is desired the pronominal object receives emphatic stress, e.g.

Wó qǐng "nǐ, bù qǐng "tā. "I invited you, not him."

If a verb has two objects, the first of which is a personal pronoun and the second a cognate object, the pronoun receives zero stress: *qǐngle ta sāncì* "invited him three times", *děng women yìhuǐr* "wait a while for us".

In other cases where pronouns occur in post-central position, they receive stress according to the normal stress pattern of the phrase or sentence.

2. CLASSES OF PRONOUNS

a. **Specific personal pronouns.** Common personal pronouns are *wǒ* "I", *nǐ* "you", *tā* "he, she, or it". Forms corresponding to our pronouns in the plural are made by adding the suffix *-men*, e.g. *wǒmen* "we", *nǐmen* "you", *tāmen* "they". In polite speech *nín* is used instead of *nɪ*, but the corresponding plural form, *nínmen*, is only to be found in the written language. In addition to the pronouns listed above, we have *zámen*, which is also translated as "we".

Wŏmen ("the exclusive we") includes the speaker and the person or persons spoken of. It does not include the person spoken to or addressed.

In contrast to *wŏmen, zámen* ("the inclusive we") includes not only the speaker and the person or persons spoken of, but also the person addressed by the speaker. Examples:

> *Wŏmen zuótian yóuyŏng le, nĭ yīnggai yĕ gēn wŏmen lái de.* "We went swimming yesterday, you should have come with us!"
> *Zámen de zhíyè xiànzài bu dà zhòngshì, nĭ zhīdao.* "You know, our profession is presently not so highly esteemed."

The person spoken to is obviously not included in the *wŏmen* of the first sentence. The use of *zámen* in the last example indicates quite clearly that the person addressed belongs to the same profession as the speaker. The semantic distinction between these two forms is now disappearing and a general use of *wŏmen* in both meanings has become quite frequent in everyday speech.

The pronoun *tā* is used with animate as well as inanimate referents. When *tā* translates as "it" with reference to something inanimate it is largely limited to the object position:

> *Zhèijiàn shìqing nĭ bu yào xiăng ta le.* "As for this matter, you need not think about it anymore."
> *Nĭ kànjian wŏ de zìdiăn ma. Zhăobudào ta.* "Can you see my dictionary? [I] cannot find it."

In both these sentences, however, *tā* in the object position is omissible.

Tā and *tāmen* may both be used to personify inanimate objects, mostly in stories and fables, but also in a case like the following, where a teacher is saying to his class:

> *Mĕige Hànzì, tāmen dōu shi nĭmen de péngyou a!* "Every Chinese character, they are all your friends!"

The pronoun *tāmen* should not be confused with the suffix *-tamen*, which means "et cetera".

b. General personal pronouns. A small class of pronouns may be termed general personal pronouns. They are used with reference to any of the specific pronouns already mentioned. Some of them (*zìjĭ, yígeren, liăngren*, etc.) occur exclusively or mostly in apposition to personal pronouns, while others occur independently.

In the following examples *liǎngr* and *zìjǐ* stand in apposition to *wǒmen* and *tā* respectively:

Wǒmen liǎngr shuō Fǎguohuà. "We both speak French."
Tā zhēn lǎole kěshi tā zìjǐ bu zhīdao. "He has indeed become very old but he does not know it himself."

(1) *zìjǐ* "self". This pronoun is used in apposition to all the personal pronouns as well as nouns and proper names.

Wáng tàitai zìjǐ xiūli qìchē. "Mrs. Wang herself is repairing the car."
Wǒ zìjǐ chángcháng xiǎng xué fǎlü. "I myself often want to study law".

Taken as separate items *zì* and *jǐ* are literary forms. In modern spoken Chinese they are bound morphemes.

(2) *yìgeren* "alone" is used in apposition to a noun, a proper name or pronoun, e.g.

Lǐ Xiānshù yìgeren gēngzhòng nèmme dà tiándi. "Li Hsien-shu is farming such a big piece of land all alone."
Nèige guānfū yìgeren zhēn wúzhùde. "That widower is really helpless (being all alone)."

(3) *měige, měiren, gèren* and *gègè* are all translatable as "each". They are used without restriction in connection with nouns, proper names and pronouns.

Wǒmen měiren dōu yǒu sīrén de bàngōngshì. "[Among us] each has a private office".
Wáng xiānsheng Lǐ xiānsheng gègè dōu yǒu zìjǐ de zhíwù. "Mr. Wang and Mr. Li have [each] his own business".

(4) *liǎnggeren, liǎngr* and *liǎngren* mean "both". Examples:

Wǒmen liǎngren qù kàn diànyǐngr. "We [both of us] are going to see a movie."
Tāmen liǎngr hē chá. "Those two are [both] drinking tea."

(5) *rén, rénjia, biéren* and *biérenjia* are used synonymously to express "other", or "others".

Biéren de shìqing méi you guānxi. "The affairs of others do not interest [me]."
Nǐ de chéngjiù, nǐ yīnggai xièxie rénjia. "As for your success, you must thank other people (others)."

As a pronoun, *rén* is seldom used in modern speech. It is preferable to use for instance *rénjia* or *biéren*, which are the most frequently used forms in speech.

(6) *dàjia* is used as a pronoun meaning "all". In everyday language, however, the adverb *dōu* expressing "all" is more common.

Zuótian zài fànguǎn dàjia chī hóngshāo yú le. "Yesterday, at the restaurant, all [the guests] were eating red cooked fish.", or
Zuótian zài fànguǎn kèrén dōu chī hóngshāo yú le. "Yesterday, at the restaurant, all the guests were eating red cooked fish."

(7) The reduplicated forms *rénrén* and *gègè* function as pronouns and are translated as "everyone".

Lǐwù gègè dōu shi hěn guì. "Every gift was expensive."
Rénrén dōu xūyào xīnxian kōngqì. "Everyone needs fresh air."

c. **Demonstrative pronouns.** *Zhè* "this, these" and *nà* "that, those" are pronouns which indicate the relative distance, in space or in thought, between the speaker and the objects spoken of. *Zhè* and *nà* are free words, and they should not be confused with the demonstratives *zhèi-* and *nèi-* occurring in determinative compounds, e.g. *zhèige* and *nèige.*

Zhè is used in reference to an object which is close to the speaker either literally in space or time or in his thoughts and present interests, e.g.:

Zhè shi wǒ de xīn fángzi. "This is my new house."
Zhè shì bu shi shū. "Is this a book?"
Zhè shi hén yǒu yìsi. "This is very interesting."

Nà is used when the speaker is referring to an object in space or time which is at a distance relative to himself. In other words, *zhè* and *nà* are mutually exclusive:

Nà shi Zhōngwén shū, zhè shi Déwén shū. "That is a Chinese book, this is a German book."
Nà bu hǎo, kěshi zhè zhēn hǎo. "That is not good, but this is very good."

When the speaker is thinking of objects or situations removed from his present interests and of small importance to himself, *nà* is used, e.g.:

Tā qùnian gēn lìng yíge rén jiéhūn le. Nà méi yǒu guānxi. "Last year she married another. That doesn't matter."

Zhè and *nà* are ordinarily restricted to precentral positions, and are usually found at the beginning of the sentence. They do not occur as modifiers or in postcentral positions. Thus, a sequence like **Wǒ tīngbudǒng zhè* "I do not understand this.", does not occur.

Nà is often encountered as a topic subject before a predicate containing a subject-predicate construction. In these cases, *nà* is translatable as "as for that", e.g.

Nà wǒ bu zhīdao. "As for that, I do not know".
Nà, tā kāi chē, kāi de hén hǎo. "As far as his driving is concerned, he drives very well."

The demonstratives *nèi-* and *zhèi-* are treated elsewhere (cp. p. 234).

d. Interrogative pronouns. *Shémme* or *shémmo* "what" and *shéi* "who" (always stressed) are pronouns functioning as interrogatives. Generally, they can substitute for any nominal in any position. Such a substitution changes a declarative sentençe into an interrogative sentence:

Tāmen shi Yīngguo mǎimairén. "They are English tradesmen."

This sentence can be transformed into several questions, depending on which word is being replaced by *shémme* or *shéi*:

Tāmen shi shéi. "Who are they?"
Tāmen shi shémme mǎimairén. "What kind of tradesmen are they?"
Shéi shi Yīngguo mǎimairén. "Who are English tradesmen?"
Shémme shi Yīngguo mǎimairén. "What is (for instance, what is meant by) English tradesmen?"

Shémme and *shéi* tend to occur in postcentral positions, but are occasionally found in precentral positions.

Shéi (sometimes, more formally, *shuí*) "who?" refers to persons and animate objects and is translated as "who?", "whose?" or "whom?" depending on the sentence position.

Zhèibén shi shéi de. "Whose book is this?"
Xiànzài shéi yào chī fàn. "Who wants to eat now?"
Nǐmen shi shéi. "Who are you?"
Shéi tīngle tā de yánjiǎng. "Who was listening to his lecture?"

Shémme "What, which" is used in reference to inanimate objects. *Shémme* is used either independently or in conjunction with another nominal: *shémme* "what?", *shémme rén* "which person?" or "what man?". In the latter case, *shémme* may be followed by the subordinating marker *de*. *Shémme de x* means "of what" or "belonging to what", e.g. *shémme de dōngxi* "of what thing?", *shémme de huǒchē* "belonging to what train?"

Shémme x is translated as "what kind of" or "of what nature", e.g. *shémme guànjūn* "what kind of first prize?", *Tā yǒu shémme máobing.* "Of what nature is his disease?"

In addition to the interrogative use of *shéi* and *shémme* the following functions should be noted:

1. *Shéi* and *shémme* (with *primary* stress and *full* tone) take on special meanings when followed by the adverbs *dōu* "wholly" or *yě* "also" + a verb. Note the following combinations:

Shéi dōu . . . "everyone, anyone, everybody, anybody".
Shémme dōu . . . "everything, anything" etc.
Shéi dōu (or: *yě*) *bù* . . . "no one, nobody".
Shémme dōu (or: *yě*) *bù* . . . "nothing".
Examples:
Shémme dōu hǎo. "Everything (anything) is all right."
Shéi dōu rènshi ta. "Everybody knows him."
Wǒ shémme dōu chī. "I'll eat anything."
Wǒ shémme dōu bú pà. "I am not afraid of anything."
Tāmen shéi yě bù qǐng. "They invite no one."
Zhèr yíge rén yě méi yǒu. "There is not a single person here."

As seen from the examples, the expression *shéi dōu* etc. always comes before the verb.

2. *Shei* and *shemme* (with *zero* stress and *zero* tone) are used in the indefinite sense, meaning "someone" and "something" respectively:

Wǒ bù zhǎo shei. "I'm not looking for anyone."
Yǒu shei lái. "Someone is coming."
Fángzi wàitou yǒu shei kūku. "Outside the house there is someone crying."
Zài chízishang yǒu shemme a! "There is something in the pond!"

When functioning in this way *shei* and *shemme* rarely occur at the beginning of a sentence, but are frequently introduced by the verbs *yǒu* "there is" or *shì* "it is".

3. Finally, note the special form *shemmede* (with *zero* stress and *zero* tone), which is translated as "and so forth" or "et cetera":

Máobǐ gāngbǐ qiānbǐ shemmede wǒ dōu yǒu. "Brushes, pencils, pens and so forth, I have all [everything].

D. Determinative Compounds

1. GENERAL

Determinative compounds consist of either a demonstrative followed by
a measure, or a numeral followed by a measure. The compounds are of
the subordinative type in both cases; the first element (a demonstrative
or a numeral) modifies the second element. Determinative compounds
occur either independently or in conjunction with a following nominal.
Examples of a demonstrative followed by a measure: *nèige* "that one",
zhèiwèi "this one [person]".

Examples of a numeral followed by a measure: *wŭge* "five pieces [of
something]", *qiānge* "a thousand pieces [of something]".

A determinative compound consisting of a numeral and a measure is
modifiable by a demonstrative: *zhèi wŭge* "these five pieces [of some-
thing]", *nèi liǎngkuài* "those two pieces [of something]".

Determinative compounds are nominals; they function in precentral as
well as postcentral position, i.e. as topic subjects, as objects or as
modifiers in nominal constructions:

> *Wŏ bu yào nèi liǎngge.* "I do not want those two pieces [of
> something]."
> *Zhèige bu tài hǎo.* "This one is not so good."

One of the primary functions of these determinative compounds is to
modify other nominals, mostly nouns, e.g.: *zhèiwèi xiānsheng* "this
gentleman", *nèi wŭge rén* "those five people", *zhèitiáo gǒu* "this dog".

The resulting nominal phrases can in turn modify another nominal
expression. Examples: *Nèi wŭge rén de qìchē.* "Those five people's car."
Zhèitiáo gǒu de cháng wěiba. "The long tail of this dog."

Determinative compounds do not ordinarily permit the insertion of
other morphemes into the compound construction. In the case of a noun
further modified by a word, a phrase or a clause-like sequence, the
modifier must be inserted between the determinative compound and the
noun, e.g. *Zhèiwèi Yīngguo xiānsheng.* "This English gentleman." *Nǐ
zuótian jiè de nèi wŭběn shū.* "Those five books which you borrowed
yesterday."

Occasionally, however, expressions like *yídàkuài táng* "a big lump of
sugar" occur. Here the quality verb actually modifies *kuài*, not *táng*.

Determinative compounds are free words. They form a semi-closed class; the number of members, though limited, is hard to state in exact terms, since nouns occasionally serve as temporary measures. Demonstratives, on the other hand, form a closed class of free words.

2. SPECIAL PROPERTIES

One might expect that the marker *de* would have to be inserted between the determinative compound and the noun or nominal expression it modifies. However, the possible use of *de* depends on the kind of measure used in the determinative compound. The use or non-use of *de* will be treated in more detail later in connection with the discussion of classes of measures. Only one fact should be emphasized here because of its general importance.

A subordinating *de* is never employed between an individual noun and a determinative compound containing the specific measure which goes with the noun in question. Thus, sequences like the following do not occur: **zhèizuò de miào* "this (item of) temple", **nèipī de mǎ* "that (item of) horse". *Miào* "temple" and *mǎ* "horse" are individual nouns and *zuò* and *pī* are their specific measures or classifiers.

The numeral *yī* "one" is sometimes omitted before the measure in a determinative compound if the determinative compound occurs in a postnuclear position as part of a noun-object.

Tāmen mǎi (yì-) shēng mǐ. "They buy a peck of rice."
Lǐ xiānsheng hē (yì-) bēi jiǔ. "Mr. Li is drinking a glass of wine."

As already pointed out, a determinative compound ordinarily resists the insertion of modifying elements. In some cases, however, the measure can be immediately preceded by and modified by an element which is not part of the original determinative compound. Thus, *yìzhāng zhǐ* "a sheet of paper", can be expanded by a modifier before the measure *-zhāng*, e.g. *yí-dà-zhāng zhǐ* "a large sheet of paper." This phrase can be analyzed by assuming that the numeral *yī-* modifies *dàzhāng* "big sheets", which is here taken as a temporary measure.

When a noun is modified by a determinative compound, the word order is generally the same as in other cases of subordination: the noun is preceded by its modifier. Sometimes an inverse order is employed, i.e. the noun comes before the determinative compound. This is most common when enumerating items, as for instance in invoices: *yǐzi sānbǎ, chuáng wǔzhāng, zhuōzi yìzhāng* "chairs: 3 (pieces); beds: 5 (pieces); tables: 1 (piece)". This construction is best described as a case of a noun functioning as a subject, with a determinative compound as a nominal predicate.

Two determinative compounds do not ordinarily modify each other, but two or more determinative compounds may occur in coordination:

Bākuài bākuài (*shi*) *shíliùkuài.* "Eight dollars [and] eight dollars is sixteen dollars."

Zhèihú nèihú dōu hǎo. "[The wine from] both this and that jar is good."

In both these examples two determinative compounds in coordination function as subject to a predicate, which, in the first case, is a nominal predicate consisting of a determinative compound, and in the second case is a verbal predicate. Two or more determinative compounds in unmarked coordination may convey the impression of vividness and rapid succession in connection with descriptive phrases: *yízì yízì de xiě* "write one character after the other".

In expressions which indicate speed, weight, price, etc., two determinative compounds may occur in succession, separated by an optional pause, and followed by a noun: *sānge sìkuài qián* "three pieces [cost] four dollars"; *sìkuài qián sānge* "[for] four dollars [you get] three pieces"; *yìdiǎn zhōng wǔshí gōnglǐ* "one hour fifty kilometers", i.e. "fifty kilometers an hour".

In such cases the first determinative compound forms the topic subject, and the second, together with the noun, makes up a nominal predicate.

3. DEMONSTRATIVES

a. **General properties.** Most demonstratives are end-bound morphemes occurring as first constituents in a determinative compound. A few demonstratives of the quantitative type (discussed below) are disyllabic free words, e.g.:

Nǐ yào duōshao. "How many do you want?"

The morpheme class called "demonstratives" includes the demonstratives proper, (*zhèi-* "this", *nèi-* "that" and *něi-* "which" or "what"), the specifying demonstratives (examples are *měi-* "each", *bié-* "another" and *xià-* "next"), and the quantitative demonstratives (for instance *quán-* "entire" and *bàn-* "half"). Demonstratives constitute a listable class of morphemes.

b. Demonstratives proper. We have already mentioned the three demonstratives proper, viz. *zhèi-* "this, these", *nèi-* "that, those" and *něi-* "which" (alternative forms *zhè-, nà-,* and *nǎ-*). The demonstratives *zhèi-* and *nèi-* must not be confused with the pronouns *zhè* "this, these" and *nà* "that, those" which are free words (cp. p. 229). The demonstratives proper have a very high frequency of occurrence in modern speech due to their great versatility. They enter readily into determinative compounds with all classes of measures (cp. p. 243).

Examples of the use of demonstratives: *nèijiàn jiàoshì* "that class-room", *zhèiliè huǒchē* "this train", *nèipiān wénzhāng* "which article?", *zhèlèi huòwu* "this kind of goods", *něifú huàr* "which painting?"

A demonstrative proper may enter into a determinative compound with a standard measure like *-gōngfēn* "centimeter" or *-diǎn* "hour", or with temporary measures like *-shǒu* "hand" or *-kǒu*, lit. "mouth", but used with the meaning of "piece" or "item", *nèikǒu* "that piece". The preferred construction, however, is that of a demonstrative modifying a numeral + measure determinative compound. In other words, a numeral is inserted into the original compound, changing the whole expression into a subordinative construction, e.g. *zhèigōngfēn* "this centimeter" becomes *zhèi yìgōngfēn* and *nèikǒu de zāng dōngxi* "that mouthful of dirt" is turned into *nèi yìkǒu de zāng dōngxi*.

Proper demonstratives are turned into complex place words by adding the suffix *-r* (cp. p. 206), e.g. *zhèr* "here", *nèr* "there", and *nǎr* "where?".

c. Specifying demonstratives. The specifying demonstratives form a closed class of morphemes. These morphemes are less versatile than the demonstratives proper in regard to possibilities of combination with measures in order to form determinative compounds.

The specifying demonstratives are *běn-* "the present one, this", *bié-* "other, different", *gè-* "the various", *hòu-* "after next", *jīn-* "this", *lìng-* "other, separate", *měi-* "each", *míng-* "next", *mǒu-* "a certain", *páng-* "other", *qián-* "previous to last, previous", *qù-* "last", *shàng-* "former, last", *xià-* "next", and *zuó-* "yester-".

(1) The specifying demonstratives *měi-* "each", and *gè-* "the various" are the most versatile members of this morpheme class. *Gè-* ordinarily combines with all kinds of measures except with the measure *-gè* "piece, item", since the combination would be homophonous with *gègè* "everyone".

Měi- does not form determinative compounds with temporary measures, but combines freely with individual measures (*měikē zhūzi* "each pearl"), group measures (*meishuāng xiézi* "each pair of shoes"), partitive measures (*měikuài shítou* "each stone"), container measures (*měihé yánghuǒ* "each box of matches"), standard measures (*měikē de fàn* "each grain of rice"), quasi-measures (*měifāngmian* "each aspect"), and verbal measures (*měicì* "each time" or *měidùn* "each meal").

(2) The demonstratives *běn-, bié-, lìng-, mǒu-* and *páng-* combine only with verbal measures and with some quasi-measures. Determinative compounds with verbal measures are, for instance, *běnbiàn* "the present turn", *biéhùi* "another time", *lìngfān* "a different turn", *mǒushēng* "a certain voice", *pángquān* "another round (turnover)".

As examples of specifying demonstratives in determinative compounds with quasi-measures, we have *běnguó* "this country", *biémiàn* "another direction", *lìngkē* "another branch (of learning)", *móuzhǒng* "a certain type", *pángdiǎn* "another point (or stroke)".

When the numeral *yī* forms a determinative compound with an individual measure, this determinative compound can be modified by a specifying demonstrative of the kind discussed here. The demonstrative *běn-* "this, the present one", does not, however, enter into these combinations. Examples: *bié yíjiàn shìqing* "another matter", *lìng yìbá fūzi* "another axe", *mǒu yízuò háidǎo* "a certain island".

(3) The function of the specifying demonstratives *hòu-, jīn-, míng-, qián-, qù-, shàng-, xià-, zuó-* is primarily to form relative time words (cp. p. 259) and relative place words (cp. p. 252). They are dealt with in detail in the section on time words and place words.

d. Quantitative demonstratives. Quantitative demonstratives form a closed class of morphemes expressing relative or indefinite quantities. Some of them are bound morphemes, others are free words. The class of quantitative demonstratives includes *bàn-* "half", *duō-* "many, which", *duōshao* "how many, many", *háojǐ-* "quite a few", *hǎoxiē* "a good deal of", *jǐ-* "how many, which, a few of", *mǎn-* "full", *quán-* "entire", *xǔduō* "many, much", *yī-* "all", *zhěng-* "whole".

(1) *bàn-* "half". This bound demonstrative should not be confused with the homophonous start-bound measure *-bàn* (cp. p. 247). *Bàn-* forms determinative compounds with individual measures, e.g. *bànpiān wénzhāng* "half an essay", *bànshǒu shī* "half a poem"; with standard measures, e.g. *bàndóu mǐ* "half a peck of rice", *bàndiǎn zhōng* "half an hour"; with container measures, e.g. *bànguō miàn* "half a pot of noodles", *bànwǎn fàn* "half a bowl of rice"; and finally, not so frequently, with quasi-measures, e.g. *bànbèizi* "half a lifetime".

(2) *duō-* is translatable both as a demonstrative of indefinite number,

"many", and as an interrogative "when" or "which". It is a bound morpheme, not to be confused with the free verb *duō* meaning "to be many, much" (cp. p. 170). This demonstrative is restricted to a few determinative compounds. It combines with these three quasi-measures *-nián* "year", *-huǐ* "moment" and *-zǎn* "moment", e.g. *duōnián* "many years", *duōhuǐ* "which moment?" and *duōzǎn* "which moment?"

(3) *duōshao* or *duóshao* is a disyllabic free word. We shall use the form *duōshao*, but *duóshao* is always understood to be an alternative pronunciation. *Duōshao* occurs either as a free word (pronoun) modifying nouns directly, e.g. *duōshao mǎ* "many horses", or as the demonstrative which we are concerned with here. It is pronounced with primary or secondary stress. With primary stress, ˈ*duōshao* means "how many", and functions as an interrogative demonstrative. *Duōshao*, with secondary stress, is translated as "many", denoting an indefinite quantity.

This demonstrative, interrogative and indefinite, produces determinative compounds with all classes of measures, with the exception of temporary measures, i.e. with classifiers (ˈ*duōshaoliàng chē* "how many cars?"), with group measures (*duōshaoyàng rén* "many kinds of people"), with standard measures (ˈ*duōshaogōnglǐ* "how many kilometers?"), with partitive measures (ˈ*duōshaocéng lóu* "how many stories [in the building]?"), with quasi-measures (*duōshaosuì* "many years old"), and with verbal measures (*Nǐ shuō* ˈ*duōshaocì*. "How many times did you speak?").

(4) *háojǐ-* "quite a few" is a bound bimorphemic unit which combines with all measures except temporary measures, to form determinative compounds. Examples of the use of *háojǐ-*: *háojǐge* "a few, some" (with an individual measure); *háojǐshuāng kuàizi* "quite a few pairs of chopsticks" (with a group measure); *háojǐkuài shítou* "quite a few stones" (with a partitive measure); *háojǐcùn* "quite a few inches" (with a standard measure); *zǒu háojǐbù* "walk quite a few steps" (with a verbal measure).

(5) *hǎoxiē* "a good deal of", "a lot of", is a demonstrative and can also modify nouns directly (*Tā bàozhe hǎoxiē dōngxi.* "He is carrying a lot of things."). The demonstrative *hǎoxiē* is very versatile and combines with all kinds of measures to make determinative compounds. Examples: *hǎoxiēběn shū* "a lot of books" (with an individual measure); *hǎoxiēháng zì* "a lot of columns of characters" (with a group measure); *hǎoxiēdiǎn zhōng* "quite a lot of hours" (with a standard measure); *hǎoxiēshěng* "quite a lot of provinces" (with a quasi-measure).

(6) *jǐ-*, a bound morpheme, is pronounced with primary stress ˈ*jǐ-*,

meaning "how many?" or "which?". If pronounced with secondary stress or optional zero stress, *jǐ-* or *ji-*, it receives the meaning of "a few", i.e. it functions as an indefinite demonstrative. Both ˈ*jǐ-* "how many?" and *jǐ-* "a few" are versatile morphemes, and they are found in determinative compounds with all classes of measures except the temporary measures. Examples:

i) With an individual measure, *jǐfēng* (*xìn*) "how many (letters)?", *jǐzhī bǐ* "a few pens";
ii) with group measures, *jǐduì gēzi* "a few pigeons";
iii) with partitive measures, ˈ*jǐchóng* "how many layers?"
iv) with standard measures, *jǐgōnglǐ* "a few kilometers";
v) with verbal measures, *jǐcì* "a few times";
vi) with quasi-measures, ˈ*jǐkè* "how many lessons?"; and
vii) with container measures, *jǐkuāngzi* "a few baskets".

(7) *mǎn-* is a bound morpheme. *Mǎn-* is not very versatile in producing determinative compounds. In fact, *mǎn-* is restricted to compounds with temporary measures, e.g. *mǎndùzi de sīxiǎng* "a bosomful of thoughts", and container measures, e.g. *mǎnxiāngzi de yīfú* "a trunkful of clothes". Ordinarily, the determinative compound modifies the following noun with the insertion of the subordinating *de* as in the examples given above.

(8) *quán-* "entire", is a bound morpheme that enters into determinative compounds, in most cases with a quasi-measure, e.g. *quánguó* "the entire country", *quánnián* "the entire year", *quángōng* "the entire day's work". *Quán-*, although less frequently, may occur with group measures, e.g. *quánbù* "the whole set [of books]", *quánshēn* "the whole body", and with temporary measures, e.g. *quányuànzi de háizimen* "all the children in the entire courtyard".

(9) *xǔduō* is a free word; it serves as a demonstrative with the meaning of an indefinite quantity, "many, much", "quite a few". It cannot be used as an interrogative demonstrative. *Xǔduō* occurs in construction with all classes of measures and, as regards versatility, is comparable with *duōshao, háojǐ-* and *hǎoxiē*. Examples of determinative compounds with *xǔduō*: *xǔduōdào cài* "many dishes of food" (with an individual measure); *xǔduōgōngchǐ* "many meters" (with a standard measure); *xǔduōhuí* "many chapters" (with a quasi-measure); *kàn xǔduōbiàn* "read over several times" (with a verbal measure).

Xǔduō does not usually enter into determinative compounds with temporary measures and container measures.

(10) *yī-* is a bound morpheme functioning as an indefinite demonstrative. It receives normal stress.

Yī- means "all", "the whole extent of"; it enters only into determinative compounds with temporary measures, e.g. *yìfànguǎn de rén* "the whole restaurant's people, i.e. the people of the entire restaurant" and with container measures, e.g. *yìchōuti de chāzi* "a whole drawer of forks". As can be seen from the examples quoted, the subordinating marker *de* is usually inserted between the noun and the determinative compound.

It is necessary to distinguish between the demonstrative *yī-* and the numeral *yī-*.

(11) *zhěng-* is a versatile bound indefinite demonstrative meaning "the whole of" or "all of". With the exception of verbal measures it is readily found with all classes of measures, e.g. with individual measures *zhěngdùn fàn* "the whole meal", with group measures *zhěngqún rén* "the whole group of people", with partitive measures *zhěngbùfen zérèn* "the whole responsibility", with container measures *zhěngshūjiàzi* "the whole bookcase", with temporary measures *zhénglián de zāng dōngxi* "the dirt of the whole face", with standard measures, *zhěngbàng* "the whole pound", and finally with quasi-measures, *zhěngshēng* "the whole lifetime".

4. Numerals

a. **Simple numerals.** The class of numerals contains both bound morphemes such as *sān-* "three" and *qiān-* "thousand", and free words like *sānbǎi* "three hundred" and *shíèr* "twelve". Numerals of all kinds form determinative compounds with measures, e.g. *sānbǎige rén* "three hundred people" and *sānbá yǐzi* "three chairs".

We shall distinguish between simple numerals and compound numerals. Simple numerals constitute a closed class of end-bound morphemes, and compound numerals are polysyllabic free words.

Simple numerals are *yī-* "one", *èr-* "two", *liǎng-* "two", *sān-* "three", *sì-* "four", *wǔ-* "five", *liù-* "six", *qī-* "seven", *bā-* "eight", *jiu-* "nine", *shí-* "ten", *líng-* "zero", *bǎi-* "hundred", *qiān-* "thousand", *wàn-* "ten thousand" and *yì-* "100,000,000".

-shí "ten", *-bǎi* "a hundred", *-qiān* "a thousand", *-wàn* "ten thousand" and *-yì* "100,000,000" are start-bound group measures (cp. p. 246), used in forming compound numerals (cp. p. 241).

The simple numerals may be said to acquire a status as free words in counting (*yī, èr, sān, sì,* etc.) and in naming numbers, e.g. when naming the numbers in a year like 1974 in rapid succession *yī jiǔ qī sì.*

Simple numerals, in counting and in determinative compounds, function as cardinal numbers, e.g. *sì* "four". Ordinal numbers are formed by means of the ordinal prefix *dì-,* like *dìyī* "the first", *dìsì* "the fourth", or a determinative compound consisting of an ordinal numeral and a measure, e.g. *dìsānběn* "volume III". These ordinals have been treated in detail elsewhere, cp. p. 212.

A determinative compound consisting of a measure and *yī-* "one" has alternative stress patterns, depending on its position relative to the central of the clause or sentence. If a determinative compound occurs in a postnuclear position in a verbal phrase (as an object), it receives secondary or even zero stress, e.g. *hē yìbēi jiǔ* or *hē yibei jiǔ* "to drink a cup of wine". If the object is emphasized, the stress will naturally be *hē|yìbēi jiǔ.* When the determinative compound is in a postnuclear position with secondary or zero stress, it acquires the indefinite sense of "a cup of wine" rather than the definite sense of "the cup of wine". With zero stress, the numeral *yī-* may even be omitted, *hē bei jiǔ* "drink a cup of wine". This is not the case, however, with determinative compounds containing temporary measures or quasi-measures.

In a precentral position, a determinative compound with *yī-* receives primary or emphatic stress depending on the context and the speaker's intentions: *yìbēi jiú hǎo* "one cup of wine is good" or *||yìbēi jiú hǎo* "*one* cup of wine is enough [not two or more!]." *Yī-* can be omitted only in postcentral positions.

The choice between *èr-* and *liǎng-,* both meaning "two", is subject to special rules. Generally, *èr-* is used as an independent numeral, when counting or naming the figure "2", and in compound numerals, *shíèr* "twelve", *èrshí* "twenty", *èrqiān* "two thousand". *Liǎng* is used more frequently than *èr-* as the common numeral used to denote "two".

In determinative compounds the choice between *èr-* and *liǎng-* is determined by the measure used. *Liǎng* is ordinarily employed with individual measures, e.g. *liǎngge rén* "two people" and *liǎngtiáo gǒu* "two dogs", with standard measures, e.g. *liǎnggōnglǐ de lù* "a two-kilometer road" and *liángchǐ* "two feet", with quasi-measures, e.g. *liángbǐ* "two strokes" and *liǎngkè* "two lessons", and with verbal measures, e.g. *tā xiě liǎngcì* "he writes twice". *Èr-* is used, however, before the standard measure *-liǎng* "ounce".

Both *èr-* and *liǎng-* alternate freely in use in connection with the other classes of measures; e.g. with group measures, both *liǎngqún de yáng* and *èrqún de yáng* "two flocks of sheep" are common. Similarly, it is possible to have *liǎnglánzi* as well as *èrlánzi*, "two baskets (of something)".

Liǎng- is employed in determinative compounds to mean "a couple of", e.g. *Jīntian wǎnshang wó qíng liǎngge rén.* "I invited a couple of people tonight".

Liǎngge "two pieces of" may have a short form, *liǎ*, e.g. *liǎ rén* "two people". It should be remembered that *-ge*, the general measure, is to be used only with *liǎng-*. There is no **èrge*.

b. Compound numerals. Compound numerals are polysyllabic free words.

The numbers 11 to 19 are formed by the numeral *shí-* "ten" followed by one of the numerals from *yī-* to *jiǔ-*, e.g. *shíyī* "eleven", *shíèr* "twelve" and so on to *shíjiǔ* "nineteen".

Integral multiples of ten from 20 to 90 are formed as subordinative compounds consisting of one of the simple numerals from *èr-* to *jiǔ* and the group measure *-shí* "ten", *èrshí* "twenty", *sānshí* "thirty" and so on to *bāshí* "eighty" and *jiǔshí* "ninety".

The remaining mixed numbers between 20 and 100 are formed as compound numerals. They consist of an integral multiple of ten, e.g. *wǔshí* "fifty", and one of the simple numerals from *yī-* to *jiǔ-*. Examples: *èrshíèr* "twenty-two", and *wǔshísì* "fifty-four".

Note that if one of the simple numerals from *yī-* to *jiǔ-* stands *before* *shí-* "ten", the relation between the constituents is one of multiplication. If the simple numeral comes *after* *shí-* the relation is that of addition. Thus, we have the difference between *sānshí* "thirty" and *shísān* "thirteen". There is a combination of multiplication and addition in mixed numbers like *sānshísān* "thirty-three".

We have already mentioned the monosyllabic group measures *-bǎi* "100", *-qiān* "1000", *-wàn* "10,000" and *-yi* "100,000,000". Multiples of these numbers are made in the same way as multiples of ten. A simple numeral combined with these group measures can form subordinative compound numerals, e.g. *sìqiān* "4000", *wǔwàn* "50,000", etc.

In addition to these monosyllabic group measures, there are bisyllabic group measures for the remaining multiple figures, *-shíwàn* "100,000", *-bǎiwàn* "one million", *-qiānwàn* "ten million", *-wànwàn* "100,000,000". The group measure *-wànwàn* and the simple numeral *yi-* are synonyms. These group measures form compound numerals with any of the simple numerals from *yī-* to *jiǔ-*. Thus *èrshíwàn* "200,000", *bābǎiwàn* "eight million", *bāqiānwàn* "eighty million", *bāwànwàn* "eight hundred million"; the latter number can also be expressed as *bāyi* using the group measure *-yi*.

Mixed numbers above 100 are formed in the same way as those below 100. Thus, "1234" is expressed as *yìqiān èrbǎi sānshísì*, "35,473" is *sānwàn wǔqiān sìbǎi qīshísān*.

The simple numeral *líng-* "zero" can be used for intermediate zeros when reading numbers cipher by cipher: "400367" can be read *sì líng líng sān liù qī* (for example, when giving telephone numbers). As mentioned above, the simple numerals, which are normally bound morphemes, in this case become quasi-free words.

c. **Fractions and decimals.** A fraction is expressed with the help of a simple standard formula *m-fēn zhī n*, which translates as n out of m, n/m or n parts of m. *Zhī* is a classical marker of subordination; its function is, in this case, similar to that of the modern language marker *de*, and *-fēn* is a quasi-measure meaning "part, division". Examples: *sìfēn zhī sān* "3/4", *qiānfēn zhī sānbǎi èrshí* "320/1000", etc. When *-fēn* occurs modified by a simple numeral from *yī-* to *jiǔ-* outside the standard formula of a fraction, it means "1/10". Forms like *wǔfēn* and *qīfēn* when used alone mean "5/10" and "7/10" respectively. Thus: *shífēn* "(10/10 =) all".

Percentage expressions are formed as fractions of *bǎi-* "hundred", e.g. *bǎifēn zhī èrshí* "20%" and *bǎifēn zhī liùshísān* "63%". The quasi-measure *-fēn* can also mean "one hundredth". In this case percentages can be expressed more simply as *shífēn* "10%" and *sānshífēn* "30%".

Decimals are expressed with *diǎn* "point", e.g. *sān diǎn sì* means "3.4" and "24.56" is *èrshísì diǎn wǔshíliù*.

d. **Complex ordinal numerals.** As already pointed out, the cardinal numbers, expressed by simple and compound numerals, can be transformed into ordinal numbers by adding the ordinal prefix *dì-*. The resulting forms are complex numerals expressing ordinal numbers, e.g. *dìsān* "the third", "number three", *dìjiǔshí* "the ninetieth", "number ninety".

These complex ordinal numerals are free words, and are employed in both pre- and postcentral positions, e.g.

Wǒ xuǎnzé dìsì. "I am choosing the fourth."
Dìsān bu hǎo. "The third is not good."

Ordinal numerals are not modifiable by other words or morphemes, however. They are used when enumerating items, e.g. *dìyī, dìèr, dìsān, shémmode* "the first, the second, the third and so forth". The most common use of these numerals is, as with cardinal numerals, to form determinative compounds in which they modify measures, e.g. *dìsānge* "the third one", *dìshítiáo hé* "the tenth river".

Dì- is also found in two special words, viz. *dìmò* "the last one" and *dìjǐ* "which one?", e.g. *dìjǐge* "the one occupying which place in the series?"

5. MEASURES

a. General properties. Measures are start-bound morphemes. They form determinative compounds with numerals or with demonstratives, e.g. *sāngōnglǐ* "three kilometers" and *měigōnglǐ* "each kilometer". Measures form a rather large class, and a complete enumeration will not be attempted here. For our purposes the class will be divided into eight groups. The division of measures depends on 1) whether the measure can form distributive reduplicates or not, (cp. p. 219), 2) whether a subordinating *de* between the determinative compound and the noun is optional, obligatory or impossible, and 3) what kind of numerals can go with the measure. A number of measures are members of more than one class. The classes are 1) standard measures, 2) individual measures, 3) group measures, 4) partitive measures, 5) container measures, 6) temporary measures, 7) quasi-measures, and 8) verbal measures.

Some nouns serve as temporary measures, e.g. *zuǐ* "mouth", which is both an individual noun and a temporary measure. Examples: *yìzhāng zuǐ* "a mouth" and *yìzuǐ huà* "a mouth of words".

Individual nouns have a specific measure, an individual measure. Some individual nouns are also modifiable by measures other than the specific measure, e.g. *yìsuǒ fángzi* "a house" and *yìjiān fángzi* "a room".

A noun cannot be modified directly by a numeral or a demonstrative alone, only by determinative compounds. Four classes of nouns have been set up and defined above (cp. p. 222), according to the classes of measures that can enter into the modifying determinative compound before the noun.

In the following we shall discuss the characteristic features of each class and give examples of nouns with which they can combine. The list of measures is not exhaustive; only the most common items are mentioned. A detailed treatment is found in Chao (1968).

b. Standard measures. Standard measures are units of weight, currency, etc. They form a listable class of morphemes. Standard measures are usually modified by numerals, and they are frequently followed by the subordinative *de, shígōnglǐ de lù* "a road ten kilometers long". Most of the standard measures are monomorphemic, *-chǐ* "a foot"; some are polymorphemic, *-gōngfēn* "centimeter". Monomorphemic measures form distributive reduplicates: *cùncùn* "every inch", *diándiǎn* "every hour". Determinative compounds containing standard measures most commonly modify individual nouns and mass nouns.

-bàng "pound", a weight unit, *yíbàng chá* "a pound of tea", *-chǐ* "foot", a Chinese unit of length, *sānchǐ de miánbù* "three feet of cotton", *-cùn* "inch", a Chinese unit of length, *wǔcùn de chóuzi* "five inches of silk", *-diǎn* "hour", *sìdiǎn zhōng* "four o'clock", *-dǒu* "a peck", a Chinese unit of volume, *yìdǒu hújiāo* "a peck of pepper", *-dún* "ton", a unit of weight, *sìdún shízǐr* "four tons of gravel", *-fēn* "minute", *èrshífēn zhōng* "twenty minutes", *-fēn* "cent", unit of money, *bāfēn qián* "eight cents", *gōngchǐ* "meter", *bǎigōngchǐ de píngguo shù* "a hundred meters of apple-trees", *-gōngfēn* "centimeter", *bǎigōngfēn shi yìgōngchǐ* "a hundred centimeters make one meter", *-gōngjīn* "kilogram", *yìgōngjīn de miànfěn* "one kilogram of flour", *-gōnglǐ* "kilometer", *sāngōnglǐ, tài yuǎn* "three kilometers, that is too far away", *-jīn* "catty", *sānjīn de zhūròu* "three catties of pork meat", *-kè* "quarter of an hour", *sānkè zhōng jiù lái le* "[he] will come in three quarters of an hour", *-kè* "gram", *bǎikè de kāfēi* "a hundred grams of coffee", *-kuài* "dollar", unit of money, *yíge sānkuài qián* "three dollars for one piece", *-lǐ* "li", a Chinese unit of length, *shílǐ de lù* "a road of ten li", *-liǎng* "ounce", a Chinese unit of weight, *sānliǎng de shuǐ* "three ounces of water", *-máo* "ten cents", *sānkuài bāmáo qián* "three dollars and eighty cents", *-miào* "second", *shíliùmiào zhōng* "sixteen seconds", *-pǐ* "bolt", *yìpǐ bù* "one bolt of cloth", *-shēngdì* "centimeter", *-yīngchǐ* "an English foot", *-yīngcùn* "an English inch", *-yīnglǐ* "an English mile", *-yīngliǎng* "English mace or ounce", unit of dry volume, *-zhàng* "ten Chinese feet", *shíchǐ shi yízhàng* "ten *chǐ* make one *zhàng*".

c. Individual measures. Each individual noun (cp. p. 222) has a specific measure called an individual measure. Several nouns may share the same individual measure.

A general measure *-ge* is applicable to all individual nouns. It serves as a substitute for all the individual measures.

Individual measures form a closed class. Reduplicated forms with a distributive meaning are common: *tiáotiáo* "each river", *piānpiān* "each essay", *kóukǒu* "each opening".

A subordinating *de* is never inserted between an individual noun and the preceding determinative compound. A sequence like **sānpǐ de mǎ* "three horses" does not occur. Note the form *liǎngmiàn de jìngzi* "a two-faced mirror", where *liǎngmiàn* is a descriptive term, not a quantifier.

-*bǎ*, individual measure for *yǐzi* "chairs", *jiǎnzi* "a pair of scissors", *dāo* "knife, sword", *fǔzi* "axe", and *shànzi* "fan", e.g. *shíbǎ dāo* "ten knives"; -*běn, běr*, individual measure for *shū* "books", *zhàng(běn)* "account book", *rìjì* "diary" and *huàr* "(bound volume of) pictures", e.g. *sìběn shū* "four books"; -*bù*, individual measure for *shū*, "book (as a work)"; -*dào*, individual measure for *hé* "river", *qiáo* "bridge", *xiàn* "thread, line", *cài* "dish of food", e.g. *biédào hé* "another river"; -*dīng* individual measure for *màozi* "hat", *jiàozi* "sedan chair", e.g. *néidīng màozi* "which hat?"; -*dùn*, individual measure for *fàn* "meal" and *diǎnxīn* "snack, dessert", *yídùn hén hǎo de fàn* "a very good meal"; -*fēng*, individual measure for *xìn* "letter", *Wó gěi ta yìfēng xìn*. "I am giving him a letter."; -*fú*, individual measure for *huàr*, "painting"; -*gǎn*, individual measure for *qiāng* "rifle", *Wǒ nálai sāngǎn qiāng*. "I am bringing with me three rifles."; -*gè*, the general individual measure that is used with most nouns, *sānge hé* "three rivers", *shíge rén* "ten people"; -*gēn*, -*gēr*, individual measure for *shéngzi* "rope", *xiāngyān* "cigarette", *gùnzi* "rod" and *gēr* "root", e.g. *èrshígēn xiāngyān* "twenty cigarettes"; -*guǎn*, individual measure for *bǐ* "pen" and all the different kinds of pen, e.g. *yìguǎn máobǐ* "one pencil" (*yìzhī máobǐ* is also possible); -*jià*, individual measure for *fēijī* "airplane", *wàngyuǎnjìng* "telescope"; -*jiā*, individual measure for *rénjiār* "household", *pùzi* "store, shop", e.g. *Tā zài nèijiā pùzi zuò gōng* "he is working in that shop"; -*jiàn*, individual measure for *shìqing* "affairs, matters", *dōngxi* "things", *jiāhuo* "tool", *yīshang* "garment", e.g. *mǒujiàn shìqing* "a certain matter"; -*kē*, individual measure for *shù* "trees", *huār* "flowers" and *cǎo* "grass", e.g. *yìkē hěn piàoliang de huār* "a very beautiful flower"; -*kē*, individual measure for *zhūzi* "pearls"; -*kǒu*, individual measure for *jǐng* "well" and *zhōng* "bell"; -*liàng*, individual measure for *chē* "car, vehicle"; -*miàn*, individual measure for *qízi* "flag", *jìngzi* "mirror", *luó* "flat gong", e.g. *Zhèimiàn jìngzi tài xiǎo*. "This mirror is too small."; -*pī*, individual measure for *mǎ* "horse", *luózi* "mules" and *lǘ* "donkeys"; -*piān*, individual measure for *wénzhāng* "articles, essays", *yìlùn* discourse, theory"; -*shàn*, individual measure for *mén* "door (the thing)"; -*suǒ*, individual measure for *fángzi* "houses" and *gōngyù* "apartment houses", e.g. *Wǒmen mai nèisuǒr fángzi le*. "We have bought that house."; -*tiáo*, individual measure for *shé* "snake", *yú* "fish", *gǒu* "dog", *yǐba* or *wěiba* "tail", *shéngzi* "rope, cord", *hé* "river", e.g. *Wǒ kànjian yìtiáo shé*. "I see a snake."; -*tóu*, individual measure for *niú* "cattle", e.g. *liǎngtóu niú* "two head of cattle"; -*wèi*, individual measure for *xiānsheng*, "gentleman", *tàitai* "lady", *xiǎojié* "unmarried lady", *láibīn* "visitor"; -*zhǎn*, individual measure for *dēng* "lamp or light"; -*zhāng*, individual measure for *chuáng* "bed", *zhuōzi* "tables", *dèngzi* "stools", *yǐzi* "chairs", *zhǐ* "papers", *báobǐng* "thin cake", e.g. *Shū zài něizhāng zhuōzi*. "On which table are the books?"; *-zhǐ*, individual measure for *bǐ* "pens", *jiàn* "arrows" and *qiāng* "rifles", e.g. *Tā yào sānzhǐ gāngbǐ*. "He wants three pens."; *-zhǐ*, individual measure for *shǒu* "hands", *é* "geese", *gǒu* "dogs" and *chuán* "boats", *yìzhǐ hěn bu-hǎo píqi de gǒu* "a very bad-tempered dog"; *-zuò*, classifier for *shān* "mountains", *háidǎo* "islands", *yángfáng* "foreign-style house", *zìmíngzhōng* "clock (which rings)", i.e. "alarm clock".

d. Group measures. Group measures form a listable class of measures used to designate a collection of items or a group of objects. They are usually combined with individual nouns and abstract nouns (cp. pp. 222, 224). Several group measures form distributive reduplicates, like *páipái* "row by row" and *lǘlǘ* "each donkey". In the majority of cases the subordinating *de* can be inserted between the determinative compound and the noun.

-bǎi "one hundred", *sānbǎizuò shān* "three hundred mountains"; *de* does not occur in combination with this measure; *-bǎiwàn* "one million"; *-bān* "squad", *yìbān bùbīng* "one squad of soldiers"; *-bù* "set", *měibù shū* "each set of books"; *-chuàn* "string", *zhèichuàn zhūzi* "this string of pearls"; *-dá, -dǎ* "dozen", *sìdá lí* "four dozen pears"; *-duì*, "squadron", *yíduì de zhànzhēng fēijī* "one squadron of fighter-planes"; *-duì* "pair", *Zhèiduì gēzi hěn xuānzàode*. "This pair of pigeons is very noisy."; *-fù* "a set of something", *yífù zhuózi* "a set of bracelets", *shífù de shǒutào* "ten pairs of gloves"; *-háng* "row, column", *yìháng de túhuà* "a row of pictures"; *-lèi* "a kind of, a category of", *něilèi dōngxi* "what kind of things?"; *-liú* "type or class", *yìliú rénwù* "a class of personages"; *-pái* "row", *Wó yǒu sānpái de sōng shù*. "I have three rows of pine trees."; *-pī* "batch", *yìpī huò* "one batch of goods"; *-qiān* "one thousand", *sānqiān rén* "three thousand people", *de* is not combined with this measure; *-qiānwàn* "ten million"; *-qún* "crowd, flock", *Zhèiqún de pìnniú hěn dà*. "This herd of cows is very large."; *-shí* "ten", *èrshí xuésheng* "twenty students", the insertion of *de* is impossible in connection with this measure; *-shíwàn* "100,000"; *-shuāng* "pair", *Zhèishuāng wàzi wūhuìde*. "This pair of stockings is dirty."; *-táng* "hall", *měitáng jiāju* "each set of furniture"; *-tào* "set", *Nèige háizi yóu jǐtào wányìr*. "That child has several sets of toys."; *-wàn* "ten thousand", *de* is not combined with this measure; *-wànwàn* "100,000,000", synonymous with the group measure *-yì*; *-yàng* "kind, sort", *zhèiyàng de rén* "this kind of man or people"; *-yì* "100,000,000"; *-zhǒng* "kind, species", *gèzhǒng de dòngwù* "each kind of animal"; *-zǔ* "section, group", *zhèizǔ de jǐngguān* "this group of policemen".

e. **Partitive measures.** Partitive measures form a closed class. While group measures are used to denote groups or collections, partitive measures indicate parts or portions. They do not usually form distributive reduplicates, but most of them allow the insertion of the subordinating marker *de* before the noun. All classes of nouns, i.e. individual, abstract, collective, and mass nouns, can be combined with partitive measures.

-bǎ "a handful, a bunch of", *yìbǎ huángdòu* "a handful of soybeans"; *-bàn* or *-bàr* "half", *yíbàn lìliang* "half of the strength"; *-bùfen* "part, fraction"; *-céng* "layer, story of a building", *shícéng de lóu* "a ten-story building"; *-dài* "belt, zone", *zhèidài zhǎozé* "this belt of marshes"; *-dī* "drop", *yìdī shuǐ* "a drop of water"; *-diǎr* "a little, a few", *yìdiǎr miànbāo* "a little bread"; *-duàn, -duàr* "section, (short) length", *Něiduàn wénzhāng.* "Which part of the text?"; *-duī, -zuī* "pile", *yìduī shítou* "a pile of stones"; *-fèn* "portion, share", *yífèn qián* "one portion of money"; *-jì* "dose, prescription"; *-juǎn, -juǎr* "a roll", *qījuǎn huàr* "seven rolls of paintings"; *-kuài* "lump, piece", *zhèikuài shítou tài zhòng* "this stone is too heavy"; *-lán* "a section"; *-piàn* "a slice", *Wǒ yào shípiàn de zhū huótuǐ.* "I want ten slices of ham."; *-piār* "sheet, leaf", *zài shūshang yìpiār mílùde* "one page of the book is missing"; *-tuán* "a lump or mass", *zhěngtuán de shāzi* "the whole lump of sand"; *-xiē* "some, an amount of", *Zhèixiē shìqing hěn máfan.* "These matters are very troublesome."; *-yè* "leaf, double-page".

f. **Temporary measures.** Temporary measures are nouns which temporarily function as measures, and thus form an open class. They are modifiable only by the simple numeral *yī-* "one". Temporary measures do not form distributive reduplicates. They are commonly followed by *de*. Examples: *yídùzi de sīxiǎng* "a stomach full of thoughts", *yìliǎn de hàn* "a face full of sweat", *yìzuǐ de tuòyè* "a mouth full of saliva", *yíyuànzi de háizimen* "a courtyard of children".

g. **Container measures.** The class of container measures resembles that of temporary measures in that it forms an open class of nouns serving temporarily as measures. They differ from temporary measures in being modifiable by all kinds of numerals and demonstratives. They are usually associated with *de*. Like temporary measures, the container measures do not form distributive reduplicates. Mass nouns and individual nouns are the two groups which are most often modified by the container measures. Examples: *sìbēi jiǔ* "four cups of wine", *yìchōuti de wàzi* "a drawer of stockings", *zhèidiàozi de rèshuǐ* "this kettle of hot water", *sānguànzi de qìyóu* "three cans of gasoline", *jǐguō de fàn* "several pots of rice", *mǎnhé de yánghuǒ* "a box full of matches",

shíkuāngzi de méi "ten baskets of plums", *něilánzi* "which basket?"
zhèipánzi de diănxīn "this tray of refreshments", *zhèipíngzi de huār*
"this jar of flowers", *shíwăn de fàn* "ten bowls of rice".

h. **Quasi-measures.** Quasi-measures are also called autonomous
measures because they are not ordinarily followed by a noun. They form
determinative compounds and distributive reduplicates, (*xiànxiàn* "every
district"). The quasi-measures form a listable class.

-*bèi* "double, times, -fold", e.g. *yíbèi* "twice", *liăngbèi* means either
"four times" or "twice"; -*bèi* "generation"; -*bèizi* "one's lifetime",
shēngbèizi "the whole lifetime"; -*biān* "part of a book"; -*biān, -biār*
"sides"; -*bù* "department, ministry of a government"; -*cè* "volume,
pamphlet", *Nèiběn shū yóu wŭcè.* "That book has five volumes."; -*cūn*
"village", *cūncūn* "village by village"; -*dài* "generation", *yídài yídài*
"generation after generation"; -*děng* "class, grade"; -*diăn* "a stroke of
some kind"; -*dù* "degree of temperature or angle"; -*fān* "double times"
or just "times"; -*fāngmiàn* "aspect"; -*fēn* "the hundredth" or "the
tenth"; -*guó* "country, nation", *quánguó* "the whole country"; -*huà* "a
stroke"; -*huí* "chapter of a novel"; -*huĭr* "moment", e.g. *Qíng nĭ jiù děng
yìhuĭr.* "Please wait just one moment."; -*jì* "season, quarter", *chūnjì*
"spring"; -*jí* "class, step", *èrniánjí* "second-year grade"; -*kè* "branch of
learning, course of study"; -*kè* "lesson", *biékè* "another lesson"; -*lĭbài*
"week"; -*miàn, miàr* "side, face, direction", *Zài zhèimiàn nĭ kànjian
Húběi.* "In this direction you can see Hupeh."; -*míng* "name, person",
xuésheng sìmíng "four students"; -*nián* "year", *něinián* "which year?";
-*shēng* "one's lifetime", *quánshēng* "the whole lifetime"; -*shěng* "pro-
vince"; -*shì* "one's lifetime"; -*shìjì* "century", *běnshìjì* "the present
century"; -*suì* "years old", *Tā jĭsuì.* "How many years old is he?"; -*tiān*
"day", *sāntiān* "three days"; -*xì* "department of a university"; -*xiàn*
"district", *Nĭ zhùzài něixiàn.* "In which district do you live?"; -*xīngqī*
"week"; -*xuéqī* "semester, term"; -*yè* "night"; -*yuán* "dollar"; -*yuàn*
"main branches of the government"; -*yuè* "month", *Tā bìyè zhèiyuè le.*
"He graduated this month."; -*zhàn* "station (on railways and tram-
ways)".

A number of quasi-measures for foreign currency units belong to this
class, e.g. *măkè* "mark", *xiānlíng* "shilling", and *făláng* "franc".

i. **Verbal measures.** Verbal measures are specific measures for verbs
of action and form a listable group. They are modifiable by demonstratives and numerals, and most of them can occur as distributive
reduplicates. The verbal measure is actually part of a cognate object in
the form of a determinative compound. These determinative compounds,

consisting of a numeral or a demonstrative and a verbal measure, give some supplementary information as to how the action of the verb takes place (how long it lasts, by what kind of instrument it is performed, or the number of occurrences).

As a cognate object, the verbal measure may be accompanied by another object to the same verb. If this object is a pronoun, it always precedes the determinative compound, *Wǒ yùjian ta yícì le.* "I have met him once." If the object is a noun, however, the noun follows the determinative compound: *Tā kànle yíkàn zhèibĕn zázhì.* "He took a look at this magazine."

In general an action verb can serve as its own verbal measure, in the position of a cognate object, e.g. *shuō yishuo* "say a saying"; *dǎ yida* "to strike a stroke"; *xiě yixie* "to write once".

-bǎ "a grip", used with verbs like *lā* "pull", *zhuā* "grasp", *qiā* "pinch", *níng* "wring, pinch", *niŭ* "wring" and *niè* "pinch"; e.g. *Tā qiāle wǒ yìbǎ.* "He pinched me in a grip."; *-bāzhǎng* "a slap of the palm", used with verbs like *dǎ* "hit, strike", *pāi* "beat", *chuí* "beat", *dá jǐbāzhǎng* "strike several slaps"; *-bàng* "a hit with a club", used with verbs like *dǎ* "hit, strike" and *chuí* "beat"; *-bǎnzi* "a hit with the board", used with *dǎ* "hit, strike"; *-biàn* "once over, one turnover", used with several verbs, for instance *shuō* "say, speak", *fānyi* "translate", *qǐng* "invite", *jiĕshi* "explain", *Wǒ de jiàoshòu jiĕshi jǐbiàn zhèige wèntí.* "My teacher explains this problem several times."; *-biānzi* "a whip", used with verbs like *dǎ* "hit, beat" and *chōu* "whip, lash"; *Wǒmen chōu jǐbiānzi mǎ.* "We whip the horse several times (several whips)."; *-bù* "step", used with verbs like *pǎo* "run", *zǒu* "walk", *mài* "step", *jìn* "to advance", *chū* "to go out", *Tā jìnle sìbù.* "He advanced four steps."; *-chuízi* "a hit with the mallet, hammer", used with *dǎ* "to strike, hit"; *-cì* "number of times", this measure is very common and is used in connection with almost any action verb, e.g. *Wǒ gēchàng liǎngcì le.* "I sang twice.", *dào Rìben lǚxing jǐcì* "to travel many times to Japan"; *-dùn* "spell, meal", used with verbs like *chī* "eat", *mà* "scold" and *dǎ* "beat"; *-fān* "once over", used with verbs like *shuō* "say", *xiǎng* "think", *quàn* "admonish", *xiǎng yifān* "think once over"; *-guān* "a barrier, a pass", used with the verb *guò* "to pass"; *-gùnzi* "a hit with the rod", used with *chǔ* "to poke" and *dǎ* "hit"; *-huí* "number of times" (cp. *-cì*). *-huí* can be used with all verbs, e.g. *bàiwàng yìhuí* "call on (someone) once", *dǎ yìhuí* "hit once", *huíhuí yùjian tā* "meet him every time"; *-jiǎnzi* "scissors", used with verbs like *jiǎn* "cut, shear" and *jiǎo* "shear, cut"; *-jiǎo* "a step or kick of the foot", used with verbs like *tī* "kick" and *cǎi* "tread", *Tā tī ni jǐjiǎo le.* "How many times did he kick you?"; *-jiào* "a nap", used with *shuì* "to sleep", *Wǒ yào shuì yíjiào.* "I want to have a nap."; *-kǒu* "a mouthful, a bite",

used with *chī* "eat", *yǎo* "bite"; -*qiāng* "a shot of the gun or rifle", used
with *dǎ* "hit, beat", and *fàng* "shoot"; -*quān* "a round", used with verbs
like *zhuàn* "revolve", *rào* "wind", e.g. *Tā bǎ shéngzi ràole jǐquān.* "He
wound the rope several rounds."; -*shēng* "a voice", used with *jiào* "to call",
Nǐ jiàole ta sānshēng jiù lái. "If you call him three times, he will come.";
-*tàng* "trip, tour", used with verbs like *lǚxing* "travel", *qù* "go there",
zhuàn "revolve", *pǎo* "to run", e.g. *Wǒmen yào lǚxing yítàng.*
"We want to travel one trip."; -*xià*, -*xiàr* "stroke", used with verbs like *dǎ*
"hit", *wèn* "ask"; -*xiǎng* "sound", used with *xiǎng* "to sound", *hēng*
"hum", *chàng* "sing", *Tā píqi hǎo jiù hēng liángxiǎng.* "If he is in a good
temper he will hum a couple of bars."; -*yǎn* "an eyeful, a look", used
with verbs like *kàn* "to see", *dèng* "stare", *chǒu* "to look at", *qiáo* "to
look at", *Yíge rén jīngyíle, jiù dèngzhe yìyǎn.* "If a man becomes
alarmed, he stares (a look)."; -*zhàng* "a battle", used with *dǎ* "hit".

E. Place Words

1. GENERAL

Place words share the general properties of nominals. They are
distinguished from other nominals by the fact that they occur as objects
to the set of verbs listed below. Any nominal which can serve as an
object to these verbs is defined as a place word. In the following patterns
'x' marks the position of a place word.

(1) *zài x* "to be at x", e.g.
   Fàn zài zhuōshang. "The food is on the table."
(2) *dào x* "to arrive at x", e.g.
   Tā dào Zhōngguo le. "He arrived in China."
(3) *dào x qù* "to go to x", e.g.
   dào túshūguǎn qù "to go to the library",
   Tā dào shānshang qù. "He is going to the mountaintop."
(4) *cóng x lái* "to come from x", e.g.
   Nǐ cóng nǎr lái. "Where are you coming from?"
   cóng nèr lái "to come from that place".
(5) *shàng x qù* "to go to x", e.g.
   shàng Tàishān qù "to go to T'aishan".
(6) *wàng x zǒu* "go toward x", e.g.
   wàng héshang zǒu "to go towards the river".

Place words are used as sentence topics to indicate the general circumstances or the location of the action expressed in the sentence predicate. If a time word (cp. p. 255) as well as a place word occurs as part of the sentence subject, the time word generally precedes the place word:

Wǎnshang fànguánli yǒu hěn duō rén. "There are many people in the restaurant in the evening."
Bādiǎn zhōng fàntīngli wǒmen chī wǎnfàn. "At eight o'clock we eat in the dining room."

In these examples, *wǎnshang* "evening" and *bādiǎn zhōng* "eight o'clock" are time words while *fànguánli* "in the restaurant" and *fàntīngli* "in the dining-room" are place words.

Place words are divided into several groups. Most place names are place words (*Shànghǎi, Měiguo* "the United States"). Note that monosyllabic place names are not free words.

Place words which are not place names are words which designate "places" in general; they are noun-like units, subject to the restrictions pointed out above. According to their morphological structure, we distinguish between compound place words (*fēijīchǎng* "airport") and complex place words (*fàntīngli* "in the dining-room"; *shānshang* "on the mountain"; *wǒzhèr* "(here) where I am"; *nǐnàr* "(there) where you are").

2. PLACE NAMES

Proper nouns (cp. p. 224) have a geographical location or area (including institutions and agencies) as their referent, e.g. *Fǎguó* "France", *Běijīng* "Peking", *Guǎngdōng Dàxué* "The University of Kwangtung", *Yuǎndōng Lǚxíngshè* "Far East Travel Agency". Since they are proper place names they cannot be modified by determinative compounds, but this does not exclude the possibility of modifications marked with *de.*

Place names designate, for example, names of countries, mountains, cities, lakes, rivers, subdivision of countries, etc. Place names may also refer to churches, temples, factories and occasionally to private houses.

Further examples are: *Sūzhōu* "Suchow" and *Hànxiàn* "the county Han"; *Bǐlìshí* "Belgium", *Xīndélǐ* "New Delhi", *Shǎnxi* "Shensi".

In connection with *zài*, names of rivers, mountains and lakes regularly need a place word suffix in order to serve as a place name.

Zài Huánghé-shang yǒu duō chuán. "There are many boats on the Huangho river."

Zài Nánshān-shang shōují húdié. "To collect butterflies on the mountain Nanshan."

Names of this category function as place names without the use of a place word suffix in connection with *dào* and *cóng x lái:*

Wǒmen wǎnshang dào Huánghé. "We are coming to Huanghe river in the evening.",
cóng Nánshān lái "to come from Nanshan mountain".

3. RELATIVE PLACE WORDS

a. General. Relative place words are nominals expressing the general location or position of objects in space in relation to one or more other objects in space. Relative place words are *wàitou* "outside", *lǐtou* "inside", *biéchu* "elsewhere", *dǐxia* "below", *shàngtou* "above", *xībian* "the west side", *hòutou* "behind". Relative place words form a listable class.

Relative place words are commonly modified by another nominal or by nominal expressions, with or without the insertion of the subordinating marker *de*. The result is usually a phrase. Examples: *fángzi (de) lǐtou* "inside the house", *piàoliang nǚren de zuǒbian* "the left side of the beautiful woman", *gāo shān (de) dǐxia* "below the high mountain".

Relative place words are also used in subordination (with or without *de*) with other nominals, particularly nouns. Examples: *shàngtou de háizimen* "the children above", *lǐtou de huǒlú* "the stove inside".

Both relative place words and place phrases occur as objects to the verbs given above, e.g.

Zài piàoliang nǚren de zuǒbian yǒu yíge háizi. "There is a child on the left side of the beautiful woman.",
Wǒmen wàng gāo shān dǐxia zǒu. "We are walking towards the foot of the mountains."

b. Complex relative place words. Most of the bisyllabic relative place words are complex words consisting of a locator stem and a place word suffix, and only a few are compound words. The place word suffixes are *-bian*, *-biar* "side, border", *-li*, *-r* "in", *-mian*, *-miar* "side, face" and *-tou* "end". The locator stems form a closed class. They should be distinguished from the suffixes as, for example in *fángzili* "inside the house", as well as from certain demonstratives with which they are homophonous. The locator stems are listed here together with examples of complex relative place words which they form.

(1) *běi-* "north", *běibian* or *běibiar* "north side", e.g. *běibian de fángzi* "the houses in the north".

(2) *qián-* "front", *qiántou, qiánbian* and *qiánmian* "the front side or front direction". *Nǐ kànkan qiánmian.* "You look forward (in the forward direction)."

(3) *dōng-* "east", *dōngbian* "the east side".

(4) *hòu-* "back", *hòutou, hòubian* and *hòumian* "behind" or "at the back of", *Tā hòutou yǒu sānzhī shīzi le.* "There were three lions behind him."

(5) *lǐ-* "inside", *lǐtou, lǐbian* and *lǐmian* "inside", *cóng lǐtou lái* "come from the inside", i.e. "to come out of".

(6) *nà-* "that", *nàbian, nàmian* "that side", *nàr* or *nàli* "that place" or "there", e.g. *nàbian de xiānsheng* "the gentleman on that side", or "over there".

(7) *nǎ-* "which", *nǎbian, nǎmian* "which side?", *nǎli* or *nǎr* "where, which place?". *Tā dào nǎr qù.* "Where is he going?"

(8) *nán-* "south", *nánbian* "the south side"; *Nánbian hěn rè.* "In the south it is very hot."

(9) *shàng-* "above", *shàngtou* "above", *shàngbian, shàngmian* "the up-side", *zhuōzi shàngtou* "on the table".

(10) *wài-* "outside", *wàitou, wàibian* and *wàimian* "outside"; *Wàitou xià yǔ.* "It is raining outside."

(11) *xī-* "west", *xībian* "the west side".

(12) *xià-* "below", *xiàtou, xiàbian* and *xiàmian*, "below" or "at the bottom of".

In the Peking dialect, "below" (= "under") is usually expressed by *dǐxia* "below", which is a complex place word consisting of the noun *dǐ* and the place word suffix *-xia*.

Some of the locator stems form compounds meaning "thereabouts", viz. *-zuǒyòu, -shàngxià* and *-qiánhòu.* They are still bound morphemes, e.g. *Wǒmen zài túshūguǎnshàngxià yùjian le.* "We met by the library or thereabouts."

    c. **Compound relative place words.** We shall give a few examples of the most common relative place words, which are, morphologically speaking, compound words.

The bound morpheme *-chù* "place, locality" is part of four compound relative place words: *yuǎnchù* "distant place", *jìnchù* "near place" and *dàochù* "everywhere", where the other component parts are verbs, e.g. *jìn* "to be near". *Biéchù* "elsewhere", is a determinative compound acting as a place word, e.g. *zài biéchù chī fàn* "to eat at another place".

-chù also forms a distributive reduplicate which functions as a relative place word: *chùchù* "everywhere".

Pángbiān "by the side of, beside" is another compound relative place word in common use:

Zài wǒ pángbiān yǒu Hán jiàoshòu. "Professor Han was by my side."

Some compass directions are expressed by bisyllabic compound relative place words, consisting of combinations of the four morphemes *nán-*, *běi-*, *xī-* and *dōng-*, i.e. *dōngnán* "south-east", *dōngběi* "north-east", *xīnán* "south-west" and *xīběi* "north-west".

Finally, there are three compounds expressing "middle" or "between", viz. *dāngzhōng* "right in the middle", *zhōngjiār* "middle space", *dāngjiār* "right in the middle space", e.g. *kètīng dāngzhōng* "right in the middle of the living room".

d. Monomorphemic relative place words, We have already dealt with the complex relative place words *zhèr*, *nàr* and *nǎr* (cp. p. 253). These are monosyllabic and bimorphemic words.

Other relative place words are monomorphemic. These are bound words and form a closed class: *běi* "north", *dōng* "east", *hòu* "back", *lǐ* "inside", *nán* "south", *nèi* "inside", *qián* "front", *shàng* "above", *yòu* "right", *wài* "outside", *xī* "west", *xià* "below", *zuǒ* "left". These monomorphemic words may occur in fixed phrases of literary origin, e.g.

Shàng yǒu tiāntáng, xià yǒu Sū-Háng. "Above is Heaven, (here) below are Suchow and Hangchow."

They are also employed as objects after the verbs *wàng* "towards", *zài* "at" and *cóng* "from", e.g. *zài shàng* "above"; *cóng yòu* "from the right"; *wàng qián* "forwards". *Zàinèi* and *zàiwài* are compounds with the special meanings "included" and "not included", respectively.

The monosyllabic relative place words do not occur in subordinative constructions, i.e. they are not modified by other nominals and cannot themselves modify another nominal. Thus, they are never accompanied by the subordinating marker *de*. Sequences like **shū de shàng* "above the book" or **shàng de shū* "the book above" do not occur.

It should be clear from this description that the monosyllabic relative place words constitute a group of place words of limited importance and restricted occurrence.

4. COMPLEX PLACE WORDS

A complex place word consists of a stem and a place-word suffix. Place words of this type are derived from nouns, pronouns, and proper names. We have already seen that certain place names sometimes take a place word suffix in order to serve as place words (cp. p. 251).

Examples of complex place words: *shānshang* "on the mountain", *chuánnei* "inside the boat", *hébei* "north of the river", *wòchēli* "inside the sleeping-car".

Complex place words derived from pronouns and proper names are formed by means of the place word suffixes *-zher* "here" and *-nar* "there", e.g. *Wáng xiānsheng-nar* "where Mr. Wang is", *wǒmen-zher* "where we are", *zài tā-zher kéyi yùjian* "(we) can meet at his place".

It is of practical importance to remember that nouns denoting "places" are not necessarily place words in the grammatical sense. Typical examples are: *jiē* "street", *jiāng* "river", *hé* "river", *hú* "lake", *lù* "road", *chéng* "city". As place words, such items take the following form respectively (only a few possibilities are mentioned): *jiēshang* "on the street", *jiāngli* "in the river", *chéngwai* "outside the city".

It has been mentioned already that words like *túshūgŭan* "library", *yóuzhèngjú* "post-office", *xuéxiào* "school", *shūfáng* "study", *kètīng* "living-room", are place words. Still, such words may take a place word suffix. Thus one may say *zài kètīng* as well as *zài kètīngli* "to be in the living-room". *Shūfáng de wàitou* and *shūfángwài* are alternative forms, both meaning "outside the study". Expressions like *yóuzhèngjú de wàitou* "outside the post-office" and *túshūgŭan de shàngtou* "on top of the library" are quite common.

F. Time Words

1. GENERAL

Time words share the general properties of nominals (cp. p. 204). Time words are distinguished from other nominals by the fact that they occur as objects to the set of verbs listed below. A nominal which serves as an object to these verbs is defined as a time word. In the following patterns 'x' marks the position of the time word.

(1) *zài x* "to be at", e.g.
    zài bādiǎn zhōng "at eight o'clock",
    zài wǎnshang "in the evening".

(2) *dào x* "reach the time of", e.g.
   dào jīnnián "to this year",
   dào xīngqitiān "to Sunday".
(3) *děngdào x* "by", "by the time when", e.g.
   děngdào zǎoshang "by morning".
(4) *cóng x V-qǐ* "to start to do V at x time", e.g.
   cóng sìdiǎn zhōng fēiqǐ "to start flying at four o'clock".
(5) *dào x wéizhǐ* "as far as", "up till".

If this set is compared with the set which defines place words, a few cases of overlapping will be noted. The verbs *zài* and *dào* take place words as well as time words as objects. The same is the case with the combination *cóng x qǐ* and *dào x wéizhǐ*. Examples: *dào Tàishān wéizhǐ* "as far as T'aishan" or *dào zuótian wéizhǐ* "up till yesterday"; *cóng Húnán qǐ* "to start from Hunan" or *cóng míngtian qǐ* "to start tomorrow".

Tàishān and *Húnán* are place words, while *zuótian* and *míngtian* are time words. In other words, any nominal which occurs as an object after *zài*, *dào* and in *cóng x qǐ* and *dào x wéizhǐ* is either a place word or a time word.

A time word frequently serves as a topic subject; it indicates the time at which the action of the predicate takes place. In such cases, the predicate often contains a minor subject. In the following examples, the time words *jīntian*, *tiāntiān* and *qīdiǎn zhōng* are topic subjects.

Jīntian wǒmen zūle liǎngjiān wūzi. "We rented two rooms today."
Tiāntiān qīdiǎn zhōng wó xí zǎo. "Every day at seven o'clock I take a bath."

When a topic subject contains a time word as well as a place word, the time word tends to precede the place word:

Jīntian shūfángli wǒmen tán yitan. "We are talking today in the study room."

Adverbs of time (cp. p. 203), e.g. *yǐjing* "already", *mǎshàng* "at once", and *likè* "immediately" should not be confused with time words.

Most time words are disyllabic free words; they are either compound words like *xiànzài* "now" or complex words like *jiār* "today". Time words refer to a point in time or to a period of time. The time scale may be that of a watch, the solar year or the moon year, an historical period, etc.

2. TIME NAMES

Time words that are proper names and that refer to a definite point or period of time, past, present, or future, are called time names. Time names include names of historical periods, *Hàncháo* "the Han dynasty", years *yī-jiǔ-qī-sì-nián* "1974", days *xīngqiyī* "Monday" and names of periods of the day and the hours of the day, e.g. *sāndiǎn zhōng* "three o'clock" and *zǎoshang* "morning".

a. **Historical periods. Years.** Time names for dynasties are bisyllabic compounds consisting of the monosyllabic bound name of the dynasty, e.g. *Zhōu, Hàn, Sòng*, and the bound word *cháo* "dynasty", e.g. *Zhōucháo* "the Chou dynasty" and *Sòngcháo* "the Sung dynasty". The bisyllabic words are free, and enter into ordinary syntactical constructions, for instance in subordinative constructions: *Zhōucháo de shíhou* "at the time of the Chou dynasty", or they can be modified by quality verbs, *yǒumíng de Sòngcháo* "the famous Sung dynasty". Bound monosyllabic names of dynasties are also combined with the time stems *qián-* "former", *hòu-* "latter", and the locator stems *dōng-* "east" and *xī-* "west". The resulting bisyllabic compounds are free words, e.g. *Qiánhàn* "the former Han (dynasty)".

Time names for reigns or eras are compounds consisting of the mono- or bisyllabic words for the period, and the compound *-niánjiān* which means "in the years of", e.g. *Lóngqìngniánjiān* "in the period of Lungch'ing" (i.c. 1567–1572) or *Tài-Zǔ-niánjiān* "in the years of T'ai Tsu" (i.e. 1368–1398). Time names for eras can also be formed as compound words with *(de)-shíhou* or *(de)-shídài* "in the time of", e.g. *Lóngqìng de shídài* or *Tài-Zǔ (de)-shíhou*.

Time names for years are determinative compounds consisting of a numeral, simple or compound, and the quasi-measure *-nián*. The numeral is an ordinary cardinal number, e.g. *yī-jiǔ-wǔ-bā-nián* "1958", *sānsì-nián* "the year '34". The measure *-nián* can never be omitted from time words naming years.

b. **Divisions and parts of the year.** The seasons of the year have time names which are free compound words consisting of the bound word *tiān* "time" and the bound words *chūn* "spring", *xià* "summer", *qiū* "autumn" and *dōng* "winter", i.e. *chūntian* "spring-time", *xiàtian* "summer-time", *qiūtian* "autumn-time" and *dōngtian* "winter-time". There is also another set of compound names for the seasons with *jì* "season" as the second component, e.g. *chūnjì* "spring", *xiàjì* "summer", *qiūjì* "autumn" and *dōngjì* "winter".

Time names for the months of the year are compound words consisting of one of the numerals from *yī* "one" to *shíèr* "twelve" and the quasi-measure -*yuè* "month", e.g. *yīyuè* "January", *wŭyuè* "May" and so forth. As with names of the years, the numerals are ordinals. "January" is also called *zhēngyuè*, a complex word made up of the ordinal prefix *zhēng*- "first" and the noun *yuè* "month".

Time names for the weeks are formed in a similar manner. They are compounds of the numerals from *yī* "one" to *wŭshíèr* "fifty-two" in the form of ordinal numbers, followed by quasi-measures -*lĭbai* or *xīngqi*, both meaning "week", e.g. *shílĭbai* "the tenth week".

Time names for the days of a week are compounds consisting of either the free word *lĭbài* "week" or the free word *xīngqi* "week", and one of the simple numerals from *yī* "one" to *liù* "six", e.g. *lĭbaiyī* "Monday", *lĭbaièr* 'Tuesday" or *xīngqiyī* "Monday" and *xīngqièr* "Tuesday". There are six time names for "Sunday", viz. *lĭbairì* or *xīngqirì* and *lĭbaitiān* or *xīngqitiān*, or simply *lĭbai* or *xīngqi*. -*tiān* is a quasi-measure meaning "day" and -*rì* is a literary quasi-measure meaning "day".

c. **Divisions and parts of the day**. Time names for hours of the day are made up of a noun, *zhōng*, meaning "hours", preceded by a determinative compound, which consists of the measure -*diăn* with the numerals from *yī*- "one" to *shíèr* "twelve", e.g. *sìdiăn zhōng* "four o'clock", *shíyìdiăn zhōng* "eleven o'clock"; *zhōng* can be omitted after the determinative compound with -*diăn*. To count the number of hours to indicate length of time, the general measure -*ge* is used with the noun *zhōngtóu* "hours", e.g. *shíge zhōngtóu*, "ten hours"; *Wó dĕngdào sānge zhōngtóu le.* "I have been waiting for three hours."

Certain periods of the day may be expressed with the help of a set of compound and complex words: *zăoshang, záoqĭ, zăochén* translate as "morning", *shănghuo* means "around noon", while *zhōngwŭ* or *zhèngwŭ* means "exactly noontime". The time before and after noon is expressed as *shàngwŭ* and *xiàwŭ* respectively, corresponding to the English "a.m." and "p.m.", and they are used in connection with the hours of the day to indicate time before or after noon, *xiàwŭ sāndiăn zhōng* "three p.m.".

Shàngbàntiān and *xiàbàntiān* mean "forenoon" and "afternoon" respectively. *Wănshang* is employed to denote "evening", and *báitian* and *yèli* are common time names for "daytime" and "nighttime"; "midnight" is expressed as *bànyè*.

The fractions of the hour are expressed by the noun *zhōng* which is optional, preceded by a determinative compound consisting of one of the numerals from *yī* "one" to *liùshí* "sixty" and one of the measures -*kè* "a quarter of an hour", *-fēn* "a minute", and *-miǎo* "a second". Examples: *xiànzài bādiǎn sìshíwǔ-fēn* (*zhōng*) or *xiànzài bādiǎn sānkè* "[the time] is now 8:45"; *qīdiǎn shísìfēn sānshímiǎo* (*zhōng*) "[the time] is now 7:14:30". Note also the expressions: *chà yíkè sāndiǎn* (*zhōng*) "a quarter to three" and *sāndiǎn bàn* (*zhōng*) "half past three".

The group of time names also includes special names for festivals or periods of the year, e.g. *shèngdànjié* "Christmas", *duānwǔ* or *duānyáng* "the fifth day of the fifth moon, the annual dragon-boat race day", *zhōngqiū* "mid-autumn festival", etc.

3. RELATIVE TIME WORDS

a. General properties. Relative time words are nominals expressing a point or a period of time which is physically measured or mentally understood. Relative time words are for instance *míngtian* "tomorrow", *qùnian* "last year", *zhèicì* "this time", and *běnyuè* "this month".

Relative time words occur in both pre- and postcentral positions, e.g. *cóng míngtian zuò qǐ* "to start working tomorrow", *Zhèicì cuòle.* "This time [I] made a mistake." Relative time words can occur as modifiers, and they are sometimes themselves modified by nominal expressions: *jīntian de tiānqi* "today's weather", *qùnian de gémìng* "last year's revolution", *zhèige shìjì* "this century".

Relative time words form a listable class of nominals, and include mostly disyllabic free words. A few of them are complex words, the majority are compound relative time words.

b. Complex relative time words. The complex relative time words consist of the time suffix *-r* and one of the time stems, *qián-* "before last", *zuó-* "yesterday", *jīn-* "today", *míng-* "tomorrow" and *hòu-* "after next". The resulting complex words are monosyllabic free words: *qiár* "the day before last", *zuór* "yesterday", *jiār* "today", *míngr* "tomorrow", *hòur* "the day after next". Examples:

Qiár wǒ de tàitai huílai le. "My wife returned the day before yesterday."
míngr de jiángyǎn "tomorrow's lecture".

c. Compound relative time words. Compound relative time words consist of the time stems and certain nouns or measures of time units, e.g. *qiántiān* "the day before yesterday", with the time stem *qián-* "before last" and the quasi-measure *-tiān* "day", and *běnyuè* "this month" with the time stem *bĕn-* "the current" and *-yuè* "month". The compound relative place words form a listable group of disyllabic and trisyllabic free nominals.

The time stems must be distinguished from some of the locator stems in complex relative place words discussed above (cp. p. 252), but the time stems form, in a similar way, a closed list of end-bound morphemes. A list of the time stems is given below together with the compound relative time words which they form.

The nouns employed in these compounds are *lĭbai* "week", *xīngqi* "week", *yuè* "month", *xuéqī* "semester", *niándù* "academic year", *shìjì* "century". The measures used in the compounds are *-tiān* and *-rì* meaning "day", *-huí* and *-cì* "time", *-huĭr* "moment", *-lĭbai* "week", *-xīngqi* "week", *-yuè* "month", *-jì* "season", *-xuéqī* "semester", *-nián* "year", *-niándù* "academic year", *-shìjì* "century".

(1) *bĕn-* "the current, this", *bĕnyuè* "this month", *bĕnniándù* "this academic year", *bĕnshìjì* "the current century", *bĕnxuéqī* "this semester", *bĕnjì* "this season".

(2) *hòu-* "after next", *hòutian* "the day after tomorrow", *hòuhuí* and *hòucì* "next time", *hòunian* "the year after next".

(3) *jīn-* "this", *jīntian* "today", *jīnnian* "this year", *jīnhuí* and *jīncì* "this time".

(4) *míng-* "next", *míngtian* "tomorrow", *míngnian* "next year".

(5) *nà-/nèi-* "that", *nèitian* or *nèiri* "that day", *nèinian* "that year", *nèihuí* and *nèicì* "that time", *nèihuĭr* "that moment".

(6) *nă-/nĕi-* "which?" *nĕitian* "which day?" *nĕinian* "which year?" *néihuí* or *nĕicì* "which time?" *néihuĭr* "which moment?"

(7) *qián-* "next to last, last but one", *qiántian* "the day before yesterday", *qiánnian* "the year before last".

(8) *qián-* "previous", *qiánhuí* or *qiáncì* "the previous time", *qiánlĭbai* "the previous week", *qiánxuéqī* "the previous semester".

(9) *qù-* "gone, last", *qùnian* "last year".

(10) *shàng-* "last", *shànghuí* or *shàngcì* "last time", *shànglĭbai* "last week", *shàngxuéqī* "last semester", *shàngniándù* "last academic year".

(11) *xià-* "next", *xiàhuí* or *xiàcì* "next time", *xiàlĭbai* "next week", *xiàxuéqī* "next semester", *xiàniándù* "next academic year", *xiànian* "next year".

(12) *zhè-/zhèi-* "this", *zhèitian* or *zhèiri* "this day", *zhèihuí* or *zhèicì* "this time", *zhèihuĭr* "this moment", *zhèinian* "this year".

(13) *zuó-* "yesterday", *zuótian* "yesterday".

In addition to the relative time words mentioned above, there are a number of other words which mark a relative position in time. They are not, however, compound relative time words according to our definition.

Jìnlái "recently", *gāngcái* "just now" and *xiànzài* "now". In object position these time words are usually only employed after the verbs *cóng* "from" and *dào* "to".

Cóngqián "formerly", *guòqù* "the past"; *dāngchū*, *qǐchū*, *qǐxiān*, *xiāntóu* and *qǐtóu* are all translatable as "at first"; *yǐqián* "before". In object position these time words are most frequently preceded by the verb *cóng* "from".

Yǐhòu "after"; *hòulái* "afterwards" and *jiānglái* "the future". In object position these time words can only be used after the verb *dào* "to".

Some of the time localizers form localizer compounds with the meaning "thereabouts", viz. *-shàngxià*, *-zuǒyòu* and *-qiánhòu*: *wúdiǎn-shàngxià* "about five o'clock".

Intervals of time are expressed with the help of four disyllabic compound words, *dāngzhōng*, *dāngjiār*, *zhōngjiān* and *zhōngjiār*, all meaning "(time) between", e.g. *zài zǎochén gēn wǎnshang de zhōngjiār*, "between morning and evening".

d. Relative time phrases. These consist of time words preceded by determinative compounds.

(1) Combinations with demonstratives proper, *zhè-* or *zhèi-* "this", *nà-* or *nèi-* "that" and *něi-* or *nǎ-* "which" form a limited number of phrases:

zhèige lǐbai "this week", *nèige lǐbai* "that week", *něige lǐbai* "which week?", *zhèige yuè* "this month", *nèige yuè* "that month", *něige yuè* "which month?", *zhèi yíjì* "this (one) season", *nèi yíjì* "that (one) season", *něi yíjì* "which (one) season?", *zhèige xuéqī* "this semester", *nèige xuéqī* "that semester", *něige xuéqī* "which semester?", *zhèige shìjì* "this century", *nèige shìjì* "that century", *něige shìjì* "which century?".

(2) The specifying demonstratives *qián-* "previous to last, previous", *shàng-* "former, last" and *xià-* "next" form a limited number of phrases:

qián yìhuǐr "the moment before last", *qián'ge yuè* "the month before last", *qián yíjì* "the season before last", *qián yíshìjì* "the century before last", *shàngge yuè* "last month", *shàng yíjì* "last season", *xiàge yuè* "next month", *xià yíjì* "next season".

4. COMPLEX TIME WORDS

Complex time words consist of a nominal, more specifically a noun, and a time word suffix. These suffixes form a listable class (cp. p. 210). Such a suffix transforms a noun into a time word.

The majority of time word suffixes can combine with nouns as far as lexical compatibility will allow. The result is a large open class of transient complex time words. Examples: *fànqián* "before the meal", *yuèdǐ* "end of the month", *shìhòu* "after the event", *yǔchū* "at the beginning of the rain", *yèlǐ* "in the night", *wǔshàng* "noon", *mùxià* "under the eyes" i.e. "currently", etc.

CHAPTER XII

NOMINAL SYNTACTICAL
CONSTRUCTIONS

A. Subject–Predicate Constructions

1. NOMINAL SUBJECTS

A general discussion of subject–predicate constructions has been given
above (Chapter II). Nominal expressions, that is, both words and phrases,
can serve as topic subjects in sentences. The various kinds of nominals
and nominal subjects are discussed below. The topic subject often
denotes the performer of the action described in the sentence predicate,
in which case nouns and personal pronouns are frequently used.
Examples:

Nèitiáo gǒu duì rén hěn xiōng. "That dog is very fierce (with people)."
Lín xiáojiě bu xǐhuan dài yǎnjìngr. "Miss Lin does not like to wear
glasses."
Shéi shi Rìběn rén. "[Among those present] who is Japanese?"

The topic subject is often the actual topic, the qualities of which are
being commented on. Examples:

Zhèikē zhūzi piàoliangjíle. "This pearl is most beautiful."
Sānkuài qián yìběn tài duō. "Three dollars [for] one volume is too
much."

Of great practical importance is the use of time and place expressions
as sentence topics expressing where and when the action of the predicate
takes place. In the first example below a time expression serves as topic
subject and in the second sentence a place word. In the last example a
time word, *jīntian*, is the topic subject, whereas a place word, *jiēshang*, is
a separate subject introducing the sentence predicate.

263

Tiāntiān bādiǎn zhōng wǒ chī zǎofàn. "Every day at eight o'clock I eat breakfast."
Sìchuān yǒu shān. "There are mountains [in] Szechwan."
Jīntian jiēshang chē hěn duō. "Today there are many cars on the street."

2. NOMINAL PREDICATES

Any nominal word and phrase can serve as a nominal predicate, i.e. the comment on the topic presented. In the following examples the nominal predicates are *Zhōngwén shū*, *wǒ de*, and *liùkuài qián*:

Zhèiběn shū, Zhōngwén shū. "This book [is] [a] Chinese book."
Zhèisuǒr fángzi wǒ de. "This house [is] mine."
Sānjīn zhūròu liùkuài qián. "Three catties [of] pork [cost] six dollars."

A nominal predicate frequently indicates the class of objects to which the topic subject belongs, e.g.

Tāmen Yīngguorén. "They [are] Englishmen."
Ní hǎoren. "You are a good man."

A nominal predicate frequently contains a specifying attribute:

Zhèige háizi gāo gèr. "This child is tall (has a tall stature)."

Nominal predicates in the form of a determinative compound consisting of a demonstrative and a measure with or without a following noun, express a quantitative specification about the topic subject, e.g.

Tuántǐ sānbǎi rén. "The organization [comprises] three hundred people."
Lǎo Wáng bāshísuì. "Old Wang [is] eighty years [old]."

A nominal predicate cannot be negated by *bu*. A sentence containing a nominal predicate must be transformed into a verbal sentence with *shì* before a negation is possible: *Tā Rìběn rén.* "He is Japanese." is changed into *Tā bú shì Rìběn rén.* "He is not Japanese." if a negation is desired.

B. Coordination

1. GENERAL

The syntactical type of construction called coordination has been dealt with above (Chapters I, II, and III). Nominal expressions are commonly used in coordinative constructions. In this example two nominals in (unmarked) coordination function as sentence topic:

Zhōngguó Měiguó dōu hěn dà. "Both China [and] the United States are very big."

Here the use of nominals in a coordinative construction serves to list a number of items in simple succession.

The order of items in a coordinate construction is in principle reversible without any change of meaning, e.g.

Wáng xiānsheng Lǐ xiānsheng hǎo péngyou. Lǐ xiānsheng Wáng xiānsheng hǎo péngyou. "Mr. Li [and] Mr. Wang are good friends."

In some cases, a fixed order is preferable or obligatory from the point of view of style or idiomatic usage, e.g. *fùqin mǔqin* "father and mother" and *xiānsheng xuésheng* "teachers and students". This is a case of a conventionally determined order of items in coordination.

The expressions joined in coordination will generally have the same number of syllables, belong to the same nominal class or type of nominal expression. All the cases of nominals in coordination discussed in the present paragraph illustrate this. The next example shows the same principle at work with two fairly complicated nominal expressions in coordination:

Shuō Zhōngguó huà de nénglì, niàn Zhōngguó shū de nénglì, zhǐ yǒu liànxí yònggōng cái néng tígāo. "The ability to speak Chinese [and] to read Chinese books, it is only a matter of practice [and] diligence before [one] can improve [it]."

2. MARKED AND UNMARKED COORDINATION

A coordinate construction is marked or unmarked. Whether or not markers are used is largely a matter of style; unmarked coordination is more common in Chinese than, for example, in English. Coordinated nominal expressions can be separated by pauses. In printing, commas are sometimes used.

There are a few connective words, connectors, serving as markers of coordination. These connectors are put between the nominal items, especially if several rather long nominal expressions occur in succession. The connectors most commonly in use are *hé, tóng* and *gēn*, all translatable as "and" or "together with". *Gēn* is most frequently used, e.g.

Wáng tàitai gēn Wáng xiānsheng dōu hěn pàng. "Both Mrs. Wang and Mr. Wang are very fat."

Wǒ gēn ta tán yitan. "I and he are talking together."

Alternative and disjunctive choice is unmarked (zero marker) or marked. The markers are, in this case, *háishi* and *huòzhě* (or *huòshi*). They are both translatable as "or", but they have different functions. *Nǐ yào kāfēi háishi chá.* means "[Which] (do) you prefer, either coffee or tea?" This is the marker of disjunctive choice. *Nǐ yào kāfēi huòzhě chá.* means "(Would) you like [something to drink, for instance] coffee or tea?" The latter sentence, with *huòzhě*, merely lists two alternatives in succession.

3. Apposition

Two or more nominal expressions occurring in coordination and having the same referent are said to form an apposition.

> *Wǒmen de xiānsheng, Lǐ jiàoshòu, bìng le.* "Our teacher, Professor Li, has become ill."

In this sentence *wǒmen de xiānsheng* and *Lǐ jiàoshòu* occur in coordination, and both have the same referent. In the following example, *Cóng Běijīng lái de rén* and *Tiě dàifu* are nominal expressions with the same referent. Thus, we have a case of apposition:

> *Cóng Běijīng lái de rén, Tiě dàifu.* "The man (who) came from Peking, Dr. T'ieh."

This kind of coordination is called apposition if there is a facultative pause, marked above with commas, between the two nominal expressions. Apposition in this sense should be distinguished from subordination, e.g. *Lǐ jiàoshòu* and *Wǔ tàitai* "Mrs. Wu", which consist of two nominals each, the first nominal being subordinated to the second.

C. Subordination

1. General

A general definition and discussion of subordination is given above (p. 77). The present section is confined to subordinate constructs which function as nominals. The head or the center of the subordination is a nominal expression, but the attribute or modifying element may or may not be a nominal expression. In the following subordinative constructs both the head and the modifier are nominals: *zhèige rén* "this man", *wǒ dìxiong* "my brothers", *bànge zhōngtóu* "half an hour", *gōngyuán lǐtou* "inside the park".

In the following examples of subordinative constructions the modifying elements are verbal expressions: *niánqīng xuésheng* "young students", *chǎo báicài* "fried cabbage", *hóng wàzi* "red stockings".

Each immediate constituent in such a subordinative nominal construct may be grammatically complex:

Qīngcháo chūnián chūbǎn de liǎngbù zuì liúxíng de báihuà xiǎoshuōr. "[The] two most popular paihua novels published in the early years [of] the Ch'ing dynasty".

In this phrase, the first constituent is *Qīngcháo chūnián chūbǎn* and all of the rest is the second constituent of this subordinative construct. The second constituent, however, consists of a head, *báihuà xiǎoshuōr* (which is itself a subordinative construct with an attribute, *báihuà*, and a head, *xiǎoshuōr*), and an attribute, *liǎngbù zuì liúxíng*.

2. COMPOUNDS AND PHRASES

A subordinative construction is either a compound nominal word or a nominal phrase. The construction is a compound nominal if one or both of the elements are bound, e.g. *wàiguó* "foreign country", *qìchē* "automobile", *chúfáng* "kitchen".

If the nominal head has a neutral tone and both the head and the attribute are free words, the resulting subordinative construct is a nominal compound word, e.g. *kèrén* "guest", *tóuténg* "headache".

The construction may be either a compound or a phrase if both the head and the attribute are free words. Criteria for making a conclusive distinction between words and phrases are difficult to establish, but for practical purposes it is sufficient to note that a construct is usually a word if it carries a specialized meaning, and if it does not permit separation or insertion of other elements. *Huángyóu* "butter" does not allow the insertion of *de*: there is no **huáng de yóu* in the sense of "butter".

Examples of subordinative phrases: *zhèige zhǎi lù* "this narrow road", *chuántǒng sīxiǎng* "traditional thought".

3. CLASSES OF SUBORDINATIVE CONSTRUCTIONS

We distinguish between several semantic categories of subordinative constructions, depending on the kinds of words which occur in them. Some of the most frequently used and well-defined categories are discussed here. Both phrases and compounds are included.

(1) The center or head is a word for a person or a thing, and the attribute denotes a quality or a material, e.g. *hǎo chúzi* "a good cook",

xiăo jīdàn "small eggs", *Yīngguó tàitai* "English lady", *jīn zhuózi* "golden bracelet". The attribute may also be a word denoting a person or a thing, e.g. *nán-yănyuán* "actor", *wŏ fùren* "my wife".

(2) The center is a word which denotes the logical goal of an action, and the attribute expresses the action, e.g. *kàn de shū* "books which are read", cp. *kàn shū* (verb + object), *shāo jī* "roast chicken". The head may indicate the "actor" and the attribute the action: *dăzìjī* "hit characters machine", i.e. "typewriter" and *láirén* "come-man", i.e. "messenger".

(3) The center is a word for a thing and the attribute specifies the thing, quantitatively or qualitatively. In its simple form such a construction may consist of a numeral or a quantitative demonstrative, modifying a measure. Such a subordinative construction is a determinative compound (cp. p. 232). Examples: *sānge* "three pieces of something", *yìnián* "one year", *zhĕngpíng* "the whole bottle of", *jǐyuè* "which month?".

If a compound which consists of a numeral or a quantitative demonstrative and a measure modifies a nominal head, the result is a subordinative phrase, e.g. *yíjù huà* "a sentence", *jiŭbēi jiŭ* "nine cups of wine", *bànge zhōngtóu* "half an hour".

(4) The attribute is an element denoting position in space with a nominal center, e.g. *shăngshēng* "upper tone", i.e. "the third tone in Mandarin", *wàiwù* "outside matters", i.e. "foreign affairs", *bĕibian de hú* "the lake on the north side", *dōngfāng* "the east". The nominal head can also express a position in space, the attribute being a word denoting a thing or a person, e.g. *gōngyuán lĭtou* "the inside of the park", *lùshang* "on the street" and *rén qiántou* "in front of the man".

(5) The center is a word denoting a point or period in time, and the attribute expresses an action or an event, or it is a word denoting a thing, e.g. *niàn shū shíhou* lit. "the time [when] reading [is being done]", i.e. "when [someone] is or was reading", *kāi chē yǐhòu* "after driving".

On the other hand, the attribute may be a time word or a time expression, and the head a noun denoting a thing or a person, e.g. *yèbàn de fēng* "the wind in the night" and *jīnnian de wăngqiú guànjūn* "this year's tennis champion".

D. The Marker of Subordination *de*

1. GENERAL

De is a marker of subordinative constructions. As a marker, it has a grammatical function without carrying a lexical meaning. In later sections, the nominalizing marker *de* and the equational *de* will be discussed.

The function of *de* is to signal that the word, phrase, or clause-like sequence preceding it is a modifier or an attribute, and that the subsequent expression is the center or head of the subordinative construction. Examples: *wǒ de xiāngzi* "my suitcase", *bù hǎo de xīnwén* "bad news", *shéi de màozi* "whose hat?"

In most of the examples of subordination given in the preceding section, the subordinative constructs appear without the marker *de*. In other words, a subordinative construction is either marked (with *de*) or is unmarked, i.e. the modifying element immediately precedes the center (= zero marker).

The difference between subordinative compounds and phrases was mentioned above (cp. p. 267). There is often a contrast between a combination without *de* and the same elements in a phrase with *de*, e.g. *hēibǎn* means "blackboard", but *hēi de bǎn* simply means "(any kind of) black planks" without any specialization of meaning. *Fēijī* "airplane" carries a lexical meaning as a compound word, but the phrase *fēi de jī* means "a (= any) machine which flies".

Not all subordinative compounds can be transformed into phrases with *de* in this way. If both constituents of the subordinative construct are free words, it is usually possible to make a phrase with *de*. However, if one or both constituents are bound morphemes, separation is impossible.

De is used in a descriptive or in a restrictive way. In the examples given above, *de* is used descriptively. The attribute gives a description of the head or center, e.g. *chuān lán yīfu de xiānsheng* "the gentleman who is wearing blue clothes".

However, if a determinative compound, e.g. *nèiwèi*, is added to the phrase above, the position of this modifier determines whether the attribute is a purely descriptive attribute or a restrictive attribute, e.g.

nèiwèi chuān lán yīfu de xiānsheng, or
chuān lán yīfu de nèiwei xiānsheng.

In the former example, the determinative compound is the first element of the modification, and the attribute remains purely a description of the man who happens to wear blue clothes. It translates as "the gentleman [over there] who is [accidentally] wearing blue clothes".

If the determinative compound immediately precedes the center, as in the second example, the attribute emphasizes that the gentleman in question is the one person who is wearing blue clothes in contrast to someone else who is not wearing blue clothes. The translation would be: "the gentleman who is [specifically] wearing blue clothes [and not, for example, white clothes, like someone else]".

In the first sentence, the use of *de* is said to be descriptive, and in the second sentence it is restrictive.

In a construction where an element A, the attribute, modifies B, the center, and the resulting construction modifies a second center, C, there are several possibilities of inserting *de* to make the construct explicitly marked as a subordination. A, B, and C may be words or phrases. The insertion of *de* between only A and B, only B and C, or between all three constituents reflects the analysis into constituents. In general, *de* is preferably used to mark off long constituents while the shorter constituents are left unmarked. "Long" and "short" are to be taken in a relative sense. *Běijīng shìnèi jiāotōng* is likely to mean "the circulation within (the city) Peking", and it would be natural to mark off the long attribute with *de*, e.g. *Běijīng shìnèi de jiāotōng*. It is also possible to use *de* as a marker between all constituents, *Běijīng de shìnèi de jiāotōng*, or only between the attribute and the center in the first part of the construct, *Běijīng de shìnèi jiāotōng*.

2. TYPES OF CONSTRUCTION WITH *DE*

(1) We shall first consider the constructions in which the head is a nominal and the modifier is a noun or pronoun, e.g. *wǒ de qián* "my money", *tāmen de fángzi* "their house" and *gēzi de yǔmáo* "the pigeon's feathers".

De is frequently omitted in cases where personal pronouns modify words indicating personal relations, e.g. *wǒ jiā* or *wǒ de jiā* "my family", *tā dìxiong* or *tā de dìxiong* "his brothers".

(2) In place expressions with a place word as a center, *de* is very often omitted, e.g. *zhuōzi* (*de*) *qiántou* "in front of the table", *Zhōngguó* (*de*) *dōngbiar* "the eastern part of China".

(3) It is important to note that if the attribute is a determinative compound consisting of a numeral and a measure, the use of *de* before the nominal head is optional in certain cases, e.g. *liǎngbàng* (*de*) *ròu* "two pounds of meat" and *bǎizhāng* (*de*) *zhǐ* "a hundred sheets of paper".

If the attribute is a determinative compound, the use or non-use of *de* depends on the kind of measure used in the compound. It should be remembered that if the compound contains individual measures, *de* is never used in the subordinative phrase, e.g. **sānpī de luózi* for "three mules" cannot occur.

Similarly, *de* is never inserted between a nominal and a determinative compound if the compound contains one of the demonstratives *zhèi* "this", *nèi* "that" or *něi* "which?" It is impossible to say **zhèizhī de hǎiōu* "this seagull".

Where the measure is a temporary measure, the insertion of *de* is almost compulsory, like *yìdǐ de shuǐ* "a floor full of water" and *sānwūzi de rén* "three rooms full of people".

(4) Subordinative constructions consisting of a nominal head modified by a transitive or an intransitive quality verb are common. The insertion of *de* is optional, e.g. *shēn (de) shuǐ* "deep waters" and *hóng (de) yánse* "red color".

If the quality verb itself is modified by an adverb, the insertion of *de* becomes necessary. Examples: *hěn pàng de xiǎohár* "a very fat child", *zuì kěxī de shìqing* "a most regrettable affair".

De is generally inserted when the attribute is an intransitive or transitive action verb. Examples: *pǎo de gǒu* "a dog which runs", *gài de gōngchǎng* "a factory which is built", *dài de yǎnjìngr* "spectacles which [he] wears".

If the attribute is a verb—object construction, where the verb is an action or a quality verb, *de* is usually inserted, and it occurs after the object, before the center. Examples: *mài shū de rén* "person [who] sells books", *tán pǐba de nüren* "woman [who] plays a pipa", *xǐhuan yìshù de tàitai* "the lady [who] likes art".

Similarly, intransitive action and quality verbs followed by cognate objects can modify a nominal head, with the insertion of *de*, e.g. *shòu shíbàng de lǜshī* "the lawyer [who has] lost ten pounds [of weight]".

(5) The attribute modifying a nominal head may be a subject—predicate construction. This kind of subordinate construction is generally explicitly marked by *de*, e.g. *nǐmen yòng de fǎzi* "the method [which] you use", *tā shuō de fāngyán* "the dialect [which] he speaks".

E. The Equational Marker *de*

The equational marker *de* has a purely grammatical function and "meaning". The sentence *Cháng de yìsi shi bù duǎn.* "The meaning of 'tall' is 'not short'.", states that *bù duǎn* is used synonymously with *cháng*. *Wó xiě xìn shi wǒ yào qián de yuángù.* "The reason [why] I write letters is that I need money." is also an example of how *wó xiě xìn* points to the same fact or object as *wǒ yào qián de yuángù.* This use of *de* in connection with statements of reason or meaning, *x de yìsi shì y* "the meaning of x is y" and *x de yuángù shì y* "the reason for x is y" illustrates the use of the equational marker *de*.

F. The Nominalizing Marker *de*

1. GENERAL

The nominalizing marker *de* is a bound morpheme with a purely grammatical function and "meaning". If the marker is attached to a verbal expression, it serves to transform it into a nominal expression. The resulting form should be regarded as a regular nominal, e.g. *xiě de* from *xiě* "to write" means either "that which is written" or "someone who is writing". The resulting nominal expression *xiě de* should not be taken to be a modifier with a zero head. Thus, the nominalizing *de* should not be confused with the subordinating marker *de* in *xiě de rén* "a man who is writing" or an abbreviated form *xiě de* of *xiě de rén*.

An expression like *xiě de* with a nominalizing *de*, functions as a nominal in serving as a subject in *xiě de hén yǒu yìsi* "that which is written is very interesting", and as an object in *Wǒ bu dǒng nǐ xiě de.* "I do not understand what you have written."

The verbal *hē chá* "to drink tea" is nominalized by *de* in the following sentence:

Tā shi hē chá de. "She drinks tea.", or literally "She is someone who drinks tea."

A common function of the nominalizer *de* is to form nominal expressions denoting the agent of an action or a profession, e.g. *xiě shū de* "make books'er" i.e. "writer"; *zhǎng guì de* "keep desk'er" i.e. "store manager" and *kāi chē de* "manage car'er" i.e. "driver". These nominals are modifiable by, for instance, quality verbs or determinative compounds:

nèiwèi xiě shū de "that writer"
Nǐ shi yíge huài (de) zhǎng guì de. "You are a bad store-manager."

The use of quality verbs to modify these nominals, however, seems rather limited. The spoken language prefers the construction involving a predicative complement, e.g.

Nǐ zhǎng guì zhǎng de huài. "You, in managing the store, manage it badly."

2. EMPHATIC USE OF THE MARKER *DE*

The general formula *X shi Y de* in which Y is a verbal expression, *de* the nominalizing marker and X is either a verbal or a nominal expression, is frequently used for emphasis. X is something or someone about whom/which a statement can be made, e.g.

> *Huà huàr shi hén yǒu yìsi de.* "To paint is very interesting."
> *Wǒ shi bú rènshi nǐ de.* "I did not recognize you."

The speaker, in using this construction, wants to emphasize a fact which he regards as important in contrast to something unimportant. In the first sentence, there is an explicit reference to painting, not to singing, dancing or sculpturing.

G. Nominal Objects

Verb + object constructions have been treated in detail above (cp. p. 192). All kinds of nominals, words or phrases, can serve as objects to transitive verbs.

(1) The object may be a single noun or a pronoun:
   Wó xǐhuan ta. "I like him."
   Wǒmen hē chá. "We drink tea.",
   or two coordinated nouns or pronouns:
   Tāmen mài zázhì gēn zhǐyān. "They sell magazines and cigarettes."
(2) The noun may be modified by a verbal expression or a determinative compound:
   Wǒ dài yíge màozi. "I am wearing a hat."
   Wó yóu hěn duō de qián. "I have a lot of money."
(3) The nominal object may be determinative compounds of different types (cp. p. 232):
   Tā mǎi sìběn. "He buys four volumes [of something]."
   Tā mǎi zhèige. "He buys this one."
(4) The object may be a subordinate construction, a phrase with or without a subordinating *de*:
   Tāmen jiànzhù yíge shícéng de lóu. "They are erecting a ten-story building."
   Wo rènshi huì shuō Zhōngguó huà de rén. "I know people who can speak Chinese."
   Nǐ zhùyì tā de huà ba. "You must pay attention to his words."

In principle the nominal object has indefinite reference, and the object is always pronounced with full tone and stress, as seen from the examples above. Pronoun objects, however, are unstressed and hence pronounced with neutral tone. The pronoun object may receive contrastive stress and in that case has a full tone:

Tā bù xǐhuan ˈ*wǒmen, kěshi tā xǐhuan* ˈ*tāmen.* "He does not like us, but he likes them."

When a noun object modified by a determinative compound denoting an indefinite quantity has special stress, the determinative compound will receive secondary stress before the fully stressed noun, e.g. *kàn liángběn shū* "read a couple of books".

Determinate compounds are frequently used as cognate objects. In these cases, the compound consists of a numeral or a demonstrative modifying a verbal measure, *zǒu sìbù* "take four steps", *chī yìkǒu* "eat a mouthful" (cp. p. 194), or a verbal stem serving as a measure, e.g. *kàn yikan* "take a look", *xiǎng sānxiǎng* "sounds three times".

In other cases, the cognate object expresses the duration or extension of an action. For this and for time and place words as objects, reference is made to Chapter VIII.

REFERENCES

Chao, Y. R. 1948. *Mandarin Primer. An Intensive Course in Spoken Chinese.* Cambridge: Harvard University Press.

Chao, Y. R. 1968. *A Grammar of Spoken Chinese.* Berkeley and Los Angeles: University of California Press.

Chao, Y. R. and Yang, L. S. 1947. *A Concise Dictionary of Spoken Chinese.* Cambridge: Harvard University Press.

DeFrancis, J. 1950. *Nationalism and Language Reform in China.* Princeton: Princeton University Press.

Huang, P. F. et. al. 1967. *Twenty Lectures on Chinese Culture.* New Haven and London: Yale University Press.

Kennedy, G. A. 1964. (Li Tien-yi, ed.) *Selected Works of George A. Kennedy.* New Haven: Far Eastern Publications, Yale University.

Kratochvil, P. 1968. *The Chinese Language Today.* London: Hutchinson University Library.

Kuraishi, Takeshirō 1968. *Chūgokugo jiten.* Tokyo: Iwanami.

Mullie, J. 1932. *The Structural Principles of the Chinese Language.* Peking.

INDEX

277